POETRY AND ITS PUBLIC IN ANCIENT GREECE

# Poetry and Its Public in Ancient Greece

*From Homer to the Fifth Century*

. . .
. .
.

Bruno Gentili

translated, with an introduction, by
A. Thomas Cole

The Johns Hopkins University Press

BALTIMORE AND LONDON

This book has been brought to publication with the generous assistance of the National Endowment for the Humanities.

Originally published as *Poesia e pubblico nella Grecia antica: da Omero al V secolo.*

© Gius. Laterza & Figli Spa, Rome-Bari, 1985, by arrangement with Eulama S.R.L., Rome

The Johns Hopkins University Press
701 West 40th Street
Baltimore, Maryland 21211
The Johns Hopkins Press Ltd., London

The paper used in this publication meets the minimum requirements of American National Standard for Information Sciences—Permanence of Paper for Printed Library Materials, ANSI Z39.48-1984.

Library of Congress Cataloging-in-Publication Data

Gentili, Bruno.
   [Poesia e pubblico nella Grecia antica. English]
   Poetry and its public in ancient Greece: from Homer to the fifth century / Bruno Gentili; translated and with an introduction by A. Thomas Cole.
      p.   cm.
   Translation of: Poesia e pubblico nella Grecia antica.
   Bibliography: p.
   Includes indexes.
   ISBN 0-8018-3290-X (alk. paper)
   1. Greek poetry—History and criticism.   2. Literature and society—Greece.   3. Oral tradition—Greece.   4. Greece—Intellectual life.   I. Title.
PA3093.G4613   1988
881′.01′09—dc19                                                                87-26852
                                                                                      CIP

*But neither can the culture of a period, however remote in time from us, be an entity closed in upon itself like a ready-made product to which the finishing touches have already been added, a thing dead and done with. . . . The unity which a given culture exhibits is an* open *unity. . . .*

*In the study of culture the perspective of distance is the most powerful tool for comprehension. A deeper, fuller view into the nature of a foreign culture only comes from the vantage point of a* different *one— though there will always be further aspects of the subject which subsequent cultures will perceive and understand more thoroughly. To plumb the depths of one meaning it is necessary to bring it into contact with another meaning—someone else's. At that point a sort of* dialogue *ensues to break down the isolation and onesidedness of the meanings and cultures involved. We ask of someone else's culture questions it could not ask of itself; we seek in it answers to these questions, and the other person's culture supplies them, revealing new aspects of itself and new depths of meaning in the process. Without asking* one's own *questions there is no creative understanding of anything about others or what pertains to them (though, naturally, the questions must be serious, genuine ones). In an inter-cultural dialogue of this sort there is no fusion or confusion: each culture preserves its own unity, its own* wholeness *and* openness, *while at the same time enriching, and being enriched by, the other.*

—M. M. Bakhtin, Reply to a Question
from the Editors of "Novyi Mir"

# Contents

# CONTENTS

. . .

# Preface to the
# English-Language Edition

The present work has no need of a lengthy introduction; the main lines of my method will be apparent from the start. If theories are understood as efforts to solve problems, then one need have no hesitation in saying that oral theory is a key that opens the door to the problem of the cultural and social function of Greek poetry from Homer to the fifth century in all of its vitality and concreteness. It is a key that allows a reevaluation of the decisive role played by audience and addressee, and with it a more precise conception of both the theoretical presuppositions of poetic activity and the symbolic, formal, and practical procedures it involved. Hence the constant attention I pay to the role of memory—the varying degrees in which traditional formulas and stylistic techniques were taken over and subjected to individual modification—to the poet's relationship to his patron and his public, and, finally, to the role of the intellectual and the economic and social factors conditioning it. My basic criteria of analysis are drawn from specialized disciplines such as philology, linguistics, anthropology, and sociology; the end toward which they are directed is, above all, a *concrete* understanding of the archaic mentality: its linguistic structures, its intellectual categories, the characteristic forms exhibited by its thought and its art. It is a basic principle of hermeneutics that to make sense any text must be read, initially, in terms of our own experience. This is the only way to arrive, ultimately, at a correct interpretation of the sense the text had for its author, or of the meaning it must have had in its original context. The guarantee of the validity of this method is the *sense of history* that it requires of the critic—an awareness of his own distance from his subject and a feeling for the unique and the particular which extends beyond the evolutionary, deterministic perspectives of traditional historicism.

The beginning of my investigation into the topics examined here dates back a number of years, to 1969. The occasion was the Fifth International Congress of Classical Studies, which marked a decisive turn in my own studies.[1] The course they have taken since then shares at a number of points the interests and perspectives of E. A. Havelock; the reader will also note the influence, though to a different degree, of Hermann Fränkel, Bruno Snell, and E. R. Dodds.

The work is the fruit of many years of close reading of Greek poetry—archaic lyric in particular. Specific investigations into different aspects of its theme were published earlier in various Italian and foreign periodicals. Some of them reappear here, reworked and expanded into a larger organic whole. The English-language version contains, as well as corrections and updatings, certain essential additions, which direct the reader's attention to disputed interpretations and to the recent scholarly literature on some of the subjects treated.[2] It omits the second appendix of the original edition, intended mainly for Italian readers: "On Translating the Lyric Poets: Some Observations on the Problem of Translation."[3]

I am especially grateful to my colleagues and to my collaborators, both Italian and foreign, at the Institute of Classical Philology of the University of Urbino, who have argued with me, both in private and in public, the issues dealt with here and contributed to their clearer formulation and presentation. My sincere thanks to my friend and colleague at the University of Urbino Professor Carlo Gasparri, who has seen to the selection of photographic material, revised and expanded for the English edition; and to Doctor Ettore Cingano, who has helped me in the revision and updating of the original Italian text. Finally, I wish to thank Professor Thomas Cole for his highly competent, perceptive translation—in gratitude and remembering, as always, our many years of friendship.

# Translator's Introduction

*I am the servant of Ares, lord of battle,*
*and I know the lovely gift of the Muses.*

So goes a famous fragment of Archilochus, composed in the early seventh century B.C. by the poet whom the Greeks of a later period regarded as the inventor of invective, satire, and iambic verse. The lines are preserved, like so much else that survives from the period, out of context, and much easier to translate than to understand and interpret. Is this Archilochus's Song of Himself—Western man wrestling for the first time with the problem of individual identity and seeking a solution along highly untraditional lines? Hermann Fränkel thought so, and developed the idea at some length in his *Dichtung und Philosophie des frühen Griechentums*—still the most ambitious interpretative history of early Greek literature yet attempted. Or is Archilochus refining and intellectualizing the Homeric ideal (*Iliad* 9, 443) of prowess on the battlefield linked to skill in deliberation, and so moving Greek morality one step further toward its ultimate, Platonic culmination? This interpretation would be in line with the view of the pedagogic function of early Greek literature advanced in the first volume of Werner Jaeger's once widely read *Paideia*. Contemporary fashion in classical studies might well lead, on the basis of the same Homeric parallel, to the conclusion that Archilochus is not saying anything in particular—merely paying himself a formulaic compliment. In chapter 10 of this work is an interpretation that is essentially different from these and, to my knowledge, from any others yet offered. Gentili takes the words not simply as a statement of individual competence but, more importantly, as an assertion of the "ability to guide and control" within one's own community. The result is almost an advertisement or an offer (my paraphrase): "Archilochus at your service, whether you need a captain to command your next campaign or a singer to supervise your next symposium."

If the reader finds this too ephemeral a remark for the inventor of invective and satire, or too speculative an interpretation for a scholar whose business is the explication of texts, he will probably not like this book. If he finds it persuasive, or intriguing, or interesting, he probably will; for the book marshals far more evidence than has hitherto been accumulated in a single volume for viewing archaic Greek poetry as composed, to a far greater extent than hitherto realized, of utterances of this sort—offers, exhortations, promises, prescriptions, prayers, curses, and the like—produced in a particular situation with particular addressees and particular practical ends in mind. The poet and public it discusses are never author and reader, but always performer and hearer: on the one hand a reciter or singer improvising in some sort of social setting—banquet, symposium, political gathering, religious rite, public festival—and, on the other, a largely or totally aliterate audience for whom such occasions function both as a source of entertainment, information, moral edification, and practical advice, and as the principal means for putting the here and now of one's day-to-day existence into some sort of larger cultural context.

The germ for this view of the basic character of early Greek literature goes back, as is well known, to a series of books and articles on Homer published by the American scholar Milman Parry between 1928 and 1935. In them Parry showed conclusively that the formulaic style of the Greek epic, the earliest Greek poetry that has come down to us, must have been in origin a technique developed to facilitate the task of oral improvisation. This demonstration was subsequently confirmed by comparative studies of Greek and south Slavic epic tradition conducted by Parry and his student A. B. Lord, and its wider implications for our understanding of archaic culture as a whole were spelled out in a series of publications beginning, in the early 1960s, with E. A. Havelock's *Preface to Plato*. It was there argued that what was true of epic was also true, by and large, of all of Greek culture until the late fifth century and that "orality" was the single most important factor in determining the character of that culture. In particular, the "didactic," community-oriented character of early Greek literature was inevitable, both because in an oral society poetry is the great repository of stored information—metrically encoded for easier remembering and recovering—on which the transmission of a culture from generation to generation rests, and because, in a world where poems and stories depend on performance before an actual audience for their transmission and survival, the purely private or personal element in literature will inevitably be eliminated or sharply curtailed. Equally difficult to develop in a purely oral context is what subsequent literary cultures know as philosophy or science; for philosophy and science require the notion of stable categories of being or constancy in nature, and such concepts are unlikely to arise before the words themselves in which they are to be couched become fixed and available for study and comparison in written form. The "ancient quarrel" between poetry and philosophy to which Plato refers in the *Republic* is only settled in favor of the latter in the fourth century, and through the activity of Plato himself, whose achievement is inconceivable apart from his ability to fix, through the composition of a set of written works, the basic curriculum and methods of investigation to be used in his Academy, the first Western university.

Havelock may be said to represent the oralist approach in its most rigorous form, a form in which it has been, probably, more widely accepted by Continental than by Anglo-American scholars, and outside rather than within the field of classical studies. It was greeted enthusiastically, for example, by Marshall McLuhan when first propounded in the early 1960s; and it has strongly influenced Walter J. Ong's wide-ranging studies (see, most recently, *Orality and Literacy* [1982]) on the interaction of orality and textuality throughout the history of the West. But the view of which Havelock has been the most vigorous and consistent proponent over the past twenty years seems well on the way to becoming, in one form or another, an essential ingredient in our conception of early Greece. It provides, for example, the point of departure for the brilliant evocation of the "song culture" of the archaic age which begins C. J. Herington's recent *Poetry into Drama* (1984).

Gentili's own work is partly a synthesis and survey of the oralist approach as it has developed over the past twenty years, enriching the discussion with far more extensive bibliographical references and a far greater amount of comparative material than any other classicist has yet brought together. At the same time, more importantly, it involves a broadening of perspective to include large areas of Greek literature where the possibilities of the method have remained, for the most part, unexplored. Earlier oralists had tended to concentrate on the study of Homer and Hesiod, where documentation was most extensive and the works involved were ones that had continued to play a significant role in the public life of Greek communities even in later antiquity. Occasional poetry from the archaic period presented a much more difficult problem. Except for the victory odes of Pindar and Bacchylides, composed toward the very end of the period, it is preserved in highly fragmentary form. And whereas the subject matter of the Homeric and Hesiodic poems had to be such that they could be understood and enjoyed by audiences all over Greece and during the course of several centuries, occasional poetry was always, in origin at any rate, meant for a particular place and time, often presupposing knowledge of local custom and local history to a degree that would make its survival, except in written form, very hard to explain. It is at this point that the distinction, drawn at the outset of Gentili's discussion, between oral composition (improvisation), oral "publication" (performance), and oral transmission (preservation, through memory, of all or part of an earlier performance) becomes crucial. We are dependent for our knowledge of Greek occasional poetry on a transmission that was, from the very beginning, at least partially written (author's copies, presumably, or official copies, when the occasion was an important one, or selections excerpted from such texts at a later date, when literacy was beginning to be more common). This does not exclude, however, oral composition or, above all, performance; and Gentili's review of large portions of the body of early lyric with the possible circumstances of performance in mind adds a new dimension to our understanding of the subject.

Here the author's own special expertise as metrician, interpreter, and textual critic—his editions of Anacreon and of the elegiac poets are standard, and an edition of Pindar's *Pythians* will soon appear—has had to be supplemented, in order to be fully effective, by other talents and attainments: a certain native *divinatio* and a more than passing acquaintance with the findings of comparative anthropology where relevant and available. The result is a rich, comprehensive, and engrossing picture of singer or reciter operating in contexts where poetry's role as a means of access to the collective memory of an entire culture is important, but probably less so than the way an individual oral performer registers, responds to, and sometimes shapes the mood or preoccupations or policy of the particular group that he is addressing. Whether the discussion involves a poem as part of homoerotic rites of passage within a women's *thíasos* (chap. 6), or a committed partisan's effort to galvanize the members of a political faction to violent actions against an opponent (chap. 11), or a campaign to expose the object of a personal vendetta to public shame and ridicule (chap. 10), Gentili is inevitably involved in a certain amount of speculative reconstruction, but reconstruction that is always as informed as the evidence will allow, never less than stimulating and often highly persuasive.

These are some of the most valuable sections of the book. They are the ones that make it, in some sense, a natural successor to the works of Jaeger and Fränkel mentioned at the outset. Nothing else has appeared in the half century since those two were written that shows the same comprehensive grasp of a whole period, or the same remarkable ability—an inheritance from the great tradition of nineteenth-century Continental scholarship which all three share—to focus on both minute philological detail and major cultural movements. The sections are also, inevitably, those that require the most formidable array of documentation and so make the heaviest demands on readers who are not specialists in the study of archaic lyric. The whole work is, in a sense, organized in such a way as to prepare gradually for this sort of coming to terms with fragmentary written texts deriving from what were themselves no more than passing moments in the life of an archaic Greek community. The first five chapters are a kind of orientation, historical and methodological. The general concept of orality and its implications are introduced in chapter 1, followed—for all Greek oral poetry was also sung poetry—by a discussion of the relation of poetic texts to the melodies and instrumentation that accompanied them. With chapters 3 and 4, devoted to early notions of genre and shifting attitudes toward poetic mimesis, one passes to a consideration of the way the Greeks themselves first divided and organized, then radically restructured their own notions of poetry as in the late fifth century oral techniques of communication began to give way to literate ones. Methodology is of central importance in the next chapter, dealing with the interconnection of synchronic and diachronic perspectives as they apply to the study of archaic poetry. Chapter 6 begins the discussion of specific genres—erotic, satirical, and encomiastic, both in themselves (chaps. 6–8) and in their larger socioeconomic context (chap. 9, where the topic is carried, for purposes of contrast and comparison, down into the Hellenistic period). Finally, there is an examination of selected individual texts and sets of texts, mostly Archilochean and Alcaean (chaps. 10–11), but culminating in the investigation of the meaning of the single word *hagnós* in a single line referring to Sappho (chap. 12).

All this will involve, for specialists, a certain amount of material with which they are already familiar; but the constant focus on what can be known or inferred about original performance situations means that the results of earlier scholarship are only reviewed to the extent that they cast light on new problems or new solutions. Here Gentili's contributions are both extensive and indispensable; and his historical orientation provides a needed corrective and counterbalance to what is probably the method of dealing with archaic texts most fashionable among classicists today. Ironically, the method, like Gentili's own, goes back to the work of Parry, though by a different route, and applies his findings in a completely different way. Parry's analysis of the formulaic character of Homeric diction was followed, in 1962, by E. L. Bundy's convincing demonstration of the equally "formulaic" character of large portions of the subject matter and thematic structure of the victory odes of Pindar and Bacchylides. A natural result, on the part of some of Bundy's followers, was a tendency to view the victory ode as totally formulaic in character—a skillful manipulation of the conventions of an elaborate encomiastic etiquette with minimal attention paid to anything beyond the identity and number of an athlete's victories that might distinguish him, the totally depersonalized *laudandus,* from any other athlete, or any one celebratory occasion from another such occasion. Epinician poetry is a succession of *topoi* capable of being used interchangeably for any *laudandus* by any poetic *laudator.* Further extension of this type of analysis to the entire corpus of early lyric—often under the influence of the essentially ahistorical perspectives of structuralist and poststructuralist criticism—can even lead to the assumption that the events and persons referred to there are purely "conventional"—fictitious exemplars of typical characters and situations. And this requires, in turn, the dismissal of much of the research of Alexandrian scholars into the background of archaic poetry. They were simply early victims of the "biographical" fallacy.

Readers must judge for themselves in any given instance how far they want to follow Gentili in his vigorous protest ("Traditional language does not and cannot mean eternal tautology" [chap. 8]) against this school of interpretation. Are Alcaeus's famous "ship of state" poems, for example, a series of exercises, ringing the changes on the process by which metaphor is extended into allegory, or an intimate part of factional strife in the city of Mytilene—a series of manifestoes in which the shifting fortunes of civil war are expressed in images only partially understandable to those not of the poet's own party or not familiar with the immediate background out of which each of his poems arises (see chap. 11)? My own position tends, in general, to be somewhere between that of Gentili and the "conventionalists"; though often there can be little doubt—as in the case of the example just cited—which approach makes for the more exciting, compelling group of texts.

*Compelling* is an adjective likely to appear more than once in describing the character of the occasional poetry of archaic Greece as it emerges in Gentili's expositions, and this impression obviously has something to do with the author's own preference, explicitly indicated on more than one occasion, for the poetry of involvement and commitment which can inspire this sort of reaction even across twenty-five centuries. There is an almost audible sigh of relief as he turns, toward the end of chapter 1, from the "bookish, solipsistic" traditions that have dominated Western poetry for over a century to a type of discourse that often, as he sees it, has little in common with what we now call poetry except the name. And a number of contemporary oralists show a similar affinity with their subject matter. It is a unifying thread running through their work quite as important as their shared intellectual assumptions. Thus Ong contrasts the "copious, warmly human, participatory" character of oral discourse with its "sparse, abstract, immobile" written counterpart (*Orality and Literacy*, p. 166); and Havelock has written an entire book to defend the practical, situation ethics that he associates with the orality of early Greece from the critique first voiced by Plato and echoed ever since by writers of treatises who share Plato's preference for an abstract ethics of moral absolutes. (Contrast in this respect the "non-oralist" perspective of A. W. H. Adkins, who is the leading Anglo-American exponent, along with Havelock, of the "developmental" view of Greek ethics first popularized by Bruno Snell, but whose analysis of pre-Platonic and even, to some degree, Platonic moral ideas is often a process by which those ideas are weighed, and found wanting, in a Kantian balance.) Even Parry's studies, concentrated though they were on certain purely formal features of epic style, go back to a fascination with formulaic language which had nothing to do with its mechanics. It was not, ultimately, the fixity and economy of the formula—the same idea always expressed in the same way when it appears in identical metrical contexts—which drew him to the subject, but the capacity of the formula for projecting the hearer at once into a world of shared values and assumptions—to be accepted or rejected as known quantities—without interference from what we would now call the self-referential or intertextual overcodings that come with the literate artist's search for individual expression and are the stock in trade of modern hermeneutics.

This shared enthusiasm coexists with varying degrees of optimism as to the prospects for reimporting certain archaic qualities of attitude and presentation into contemporary discourse. Parry himself likened the formulaic style to that of the English Augustans, and one suspects that reading and teaching Homer was for him a means of recovering some of the literary and moral certainties of the eighteenth century ("an ignoble translation" were the words with which one undergraduate's effort at colloquialism were dismissed—or so the undergraduate, the poet Robert Fitzgerald, later reported). Havelock is frankly skeptical, although in his most recent book he notes how an awareness of the growing importance of the radio for modern mass communications played a crucial role in turning his thoughts toward the phenomenon of orality in early Greece. Gentili, led—or misled—thereto by an article of Northrop Frye (see chap. 1), thought he saw in certain American poetic experiments of the late 1960s not only a reflection of renewed interest in oral forms of communication but also the direct influence of the teaching of oralists in American universities. (Like all Continental scholars, he finds it hard to realize just how little of academic *Geisteswissenschaft* is ever taken seriously by the general public, educated or uneducated, in Anglo-Saxon countries.) Yet, such differences notwithstanding, it is a fair guess that all three authors would find themselves more at home with certain aspects of the highly "politicized" writing of Latin America and Eastern Europe—its community orientation, its indifference to the distinction between popular and esoteric, rhetorical and "poetical," analysis and advocacy—than with contemporary products of their own literary tradition; and they invite us to believe that Anacreon and Alcman, Sappho and Alcaeus, Pindar and Bacchylides would feel the same way if they were in a position to make the same comparison. Like his distinguished predecessors, what Gentili offers at his best is not simply scholarly mastery but an invitation and a challenge—to reject or question both the time-honored practice of recreating archaic Greek culture in our own literate image and the equally time-honored proprietary feelings that Western men of letters have toward a culture that, by virtue of descent, they fancy themselves uniquely qualified to interpret and understand.

# Abbreviations

CALAME        *Alcman.* Critical edition with introduction, translation, and commentary, by C. Calame. Rome, 1984.

DEGANI        *Hipponax: Testimonia et fragmenta,* ed. H. Degani. Leipzig, 1983.

D.-K.        H. Diels–W. Kranz. *Die Fragmente der Vorsokratiker,* I–III. Zürich and Berlin, 1964[11].

FGRHIST        F. Jacoby. *Die Fragmente der griechischen Historiker.* Leiden, 1954–69.

GENT.        *Anacreon.* Critical edition with introduction, translation, and a study of the papyrus fragments, by B. Gentili. Rome, 1958.

GENT.-PR.        *Poetarum elegiacorum testimonia et fragmenta,* ed. B. Gentili–C. Prato. I, Leipzig, 1970; II, Leipzig, 1985.

P.        *Poetae melici Graeci,* ed. D. L. Page. Oxford, 1962.

SLG        *Supplementum lyricis Graecis,* ed. D. L. Page. Oxford, 1974.

SN.-MAEHL.        *Pindari carmina cum fragmentis,* ed. B. Snell–H. Maehler. Leipzig, 1975[4].

T .                        *Archiloco.* Critical edition with biographical and
                           literary testimonia, introduction, and translation,
                           by G. Tarditi. Rome, 1968.

V .                        *Sappho et Alcaeus.* Fragments, ed. E. M. Voigt.
                           Amsterdam, 1971.

W E S T                    *Iambi et elegi Graeci ante Alexandrum cantati,* I–II,
                           ed. M. L. West. Oxford, 1971–72.

# PART ONE

# I

. . .

# Orality & Archaic Culture

Greek poetry differed profoundly from modern poetry in content, form, and methods of presentation. An essentially practical art, it was closely linked to the realities of social and political life, and to the actual behavior of individuals within a community. It rendered the poet's own experience of human existence as well as that of others, but was not private poetry in the modern sense. It drew regularly for its themes on myth, which was at once the sole subject matter of narrative and dramatic poetry and a constant point of paradigmatic reference in lyric. It existed to inform and instruct, most explicitly so when composed with the needs of specific groups and occasions in mind: symposium, community festival (*kômos*), and male club (*hetairía*), for instance (Alcaeus and Theognis); or female *thíasos* and the premarital initiatory rites celebrated there (Alcman and Sappho); and this continued to be true when it took to the stage and adopted the modes and forms of dramatic representation. What distances it most radically from modern poetry is the medium of communication: not a written text for reading but a solo or choral performance, to the accompaniment of a musical instrument, before an audience. The regular word for poetry was *mousiké*, which designated the art in its totality, as a union of words and music; and the regular word for poet was, in the archaic period, *aoidós* (singer), or, later, beginning with the fifth century B.C., *melopoiós* (maker of songs) and *poietés*.

The sharpness of this contrast was noted as early as the turn of the century by Jacob Burckhardt.[1] Yet the differentiating features on

3

which he insisted—oral transmission and the link with music—were continually ignored by critics, especially as regards Greek lyric, on whose oral character Burckhardt had rightly placed special emphasis.

It is only in recent decades that the phenomenon of orality has become the object of extended investigations, on the part of medievalists and anthropologists as well as classicists. Among Hellenists, as is well known, it is the Anglo-American critics who have shown the greatest awareness of the problem, thanks to the decisive role played by the studies of Milman Parry, whose activity dates back to the 1930s. It may fairly be said that the whole American oralist school reflects, directly or indirectly, and with varying degrees of fidelity, the commanding influence of his teaching. This is true of A. B. Lord and even of Eric A. Havelock, in spite of the undeniable independence and originality of Havelock's approach, tending as it does to stress the role of memory in the oral process over that of improvisation.[2]

Any consideration of orality must provide at the outset a definition that takes into account both what is intrinsic and what is extrinsic to its basic nature. The phenomenon is encountered in many types of society, past and present, literate and aliterate—societies whose cultures may or may not be dependent on the circulation of books as a principal means of communication, and whose economies, developing or industrialized, differ greatly from one another. Such socioeconomic and cultural diversity makes generalization difficult and dangerous. Too rigid or restrictive a formulation runs the risk of elevating the historically determined characteristics of a particular oral culture to the level of universal definition. It is illegitimate, for example, to assume that oral poetry must necessarily belong to an oral tradition or be orally composed, or that its style be totally formulaic and paratactic. These are certainly characteristic features of many types of orality, but they do not define the phenomenon in the absolute. The critic's task is precisely this: to isolate in any given situation the distinguishing traits of the particular oral culture he is investigating.

To be called oral, poetry must meet one or more of three conditions: (1) oral composition (extemporaneous improvisation); (2) oral communication (performance); and (3) oral transmission (memorized poetic tradition).[3]

It goes without saying that oral transmission may either precede or follow the here and now of oral performance: a memorized composition may be recited or sung before an audience, or an improvised composition may be preserved through memorization. Thus, to use archaic Greek poetry as our example, it is in the light of these distinctions that

Plato's formulation in *Republic* 10, 603b is to be understood. Poetry is there defined as *aural*—created for the ear—by contrast with painting, which is created for the eye. The aurality referred to by Plato obviously belongs to the orality of communication, but also to that of transmission. The activity of the rhapsode as described and analyzed by him in the *Ion* consists in the performance, with gestures as well, of memorized passages from the Homeric poems.

The profession of oral poet calls for natural ability—or, as the Greeks would have said, *phýsis*—well beyond the ordinary, but it is equally true that the deployment of this individual talent would have been impossible without the possession of a refined mnemonic and compositional technique of great complexity. Essentially a craftsman's art, this technique was a recognized part of Greek culture from earliest times down to the end of the fifth century. Already in the *Odyssey* (17, 382ff.), Homer explicitly places the bard in the category of craftsmen (*demiourgoí*) and so in the same class as the seer, the doctor, or the carpenter. The poetic act does not take place at the level of esthetic creation, but rather at that of inventive imitation—as a reproduction of experience or of earlier poetic models.[4]

The art of memory has always been one of the fundamental means for the preservation of the information and ideas that form the fabric of a cultural tradition. The incisive ancient formulation found in the *Dissoi logoi* (fifth to fourth centuries) is still pertinent: "Memory is the greatest and most splendid of inventions—indispensable for living as well as for learning."[5] It undoubtedly provided the mainstay for the entire structure of Greek culture in its earliest phases, antedating writing in this respect, as is clear from Homer's description of the two bards Demodocus and Phemius. But even at a later period, once the practice of writing had already begun, it was felt more as a gift of the gods—and, above all, of the Muses—than as the work of men. So far as we know the first person to understand it as a genuine craft (*téchne*), articulated according to precise norms of its own that had to do with the visualization of space and images, was Simonides of Ceus (fifth to fourth centuries);[6] and his definition of poetry as "speaking painting" and painting as "silent poetry" is not simply evidence for a conception of the poet as craftsman.[7] It also provides, as Frances Yates has observed, the clearest possible indication of a unitary conception of "poetry, painting and mnemonics as a process of intense visualization."[8] All the mnemonic techniques elaborated subsequently for either words or things—from those of Aristotle, the *Rhetorica ad Herennium*, and Quintilian down through medieval and modern times to the treatise of

Leibniz—are based on a recognition of the fundamental importance of space and images.

It is necessary, of course, to draw a distinction, in theory, between memorization of topics and poetic formulas and mechanical memorization of texts preserved with word for word exactness. The matter is still the subject for debate among anthropologists and the data assembled seem to vary from culture to culture. J. Goody, for example, is inclined to recognize, in oral cultures where writing is completely unknown, only the first kind of memorization, confining the second to cultures where there is formal education in literacy.[9] Other anthropologists disagree, pointing out that "the variations both of form and content which are encountered in the ritual narratives and recited myths of illiterate nations are not in any sense the result of an inability to adhere to some optimal, canonical original—of whose existence, for good reason, there is never any trace—but rather to a conscious reworking on the part of the mythmaker which does not exclude—and often entails—glaring inconsistencies and even reversals of genealogical, circumstantial, and factual relationships."[10] The situation in Greek culture at its earliest stages seems to me precisely of this sort—as emerges also from the picture outlined with great clarity by E. A. Havelock, in specific reference to the genesis of the text of Homer.[11] The oral social context in which the Homeric poems first appeared was not, in his view, of such a sort as to allow the critic to draw a distinction between creative composition and mechanical repetition—as if two mutually exclusive categories were involved. One can only speak—at every stage in the process—of composer-performer or of aoidós (singer, bard) -rhapsoidós (professional reciter, rhapsode).

The evolution in meaning of the term rhapsoidós is relevant at this point and calls for a brief discussion. Like aoidós, the word was applied originally to poet-performers,[12] but with what some have thought was a difference in meaning having to do with the manner of performance or the relative importance of improvisation as against memorization, in which case the activity of the singer-bard would have been productive and creative, and that of the performer-rhapsode merely repetitive. In fact, however, the ancient evidence does not allow such a distinction, at least for the archaic period. Even the rhapsode's mode of performance might or might not involve the use of song. He could either sing his text to the accompaniment of the lyre, like Demodocus and Phemius, or declaim it holding the rhapsode's staff (rhábdos), like Hesiod, who in the proem to the Theogony (vv. 30ff.) depicts himself with wand in hand, a symbolic gift from the Muses on the occasion of his investiture as a poet.[13] We have Hesiod's own reference (fr. 357

Merk.-West) to himself and Homer as poets, and his description of how at Delos they both "sing" after "weaving in new hymns the fabric of their song" (*en nearoîs hýmnois rhápsantes aoidén*). It is obvious that *rháptein* is a concrete metaphor for the process of composition, describing the operation by which the strands or web of discourse are woven together.[14] In quoting the Hesiodic verses the historian Philochorus (fourth to third centuries) observes that rhapsodes were so called because it was their custom to "compose and weave the fabric of song" (*syntithénai kaì rháptein tèn oidén*).[15] He is referring to two complementary aspects of the poetic process, the putting together of the material of the story and the subsequent weaving of the plot.[16] (The type of performance to which Hesiod refers was dedicated, of course, to narrative poems composed in hexameters.)

I do not believe it possible to maintain that at the beginning of the sixth century rhapsodic activity had already degenerated into a mere execution of pieces learned by heart from the epic repertory.[17] On the contrary, we know that the rhapsode Cynaithos of Chios, who between 504 and 501 had recited Homer "for the first time" in Syracuse, was not only the performer but also the author of many epic verses that he is said to have interpolated into the corpus of the Homeric poems.[18] Creation and repetition thus continue to coexist as two aspects of the rhapsode's activity, even in the sixth century. And repetition included not simply the delivery of Homeric epic but also the oral performance of any text whatsoever drawn from the poetic tradition, in public recitations devoted not only to Hesiod and Homer but also to pieces from the repertory of iambic poetry (Archilochus, Semonides of Amorgos), elegy (Mimnermus), and lyric (Stesichorus).[19] The use of the word *rhapsoidós* is similarly ambivalent. It usually suggests epic composition[20] or recitation from Homer,[21] but is still not out of place in speaking of a rhythmical medley like the *Centauros* of Chairemon.[22]

It is difficult for the literate imagination to conceive the mental effort required for mastering and carrying out a piece of epic *mímesis*. The auditory memory may be said to be associative rather than synoptic. It lives and operates through a total but temporary immersion in one slice of mythic action before proceeding to the next. The Homeric poems offer so many possibilities for the rearrangement of episodes that no single ordering of them can be accepted as original and authentic. In each separately sung part there are allusions that presuppose the whole myth on which the epic is based. The performer is conscious of this, but his attention is absorbed by the theme of the moment and excludes everything else. A similar point is implicit in A. B. Lord's hypothesis about the way in which the poet *recalls*, rather than memorizes, the theme of his story. In thus insisting on the difference between remembering and recalling, he draws attention to the way the singer retains the myth and the basic compositional units of his narrative rather than a rigidly fixed verbal text. In Lord's view, song as creation is more important than song as repetition.[23]

It is in connection with the notion of the poet as a repository of cultural information that the concept of *divine inspiration* takes shape—as if poetry came not from the singer himself but rather by direct descent from the intervention of the divinities who are patrons of his song: Mnemosyne (Memory)[24] and the Muses. The same view appears in the *Ion*, where Plato analyzes the state of divine possession or "enthusiasm" that is characteristic of the rhapsode when reciting Homer before an audience at Panathenaic festivals. Such are the character and dimensions of the psychic tension inherent in the mind's capacity for memorization.

This nexus of ideas relating to poetry as inspired performance has a striking modern parallel. It reappears in connection with the typically and uniquely Italian phenomenon, most widely encountered in the eighteenth century, of learned poetry orally improvised and sung to the accompaniment of guitar or harpsichord. The performances were not simply for select audiences in aristocratic salons. They also appealed to the more heterogeneous groups assembled in theaters, oratories, public squares, and even hospitals. The theme of a song could involve any of the varied subjects that formed part of the general culture of the time, from classical mythology to natural science. The audience itself selected the improviser's theme, according to a precise code of conventions to which both singer and listener were bound. The character of the resulting poetic productions is known to us not simply from the press of the time but also through transcriptions made, sometimes without the knowledge of the poet, by special stenographers.[25]

The improvisation is noteworthy for the tetradic form it often took. Thus in several performances of Bernardino Perfetti, one of the most famous improvisers of the eighteenth century, a triad of alternating sacred and profane themes would be summarized in an *epilogo* or *ripetizione* and followed by a *pastorella*. The *pastorella* is a composition set off from what preceded by its playful, amorous, bucolic, or even, in some instances, scientific and didactic character, and cast in the form of a drama with two fixed characters, the shepherdess and Elpino.[26] The tetralogies, each of them composed for a single performance, varied in total length from around nine hundred to twelve hundred verses.

Of particular significance, given the oral context for which this poetry was intended, is the use of the *epilogo* or *ripetizione,* which recapitulated, with a different metrical structure, the themes already treated in a given recitation. Such a technique would serve no purpose in a piece of poetry composed for reading. Its primary function was to impress firmly on the memory of those present the context of what they had heard, forcing them to look beyond the variety of themes to the subtle connecting thread that underlay them.

In the construction of the epilogue, variations and expansions testify to the poet's capacity for innovative repetition. An analysis of the meters used is beyond the scope of the present discussion. The versification does not, however, diverge significantly from the mainstream represented by chivalric epic and "Arcadian" poetry. Ottava rima is reserved for narrative, historical, and mythological themes; the various stanzaic structures found in *canzone, pastorella,* and anacreontics are for material of ethical or scientific character, and so forth.[27] The technical competence displayed is, in general, at the same level as that of written poetry from the same period.

Various melodies, each one appropriate for a particular type of versification, were available to the improviser. Our main informant, Karl Ludwig Fernow, mentions aria structures,[28] usually of great simplicity and attractiveness, and so adaptable to a great variety of themes. Music was thus subsidiary to the poetic text: an ornament for the song and, at the same time, a means of filling the interval between stanzas or individual verses, especially when the improviser needed a moment's pause for thought. This relation between words and music recalls the phenomenologically analogous process by which melodic design was accommodated to an unfolding verbal text in the poetic productions of archaic Greece.[29] Improvised as they were, the melodies have, of course, disappeared almost completely. The only exceptions are those published by Fernow in his appendix.[30]

References in eighteenth-century Italian literary theory to the "madness" that accompanies poetic improvisation reflect a clearly formulated "poetics of divine possession" that is analogous in important ways to the Greek notion of poetic "enthusiasm."

In this connection the views of Bernardino Perfetti as reported by Domenico Cianfogni, his contemporary and the first editor of his improvised poems, are of great interest:

Thou knowest well, Lord, that Thou art the principal object—nay, sole goal—of the Song that I send forth with a pure heart, having no other aim in mind than Thy greater glory, Thy divine pleasure. *Tamquam prodigium factum sum multis.* Wherefore I am well aware, Lord, that many of those present at the singing of my Song regard it as something, if not altogether supernatural, at least *preternaturale*, that is, exceeding the accustomed order of Nature, and thereby marvel at it as a thing half miraculous. The which notwithstanding, all is owing to Thee, all is Thy gift, and pure grace of Thine vouchsafed to me, without aught that I have merited of my own.[31]

The document also has a bearing on the frequent custom of beginning a recitation with a brief invocation, to the Muse or the deity according to the character of the poet's theme.[32] The practice is, of course, exactly paralleled in the archaic Greek poet's traditional proem—his practice of beginning his song, whether epic or lyric, by an invocation to the Muses, the Graces, or some other divinity, such as Apollo or Zeus.

We thus find ourselves face to face with a veritable "theology" of the poetic process—a perfect correlate to the objective fact of the extraordinary physiological tension required of the improviser if he is to achieve a perfect performance. The whole subject is well illustrated by the vivid and detailed picture given by the Abbé Bettinelli, in his *Dell'entusiasmo delle belle arti,*[33] of the behavior and emotional state of the singer-improviser: after a hesitant beginning, slow and insecure because of the initial moment of concentration and preparation, he suddenly rouses himself, fired up to take flight on the wings of song. There are clear external signs of inspiration: a rapt gaze detached from everything that surrounds him, glances cast on high. As if oblivious of himself, he is absorbed in a new world of images and entrancing visions. His participation in the pleasure of the poetic vision excludes all else. There are even reactions of a strictly physiological character: bloodshot eyes and flushed cheeks. The tone of his voice rises and gesticulation becomes more violent, as if the performer were overwhelmed by a flood of ideas, images, and rhymes. The means of execution reflect mimetically the thematic development of the poetic message, to the point that the instrumental accompanist finds it difficult to make the music keep pace with the onrush of the meter. The enthusiasm of the poet communicates itself to his audience, who are carried away by his inspiration and his song. Emotional identification becomes absolute in the pleasure and intoxication that the occasion brings. What Bettinelli's lucid exposition is presenting thus far is evidently a sort of physiology of oral poetic communication. He goes on to tell how, when the tension has reached its highest point, the poet falls into a state of exhaustion and prostration, leaving the audience in absorbed silence. Applause follows, and an instrumental interlude, after which the singer asks the audience to set a new theme for him and the same scenario is repeated, to a maximum of four or five performances. Charles de Brosses testifies to the presence of similar ritualistic elements in the improvisations of Perfetti.[34]

Further corroboration comes from Fabi Montani's account of one of the most famous and admired of oral poets, Francesco Gianni. Active at the end of the eighteenth and the beginning of the nineteenth century, Gianni was the official singer of the victories of Napoleon and even received an annual pension from the emperor in return for his services.[35] Of his performances Montani writes that

> one had merely to look at him once he was given a subject for improvisation—the way he would gather together his energy, the flush that would come to his face and the fire in his eyes, the wild looks, the ruffled hair, arms impetuously extended and a convulsive movement imparted to the whole body—in order to be convinced that such things were not the ready-made products of art. He was truly in the grips of divine force similar to that which overpowered the pythoness in the scene which Virgil has described for us. He would not sing his verses in the way all the others were accustomed to do; rather, he would declaim with such breakneck speed that it was sometimes barely possible to follow the sequence of thought.[36]

The inventory could continue. But one more brief mention will suffice, drawn from the Countess Silvia Curtoni Verza's tribute to the inspired virtuosity of Bartolomeo Lorenzi:

> Before beginning his song he grows pale and slightly agitated, standing with a fixed gaze that seems to be looking but in fact sees nothing; then, after a few verses, his imagination takes fire, the voice becomes steady and resounding, he seems an Apollo speaking from his oracular seat and infusing the spectators with incredible ecstasy.[37]

It is pure coincidence, but a significant coincidence nonetheless, that the reference to oracular prophecy is exactly paralleled in a passage of Strabo.[38] *Apophoibázo*, a term referring to the practice of divination, is there used in connection with Diogenes of Tarsus, a poet of the second century who improvised "tragic poems" on subjects chosen by his audience. Song is understood as an immediate reflex of inspiration coming from Apollo.

The main lines of this doctrine are traced out in systematic form by Plato, especially in the passages of the *Ion* and the *Phaedrus* concerned with the phenomenon of poetic *manía*—explicitly likened by Plato to the inspired trance of the prophet (*Phaedr.* 245a). The poet, whether epic or lyric, is possessed by a divinity and becomes in the act of composing a direct intermediary for the divine afflatus, which he transmits to his audience, exactly as a magnet transmits its powers to the objects that it has itself attracted. These powers nullify all the rational faculties of the possessed, producing in him a state of hypnosis.[39] Technical expertise is a necessary but not a sufficient condition for producing a composition worth remembering: without inspiration a poet is condemned to mediocrity. Behind this theorizing, the presuppositions of which are already to be found in certain pronouncements of Democritus,[40] there lies the author's entire experience of earlier poetry, whose distinctiveness is a function of its orality.

It is primarily against the irrationality of poetry that Plato's critique is directed: its failure to provide a reasoned analysis of experience or a genuinely dialectical development of thought through a logical sequence from cause to effect.[41]

Even this polemical aspect of Plato's analysis has parallels in the eighteenth century. For much as the extemporized poetry of the period was admired, critics were still capable of noting certain of its limitations, and the limitations involve precisely the absence of rational coherence of which Plato had complained. No one was better qualified to voice this charge than Metastasio, who in his youth had practiced the art of improvisation with great success, even participating in poetic contests with one of the most famous virtuosos of the day, Bernardino Perfetti. A letter to Francesco Algarotti, dated 1 August 1751 and written in Vienna, notes that his teacher, Gravina, was the one who induced him to stop the practice of that art, considering it harmful to his formation as a poet. It was always the case, he explains, that

> agitated as I was in the process by the violent conflict of my spirits, my head would become feverish and my countenance flushed to a degree that was incredible, my hands and other extremities remaining all the while as cold as ice. For this reason Gravina decided to use all his teacher's authority in enforcing upon me a rigorous abstention from improvisation in the future—a prohibition which from the age of sixteen I have always scrupu-

lously observed and to which, I am convinced, I owe what little of rational clarity and logical coherence is to be found in my writings. For, upon mature reflection as to the mechanism of that useless and brilliant calling, I have become fully persuaded that the mind condemned to perform in such bold, unpremeditated fashion must of necessity take on a habit of thought that is diametrically opposed to reason. The poet who writes at his leisure chooses the subject and end of his labors, regulates the continuous chain of ideas which leads thither by a natural progression, and only subsequently avails himself *of meters and rhymes as faithful agents in the execution of his design* [italics mine]. He who, by contrast, exposes himself to the venture of poetic improvisation becomes the slave of those tyrants and before thinking of anything else must use the brief time at his disposal for the purpose of marshaling up rhymes to fit the scheme that the other contestant has bequeathed him and into which he has fallen unawares. He must then take up the first thought that comes into his head capable of being expressed with those rhymes, bizarre though they are for the most part and sometimes totally out of keeping with the subject matter.[42]

Metastasio is being purely autobiographical here, but in speaking of his decision to give up the practice of improvising he adduces arguments almost identical to those developed many centuries earlier by Isocrates concerning his own youthful choice of a career as writer rather than public speaker. There is the same reference to the degree of physical and spiritual commitment required by the oral performer, just as there is to the inherently rational, reflective character of the writer. And there is the same recognition of the unquestionable advantages that are part of the very nature of oral discourse.[43]

The improvised poetry of the eighteenth century provides evidence that has an undeniable bearing on two fundamental problems: one has to do with compositional technique and style, the other with the relationship between spontaneity and tradition. It is obvious that formulaic technique is not a characteristic feature of all extemporized poetry. It may be replaced, depending on the possibilities a particular cultural situation offers, by other devices, such as rhyme and assonance. And it is equally obvious that the terms in which the relationship between spontaneity and tradition presents itself will be very different in a culture where literate communication is unknown from what they are in a culture where oral poetry flourishes alongside a well-developed literary tradition. In the second instance it is clear that the repertory on which the "spontaneity" of the improviser is based is supplied by extensive reading and memorization of poetic texts—in particular, in the case of the extemporizers of the eighteenth century, by a reading of Dante, the chivalric epic of the fifteenth and sixteenth centuries, and Renaissance and Arcadian lyric. This can be demonstrated in detail by lexical and stylistic analysis and was perceived even at the time. A contemporary critic observed of the poet Sante Ferroni that "he combined the fire of extemporization with a refinement and polish that make his improvised verses almost seem as if they had been written."[44]

On the other hand, given a culture which, though it may know the alphabet, has not come to be based on literacy, the poet will spend his apprenticeship on the learning and memorization of traditional songs, orally transmitted. The tradition, it should be stressed, is not a closed, static one—not a finished product or a repertory of fixed conventions. It is dynamic and open to the innovations in vocabulary, formulaic technique, and narrative which each poet introduces to fit his songs to the particular needs of performance on different occasions and before audiences with differing expectations. The process involves a craftsman's highly specialized technique, poised as it is at the moment of intersection between tradition and innovation or, in Saussurian terms, between *langue* and *parole*.[45] Our own tradition of poetry—bookish, solipsistic, a product of desk and study—has unaccustomed us to the social dimensions of a poetry that is *actually created* through a process of collaboration and interaction between artist and public.[46]

It is in precisely such terms—as expertise in public discourse, whether poetry or prose, pertaining to history, religion, or the nature of the physical world—that the activity of the "wise man" (*sophós*) is conceived in Greece from the earliest period down to the end of the fifth century.[47] This is true for all the varieties and phases of orality which are encountered over the course of time and which may be distinguished from each other according to whether they meet one or more of the three conditions set forth at the start of our discussion: orality of (*a*) composition, (*b*) communication, and (*c*) transmission.

In the earliest phase of epic, song was certainly the product of what we have defined as compositional orality—that is, improvisation. Book 8 of the *Odyssey* presents a detailed picture of precisely such a singer, exercising his calling in the restricted context of a royal banquet (v. 62ff.) or in the larger one of public performance before a large audience (v. 258ff.) and to the accompaniment of a silent chorus of young men who do dances to the rhythm of the lyre and the song. The singer is the bard Demodocus, and his songs are monodic renderings of epic poetry dealing with the deeds of gods and heroes during the Trojan War. But there is another element in the picture which emerges from

Homer's account. The bard's song has a strophic structure, as is clear from the presence of the chorus of dancers. As I have shown in a study of the prehistory and genesis of the hexameter,[48] this epic-lyric type of sung performance antedates purely recitational performances in the normalized hexameter form in which the Homeric poems have come down to us.

There can be no doubt that the composition that figures in the Homeric account is a piece of oral improvisation, given Demodocus's ability to change the content of his song according to the requests of his audience. The professional competence of the poet consisted in his ability to extemporize a song on episodes of which he knew only the basic narrative outline (*oíme*).[49]

Demodocus's mode of delivery, as described by Homer, presents the distinctive traits of the type of poetry known as citharoedic.[50] Heraclides Ponticus, writing in the fourth century, traced a continuity of poetic tradition between this type of pre-Homeric composition and the post-Homeric lyric narratives of Stesichorus;[51] and in the light of the Homeric evidence, his view should be accepted as historically valid, both as pertains to subject matter (heroic narrative) and to form (strophic song construction) and meter (dactylo-anapests and epitrites "in the enoplion manner" [*kat' enóplion*]).

Viewed from this standpoint Milman Parry's theory of formulaic technique requires reexamination in a new light: what emerges for the earliest phase of the tradition is not necessarily composition in hexameters but versification based on a looser association of the *cola* that gave metrical shape to the eight types of formulaic structure isolated by Parry.[52]

Demodocus, like Phemius, the other bard who appears in the *Odyssey*, belongs to the earliest, oral-aural phase of development, for whose existence all three of the conditions for orality had to be met. At a second stage, after the introduction of the alphabet—usually assumed to have occurred between the middle of the ninth and the middle of the eighth century[53]—it is possible that pieces of the epic repertory were sporadically committed to writing, to facilitate memorization of the main elements in the story or the beginnings and conclusions of a song. It has been suggested,[54] for example, that the Catalogue of Ships in book 2 of the *Iliad*, or the two councils of the gods in the *Odyssey*, which provide the starting point for a whole series of episodes, may have been among the earliest pieces so transcribed. The technique of writing could have served at the beginning as a mnemonic aid.

The hypothesis of a partial transcription for mnemonic purposes certainly seems far less fanciful and unfounded than others, which date the fixing of epic material in written form to the remote epoch of the Mycenaean syllabary (Linear B), in use between the fifteenth and the thirteen centuries, or posit a written redaction of the *Iliad* and the *Odyssey* at the end of the eighth century, only a generation after the introduction of the alphabet.[55]

As far as the first hypothesis is concerned, it is impossible to believe that Mycenaean scribes, employed to compile palace catalogues and inventories and using syllabic script, would have been able to come up with a redaction of epic songs; they would have produced, if anything, reduced and simplified texts, compatible with the inherent limitations of the mode of writing they employed. These limitations

> would require economy and repetitiousness of vocabulary with minimum variation in types of statement. Catalogues and quantities would abound, psychological analysis would be absent. Though metre might be retained, performance would be not popular but liturgical, reserved for high occasions. Meanwhile "Homer" would have continued in composition and recitation among the people, but with the likelihood that the quality of oral art practiced would have suffered because the linguistic brains were being drained off into the scribal centers. Homer's formulaic complexity, unique among the surviving remnants of oral poetry, bespeaks a culture totally non-literate, in which a monopoly of linguistic sophistication was vested in the bard.[56]

Seen in this perspective the continuity of poetic tradition between the Mycenaean and archaic Greek periods becomes more evident, and Heraclides Ponticus's testimony of particular relevance when he makes Stesichorus the heir, in epic content and metrical structure, to the citharoedic tradition in its most ancient, "pre-Homeric" form. If the Mycenaean scribes had produced transcriptions of epic materials for the exclusive use of palace or temple, the collapse of Mycenaean civilization would have brought with it the irrevocable destruction of the earliest Western epic as well, or at any rate a burial for centuries from which it would only now be emerging—along with the clay tablets devoted to lists and inventories. In fact, however, it survived the Greek dark ages and was able to flourish in the archaic period precisely because of the persistence of an oral mode of life and thought and through the creative vitality of the bardic tradition. Whatever the outcome of the contemporary debate on the continuity between Mycenaean and archaic Greece on the level of socioeconomic or political structures,[57] it is impossible to doubt the objective evidence for the persistence of Mycenaean traditions, mythical and historical, in the memory of the bards.[58] Recent archaeological discoveries attesting to Mycenaean presence in Sicily and south-central Italy before the era of Greek colonization[59] provide further confirmation of ancient traditions of heroic voyages in the western Mediterranean and of all those legends out of which, for example, the narrative fabric of the poetry of Stesichorus is composed.

Concerning the other hypothesis—that which posits a Homeric text already committed in its entirety to alphabetic script at the end of the eighth century—it is obvious that we are not in a position to know the scope and extent of the two poems at that time. If transcribed in their entirety, in the form in which they have come down to us, on what material were they written? Certainly not papyrus, which was not yet in common use at that time and only became so, as is well known, in the final quarter of the seventh century, when Egypt established conditions favorable for its export to foreign markets. Herodotus (5, 58) tells us that, when the Phoenician alphabet was introduced into Greece, the writing material used was not papyrus, which was hard to obtain, but skins of goats and sheep. Can one really suppose that the twenty-four books of the *Iliad* and the twenty-four books of the *Odyssey* were first permanently transcribed, in an era when written technology was as yet inadequate to the production of large-scale works, *on skins?*[60]

The material conditions of cultural development at the end of the eighth century seem to impugn rather than support the thesis of a complete Homeric text already prepared and transcribed for use by rhapsodes. And one cannot help but be struck, in reviewing the ancient critical testimony, by the categorical assertion (*Contra Ap.* 1, 12) of the late Jewish writer Flavius Josephus, one of the pieces of evidence on which Wolf made his whole theory hinge:

> Nowhere in Greece can there be found a piece of writing which is considered more ancient than the poetry of Homer. It is clear that he lived after the Trojan War; it is said that he left his poetry, not in written form, but committed to memory in a version which was later arranged into books, and that it is for this reason that many variants are encountered in the text.[61]

Whatever value one attaches to Josephus's testimony, no piece of historical or achaeological evidence has yet turned up to invalidate it. On the contrary: the picture presented here of an epic based exclusively on extemporaneous composition, memory, and oral transmission has been fundamental to all of modern oral theory. As to the question of where and when the two poems were given unified, written form, one can only reply with hypotheses based in various degrees on evidence external to the poems themselves. Rather than retrace the peregrinations of an endless discussion, carried on for centuries from postclassical antiquity down to our own day, I will limit myself to a few essential points. Obviously, given the nature of the topic, they will not be universally accepted. But creative understanding, whether in the study of nature or of man, springs more from disagreement than agreement.

The usual point of departure for the discussion are two notices found in the pseudo-Platonic *Hipparchus* (228b) and Cicero's *De oratore* (3, 137). We know from the first that Hipparchus, the son of Pisistratus, introduced the poems of Homer into Attica, along with the practice of having them recited in shifts, without interruption, at the Panathenaic festival. The second,[62] on the other hand, credits Pisistratus with bringing together the "scattered songs" of Homer and arranging them in the form in which they came down to Cicero and his contemporaries.

Even if we ignore the problem of the authenticity of the two notices (particularly that transmitted by Cicero)[63] and their contradictory character, and admit the possibility that in the sixth century, in the time of Pisistratus or his sons, Homer's work was available in writing, we still do not know whether this "proto-historic"[64] edition already had the canonical form with which we are familiar. We cannot even be sure that this was true of the personal edition possessed by the Sophist Euthydemos of Chios,[65] a contemporary of Socrates, even though it is explicitly stated to have contained "all the verses of Homer." What were the character and contents of the complete Homer, memorized by Niceratos, the son of Nicias,[66] or the Homer owned by the teacher who dumbfounded Alcibiades with the textual corrections he introduced?[67] Chance factors must have entered significantly into their formation if they were subject to tampering from a schoolmaster; and it is hard to imagine any comparable work more subject than the Homeric epic in fact was in the course of its long history to manipulation of the most diverse sorts, with or without political motives, to meet the needs of situation or audience, and on both the part of public performers and those who made transcriptions for private use.[68] The fluidity of the Homeric "text" down to the time of the canonical Alexandrian edition bears witness to the characteristic vitality and scope of a cultural phenomenon that revealed to the Greeks over the course of many centuries their distinctive cultural identity.

The questions posed here are timely ones in the context of contemporary Homeric criticism, inclined for the most part to the view that Greece had attained *full* literacy before the beginning of the fifth century. The invention of alphabetic writing and its initial use on more or less durable materials for sepulchral and votive dedications, or for fixing the contents of social and legal codes, was one thing; the practice of large-scale composition and diffusion of texts—sufficient to allow for the fixing in writing of a vast work like the Homeric poems—was a different matter. The production and circulation of books did not become current until the second half of the fifth century;[69] it is no accident that references to the practice of reading and the new function of the written word as symbol begin to proliferate in poetry[70] and art[71] precisely in this period—from the second quarter of the century on.

The acquisition of literacy was a much slower process than anything we can readily imagine, and the gradual course of its development within a society that remained for the most part aliterate did not substantially change the system of communication or the psychology and mode of thought that were part and parcel of traditional oral culture. The power of memory remained unaltered, as did the oral character of poetic communication and transmission. The most significant fact here is the presence in epigraphic versification of formulas, stylistic features, and meters that belonged to the repertory of citharoedic or choral poetry.[72] (It is purely gratuitous skepticism to deny a priori, as some scholars have done, the very possibility of such an epigraphic use of lyric meters.) The authors responsible for the inscriptions, sometimes professional poets themselves, operated within an orally disseminated tradition whose formulary, style, and versification were a common patrimony, learned aurally and reutilized for epigraphic composition. It is impossible to imagine these authors bent over papyrus rolls of Homer and the lyric poets in order to copy out words and phrases for their own use.

The roots of this orality held firm until the end of the fifth century. Even the drama was a performance to hear, see, and memorize;[73] and such it remained for several centuries more, even when writing had come to be felt, in the context of later book culture, as a genuinely and specifically literary activity.

As far as the modes of poetic composition are concerned—the crux of the ongoing debate on orality—it is important to note that there is no significant break in continuity between the world of epic and the age of lyric. If there was any break at all, it must have manifested itself elsewhere, in an increased tendency to record and preserve by means of written technology—the art that Aeschylus calls "the putting together of letters," "universal memory," and "hard-working mother of the Muses" (*Prom.* 460ff.). There is no need to doubt that Archilochus was an oral poet like the Homeric bard;[74] his language and modes of thought still followed along for the most part in the wake of epic diction.[75] The creative aspects of his work are closely linked to particular situations and events in the varied course of his career as a poet and do not constitute a valid objection to the thesis of oral composition. For oral poetry is no less creative than written. Given the added fact that they are, by epic standards, very brief, the poems of Archilochus were perhaps written down by the poet or others after being composed, then memorized and diffused, like Homer, through the performance of rhapsodes.[76] From the reference in fragment 188 T. to the messenger's stick or *skytále*,[77] one may assume that the normal writing material was skin.[78] Similar conclusions about the orality of Hesiod and the Homeric hymns may be drawn from the results of recent research on their formulaic systems.[79] For the Hesiodic poems in particular the most plausible hypothesis is that their transcription formed the intermediate stage between composition and oral transmission.

The same must have held true in the archaic period for elegiac and iambic composition and for the solo song with string accompaniment, poetic genres destined for performance at symposia or some other type of social gathering. Many poems in Alcaeus, Sappho, Solon, the Theognidean collection,[80] and Anacreon must have been composed in the immediate *hic et nunc* of a particular occasion. Even some of the brief odes, without a myth, of Bacchylides and Pindar (Bacchylides 4, for Hieron; 6, for Lacon; Pindar *Ol.* 11 and 12; *Pyth.* 7) were evidently improvised immediately following the victory of the athlete and taught by rote to the chorus that was to perform them. Recent investigations into methods of poetic composition and performance in the Gilbert Islands of the South Pacific[81] have shown how oral poets of the region elaborate their songs through a long process of solitary meditation supplemented by sessions especially convoked for the purpose, in which they listen to the opinion and advice of colleagues. They devote particular care to diction, following the canons of a demanding and refined technique. Once he has composed the poem, the poet teaches it to those who will perform it; the chorus learns the piece phrase by phrase and executes the accompanying dance movements. Even rehearsals are long and elaborate. The comparison can give an idea of how the Greek choral poet—who might also be his own chorus master[82]—prepared his choir for the performance of the song, having them memorize the text and indicating the musical "modes" and melodies that were to accompany it. One should remember that written musical notation did not antedate the second half of the fifth century.[83]

The suggestion that oral techniques of composition were used in lyric poetry is not a mere hypothesis. Even in the Hellenistic period, Diogenes of Tarsus would improvise tragedies on themes proposed by the audience[84] – just as his distant successor Tommaso Sgricci was to do for the theater public of the eighteenth century.[85] The skepticism that the idea arouses in some scholars is based on a preconceived identification of orality with oral composition alone, an identification excluding the possibility of compositional structures influenced by orality of performance and transmission. Yet these two elements are an undeniable part of the phenomenology of the lyric; and even the basic linguistic structures of lyric continue to show, down to the late archaic period, the unmistakable marks of origin in oral tradition.

The practice and theory of poetic improvisation in the eighteenth century is, as we have seen, a phenomenon of the highest interest, both for oralists and classicists. But it is also significant for what it tells us about the history of the developing awareness, in modern Europe, of the cultural experience of Greece. What is involved is a clear recognition – for the first time in the history of the West – of the oral character of large portions of the Greek poetic tradition.

The recognition is already implicit in G. B. Vico's intuition of the orality of the Greek epic,[86] but the same vision of Greek poetry also pervades the extensive body of publications which accompanied and sustained the activity of the improvisers of the eighteenth century. Hence the emphasis that certain key aspects of ancient poetic theory receive – for example, its conception of the relationship between artistic skill and natural talent, and the notion of inspired composition in a state of poetic and artistic possession. The continuity of Greek and Italian traditions in this respect was the object of a far-reaching analysis on the part of Saverio Bettinelli, who maintained that the Greeks and the Italians were the only two peoples with an unusual natural propensity for inspired creativity in music, poetry, and the figurative arts.[87] The very lively attention paid in this period to the poetic activity of the Greeks and to their innate artistic gifts was less the result of the reconstructions of scholars than a "rediscovery" linked closely to the direct experience of poetic improvisation.

The awareness of this phenomenon was not confined within the boundaries of Italy; it involved all of European culture, English, French, and German, as well as Italian, at the turn of the century,[88] and it lies behind Wolf's intuitions as to the oral character of Homeric poetry.[89] I do not, of course, mean to suggest that the theory of Milman Parry is already present in the ideas of Wolf or some other scholar of his time. Parry alone should have the credit for having offered for the first time a coherent and systematic conception of formulaic technique and its function.[90] I only wish to emphasize the importance of these first approaches to the problem of orality, approaches subsequently lost sight of as research on Homer came to be dominated by the perspective of nineteenth-century analysts.

The vision of Greece which, beginning with Winckelmann, neoclassicism appropriated as its own was, as is well known, an elaboration based on models drawn from Hellenistic art—and as such a fundamental misrepresentation of the historical reality of the archaic and classical periods. Its influence on all subsequent European culture has been enormous, not only in the realm of philology and ancient history but also in that of education. Certain aspects of Greek poetry from Homer to the time of the tragedians have become accessible only in this century, thanks to Parry's theory. The notion of a traditional poetry, formulaic in its technique, social in its orientation, and dependent in the last analysis on a process of interaction between singer and audience, provides the indispensable key for a correct understanding of the Greek cultural achievement in its pre-Platonic, preliterary stages.

A number of indications suggest that the time may be at hand for the recovery of Greece as it existed at an earlier period, in the ripe vitality of archaic modes of thought and communication. There is a kind of bridge that passes over the neoclassicism familiar to an earlier generation and nineteenth-century idealism in its various manifestations to form a direct link between the earliest stages of Western poetry and the requirements of a new orality whose outlines are now beginning to take shape—as a challenge to the bookish exclusiveness that has been characteristic of modern poetry. The prospect thus opened up is the one described by Northrop Frye:

> But the cultural changes of the last two decades or so make it obvious that we are beginning to move into a different cultural orbit, and one which is recapturing many of the qualities of pre-literate culture. The revival of oral poetry is the most obvious of these new factors: poetry read or recited to groups which is close to improvisation, usually has some kind of musical accompaniment or background, and often takes the form of commentary on a current social issue. . . . Poetry which addresses a visible audience must win the sympathy of that audience, and hence a surface of explicit

statement embodying social attitudes that the audience can share comes back into poetry. Of the characteristics of an oral culture that are once again with us, one is what Wyndham Lewis recognized and deplored as the "dithyrambic spectator." Such poetry demands a consolidation of public opinion. We shall not, I hope, go so far as to retribalize our culture around formulaic units. . . . But a similar oral context, and a similar appeal to immediate emotional response, is obviously reappearing in our literature.[91]

Frye's interesting prediction was in effect borne out with the appearance, in the America of the 1970s, of a poetic avant-garde defining itself as "postmodern" and drawing on the picture of oral poetry built up in recent decades, not only by cultural anthropologists but, above all, by the most widely influential of American philologists—those belonging to the tradition represented by the works of Parry, Lord, and Havelock. In its well-manned ranks are to be found poets and theoreticians who have opened a lively and stimulating debate on what they call "open" poetry, or poetry of "dialogue" and "process."[92]

# II

· · ·

# Poetry & Music

*Compromise between sound and meaning does not admit of partial solutions in favor of the one or the other.*

*Poetry . . . is music composed with words and even with ideas: it happens the way it happens, born out of an initial intoning of which there is no hint until the first verse is formed.*

—*Eugenio Montale,* Sulla poesia

From earliest times, public performances in Greece were a matter of words linked to music and dance. It is no accident that poetry, at least in the case of certain melic forms like the hyporcheme, was called a "speaking dance,"[1] so close was the association of the verbal sign with the musical and gestural one. This is why the term *mousiké*, "the art of the Muses," was taken over to indicate not only the art of sounds but also that of poetry and dance—the basic means of communication in a culture that transmitted its messages publicly, through the medium of performance. The composer of choral songs for festivals and the poet-performer of solo pieces for various social occasions in the life of the community were agents in the diffusion of a culture that used the resources of poetic language and the harmonies of rhythm and melody to facilitate listening and memorizing.

The paideutic possibilities of this combination of word, melody, and dance were obvious. *Mousiké* was felt to be the most efficacious of all the arts that the educator had at his disposal. In sketching its relationship to painting and sculpture, the musicologist Aristides Quintilianus (second or third century A.D.) observes (*De musica* p. 56, 6ff. W-I.) that the latter have a limited effectiveness, presenting as they do a purely visual, static representation of reality; and that poetry without melody and dance acts on the soul through the auditory faculty but is unable to arouse *páthos*. *Mousiké*, on the other hand, by means of words, melody, and dance (the last a mimetic, rhythmic representation of action), acts on both sight and hearing to achieve in dynamic rather than static fashion the highest degree of mimesis. Aristides' remarks on the communicative aspects of *mousiké* are applicable *tout court* to the culture of archaic Greece, based almost exclusively on oral communication of the poetic message, and on its aural, visual reception—a combination of poetry and spectacle which becomes the principal means for the diffusion and transmission of knowledge. The paideutic potential of an art whose mimetic qualities allowed it to create public involvement on an emotional as well as intellectual level had become an object of theorizing as early as the fourth century. Plato saw its effect as a negative one: it made the soul unamenable to control by reason;[2] Aristotle by contrast felt that art's ability to arouse strong emotions could perform a cathartic function, cleansing the soul and making its passions harmless in real life.[3]

None of the melodies performed in Greece during the archaic and classical periods has come down to us. We know only their names and, for some of them, certain details of a technical or sociological character: the sacral or ritual purpose that each was felt to have, and its paideutic role in arousing in an audience emotions and attitudes conducive to the development of character and citizenship.[4]

The Greeks were completely unfamiliar with harmony and polyphony in the modern sense of the terms. Music for them was pure melody and excluded simultaneous combinations of sounds. *Harmonía* was accordingly a technical term referring to the tuning of an instrument, or, more inclusively, to the disposition of intervals within a scale, the pitch of the notes, and the melodic progressions, colors, intensities, and timbres of a given musical piece.[5] The words *polyphonía* and *polychordía* designated the multiplicity of sounds encountered within a single piece or produced by a single instrument. Instrumental accompaniment faithfully followed the song line.

Airs or musical compositions were called *nómoi* (norms, laws, conventions). The ancient musicological treatise falsely ascribed to Plutarch offers the following explanation for the use of this term, which applies to the sphere of law and custom as well as that of music and song:

Singing to the accompaniment of the lyre [citharoedy] remained totally simple from the time of Terpander down to that of Phrynis: citharoedic composition in the modern manner was not allowed in early times, nor was passing from one harmony [or musical scale] to another, or from one rhythm to another. Each *nómos* maintained the string tension [tuning] proper to it throughout. Hence the designation *nómoi*, so-called because it was not permitted to disregard the tuning established as canonical for each one of them.[6]

Plato makes the same point in his discussion (*Leg.* 3, 700a–c) of the fixed norms that governed music from earliest times, norms that later ages, his own in particular, swept aside: music had formerly been divided into definite genres and modes. One involved prayers to the gods ("hymns"); the second, songs in honor of the dead (*thrênoi*); the third was for the "paean"; and the fourth for the "dithyramb." Finally there were all the *nómoi* used for some other type of song. Once these categories were established, it was no longer permitted, as had become the practice in Plato's own day, to pass improperly from one melodic mode into another. Violators of this rule were punished; and the audience itself listened in silence, not disturbing the performance with whistling and applause.

The four basic types of *nómoi* were: (1) citharoedic (*kitharoidikós*), a solo song to the accompaniment of a stringed instrument; (2) aulodic (*auloidikós*), solo song to the accompaniment of the *aulós* (flute); (3) auletic (*auletikós*) for solo *aulós;* and (4) citharistic (*kitharistikós*), for solo lyre (also called *psilè kithárisis*). Every *nómos* was given its own name according to criteria such as region of origin,[7] rhythmical form, intonational range,[8] or ritual purpose;[9] and each one had its own tuning.

Down at least to the first decades of the fifth century, combining poetry and music was a matter of adapting musical design to the sequence of words and thoughts. This is the sense of the invocation to "hymns that are lords of the lyre" in the incipit of Pindar's second *Olympian.* Music was a matter of simple melodies sustained by the rhythmical beat of the verse and improvised on the basis of the musical modules that oral tradition supplied. Its primary purpose was to provide the poetic text with a set of overtones in keeping with the purpose and occasion of its performance. But one can observe, even before Timotheus, the beginnings of an attempt to free music from the text.

The prevalence of the new taste for soft, sensual melodies of Asiatic origin—the Ionian and the Lydian—and for Oriental instruments—the *sambýke* and the *trígonon*—led to a progressive rejection of the simple, solemn austerity of traditional Dorian and Aeolian harmonies. Audiences wanted to hear, rather than the old-fashioned airs of Alcman,

Stesichorus, and Simonides, the obscene songs of Gnesippos, executed in Lydian harmony.[10] In the *Clouds* (vv. 1355–58, 1362) of Aristophanes, the young Pheidippides passes a harsh judgment on the songs of Simonides, a bad poet in his eyes.

A typical aspect of this phenomenon was the adoption of a complicated, tortuous melodic line full of adornments—the sort of thing that suggested to comic poets an unfavorable comparison with the "trackings" or "tunnelings" of ants.[11] The increased freedom and expressivity thus obtained inevitably involved less subordination to the metrical and rhythmical structures of the verbal text. Evidence for this is already detectable for performances prior to 450. Pratinas of Phlius, a writer of tragedies and satyr plays, complains in a hyporcheme fragment (fr. 708 P.) that the sound of the flute is so prominent that the words cannot be heard during the singing of the song and that the chorus is forced to follow the flute player. Hence the poet's reminder that "it is the Muse who has enthroned Song as king; let the flute take second place in the dance" (vv. 6–7).

Melic forms, in which the new music found the widest scope for its expressive virtuosity, were now the ones most extensively cultivated, in particular the dithyramb and the citharoedic *nómos*.[12] In his *Chiron* (fr. 145 Kock), the comic poet Pherecrates launches a vivid polemic against the outrages that the protagonists of the new forms (Melanippides, Cinesias, Phrynis, and Timotheus) have perpetrated against music, represented as a battered, tattered woman who describes the sorry state to which she has been reduced.

Melanippides, the most admired of the new, fifth-century, dithyrambists,[13] was the first to eliminate the constraint of strophic responsion, introducing the so-called *anabolaí*, astrophic solo lyrics serving as preludes.[14] In tracing the gradual advance of solo at the expense of choral lyric, the author of the pseudo-Aristotelian *Problemata* (19, 15) cites as an explanation the greater imitative possibilities of astrophic song by comparison with choral strophe and antistrophe, where rhythmic and melodic uniformity tends to guarantee a corresponding uniformity of *êthos*. The absence of responsion allowed a richer variety of rhythms and melodies and a more realistic emotional expressivity, enhanced by the abrupt and frequent changes in harmonies. The preeminent role assigned by Melanippides to the flute player also contributed to the increasingly mimetic character of solo song. In earlier times, as pseudo-Plutarch explains, the flute player was at the mercy of the poet, thanks to the guiding role assigned to poetry and the corresponding obliga-

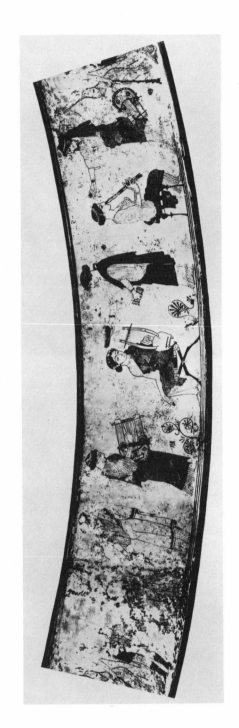

FIGURE ONE. Pyxis by the Hesiod painter. Mid-sixth century. Museum of Fine Arts, Boston.

tion of the accompanist to follow the author's instructions. With Melanippides, however, the roles are reversed and the text becomes the humble servant of the music.[15]

Cinesias (second half of the fifth century), one of the favorite targets for Aristophanes' satire, distinguished himself for his indiscriminate use of vocalized modulations on the melodic line;[16] Phrynis (middle of the fifth century) for his use of the *stróbilos,* a bridge modifying the tuning of the lyre in the performance of *nómoi.*[17] The number of harmonies possible with only five strings was thereby increased. Phrynis also raised the maximum number of strings on the lyre from seven to nine, and, while remaining faithful to Terpandrian rhythmical and metrical canons in his use of dactyls, he seems to have combined them with "free" forms, probably meters akin to those that recur in the *Persians* of his pupil Timotheus of Miletus.[18]

Two other noteworthy innovations in the realm of the dithyramb are attributed to Crexos (fifth to fourth centuries) and his contemporary Philoxenos of Cithera. Crexos introduced the use of recitative and of accompaniment at a higher pitch than the vocal line, against the hitherto prevailing practice of unison accompaniment.[19] Philoxenos inserted solos into choral passages,[20] thereby creating lyric dialogue.[21] This does not, of course, mean that Philoxenos was the creator of the dramatic dithyramb. The *Theseus* of Bacchylides (*Dith.* 18 Sn.-Maehl.) is already a true lyric dialogue, monostrophic in structure, between one character, King Aegeus of Athens, and the chorus. The innovation that the ancients attributed to Philoxenos must have involved the use of a solo lyric different in its metrical structure from the song of the chorus, something similar to the lyric monodies of Attic drama.

But the leading role in the history of the new music, and a role of which he was fully aware, belongs to Timotheus of Miletus (c. 450–360). "I sing not old melodies," he writes (fr. 796 P.). "My new songs are better. Zeus is the new king: Cronus's rule is a thing of the past. Away with yesterday's Muse." In the concluding section of his famous *nómos,* the *Persians* (fr. 791, 229ff. P.), he claims credit for having given greater possibilities of expression to the lyre "by meters and rhythms resounding elevenfold"; that is, by raising to eleven the number of strings on the instrument. The number twelve attributed to him in this connection by Pherecrates should be understood in a generic sense as meaning "many-stringed."[22] Timotheus's reference in this passage to both meters and rhythms is important: it is the first clear testimony to the divorce between metrics and music. The metrical scheme of the verse no longer constitutes, as it did in the past, the rhythmical basis for musical performance. The quarrel between the two arts, already under way in the time of Pratinas, moved first in Melanippides and then in Timotheus toward a definitive solution: ultimately music was to have unchallenged supremacy over poetry, with the text becoming a libretto for the music. As the long surviving fragment of the *Persians* shows, Timotheus, no less than Phrynis, combines dactyls with various other meters: iambs, trochees, cretics, and aeolic forms. The last, in particular, were probably what gave the versification of Timotheus's *nómos* its own character in the context of the Terpandrian tradition. The distinction between the two melic forms, dithyramb and *nómos*, was by now so faint that it was hard to tell one from the other. Henceforth the new dithyrambic style, with its free use within one and the same song of Dorian, Phrygian, and Lydian harmonies in three different modes — enharmonic, diatonic, and chromatic — was to prevail completely over the ancient *nómos*.[23] Music had reached its high point of mimetic expressiveness — a conclusion that follows not only from the testimony of Timotheus's contemporaries[24] but also from the bold innovations, stylistic and lexical, that characterize his poetic text.

It is significant that the triumph of the new music at the end of the fifth and the beginning of the fourth centuries coincides with the definitive establishment of writing and the practice of composing works in prose, subject to the planning and control that writing makes possible. The new art of dithyramb and *nómos*, relying as it did on daredevil strokes of musical boldness, strictly limited the role of the verbal text — to the point of reducing it to a simple *testo per musica*. With the decline of orality and the creative energy that generated the spell of improvised performance, the suggestive and emotional power of poetry had to be replaced from some other source. And this the new music did, through the appeal of its experiments in mimesis.

It is no accident that Plato,[25] in speaking of the educational function of rhythms and melodies, reiterates his condemnation of the new musical forms with the same arguments he uses in rejecting all the poetry of the past. The arguments are at once psychological and political in character — having to do, we would now say, with the sociology of communication. Through their mimetic power the new melodies do harm to the citizen: they arouse emotions that disturb the rational equilibrium of the soul. Hence the injunction (*Resp.* 3, 399e–400a) to eschew rhythms and measures that are varied and heterogeneous in character,[26] to distinguish those that are proper to an ordered, manly existence, and to require that melody and measures match the words, not vice versa — translated into technical terms, a peremptory invitation to compose music for texts and not texts for music.[27]

Plato, however, no less than the comic poets, the most tenacious and belligerent defenders of the old music, was too occupied in defending a rear-guard position to see the irreversibility of a phenomenon preconditioned in part by a radical transformation in the communicative system of an entire culture. By the third century, with the new forms of spectacle that arose in the Hellenistic period, the break between the two systems, linguistic and musical, had become definitive, leading to the absolute predominance of music over words.[28]

Although music and poetry from the archaic period to the end of the Hellenistic age offer the picture first of a homogeneous association, then of a heterogeneous marriage, between two diverse systems, it is obvious that poetic meter preserved a characteristic autonomy through the whole process. This was true even in the case of those vocal-instrumental renditions in which music availed itself more freely of its own rhythmical design and heightened capacity for imitative emotional effects in order to contribute to the total expressivity of a poetic text. The loss of the melodies of the earliest monodic and choral lyric makes it impossible to know in any detail how language and music were integrated in the practice of performance—how, for example, the rhythmico-musical design might have operated in connection with the text to produce a particular set of intonations, colorings, or emphatic underlinings. This loss limits our understanding of the way Greek poetry functioned alongside song and dance as part of a communicative whole. It does not, however, prevent us from interpreting the rhythm of the verse as a formal structure in its own right or from analyzing its function as part of the semantics of the text. And this is true even without taking into account the fact that the musical system of the Greeks, founded as it was on a succession of melodic progressions, never involved—even at the height of its mimetic, technical capabilities—a relation to poetry in which the means of integrating the two structures were articulated with the same sort of complexity as is found in the vocal-instrumental music of modern Europe.

# III

· · ·

# Modes & Forms
# of Communication

In its technical sense the Greek word *lyric*[1] designated poetry sung to the accompaniment of the lyre (*lýra*) or some similar stringed instrument (*mágadis, kítharis, bárbiton, phórminx*). This meaning is confirmed by the Alexandrian lyric canon, which contained only authors of monodic and choral song, to the exclusion of iambic and elegiac poetry, where the accompanying instrument was the flute. The modern tendency to include the latter two genres within the category of lyric is thus incorrect so far as Hellenistic terminology is concerned. In the light of their content, however, and the sort of poet-audience relationship they involve, the designation lyric is not an improper one.[2]

The name *elegy* comes from *élegos* (funeral lament),[3] whence the word *elegeîon* to designate the second verse (the pentameter)[4] of the elegiac distich, the distich itself, or a short piece composed in such distichs.[5] The form was not originally threnodic—not, that is, exclusively devoted on first appearance to themes connected with lamentation for the dead. That this was its original use is a view that goes back to ancient lexicographical and grammatical tradition[6] and received its most explicit formulation in the *Ars Poetica* of Horace (v. 75ff.). The theory seems to have arisen in close and direct connection with the use of *élegos* to mean a plaintive song of lamentation; but it is an unconvincing one, to which fundamental objections have been raised—by Richard Reitzenstein[7] and, more recently, Paul Friedländer.[8]

The most pertinent objection is that the most ancient funerary inscriptions are in hexameters, not elegiacs, some of them from the same Dorian areas in which the elegiac *thrênos* flourished.[9] Moreover, the geographical distribution of sepulchral inscriptions in elegiacs, unlike that of inscriptions in hexameters, is largely Iono-Attic, not Dorian. Another difficulty, rightly emphasized by Page,[10] is the absence of any real internal link between the archaic funerary epigram and the elegiac *thrênos* found in the *Andromache* of Euripides (v. 103ff.). Above all, the theory of an originally threnodic elegy is inconsistent with the whole developing panorama that the genre presents in its archaic, seventh-century form. Here the range and complexity of themes are already sufficient to exclude the possibility of evolution from a threnodic original. Even the flute used to accompany elegiac songs was capable of a wide gamut of tonalities and modulations,[11] according to whether the subject matter was threnodic or martial, erotic, or social and political. There certainly was a period when elegiacs were the chosen meter for laments, but this does not mean that they were the only one. If, moreover, one wishes to localize the vogue of the threnodic elegy, it is impossible to ignore the testimony of pseudo-Plutarch,[12] who in his review of the authors who wrote this type of work makes no mention of Ionian elegists but confines himself to poets who were active in the Peloponnesus. But if epigram and threnody were completely independent of each other in the archaic period, the ancient theory of a common origin for the two forms alluded to in the *Ars Poetica* must have arisen later—with the Alexandrian theorists, or at any rate during a period when the threnodic character of the elegiac epitaph could be argued on the basis of a whole repertory of epigrams in which funerary elegies containing both threnodic and narrative elements were not hard to find. It is interesting to note how words such as *thrênos* and *threneîn* begin to appear in fourth-century epitaphs, at a time when, as is well known, even the private epitaph was acquiring, in thematic structure, vocabulary, and style, the more ample dimensions that would make it a genuine literary genre.

It is thus more reasonable to suppose an original plurality of themes and functions for elegiac poetry[13] than have recourse to the artificial hypothesis of development from a form destined exclusively for funerary contexts. *Elegeîon*, as was already acknowledged by ancient grammarians, must have been a reference to meter, not threnodic content.[14] The fact that the lament could become formalized in elegiacs, as in the case of the Peloponnesian *élegoi* of Clonas and Sacadas[15] and the "surpassingly sad songs" of Echembrotos (Paus. 10, 7, 4ff.), does not mean that this was the only form it could take. For threnodic songs were not always composed in elegiac meter, and only in that case could the form have been in itself a signifier for the content. The only certain examples of elegiac *thrénos* that we possess are the heroine's aria in Euripides' *Andromacha*,[16] whose immediate antecedents come from the Peloponnesian tradition, and the "song of the fig tree" (*nómos kradías*) of Mimnermus,[17] a special type of *nómos* sung in connection with the grim expiatory ceremony during which the unfortunate victims chosen to serve as scapegoats (*pharmakoí*) were beaten with fig branches.[18] The "song of the fig tree" was a poem with the distinctive characteristics of a threnodic elegy,[19] one marked from the start as a genuine *élegos*[20] by the context for which it was intended.

The flute music that accompanied elegy is excluded from the heroic world described in Homer, and elegiac verse stands in similar contrast to the epic hexameter as a form more suitable for realistic subject matter and for the new modes of experience, individual and collective, which came with the changed socioeconomic conditions of the archaic Greek *pólis*. Developed in symposiastic contexts and in close relationship to issues and events, whether civic or military, it is a type of poetry we would call practical, both in its function and in its persuasive, didactic purpose. Deeply involved with the social problems of the community in Tyrtaeus, anticonformistic in its choice of values in Archilochus, inclined toward meditation on the meaning of life in the short elegies of Mimnermus, it may also seek to combine past history and present events in a single perspective—as in Callinus and in Mimnermus's *Smirneid* or his fragment on the early colonization of Colophon (Mimn. 3 Gent.-Pr.). What Santo Mazzarino has defined as. the poetic discovery of history is a discovery made by Ionian elegy.[21] With Solon it assumes a new dimension, becoming a vehicle for exhortation to a life of political commitment.

The problem of the presumed threnodic character of the earliest elegy is linked to another regarding its supposed Ionian origin. The argument, which has become a commonplace in scholarly discussions,[22] rests primarily on the Ionic form in which the text of archaic elegy has come down to us. But the conclusions drawn from the position of Ionic as the traditional dialect for elegy cannot be reconciled with the linguistic character of elegiac inscriptions from non-Ionian areas. These use the local dialect. The position of the Spartan Tyrtaeus remains problematic, because his elegies are preserved in an Ionian redaction. There are, however, good grounds for believing that this redaction is not the original one. It is difficult to believe that elegies sung at Sparta in the seventh century to exhort soldiers to a display of

civic and martial prowess could have been composed in anything but
the local dialect. The three isolated non-Ionic forms preserved by the
tradition are an obvious indication that the original Laconian forms
survived only in cases where the process of Ionization that took place
in Athens in the fifth and fourth centuries would have interfered with
the meter. This hypothesis is supported by a comparison with the famous inscription for the Corinthians who died at Salamis,[23] which has
come down to us in a double redaction, Doric (epigraphical) and Ionic
(literary).[24]

Elegy shared with iambic poetry its practical function, but was distinguished by a greater elevation and dignity of tone, thanks to a
formal structure that preserved, through its hexameter component, a
kind of link with the epic. This structure, by contrast with the open,
continuous forms of hexameter and iambos, had the advantage of concluding any message it conveyed with the epodic line of a distich. The
result was a formal closure well suited to the autonomy and absoluteness of poetic expression compressed within the dimensions of two
verses. This was the ideal form for the epigram-inscription, not only in
the light of the practical nature of its contents but also given the immediate necessity—based on economic considerations—of achieving a
maximum of completeness and concision in the minimum of space
that the stone, metal, or ceramic writing surface allowed. If in spite of
such differences elegy and iambos still came into contact at so many
points, it was because they arose, as has been correctly observed, in
connection with the same occasions and out of the same social context.[25] The words *iambós, iambikós* could refer to the contents of elegy
as well, a usage found in Aristotle (*Rhet.* 3, 1418b), Hermias of Alexandria,[26] and the inscription of Mnesiepes,[27] in which the licentious
subject matter of an Archilochean elegy dedicated to Dionysus is characterized as "iambic."[28]

Elegy was also distinguished from iambos by its method of performance. The text was usually sung, as can be inferred not only from
certain verses in the Theognidean collection[29] but also, in the case of
Mimnermus, from a precise ancient reference to sung performances[30]
and from the picture of the poet himself as a professional *auletés* which
appears in Hermesianax.[31]

Iambic poetry was performed in *parakataloge*, a type of rendition
that may be compared, musically and technically, to the plain (*secco*)
recitative of modern opera, and perhaps to accompanied operatic recitative as well. Archilochus is considered its "inventor," by virtue of
having introduced it into the performance of his iambics.[32]

On the level of content, however, iambic poetry, like elegy, is recep-
tive to a vast range of themes and topics—civil, political, didactic,
autobiographical—sometimes displaying the specifically seriocomic
character that justifies the explanation of the words *iambós* and *iambízein* which later ancient commentators were to provide.[33] The same
diversity of subject matter appears in the poetic types that on the basis
of their metrical structure would be called trochaic and epodic.[34] Some
of Archilochus's trochaic-tetrameter poems show a striking concern
with contemporary or recent events: for example, those that made up
the bold enterprise of the colonization of Thasos—a tetrameter epic, as
it has been called, comparable to the elegiac history composed by
Mimnermus.[35] The longest "legible" fragment of Archilochus, the
Cologne papyrus, allows us to form a clear idea of several aspects of an
episode that belongs completely to the realm of the current and the
everyday.[36]

It is clear that the differentiation between elegy and iambos is maintained solely at the rhythmical level, where the setting chosen would
vary according to the immediate purposes of the performance. In "lyric"
poetry, however, there was a dynamic interrelationship between different melic genres—one that operated more at the functional level than at
that of external stylistic structure and internal stylistic organization.[37]
Song achieved its generic character in connection with the social circumstances out of which it arose and the type of vocal and instrumental rendition required by a given occasion.

Plato's remarks (*Laws* 3, 700b ff.) on the musical norms that had
once differentiated the various types of poetry are of fundamental
importance for the earliest history of lyric genres. His reference to
hymns to the gods, funeral lamentations, citharoedic *nómoi*,[38] and
other types of song shows, first, that articulation into genres was something that had existed in the archaic and classical periods, even if it
operated within what was in effect a larger melic unity designated by
the all-inclusive term *hymn*.[39] (The term assumes, to be sure, a more
precise meaning in Plato, where it can refer specifically [*Resp.* 10, 607a]
to prayer to the gods, by contrast to the *enkómion* sung in praise of
men, either before the restricted audience of a symposium or the
larger one at a solemn ceremony honoring athletic victory.) Second,
the passage documents a state of crisis which must have existed between the fifth and fourth centuries, one that affected both the content
and the melic form of traditional poetic genres. The real object of
Plato's polemic was the so-called new dithyramb, which had effectively
absorbed all of its competitors by its free use of divergent harmonies

in combination: enharmonic, diatonic, and chromatic.[40]

Plato goes further, however, and elaborates (*Resp.* 3, 392d–394c) a theoretical typology of narrative which allows a triple division of poetry into categories based on internal structure: (1) "simple" narration in the third person, (2) mimetic narration with dialogue, and (3) "mixed" narration. To the first category belongs dithyramb, conceived as choral narration of mythical events; to the second, dramatic poetry, both tragedy and comedy; to the third, epic and other genres that associate and alternate narration and dialogue. It is obvious that by "other genres" Plato means specifically all those forms of iambic, elegiac, and lyric poetry containing a mixture of dialogue and narration. This is confirmed by the further division into subtypes which the grammarian Diomedes set forth[41] by way of elaboration on Plato's basic system. His categories are narrative-exegetic, dramatic or "active," and "common." The last is the mixed type, and within it Diomedes includes, in addition to epic, lyric poetry as exemplified by Archilochus and Horace.

The genre theory elaborated by the Alexandrian scholars maintains the essentially rhetorical orientation of its Platonic predecessor. In an epoch in which its original contexts and immediate referents were no longer forthcoming, the poetry of the past had come to be read as literature pure and simple. The pragmatic and functional criteria that determined earlier classifications were now irrelevant and so replaced by internal, rhetorical ones, concerned with the structure and content of the discourse. Hence the isolation and identification of genres and subgenres in the abstract, a frequent source of uncertainty and dispute when it came to classifying particular texts of archaic and late-archaic lyric. Witness the controversy between Callimachus and Aristarchus over the *Cassandra* of Bacchylides, which seemed a dithyramb to Aristarchus but was classified by Callimachus as a paean—on the basis of the recurring ritual cry *ié* that it contained.[42]

The Alexandrian classification of genres was the bookish work of a literate age: analytic in its fundamental approach and closely linked to the practical needs of editing and libraries. It was devised above all to offer a rational system for cataloguing ancient texts; but in the end it exercised a decisive influence on the literature of the time, leading critics to the elaboration of complex theoretical structures, and practicing poets to sophisticated experiments in the contamination and combination of literary genres.[43]

Plato's attacks against poetry in book 10 of the *Republic* (595a–607a) follow fairly clearly from his basic tendency to see it as a form of mimesis, like the figurative arts. For every object three different arts exist:

the art that utilizes it, the art that produces it, and the art that imitates it (601d). Painting and poetry, appealing respectively to the senses of sight and hearing, are the arts of imitation *par excellence*. But the activity of imitation does not presuppose a knowledge of the objects imitated. The painter, for example, is unable to tell whether the object he imitates is well made or not. This is a matter that requires neither direct experience nor correct opinion. Basically, imitation is only a pastime and a game, for it stands at two removes from nature; it does not create reality, but only its show or appearance. When he produces a picture of an object, the painter achieves a second-order mimesis: he imitates a particular object, which is in turn, through the work of the craftsman who made it, an imitation of the unique form of that object. The discussion hinges on the distinction between mimesis as a perfect reproduction of the real and a secondary mimesis that distorts the real for the sake of perspective illusion, representing distant objects as smaller and near objects as larger, or even, through tricks in the use of color, showing objects as bent or straight, concave or convex (*chiaroscuro* painting [*skiagraphía*]: 602d). The art is one of deceptive verisimilitude, intimately linked to that part of us which is recalcitrant to reason and devoid of all striving toward the wholesome and the good. By its skillful chromatic artifices it wreaks havoc in the soul of the beholder.

The poet is likewise an artisan of images (599d), and his mimetic activity is also at two removes from reality. His expertise relates to what seems to be, not what is; it produces mere impressions of moral qualities, actions performed, and everything else. If the poet had any knowledge of the real he would prefer to create rather than imitate, to be the subject of a poetic encomium rather than its author.

Through the suggestiveness of rhythm, meter, and music the poet exercises almost the same seductive power over his audience as does the painter through shapes and colors—so great is the natural fascination aroused by the use of these expressive media. Stripped of its ornamentation and colors, poetry becomes nothing but language pure and simple (601b).[44]

The objects of the poet's mimesis are all those actions, voluntary or involuntary, that cause men to consider themselves fortunate or unfortunate, and to experience suffering or pleasure. The poet, like the painter, is naturally inclined to imitate the irrational (*alógiston*), foolish, base element in our nature in which the wholesome and the genuine form no part—all those painful and pleasurable appetites of the soul which accompany our every action. These readily lend themselves to a multitude of various representations, whereas it is no easy task to represent a wise, tranquil, unchanging psychic disposition; and once it is produced, such a representation cannot be easily taken in by a heterogeneous festival or theater audience. It is clear, then, that the poet has no natural affinity for the rational part of the soul, and will not be inclined to satisfy its demands if he wishes to attain the approval of the crowd. His art is harmful because it establishes within the soul of each of us "an evil state of affairs, gratifying the foolish part of it that cannot distinguish more or less and judges the same things to be now greater, now smaller. It is a fabricator of phantoms, far removed from the truth" (605bc). What is involved is an art of deception, capable only of appealing to the hearer's passions through the pleasure of song and movement, and of engaging him emotionally in the mimetic world of its narrative. By granting admission to the lovely muse of poetry, the state will be putting pleasure and pain in charge of enforcing its decisions, not reason and law (607a). The hymn of invocation to the gods and the song of praise for distinguished men are the only poetic forms that the state will be able to permit, for they are the only ones that involve no use of mimesis and hence no potential harm for the citizen.[45]

Plato's insistence on the hedonistic purpose of poetry is understandable only with reference to the technology of oral communication that was an indispensable part of every occasion in the cultural life of the Greek world.[46] The poetry performed on those occasions, precisely because of the direct rapport it establishes with the listening public, involves modes of expression and states of mind different from those of poetry for a reading public.[47] We are dealing with a technique of communication whose psychological and linguistic profile can be detected in the poetry of other oral cultures and also, we might add, in the stylistic structures—already studied by contemporary linguistics—of texts composed for radio broadcast or delivery in public: brief sentences and parataxis rather than hypotaxis, absence of expressions of an "intellectual" character, avoidance of any idiosyncratic—hence exhibitionist and indiscreet—use of the first person, absence of syntactic hyperbaton, and, in general, clear, concrete language used for the exposition of ideas and attitudes that are immediately comprehensible to an audience and that encourage it to listen. These are unbreachable norms, to be observed in any piece of oral communication.[48]

The activity of the poet took the form of a performance during which he mimed his narrative to the rhythm of verse and music. The role of the spectator in this process was not a purely passive one;

rather, through the psychosomatic pleasure inherent in the visual (gestural) and auditory (musico-rhythmical) aspects of the spectacle, he became involved to the point of being himself actor and participant in the mimetic action. Identification between the hearer-spectator and the various characters in the narrative was complete.[49]

The particular function performed by the epic poetry that continued to be recited even in Plato's day by rhapsodes before Athenian audiences has been exhaustively documented by Havelock. He shows how the epic singer, through the narration of episodes from the heroic past, transmitted to his public the basic contents of current juridical, religious, scientific, and technical knowledge. This knowledge was not set forth abstractly and systematically, or by way of digression, but was woven into the very fabric of the narration. Hence the felicitous definition of Homeric epic as the encyclopedia of the Greeks, an organized compendium of their knowledge and wisdom.

Havelock concentrates, rather too exclusively, on Homer; but his general theory, which uses the notion of mimesis as an intellectual tool to account for both the relation between poetry and life and the participation of audience and poet in a single emotional state, also applies equally to all the forms of archaic poetry—elegiac, iambic, lyric, as well as epic.

The originality of the argument lies in its having isolated in the very cultural structures represented in Homeric epic the underlying reasons for the harshness with which Plato attacks artists and poets for producing a reelaboration of experience doubly removed from reality. Such reelaboration was especially dangerous for scientific and moral philosophy in that it encouraged the audience to a mnemonic and hedonistic, hence uncritical, reception of a poetic tradition that was at once cause and effect of the consolidation of public opinion (*dóxa*). Plato had seen clearly the radical opposition between this type of culture and that envisioned by his own educational and political program. There the word was to represent the embodiment of a thought rather than (Karl Kraus's phrase) the vehicle for socially acceptable opinion.[50] What Plato did not see clearly was that the culture he was rejecting was intimately bound up with the technology of oral communication. Plato's explicit proclamation of his own preference for oral discourse means nothing more than that he was unable to comprehend all the historical implications of the two communicative technologies, oral and written, coexisting at a moment of transition from one to the other. Hence his contradictory, rear-guard position in defense of orality and against the use of writing, on which he in fact proceeded to rely for the transmission of his own dialectic. At a later period—and this tends to confirm Havelock's approach in the face of the criticisms leveled against it—Aristotle was to draw a clear opposition, in his *Rhetoric* (3, 1413b ff.), between the structures and functions of oral (or agonistic) discourse and the very different ones of written (or graphic) discourse. The latter is less emotional, more precise and coherent in content, and more polished in form, but at the same time less lively—without the expansiveness and vigor that appeal to an audience.

Anticipations of Plato's attitude toward traditional culture can already be seen in the tragedies of Euripides, which reflect the intellectual climate of the age of Sophists. In the *Medea* (v. 190ff.) the condemnation of the poetry of the past is based on the premise that it has not fulfilled its principal function of lightening human suffering. In thus conceiving of poetry in ethical terms Euripides was not departing from established tradition, which accorded the poet a preeminently social role as master of truth and wisdom.[51] What he was denying was that poetry had fulfilled this function. It made no effort to probe the depths of human experience in the way demanded by the dialectical modes of thought and language characteristic of the new philosophical culture of the fifth century. The only purpose it achieved was the purely hedonistic one of delighting an audience at a banquet or festival celebration with the pleasure of song—not the essential one of a true liberation from suffering.[52] It was, to use a metaphor of Bertolt Brecht, "gastronomic" poetry.

The critical positions of Euripides and, later, that of Plato are perfectly coherent with the cultural needs of their time, but neither author was aware—nor could he have been aware—of the underlying reasons for the forms of thought and the attitudes of mind exhibited by the poetry of the past.

Thucydides conducted a similar polemic against the hedonistic purposes of oral narrative aimed at audience gratification rather than the rigorous investigation of truth that was the goal of his own historiography. Unlike Plato, however, he had clearly isolated the link between the rational bases of his investigation and the methods of communication chosen for presenting its results. His polemic defines both purposes and methods in no uncertain terms by insisting that his work is not composed for the brief duration of a public speech in front of the audience of the moment, but rather as a permanent intellectual achievement, preserved in writing and destined for careful, attentive reading.[53]

In Plato, however, the rejection of poetry was not total, and it did not exclude a precise analysis of those forms that were neither useless nor harmful for the education of the citizen, and so acceptable within his own cultural system. The song of praise (encomium) for a famous man and the hymn of invocation to the gods could have a legitimate paideutic function of their own, complementary to that of philosophy (*Resp.* 10, 607a): they lacked the narrative element of myth and precisely for this reason were free from the dangerous hedonism of mimesis.

Seen simply as forms of oral communication, Homeric epic and archaic lyric are part of a continuous line of development. Snell's observations on the concreteness of Homeric terms for mental processes[54] also apply to the language of lyric. The Homeric tendency to represent emotions and states of mind in the personified form of a dialogue between hero and god or between hero and one of his organs of consciousness (*thymós, kradíe*)[55]—in effect a kind of soliloquy between a person and a part of himself—is still operative in early lyric. It appears, for example, in Archilochus's apostrophe to his own *thymós* (fr. 105 T.).

What is involved is a mental attitude focused on performance—a "performance psychology" aimed at giving public dimensions to what is personal and subjective and so setting up an emotional rapport between speaker and audience.[56] Hence the frequent use of metaphors, images, and similes that in particular social contexts were able to take on connotations relevant only to the individual or collective aspects of the life of a single small community—an esoteric coterie language, so to speak, evident above all in the allegories of Alcaeus.[57]

Alcaean poetry, born out of and for action and intended for restricted hearing by an aristocratic club, bears the unmistakable mark of lively, direct, and immediate participation in the events that inspired it. It reflects the tumultuous life of an archaic political club (*hetairía*) committed to a combatant's role in the encounter between conflicting factions. Poetry thereby becomes an indispensable weapon in the political struggle and an expression of the joy or sorrow that the outcome of the contest inspires.

The nervous, abrupt movement of the poet's language, the aggressiveness of his violent invectives against his opponents, are part of the committed partisan's emotional reactions to the ups and downs of the civil war. Parataxis is of the essence here, to a degree unparalleled elsewhere; witness the effective description of the contents of an armory in fr. 140 V.—in effect, a call to arms issued to an audience of comrades in a moment of impending danger:

The vast hall is agleam with bronze;
 its whole length and breadth is decked out for Ares
with glittering helms, and down from their tops come billowing
 white horsehair plumes,
to grace the warriors' heads;
 hanging all around, each covering its peg,
are shining greaves of bronze, bulwark against the mighty dart of war;
 and there are cuirasses of new linen,
hollow shields strewn along the floor,
 Chalcidian swords beside them,
and many belts and tunics as well.
 These arms we must not permit to lie idle
now that we are launched upon this enterprise.[58]

The same function is performed by the recurrent expressions of an aphoristic character which appear in Alcaeus: "Money makes the man: the poor are never valued or honored" (fr. 360 V.), or "Painful, unbearable the evil which Poverty brings. She and her sister Helplessness can subdue a whole people" (fr. 364 V.). The generality of the pronouncement serves to validate the presentation of a particular situation, or the absolute allegiance that the code of the confraternity of aristocratic *hetaîroi* demands. The idea that poverty and worth are totally incompatible human conditions follows naturally from the principles of the aristocratic ethic familiar to us from the poetry of Theognis and Pindar.[59]

It was the aphoristic, allegorical character of their language which allowed the poems of Alcaeus to continue to be recited in Athenian symposia of the fifth century[60] and enter into the general repertory of banquet songs,[61] even when the subject matter itself, too closely linked to immediate aspects of precise political situations, no longer had any contemporary relevance.

Originally this allegorical mode of discourse was confined to participants in the shared life of the same *hetairía* or larger social group. Thus the "ship of state" theme, though commonplace in later political discussions, is for Theognis a symbol that is only meaningful to a small circle of aristocrats (v. 681ff.):

let these words of mine be phrased in riddles for discerning ears;
 if a person is knowledgeable he will understand both them and the evil
 (which they portend).[62]

A similar context should be understood for Pindar's polemical references to aspects of his language understandable only to those able to grasp the true meaning of what he says (the *synetoí*).[63]

The social setting for some of the metaphors of Solon is that of an animated political debate. Consider, for example, the "just sea" of fr. 13 Gent.-Pr.:

> the winds raise turmoil on the sea, but when no one
> troubles it, of all things it is the most just.

The notion of reciprocity and equilibrium which Solon has here transferred from the sphere of social life to that of nature constitutes a common element in the various archaic formulations of the idea of justice, however diverse its implications and however specific the different areas to which it is applied: sociopolitical, juridical, medical, erotic, and so forth.[64] Such is the meaning of *díke* in the cosmological system of Anaximander (12 B 1 D.-K.), a younger contemporary of Solon. Anaximander's "boundless" (*ápeiron*) is, as Vernant writes, "a sovereign entity that holds sway in the manner of a universal law imposing on all individuals an identical *díke*, maintaining every power within the boundaries of its own field of action, and guaranteeing what Alcmeon will later call the 'balance of forces' (*isonomía tôn dynámeon*) against all usurpation or abuse."[65] The function of the *ápeiron* is, accordingly, to make possible a universe founded on reciprocal equality between the elements or forces that compose it. A similar idea of *díke* is inherent in the notion of love as reciprocity, a microuniverse that joins lover and beloved in a constant equilibrium.

One can thus see how the idea of justice applies to the sea in a state of calm, not subject to any of the forces that can disturb it. The same notion is expressed in Latin by the poetic term *aequor*,[66] defined in Varro's *De lingua latina*[67] as "mare . . . aequatum cum commotum vento non est." This conception of the surface of the sea in a state of calm—*mare aequatum, aequor*—is almost identical to that of Solon, a perfect equivalent of his "just sea."

Elsewhere metaphor from the realm of nature serves as a figure for impending political disaster (fr. 12, 1ff. Gent.-Pr.):

> from clouds comes the might of snow and hail,
> from blazing lightning the stroke of thunder.

Here, too, the natural phenomenon determines the figurative equivalent to the storm in which the Athenian people, led astray by powerful leaders, become slaves to a tyrant.[68] In exactly the same fashion the metaphor of the sea—the most just (i.e., the most stable) of natural elements when the winds are not undermining its calm—serves as a figure for the steadfastness and equilibrium which exist when there is no one to stir the populace up out of its natural state.

There can be no doubt that Solon drew the materials for his metaphor from the vast repertory of poetic tradition. In book 2 of the *Iliad* the waves of the sea, stirred up and driven by the winds toward the rocks, are a *visual* and *aural* image of the obstreperous behavior of the Greek assembly (v. 144ff.) or of the cries of the Argives (v. 394ff.). But he has made functional use of the material he borrowed, constructing out of it a political metaphor that will become a commonplace comparison in later antiquity: a means of characterizing the populace as stable by nature and thus calm and innocuous when not stirred up by its leaders.[69] It also has the habit, like the sea, of assimilating the nature of its rulers to its own and thereby governing *them*.[70]

In the analogy sea : people : : winds : leaders—or powerful, factious private citizens—*díke* functions as a link between the two meanings, the literal one drawn from the realm of nature, and the figurative one to which the metaphor points. This function is inherent in the semantic possibilities of the word itself. If in the realm of sociopolitical ideas it carried the connotation of reciprocal equilibrium between the individual members of a governing class—that is, a regime dedicated to peace and law and order (*eunomía*), the ideal oligarchical regime that Solon vainly sought[71]—it could, when applied to nature, represent a condition of equilibrium, immobility, and calm.

In the erotic sphere, metaphor and image become instruments for objectifying private psychological and emotional states, creating a full figurative repertory in which animal, agonistic, nautical, agricultural, ithyphallic, and symposiastic comparisons abound; and, in which Eros is imaged as wind, carpenter, boxer, watchman, hunter, and winged boy—all efforts to suggest the nature and variety of the shifting aspects of an erotic relationship.[72]

In the sociopolitical realm metaphors and similes, drawn for the most part from the world of animals, exemplify moral and political attitudes and modes of behavior: the image of the fox in Solon (fr. 15, 5 Gent.-Pr.) and Alcaeus (fr. 69, 6 V.) concretizes the self-defeating slyness of the Athenians, or Pittacus's talent for maneuvering within the political arena. In *Pythian* 2, the metaphors of the monkey, the fox, the dog, and the wolf line up in paratactic order the contents of Pindar's advice to Hieron.

Myth functioned in the same way in maintaining the fabric of continuity within oral culture and providing a social instrument for interaction between past and present, tradition and modernity, poet and audience. The mythic episode becomes the exemplification of a norm, an aphorism, or an aphoristic introduction (*Priamel*), or the general paradigm for an action that is laudable or inauspicious within the occasional, situational context of the song. In Mimnermus (fr. 1 Gent.-Pr.) the immortal old age of Tithonus is the symbol of eternal misfortune worse than death. In Alcaeus (fr. 298 V.), the sacrilegious conduct of Ajax Oileus when he tore Cassandra away from the statue of Athena, thus provoking the anger of the goddess and the shipwreck of the Achaeans, becomes paradigmatic for an impious action by which his hated rival, Pittacus, had brought disgrace upon himself. (This line of interpretation is one we owe to Tarditi,[73] who has developed it through a detailed analysis of a series of parallels between the myth and the political situation in Mytilene at the moment when Pittacus broke his oath of allegiance to the *hetairía* of Alcaeus and allied himself with Myrsilus [fr. 129 V.].)

Pittacus's impiety is of a piece with that of Ajax, and the Mytileneans must punish him for it or suffer the same fate as befell the Achaeans, who failed to punish the sacrilege of Ajax and thus perished in the sea storm unleashed by the vengeance of Athena. Pittacus and, above all, his fellow citizens are thereby warned not to forget the sacrilege but rather to expiate it, lest the angry gods wreck the Mytilenean ship of state.

In one of the elegies in the second book of the Theognidean collection (v. 1283ff.), the lover addresses a boy who is resisting his advances as follows:

> Do not wrong me, lovely boy; I wish to remain dear to you;
>   take in graciously what I have to say:
> you cannot deceive or escape me with your tricks;
>   you have conquered and from now on the advantage is yours.
> But I shall wound you if you flee me — flee me in the way they say
>   the daughter of Iasios, virgin Iasia,
> fled the embrace of men, ripe for love though she was;
>   girt up for the hunt, busying herself with futile things,
> fair-tressed Atalanta kept far from her father's house;
>   and she went upon the high mountain tops to escape

46

the joys of love's embrace that golden Aphrodite gives;
  in the end, though, she came to know them, albeit reluctantly.

I do not accept the theory that the poem is a *collage* of two independent pieces dealing with the myth of Atalanta which were later clum-
sily joined together, perhaps for use at a symposium.[74] The suture between the two parts would, on this theory, fall in the middle of v. 1288,
"the daughter of Iasios, virgin Iasia," and the tautological character of
the line is an indication of its presence. The same is true of v. 1287
("But I shall wound you if you flee me"), which seems to contain an
implicit allusion, not to the fleeing Atalanta mentioned later, but to
the mythical chase episode in which the armed Atalanta, once having
overcome the short lead that she gave her suitors at the start, would
deal them a mortal blow.

It is equally true, however, that the element that acts as the link between the present and the mythical past is not only the act of *wound-*
*ing* but also—and most importantly—that of *fleeing*, which first (v.
1287) specifies the behavior of the reluctant boy and then (vv. 1290;
1293) the resistance of the virgin Atalanta.[75] Worth noting is the way
the poet insists on the firmness of Atalanta's refusal: though at the
moment of full sexual ripeness (*horaíen*), she engages in incessant or
pointless activity to avoid the embrace of love.[76] The sense of the term
*wound* must accordingly be metaphorical. Wounding by love will be
the proper punishment because the burning desire of the lover will
compel the boy to reciprocate against his will—as happens to Atalanta,
who, against her own will, had to surrender to the just law of Aphrodite, abandoning her virginity and accepting the inevitable fulfillment
of love.

The theme of the poem is the *adikía* of the beloved who flees his (or
her) pursuer, rejects his advances, and does not reciprocate his love.[77]
The element that connects the present situation with the mythological paradigm is the age of the boy and of Atalanta, both of them ripe
for love but obstinately rejecting it through various expedients. These
were futile in Atalanta's case, avoiding her father's house to escape
from love and living the wild, solitary life of a mountain huntress; and
the boy's tricks and deceptions will be equally futile, because sooner
or later the person who rejects love must pay the price for his own
*adikía*. The skein of parallels defines the relation between myth and
actuality in precise, unmistakable fashion. The mythological episode
will serve as a warning for the young man. Try as he may to refuse, he
too will have to submit to the same norm of "justice" that brought

marriage to the rebellious Atalanta, victorious over all her suitors in the race but eventually conquered by the one man who became her "husband."

At a compositional level, paratactic structure is the constant norm for all the linguistic codes of archaic culture, from the poetic to the cosmological and philosophical.[78] It constitutes yet another aspect, the structural one, of the underlying unity and identity of epic and lyric. The illustrative material is too abundant to be included here, but anyone familiar with lyric texts, from Archilochus to Pindar, knows that parataxis is a linguistic procedure common to all of them. Sappho, Alcaeus, and Anacreon are the most revealing examples of the workings of this norm, and of the "paratactic" state of mind that accompanies it. Rational analysis of experience is avoided; emotions and thoughts are formulated through aphorisms and categorical assertions, arranged to achieve a gradation of visual and aural effects through climax and anticlimax, and making use of stereotyped figures of polarity and analogy. Examples leap to mind: Sappho's ode on the emotions of love (fr. 31 V.); categorical assertions such as "Gold does not tarnish; Truth is sovereign; Smoke without fire can do nothing,"[79] which oppose eternal, incorruptible values to others that are transient and deceptive; and, outside the realm of lyric, the antithetical pairs Love and Strife in Empedocles, or Being and Not-Being, Truth and Opinion in Parmenides.[80] These figures of thought correspond to analogous structural configurations in the composition of poems, reducible in outline to the basic types isolated and identified by Van Groningen:[81]

1. Juxtaposition of completely autonomous component parts.

2. A "dynamic" rather than "static" method of juxtaposition in which contiguous parts are linked by a word or an expression correlative with what precedes and what follows, or else by a simple connective particle. The result is a chain structure, with purely surface coherence and unity.

3. Juxtaposition along with interpolations or parentheses, which tend to create a hierarchy between different elements. Typical of this method of structuring is the cyclical, circular, or "ring" pattern (*Ringkomposition*).[82] Here the idea that introduced a compositional section is repeated at its conclusion, so that the whole passage is framed by material of identical content.

4. Positioning of juxtaposed elements in transposed order with respect to the chronological or logical development (from cause to effect or from effect to cause) of the narrative.

5. The presence of a preamble (*Priamel*), exordium, or proem con-

taining the initial statement of theme and, occasionally, of an epilogue recapitulating the content of the piece.

6. Juxtaposition of elements—usually consisting of a single verse or a single strophe—set apart from each other by a verse that recurs like a refrain and is either an *ephýmnion*[83] not directly connected to the main content of the composition (even if relevant to the occasion on which it was performed), or an *epiphthegmatikón,*[84] which does have a direct connection to the narrative context. This interpolated element, repeated without variation, has its origin in the language of magic or ritual and performs the function of giving the song a unity that is psychological rather than rational in character, achieved through periodic evocation of the emotional situation in which both poet and audience find themselves.

Organic unity of composition was not a problem as such for the archaic poet. The practical aims of performance forced him from time to time to adapt form and content of his song to the concrete needs of the occasion and the requirements of patron and audience. In such a cultural context the attempt to restate the problem of unity in modern aesthetic terms ceases to have any meaning. The problem is obviously unsolvable, premised as it is on a methodologically false alternative between logical and aesthetic unity. Both unities are excluded by the character of the matrix out of which occasional poetry arose. Here the only unity was a thematic one, given the poet's freedom to juxtapose groups of verses relating loosely to a single theme even if there was no real logical interconnection. The technique was an associative, anthologizing one, which permitted the reutilization of texts already available, whether as part of the traditional repertory or among the works composed by the poet himself for other occasions of an analogous character. It is in this context that one should view several much-discussed poems of Tyrtaeus (frr. 6–7 Gent.-Pr.), Solon (fr. 1 Gent.-Pr.), and the Theognidean corpus, all of which, simply because of inconsistencies in their logical structure, have raised artificial problems of unity and authenticity.[85]

# IV

·  ·  ·

# The Poetics of Mimesis

*For generations poetry has been the art of arranging words of fixed meaning according to a precise pattern of sound and rhythm.*

−R. Queneau, *"La poésie,"* Front national, *19 January 1945*

The particular modes of activity chosen by the poet and his particular compositional techniques have their corresponding poetics–in this case a poetics of mimesis, laying the foundations of an art dedicated to reproducing nature in its aural and visual aspects, and to the imitation of human life. When Alcaeus (fr. 204, 6 V.) and Pindar (*Ol.* 3, 8) define poetry (*poíesis*) as "composition" or "ordered structuring of words" (*thésis*),[1] they present the poet's productions as the work of a crafts-man;[2] and the same conception lies behind the use of words and meta-phors such as "artificer," "architect," "build," "construct" in connection with the poet and his activities.[3] From a technical, compositional point of view, every piece of poetry constituted a linguistic universe (*kósmos epéon*)[4] carefully worked out and fitted together. Solon's fa-mous *Salamis* elegy was announced to its Athenian audience not as a simple speech but as a song–a "well-ordered construction of words."[5]

The act of "finding" or "devising" referred to time and again in the formulations of archaic poetics is, in a strict technical sense, one phase in the compositional process–linguistic and thematic as well as rhyth-mical and musical;[6] and so, through a pregnant use of the middle form of the verb, "devising" comes to be identified with the act of composi-tion itself, considered as a totality.[7] There remains the question of the context within which the operation of finding and devising takes place. In *Pythian* 12, 19ff. Pindar presents "invention" and "imitation" as two aspects of a single compositional process: the "Many-headed" *nómos*, or "melody for all the tones of the flute," is one that the goddess Athena devised through reproducing the anguished, resounding cries of the monster Euryale.

The actual activities of the poet—devising and constructing—are thus conceived as mimesis—the imitation of nature and human life. Conscious formulations of this idea appear as early as the fifth century,[8] presenting imitation either as a re-creation, through voice, music, dance, and gesture, of the actions and utterances of men and animals— or, with more specific reference to the figurative arts, as the production of an inanimate, visible object that is a realistic replica of something living.[9]

The concept can already be documented for the archaic period by the *Hymn to Apollo* (v. 163ff.). There the song of the chorus of Deliads is described as an imitation "of the unintelligible tongues of men"—that is, as an artistic re-creation of the voices and dialects of others before a foreign public, the assembly of Ionians convened on the island for the great Delian festival. The re-creation is so vivid and faithful that it involves the audience to the point where everyone present would say that he himself is the one speaking—so well executed are the words the chorus sings.[10] Imitative performance and ceremonial ritual combine in a kind of sympathetic "magic" that identifies chorus with audience. Mimesis as an instrumental reproduction of the voices and sounds of animals recurs in the *Lykoúrgeia* of Aeschylus (fr. 57 Radt = 71 Mette), and the idea must be an ancient one, going back in its very origins to the sacral world of orgiastic initiation rites.[11] The Dionysiac scene that his chorus of Edonians describes, likening it to the Thracian rites for the goddess Cotytos, involves ritual mimesis of the bellowings of a bull on the instrument appropriate for such representations, the grim-sounding *rhómbos.*[12]

When Alcman claims to know the modes of song and the airs of all the birds, or to "have devised text and song through putting together in words the cry of the partridges,"[13] his knowledge is called a piece of learning (*máthesis*) which makes possible "the devising of melodies."[14] It is thus a *máthesis* that occurs through mimesis. Later Democritus[15] will put forth the hypothesis that the development of human arts and crafts is based on the imitation of the work of the animals. In particular, so far as the art of song is concerned, the models were the swan and the nightingale—a piece of anthropological speculation that is not without merit as cultural history and was solidly grounded, at least for the mimetic aspects of musical *téchne*, in the earliest poetic practice of the seventh century.[16] The Alcman fragment (fr. 39 P. = 91 Calame) is expressly cited by the Peripatetic Chamaeleon[17] to show that the ancients discovered music through listening to the song of birds.

In reality, however, every form of art—figurative, poetic, musical, and even choreutic—was felt and conceived as imitation; and the word *eikón* could also be used for pictorial or plastic images that resembled their original. Poet, painter, sculptor, musician, actor, and dancer were all placed, because of the formal character of their activities, in the category of "imitators" (*mimetaí*)—a notion of the artistic process to be formalized and systematized[18] later by Plato.[19] Plutarch's reference to poetry as "speaking dance"[20] is in accord with this notion of mimetic rendering of a phenomenon that is both auditory and visual, as are the programmatic formulations "talking picture" (poetry) and "image of the thing" (the word) which appear in the poetics of Simonides.[21] The tactile quality of the poet's references to words "which stick in the ears of men" (fr. 595 P.) or the scandalmonger's "mouth without doors" (fr. 541, 2 P.), as well as the whole *Danae* fragment (fr. 543 P.), with its figurative-emotional language, are among the most telling examples of a technique that tends to visualize and describe every element in sensible experience. It is exactly this ability to represent emotional states through rhythmical and visual effects which, according to the ancient critics, Simonidean poetry demonstrated in most striking fashion. Pseudo-Longinus[22] underlines the uniqueness of Simonides' language in this respect, finding him superior even to Sophocles in the vividness with which he represents Achilles appearing from his tomb to the Greeks as they are about to begin their homeward voyage. Here is an anticipation of Damon's ethico-musical notion of song and dance as "imitations of life" (*bíou mimémata*)—a re-creation through different rhythmical and musical genres of differing human characters and moral attitudes.[23] This notion will later provide the basis for the Aristotelian theory of the nature of poetry.

The application of the concept of mimesis was not confined to the relationship between art and nature or human life: it included the poet's own position vis-à-vis poetic tradition. Like every other human activity, poetic composition was conceived as a matter of talent, ability, and mental resourcefulness (*sophía*)—hence the idea of *máthesis* as the acquiring of art through imitation of poetic models. Theognis (vv. 369ff.) is well aware that many will find fault with him, and that his songs will not please everyone: he cannot be expected to know the views of all his fellow citizens. But he also knows that no one lacking artistic expertise (*ásophos*) will be able to imitate (*mimeîsthai*) the technique of his song.[24] The same idea is clearly implied in the quarrel between Pindar and Bacchylides over what sort of poetry to compose and how.

Pindar (*Ol.* 2, 86) opposes the originality of the poet "who knows many things by nature" to the work of those among his contemporaries who are mere learners (*mathóntes*); Bacchylides, on the other hand, sees *máthesis* as the foundation for the poet's knowledge: "Poet is indebted to poet, in times gone by as well as now; it is not easy to devise a way to the gates of songs not sung before" (fr. 5 Sn.-Maehl.). The poet, in other words, stands in debt to tradition and to the achievement of his predecessors. This is true even of Pindar, especially when he is adhering most closely, as in the gnomic and encomiastic sections of his work, to the canons of "genre" composition. However, one cannot help but see an implicit justification for a different method of procedure in the polemical position that Pindar assumes with regard to the treatment of myth. The Pelops story in *Olympian* 1 is introduced (v. 36) with the proud self-consciousness of one who knows the "true" account: "Son of Tantalus, I will tell about you things different from those told by the poets who preceded me." He has no intention of outraging the divinity by repeating the impious tale of the eating of Pelops. The old version is corrected, and the boy's disappearance during Tantalus's banquet explained, by the story of the love of Poseidon. Bacchylides was to feel no such need to be silent about Tantalus's impiety in serving up to the gods the flesh of his own son: he would even go so far as to tell how Rhea set about recomposing Pelops's scattered limbs once the crime had been discovered (fr. 42 Sn.-Maehl.). Even Pindar, however, operates within the limits of the prevailing conception of poet as craftsman—despite his assertions of originality and refusal to follow the beaten Homeric path (*Pae.* 7b, 10ff.). Witness the frequency with which he uses metaphors drawn from sculpture and architecture in referring to poetic program and poetic technique.[25]

As can be seen, the notions of "knowing," "learning," "devising," and "composing" are part of a precise semantic system in which poetic activity is correlated explicitly or implicitly with the idea of mimesis, whether of man and nature, or of poetic texts drawn from the oral tradition. It is a poetics in harmony with the actual procedures followed by the poet and with his habitual compositional technique: reutilization and adaptation of materials drawn from a mnemonic repertory to provide the subject matter of myth or, at a linguistic level, lexemes and stylemes. The process of "devising" was a phase of composition or the act of composition itself; and as such it operated in two directions, toward an act of selection, variation, and combination which might be either musical or linguistic, depending on whether the starting point was a natural phenomenon such as the sound of human and animal utterance, or the lexical and thematic elements of poetic tradition.[26] In the latter case, the act of "devising" words, as in the formulation of Alcman, or "a way to the gates of songs," as in Bacchylides, consisted in a selection and combination of material from different texts—what modern theories of *Textlinguistik* would call "intertextuality."[27] Close analogies are provided by the *tropare* and *invenire tropos* of medieval poetry or the Provençal *trobar clus*—the art of devising expressive verbal and musical figures which forms part of the twelfth- and thirteenth-century poetics.[28]

It is in terms of this poetics—a poetics of heuristic imitation rather than of aesthetic creation—that an author's references to the novelty of the modes and techniques found in his own work are to be understood. Alcman's invitation to the Muses to strike up a new song[29] refers to a process of linguistic, rhythmical, and melodic selection within the mnemonic repertory, poetic and musical, available to him—a selection that would meet the needs of the new reality created by situation and audience at a given performance. To "know the songs of all the birds" (fr. 40 P. = 140 Calame) is to have at one's disposal a full assortment of natural modules to be used in devising melodies—or, more precisely, to be transposed and refashioned into melodies. In the present instance this would involve putting a personal stamp on a mode of song through an onomatopoetic verbal and melodic rendering of the *kakkabízein*[30] of partridges. The generic epic use of the phrase *ártia bázein*[31] to refer to speech or talk as an articulation or connecting of words, or of the epithet *artiepés*[32] for a good talker, is being replaced—already in the seventh century—by the narrower and more elaborate notion of poetic discourse as the arrangement and ordering of words in accordance with precise metrical and rhythmical norms.[33]

The notion of pleasure or "delight" (*hedoné*) as the effect that words in combination with song, gesture, and dance may produce on their audience was fundamental to all Greek poetics from Homer to the tragedians;[34] but it found its clearest and most explicit formulation in Gorgias:

> All poetry I consider and define as discourse in metrical form. When a person hears it there comes over him a tremor of fear and a compassion that moves to tears and a longing that issues in grief: though confronted with vicissitudes in the course of events and the lives of characters that have nothing to do with him, his soul so responds to words that it experiences the emotions of others as if they were its own. . . . The divine incantation of words gives rise to pleasure, puts an end to grief: becoming one and the

same with the soul's faculty of discernment, the power of incantation be-witches, persuades, and transforms with its magic.[35]

Elsewhere, in speaking of tragic performances, Gorgias insists once again on the illusionistic spell that poetry casts over an audience, pre-senting it this time as a mutual involvement of poet and spectator in the same emotional relationship: "The one who deceives is *juster* than the one who fails to deceive, and the one who allows himself to be de-ceived is wiser than the one who resists deception."[36] To understand the meaning of this passage one must remember that *díke* and *díkaios* (justice and just) here imply the precise notion of equilibrium in a mu-tual relationship of action and reaction between natural or human agents.[37] The violation of this principle of equilibrium is seen as an act of injustice (*adikía*) involving the necessity of an act of punishment aimed at reestablishing the norm of *díke*. The "wisdom" of the one who allows himself to be "deceived"—that is, of the spectator—lies in his capacity to place himself on the same footing as the poet and go along with the emotional requirements of the situation in the poetic text.[38] The words *sophía-sophós* as used by Gorgias still retain the mean-ings "ability," "capacity," "experience with the techniques of an art"—in this case the art of poetry.

The emotional relationship created by the performance of a poetic text would make no sense apart from the idea of mimesis—the imita-tive process that is transmitted to the audience and then itself imitated and reenacted in the form of sympathetic emotional response. But if pleasure is inseparable from emotional response and is correlated in turn to mimesis, it follows that pleasure is one of the aspects or func-tions of mimesis itself. The connection emerges clearly from Aristot-le's dictum on tragic poetry: "The (tragic) poet must arouse, through mimesis, the pleasure produced by pity and fear."[39]

Given a poetics posited in this fashion on an identification of the psychological processes involved in execution and reception, poetry became the principal means for integrating the individual into his so-cial context. The poetics of mimesis accordingly took on the character of a true aesthetics of performance, in which the audience's "horizon of expectation"[40] played a primary role. Poetic performance, whether epic or lyric, was conceived as more than a means for allowing audi-ences to see themselves in the mirror of mythical or contemporary events; it could also serve to arouse in them a new perception of reality and broaden their awareness to include the new modes of social and political activity which new needs and goals demanded. It was with some reason, therefore, that Werner Jaeger regarded archaic Greek poetry as a form of *paideía*. The weak point of his interpretation lay in its overemphasis on the individual aspects of the educational process and in its claim that the Greek educational model might provide an ethical norm for our own time. A new factor in the relation between poet and public which emerges in lyric, as opposed to epic, has to do with the specific character of the audiences involved, which from time to time must be seen as limited to the members of a given social group or milieu: a *thíasos* of girls (Sappho), or a nobleman's club (Alcaeus), or a band of warriors committed to the defense of their city (Tyrtaeus), or the world of the symposium and the festival *kômos* (Anacreon). In the case of choral lyric there is the added problem, over and above that of the audience, of the patron and the possible influence that his demands may have had on the poet.

The practice of reutilizing poetic materials drawn from the mnemonic repertory and adapting them to the singer's needs must be borne in mind if we are to understand not only the frequent parallels and shared commonplaces that link the idiom of lyric to that of epic and metrical inscriptions,[41] but also the very character of archaic poetic language itself. That language is a patrimony of stylistic and formulaic materials that could be drawn on at will and that would be worth investigating systematically from a historical perspective free of all literary or dialectological schematism. In spite of differences in metrical form and performative technique, epic, elegy, iambic, and lyric were, from the very beginning, contemporary and interdependent phemonena.[42] What distinguished Homeric epic from lyric was, over and above homogeneous composition in hexameters, its exclusively mythical content and, at the level of performative technique, a different method of musical rendition: psalmodic recitation without instrumental accompaniment, which was reserved for the brief citharoedic *prooímion*.

So far as linguistic forms are concerned, several studies produced in the last two decades[43] have placed the problem of the relationship of local dialect and literary language in a new perspective. In the case of Tyrtaeus (see chap. 3) archaic inscriptions disprove the time-honored classification of literary genres according to dialect—the theory that would make Ionic the traditional language of epic, elegy, and hexameter poetry in general, and Doric the language of choral lyric. This approach involves the preconceived conviction that the language of archaic Greek poetry was an exclusively literary language completely independent from the dialects spoken locally, and that inscriptional texts should be considered the products of a kind of subculture.[44] So formulated, in modern terms and without reference to functions assumed in a given social context, "literary" is a concept that is inapplicable to archaic Greek poetry. There are substantial difficulties confronting the thesis of certain standard dialects linked to the various poetic genres or different types of meter. If, for example, hexametric or, more generally, dactylic poetry required the dialect of Homeric epic, we will have to assume that epic poets such as Eumelos of Corinth, Kynaithon of Sparta, and Lesches of Mytilene, even though active in non-Ionic speaking areas, wrote in the Ionic of Homer, with no regard for local linguistic usage. But the hexameter fragment of Eumelos's processional hymn (*prosóidion*) for the Messenians in honor of Apollo (fr. 696 P.) shows non-Homeric forms, as do the hexameter of the Duris cup[45] and the archaic inscriptions of continental Greece. One must assume, therefore, that the two fragments of the *Korinthiaká* of Eumelos, which have been transmitted to us indirectly (frr. 2 and 9 Kinkel) owe their Ionic, Homeric form (*-e* vocalism) to a later normalization under Iono-Attic influence. The phenomenon is documented in the inscription mentioned earlier in honor of the Corinthians who died at Salamis (see chap. 3) and by the textual vicissitudes of a strophe of Alcaeus which Athenaeus transmits in a normalized version linguistically different from the direct tradition preserved in a papyrus.[46] These pieces of evidence, few as they are, are sufficient to suggest that skepticism is in order when the solution of linguistic problems depends on a textual documentation that is heavily suspect. How is one to defend the presence, even in the text of Alcman, of certain metrically interchangeable Ionic forms attested sporadically in portions of the indirect tradition?

Epicisms in Lesbian poetry are a different matter, for they appear in papyrus fragments as well as in the indirect tradition, from which one may infer that they were already accepted in the Alexandrian edition of Sappho and Alcaeus. Shall one continue, then, to accept Lobel's rigid distinction—set forth to account for precisely such epicisms—between "normal" poems, uncontaminated by linguistic features extraneous to the dialect, and "abnormal" ones?[47] Marzullo is essentially correct in rejecting the excessive abstractness of this formulation. "Sappho's epic *dictio* is not," he points out, "the result of a borrowing that presupposes the usual relationship of imitation to model. It represents, rather, an advanced and completely vital stage of that traditional process whose development is already traceable in the [epic] poems. ... The *Epithalamium* (44 V.) does not 'Homerize': it uses the same expressive means that contemporary epic, or at any rate epicizing, poetry had at its disposal. It has in common with that poetry . . . its transformed character—its participation in what amounts to a new act of historical re-creation."[48] Homeric epic is one epic tradition among a great many, all of which were cultivated with great success in the earliest age of Greece—a fact of which the Greeks themselves were fully aware. The epicisms of Sappho and Alcaeus are only understandable, in the last analysis, against a background of epic composition that is not exclusively Homeric but a living and vital part of the culture of the Aeolid as well. Two undeniable facts show this to be so: (1) the absence of Ionic -e, even in poems where there is epic coloration;[49] and (2) the presence of the -oio genitive and the form ptólis, which, as we now know, are not distinctively Homeric but attested even earlier, in Mycenaean (the -oio genitive is also preserved in the Aeolic of Thessaly).[50] The various instances of correptio, epic or Attic, should be taken not as borrowings but as phenomena inherent in the nature of the verse technique itself.

It is increasingly evident that the tendency, still persistent among "Panhomerists," to find Homeric borrowings everywhere is incapable of providing a historically valid explanation for the linguistic data and evidence from areas of archaic Greece outside the sphere of Ionic influence. Why posit a diffusion of Homeric forms through the activity of Ionian bards and their subsequent adaptation to local dialects, when a more likely explanation, historically, is to admit the presence of long-standing traditions of oral (or even written) epic composition in parts of continental Greece? The former position would be justified only on the impossible assumption that ancient local legends pertaining to gods, heroes, and kings had been completely forgotten, to be reintroduced at a later date by Ionian bards.[51] Viewing the problem from a different perspective, that of the relationship between poet and audience, one must answer the further question whether in seventh- and sixth-century Greece a Doric-, Thessalian-, or Boeotian-speaking public would have been able to understand an Ionian rhapsode reciting in the language of Homer—at a time when inscriptions aimed at a general public, regardless of social origins, were written in the epichoric dialect. Finally, the cultural "Homericity" presumed by the theory would make every author of epigrams an expert in the translation of Homeric Greek into the Greek of his own particular region.

Yet a different case is that of the -e forms in Bacchylides and Pindar and the random fluctuation, in the latter, between the pronouns min and nin, for which it is admittedly difficult to find a satisfactory explanation. Bacchylidean instances of -e are confined to two papyrus fragments (19 and 20A Sn.-Maehl.). Their occurrence there is unlikely to have anything to do with the character of a particular patron or occasion, given the presence of -a forms in poem 10, which was composed for an Athenian victor. An alternative hypothesis is that there was a deliberate effort at Ionic coloring. This would fit with the particular character of the two poems and their date of composition—late enough that one cannot exclude the possibility of a free choice among different dialectical colorations for stylistic purposes.[52]

It would be difficult to maintain such a hypothesis for Pindar, where, except in *Pythian* 4, the few instances of -e are sporadic and isolated ones. Recent attempts to defend it are based on what is at times specious argumentation in favor of presumed Homerisms[53]: -oio and -ao genitives, for example, though they are already attested in Mycenaean and in inscriptions from non-Ionian areas, hence not the exclusive property of Homeric epic.[54] The only general conclusion that could be drawn from the analysis of -e forms in the Pindaric text is that they go back to alterations in the manuscript tradition; and this is the view taken by Snell in his edition, where the corresponding -a forms have been restored in most instances.[55]

One should emphasize, in conclusion, that the problem of the formation of the language of monodic and choral lyric and its relation to that of Homeric epic must henceforth be posed in terms completely different from those sanctioned by the traditional line of interpretation. As Grinbaum rightly observes,

> it is common knowledge that the closeness of a given poet to Homer varies with the literary genre involved; greater in the case of the writers of epic, less in that of lyric poets and tragedians. The question naturally arises whether all the general similarities found in lyric and tragedy are to be explained as the result of Homeric borrowing. Admitting the obvious possibility of this or that particular reminiscence, is it not more legitimate in general to suppose that, for example, the linguistic characteristics shared between the Homeric poems and, let us say, choral lyric may be defined in terms of the derivation of both genres from a common source rather than as borrowing by one from the other? The common source in question could well have been the literary language of the Mycenaean (or pre-Mycenaean) period, whether reflected in epic or lyric.[56]

The decipherment of the Creto-Mycenaean tablets cannot help but give a decisive turn to the development of the complex question of dialect mixture in lyric and, in particular, choral lyric. The old view, propounded by H. L. Ahrens, which would make choral poetry the creation of the Dorians and its language, in essence, the Doric dialect, is now encountering increasing opposition. Over and above the substantial individual differences that appear in varying degrees within the corpus of choral lyric, even shared linguistic features should be considered with reference to the hypothesis of an ancient Mycenaean *koiné* containing both Aeolic and Ionic forms.[57] Given this hypothesis the traditional theory, which explains all parallels to the language of epic by an appeal to presumed Homeric influence, falls to the ground. Such parallels are to be explained as substrate phenomena, dating back in origin to the early *koiné* period,[58] or, in other cases, more simply— as modifications of the text produced during the course of transmission in oral or, later, manuscript form.[59] Analogous phenomena in connection with the transmission of poetic texts from one region to another can be documented in the history of other literatures: the Sicilian *canzonieri* of the thirteenth and fourteenth centuries underwent a progressive Tuscanization at the hands of copyists.[60]

# V
## . . .
# The Sociology of Meaning

*In its very elements (word, color, tone) art depends on the transmitted cultural material; art shares it with the existing society. And no matter how much art overturns the ordinary meaning of words and images, the transfiguration is still that of a given material. This is the case even when the words are broken, when new ones are invented—otherwise all communication would be severed. This limitation of aesthetic autonomy is the condition under which art can become a social factor.*

*—H. Marcuse,* The Aesthetic Dimension

An exclusively synchronistic approach cannot deal exhaustively with the problem of interpretation. It allows one to understand the shared characteristics of a mental and linguistic system and certain forms of cultural organization; but it does not define a perspective within which to grasp the changes of meanings which identical linguistic structures undergo in relation to changing situations. And Greek lyric poetry was, as we have seen, inseparable from the distinctively nonepic situational contexts for which it was created. It also dealt with a more realistic subject matter—human existence as experienced in the altered sociopolitical conditions of the archaic city-state. The diachronic setting for the phenomenon of lyric is the middle ground between tradition and innovation.[1] The semantic problems inherent in language are essentially, as ethnolinguistics has shown,[2] the same as those posed by the cultural phenomena of which words are symbols: value terms come to denote different things or to lose their traditional meaning even in contexts that repeat traditional poetic formulae.

Although Denys Page's study of Archilochus[3] seeks to show, from an exclusively synchronistic perspective, the completely Homeric character of the poet's language, it clearly reveals areas where significant linguistic innovation is taking place: on the lexicographical level, at those points where epic language lacked the vocabulary for describing contemporary situations and events; on the semantic level, where words pertaining to the emotions are involved;[4] and on the level of metaphorical transfer of meaning–not, however, on the morpho-syntactical one. Epic formulae are adapted to the individual context by means of a technique of variation that leaves their syntactic structure intact.[5] The reutilization of such expressions and stylemes in elegy and lyric has not yet been thoroughly examined; but even the partial studies now available allow one to speak of the *polyvalence* of epic diction.[6]

These common features of lyric language constitute a set of *loci communes* deriving from oral practice and reproducing, as we have seen, basic structures of oral communication. Their prominence has led–partially through the influence of ethnological research into "primitive" oral poetry–to an emphasis on the synchronic aspects of the texts the critic chooses for analysis, with the result that transformations in meaning that arise in response to varying situations tend to be minimized if not actually ignored. There is, of course, no denying that, for oral-aural man, the recurring mode of expression–the *locus communis*–remains always, as has been observed, "of a piece with his life situation," providing "a kind of raw, if circumscribed, contact with actuality and with truth, which literacy and even literature alone can never give and to regain which literate cultures must rather desperately shore up with other new resources their more spatialized verbal structures."[7] But traditional poetic materials could retain a link to fixed performance situations and still take on the new roles within the system of semantic relationships and oppositions which their reuse in new contexts demanded. Solon (fr. 3, 6–11 Gent.-Pr.) and Theognis (vv. 39–50) complain of the political misfortunes of their respective cities in practically identical language, attributing them in both cases to the folly of the city's leaders. But the political import is, in each instance, sharply different–a product of the different semantic systems of the two contexts and of the different extralinguistic realities of the Athenian and Megarian political situations to which they refer. Whereas in Theognis the two key words *astoí* (citizens) and *hegemónes* (leaders) constitute, at the most general level, the oppositional typology "wise men-fools," Solon's use of the terms makes them carry the same negative connotation of disapproval for both social groups.[8]

The metaphor of the way or path, which is a recurrent topos in choral lyric,[9] yields opposite semantic outcomes in the poetics of Bacchylides and Pindar, even though its structure is the same in both authors. For the former the "paths of song" have their point of departure in *máthesis*, the learning of one's craft through the imitation of traditional poetic models; for the latter, in the inborn "excellence" of the poet.[10]

The word *areté* in the poetry of Tyrtaeus presupposes a situation different from that which underlies Homer's use of the same term: its premise is the community-oriented ethic of seventh-century Sparta—civic "excellence" conceived as the common property of city and *dêmos* (fr. 9, 15 Gent.-Pr.). Although words such as *areté, agathós, esthlós* carry aristocratic ideological connotations when taken over by Simonides, his realistic way of thinking empties them of their fundamental semantic reference, turning them into utopian prescriptions without relevance to the actual human condition (fr. 541 P.):[11]

> [Time alone will?[12]] tell what is noble and what is base;
> if anyone . . . speaks slander, carrying about with him
> a mouth without doors,
> mere smoke means nothing, gold does not tarnish,
> Truth is sovereign;                                                   5
> but only to a few has God granted excellence that reaches its end:
> it is not easy to be a man of true worth (*esthlós*);
> he[13] is forced to yield, against his will,
> to irresistible passion for gain,
> the driving gadfly of wile-weaving Aphrodite,                         10
> and rife love of competition.
> If he [is unable],[14] living his whole life in respect for the gods,
> to move forward along the path of right,
> but nevertheless proves worthy to the limit of what is possible . . .

The contrast between the absolutes "noble" and "base" is exemplified, in usual *Priamel* fashion, by the opposition of the supreme truth of gold to the shifting inanity of the slanderer's chatter.[15]

Although excellence or prowess—like absolute beauty and like gold—is a supreme value in an agonistic context, it is a quality hard to come by in the world of ordinary men. Absolute and perfect excellence is not compatible with human nature, forced as it is to operate unwillingly within the limits imposed by certain "necessities"—passion for gain, love's gadfly (*oîstros*),[16] ambition—that are inherent in it and in the conditions of social existence.

Absolute worth is quite impossible to attain, but this need not matter, provided that man behave with due respect for the norms of right and wrong which serve the interests of the community.[17] He may, in effect, make up for his limited capacity for achievement by adhering to justice in his relations with his fellow citizens. In the aristocratic ethic of Pindar ambition and desire for gain are extremely dangerous for the genuine *agathós* (the man of true worth and noble birth). They may impel him to foolhardy acts of violence, which violate the divinely sanctioned principle of due measure. In the realistic ethic of Simonides they are simply an inevitable part of the human condition.

What is involved is a different perspective on reality, and a new measure of man, more suited to the changed political conditions of Greek society and to the continuing development of the new exchange economy that had replaced the landed wealth (*ploûtos*) of the past with a new wealth derived from colonial expansion and business (*kérdos*). In many cases the prerogatives to be claimed on the basis of inherited, inalienable power, capacity, and wealth were diminished or profoundly altered. The new plutocratic *agathoí*, unlike the aristocratic *agathoí* of an earlier age, could only boast the unstable wealth acquired through the toils and risks of trade.

In the encomium that he composed between 509 and 500 in honor of the Thessalian dynast Scopas, ruler of Crannon, Simonides returns to the same theme of the nature of *areté* and the man who is *agathós* (fr. 542 P.):[18]

> It is difficult to be a man of true worth,
> foursquare of hand, foot and mind,
> fashioned without fault.
>
> . . .
>
> Neither does the dictum of Pittacus ring true to me,
> though he was a wise man who pronounced it:
> worth, he said, is hard to attain.
> Only a god can have this gift;
> man cannot help but be unworthy
> once caught in the grip of a thing that has no remedy.
> In success every man is worthy,
> in failure unworthy, and the best, as a rule,
> are those dear to the gods.
>
> So I am unwilling to go looking for the impossible—
> the one perfect man among all of us
> whom the broad earth nourishes with its fruits—
> wasting my share of existence
> on a vain and idle hope;
> I will tell you of such a man when I encounter him.

My praise and friendship goes rather to anyone
who willingly does no wrong;
with necessity no one fights, not even the gods.

I am satisfied if a man is not evil
or hopelessly incompetent,
and knows at least the justice that serves the interests of the city—
a sound, healthy man. With him I will find no fault—
I am not given to faultfinding:
the race of fools has no end.
Fair are all things where actual baseness does not enter in.

The prospects for coming up to an aristocratic, agonistic standard of true worthiness are here evaluated in an essentially negative light. Excellence of body and mind is not only difficult to attain but actually impossible: man is by nature a frail, weak creature forced to deal with the constraints imposed upon him by social necessity and his own inner impulses. The important thing is not to do evil voluntarily (there being no way to avoid the possibility that one may still have to do it involuntarily), and to know at least the sort of right conduct that serves the interests of the community.

To the ethic of absolute values—true worth, achievement, and wealth seen as the birthright of men especially endowed by nature and blessed with the favor of the gods—the poet opposes the ethic of relative values, more human and less heroic, which moves from the lofty plane of aesthetic and agonistic striving to the broader one of ethical and social commitment in a community context. For Pindar's heroic man Simonides substitutes "Odyssean" man, who is not too "incompetent" to cope with the dangers and risks of living among his fellows. This realistic ethic, a combination of intellectual pessimism and moral optimism, amounted to a deconsecration of the loftiest ethico-religious values of the now-declining archaic aristocracies; but it too was nourished by an ideal, one that was equally lofty and more in tune with the new historical reality, the ideal of the democratic citizen living a just life in accordance with the interests of the city.[19]

The "sound and healthy man" who represents for Simonides a new human ideal is not the traditional strong man, "foursquare (*tetrágonos*) of hand, foot and mind, fashioned without fault," as he is defined in the initial verses of the poem.[20] He is the morally healthy man whose social behavior shows him to be neither wicked (*kakós*) nor incompetent (*apálamnos*)[21] and who knows the norms of justice and equity which benefit the life of the city (*onasípolis díka*). Health, however, is not simply the property of the citizen who acts in the interest of the community; it also appears in Simonides' thought as an indispensable prerequisite both for the joy of living, which is the highest value of existence (fr. 584 P.), and for the pleasure supplied by art (fr. 604 P.). The notion is a complex one, including bodily health, general well-being, and, at the same time, vital moral commitment.[22]

The conversation between Protagoras and Socrates (Plat. *Prot.* 339a–347a) on the interpretation of the poem to Scopas is a typical example of dialectical discussion deliberately "mismanaged."[23] When Socrates remarks in conclusion that it will be better to put poets aside and return to the central topic of the unity of virtue, he clearly reveals the nature of his own game, giving us to understand that he has not been talking seriously (347a–348a). The target for Plato's subtle irony is not only Protagoras but also the figure conspicuous by his absence, Simonides himself. Nor was the choice of the poem to Scopas an accidental one: it was able to provide ample material for a discussion of virtue from the point of view of the philosopher's own ideology. Plato's irony and his lack of good faith in dealing with a poet toward whom he felt little sympathy show themselves at their sharpest when Socrates flies in the face of grammar and syntax without any warning and links "willingly" (v. 14 *hékon*) to what precedes rather than what follows (345e: ". . . my praise . . . goes to anyone willingly / who does no wrong . . .), thereby making it possible to attribute to Simonides his own idea that no one does wrong willingly; or when, with the aid of Simonides' fellow Cean Prodicus, he ventures into the field of synonym analysis in order to conclude (341c) that "difficult" (*chalepón*) in v. 4 means "bad" (*kakón*) in the dialect of Ceos, which would make the polemic a completely justified attack on Pittacus for making the claim—as Simonides understood it—that it is "bad," not "difficult," to be a man of worth.[24] Socrates is still using the same method when he seeks to show that, contrary to what Protagoras said, there is no contradiction between Simonides' initial assertion ("It is hard to be worthy . . .") and his later disagreement with Pittacus for saying the same thing. Simonides, according to Socrates, claimed that it is difficult to "become" (*genésthai*) worthy, whereas Pittacus said something quite different—that it is difficult to "be" (*émmenai*) worthy.[25] Through the deftest of hermeneutic maneuvers, based on forced meanings of words and distortions of syntax, Plato achieves a double goal. He shows that his master, Socrates, has at his disposal, should he so desire, all the dialectical means necessary to fight and win on the same sophistic ground as his adversary; and, at the same time, he distorts for his own ideological purposes the thought of a poet whom he considered, not entirely without grounds, a proto-Sophist—a precursor of Protagoras (cf. 316d; 340a) in the dissemination of unclear and self-contradictory doctrines.

There was no room within Plato's aristocratic ideology for the realistic ethic that Simonides propounded through his analysis of man as he is rather than as he ought to be. The "humanness" (*anthrópeion*) of man (cf. fr. 521 P.: "You who are a man [*ánthropos* not *anér*]") in all his weaknesses and limitations, which the Scopas poem delineated so well, could not help but appear, from Plato's elitist perspective, the expression of a permissive moral empiricism. It is this hostility that willingly distorts and subverts the meaning of the poem.

Simonides' deconsecration of aristocratic values is well documented in other ways as well. According to Aristotle (fr. 92, 15 Rose), he was responsible for the acute observation that "those of noble birth" are "those whose wealth is of long standing."

The panorama of problems raised by this issue is a vast one, conditioned as it was by an irreversible process of evolution in Greek society. One of the problems is that of being and becoming, Truth and Opinion. Discussion of this important topic plays a crucial role in archaic thought from Simonides to Parmenides, taking as its point of departure the same general terminology, metaphors, and characteristic expressions (the verbs meaning "violate," "do violence to," for example)[26] but with different and opposite artistic and ideological outcomes. The being-appearance antithesis was already operative in the earliest period of the archaic age, even if not explicitly formulated.[27] It has its matrix in the Homeric idea (*Od.* 18, 130–37) that man's character is inconstant and changing. The flux of human thoughts and experience, the process of perpetual becoming that makes of man a "dreaming shadow" that both is and is not (*Pyth.* 8, 95ff.), is contrasted in Pindar with the solidly grounded consistency and eternal certainty of the True: "principle and beginning of great excellence" on both the mythical and the human level (fr. 205 Sn.-Maehl.). Simonides sets the True in opposition to the power of opinion (fr. 598 P.) and—given the rapid changeability of human affairs (fr. 521 P.)—the certainty of today to the mere promises of "the god called Tomorrow" (fr. 615 P.). Two opposed visions of the world are involved, one conservative, the other dynamic and realistic, and, corresponding to them, two precise political and cultural positions. The irreconcilability of these two views of reality is conceptualized in Parmenides by what may be called an oppositional logic of the real, positing the identity of the true with being, which alone is knowable, and of opinion with not-being—mere nothingness.

Style is also a coexistence of old and new. In Simonides the paratactic structures of antithesis and analogy are juxtaposed with the free flow of discursive presentation and eristic formulae, introduced polemically to mark an ideological and stylistic breaking point. The general perspective and movement of thought in the Scopas poem are emblematic of a polemical spirit that in order to assert a highly personal point of view must proceed through contrasts and antitheses, setting its own idea in opposition to another that serves as antagonist or term of comparison. One almost has the impression that the argument can only advance in response to the stimulus of the contrary idea, and that its ethical formulations, which touch on different aspects of the same general thesis, are true and proper replies to an interlocutor who is taking the role of antagonist. This diatribistic mode of thought is faithfully reflected in the language and the rhythm: an eloquent upward movement to the emphatic solemnity that underlines an aristocratic but abstract conception of man; then a descent, with sharply marked rhythmical breaks, in the direction of the discursive— that is, toward the more specifically personal tone that proclaims the poet's own conviction.[28] The style is characterized by the presence of several rhythmical phrases that appear only once within the stanza. They are introduced as vehicles for a heightened semantic density, or for stronger differentiation of meaning. One rhythmical sequence, the encomiologus, appears both here and in fr. 541 P.; it coincides in the one instance with the use of the same conceptual nucleus to open the strophes of two successive triads, and in the other (v. 7) with the point of ideological rupture, where absolute values give way to relative ones and the language relaxes into movement at a freer, more colloquial pace. In the poem directed at Cleoboulos of Lindos[29] the rhythmical jolt introduced by the glyconic with spondaic close that concludes a series of uniform dactylo-epitritic phrases serves a precise expressive function: it underlines the contemptuous irony that pervades the reference to Cleoboulos and his views.

Similarly in Parmenides, the verb *noeîn* is used both in the archaic sense, defined by von Fritz,[30] of "perceive," "plan" (28 B 2, 2 D.-K.), and in the new one of "know" (28 B 3 D.-K.): "since it is the same thing to know and to be";[31] and in Simonides the adjective *kakós* has both the archaic, agonistic meaning of "lacking in ability," and that of "bad" in an ethical sense.[32]

Innovation coexists with tradition in such contexts, but the goal— however diverse the directions taken—is always to arrive at a new awareness of the problem of reality and a new method of thought. Simonides re-poses the problem of the will in human action and offers a radical solution: voluntary moral choice that does not lose sight of the norms of justice which serve the interests of the city. In examining this Simonidean notion of justice one cannot ignore Plato and, in particular, the definition that Polemarchus attributes to Simonides at *Republic* I, 331e: "the just (*díkaion*) is rendering to each person his due" (= fr. 642 P.).

The discussion conducted by Socrates in the Platonic passage—first with Cephalus, then with Polemarchus—turns initially on a particular aspect of justice, that which involves repaying one's debts.[33] These may take the form of sacrifices owed to a god, money owed to a person (331b), and even weapons (331c) or any other objects kept as a deposit by someone who is obliged to return them upon demand (331e). It is in just this sense that Polemarchus understands the Simonidean maxim. But when Socrates shows him that Simonides meant something very different, Polemarchus proposes a second interpretation: justice consists in doing good to one's friends and harming one's enemies. Even at this point, however, Socrates' attitude turns out to be no different from that which he takes in the *Protagoras* when explicating the Scopas poem. Using the same sort of interpreter's virtuosity, this time based on a paradoxical use of analogy, he ridicules the identification of justice with helping friends and harming enemies (322d)—or, worse, with the art of robbing to the profit of friends and the disadvantage of enemies—and concludes, not without irony, that such a formulation could not possibly be genuinely Simonidean. In fact, as Socrates says to Polemarchus (335e), "the two of us, you and I, are opponents of anyone who maintains that this was said by Simonides or Bias or Pittacus or any member of that group of wise and venerable men."

What emerges from Plato's discussion is that Simonides' maxim bases justice on the principle of *reciprocity* and *equilibrium,* a principle that seeks to insure that identical or corresponding situations and ways of personal behavior are dealt with in the same way. This principle— or general norm—of justice was operative at all levels of Greek thought in the pre-Platonic period. It is clear, therefore, that the ultimate purpose of the Platonic debate on justice is to invalidate a traditional norm of social and political behavior and replace it with something different, a norm of political and personal justice, to be conceptualized in the fourth book of the *Republic* (432c–434c; 443c ff.). On the political level the citizen will be obliged to perform the single activity for which his natural capacities suit him, without moving outside of his own social class. On the personal level, which is that of the inner man, he will be obliged to fulfill his duties to himself by acting in such a way that each of the three parts of his soul performs its own proper function. The just man, through disciplining and harmonizing the three parts of his soul, establishes an inner counterpart to the same order that governs all his exterior actions, from the acquiring of material goods and tending to his physical well-being to participation in public life and contractual dealings with other individuals.

The norm of reciprocity, which in all its various applications had hitherto constituted the moral basis for human action, is thus rejected in favor of the principle of distributive justice. Man must operate in accordance with this principle in order to construct a just state and a just inner life; the action that contributes to the realization of inner harmony is just, and knowledge is the science that directs such action. Justice is at once a blueprint for society and a virtue of the soul.[34]

It is thus clear that the maxim of Simonides does not pertain to a single act or action, such as the payment of debt, but includes all aspects of human behavior and attitudes.

The application of this principle of reciprocity and just equilibrium constitutes political excellence (*onasípolis díka*)—the only type of excellence attainable, according to the Scopas poem. Its prerequisite is moral health, for only the sound and healthy man (*hygiés*) can master and apply it.

This use of *hygiés* in an ethical sense is first attested in Simonides, but it became common later, particularly in the second half of the fifth century.[35] It is implicit, for example, in the *Persians* of Aeschylus, where the folly of Xerxes, who nourished the illusion that he could defeat the gods, is judged a *sickness of the mind* (v. 750 *nósos phrenôn*) by Darius; and in the second stasimon of the *Eumenides*, where the rejection by the chorus of a life without laws and liberties in favor of one in which due measure prevails stems from their conviction that Insolence is the daughter of Impiousness and that well-being is the fruit of a *healthy mind* (v. 535 *ek d' hygieías phrenôn*). The ethical connotations of "healthy and sound" carry with them the notion of equity and equilibrium, the very things that, in Hippocratic medicine, are the indispensable precondition for physical health.

One can now understand why Plato's discussions of virtue and excellence in the *Protagoras* and of justice in the *Republic* take as their point of departure precisely these formulations of Simonides, his direct predecessor and antagonist in the consideration of ethical and political problems. The frequency with which the poet is cited in the work of the philosopher constitutes a telling testimony to the importance that Simonidean thought had in the fifth and fourth centuries and to the popularity of some of his vivid phrases. They had acquired the status of true proverbs, like the maxims of the Seven Sages.

So far as the useful is concerned, Simonides' observations are in line with those of his contemporary Xenophanes, who contrasted the useless *areté* of the athlete with the *sophía* of the poet, whose value to the community makes poetry the highest form of excellence (fr. 2, 1 Gent.-Pr.). But his observations are more radical and forward-looking in that they recognize civic excellence as the only type possible, a type that is, moreover, the property of the ordinary man rather than an intellectual elite and is taught by the *pólis:* the community is the formative instrument in the education of man.[36] It is in the uncertain climate of this crisis in traditional values that the modes of thought and language associated with the new culture of written communication favored by the Sophists and Plato make their appearance. A more than accidental indication of the change is the transformation that *Mnemosyne* undergoes at the hands of Simonides,[37] reduced from the status of goddess to that of mnemonic technique, the exercise of which is considered a purely psychological phenomenon.

Human personality in this period still tended to be felt as what Fränkel precisely terms "an open field of forces," rather than "a closed, compact entity"[38]—a situation that comparative studies of the sort done by anthropologists can help us to understand. Thus Sappho could speak of the human "I" as being party to knowledge with itself, or of the "I"'s inner consciousness of some thing or some act potentially offensive to the self.[39] One can also understand, without recourse to the outmoded contrast between "mythic" and "rational" mentality,[40] that the absence of the word for a thing does not necessarily imply the absence of the corresponding idea. The phenomena under discussion were known to the archaic poet; but they were expressed in language appropriate to a psychological and intellectual life[41] in which, as we have seen, the tendency to objectify and externalize the idiosyncratic and personal was very strong. In this way one can understand the coexistence, within Sappho's poetry, of modes of expression in which the self is understood, now as an open field for the free play of objective psychic forces, now as internal consciousness and awareness. It is obvious that the latter attitude is closely bound up with poetic situation and with poetic tone and subject matter in their more personal and confidential moments.

# VI

# The Ways of Love in the Poetry
## of *Thíasos* & Symposium

One of the problems that recent scholarship has restored to its proper
historical dimensions—partially through application of data from the
study of comparable phenomena in other cultures—is that of the character, various manifestations, and ultimate purpose of the Sapphic
*thíasos*. The basic premises of its existence were to be found in the social structure of women's life in antiquity,[1] just as the Alcaean coterie
derived its organization, conventions, and goals from the life of the
aristocratic male club. But any social organization, whether of men or
women, would have been unthinkable in seventh-century Greece
apart from the common worship of some god (or, at any rate, some
shared religious activity), common observances, common ceremonies,
a common "conventional" language, and, finally, common ethico-
political assumptions and purposes. It is difficult to believe, particularly in the light of the partheneia of Alcman, that the essential purpose
of the Spartan *thíasos* was nothing but cult recitation of choral songs
and the accessory things that went with it: participation in the same
religious rites, personal relationships, affections, rivalries, and the like.[2]

As is well known, the debate on the nature and function of partheneia is still very much an open one. The addressees in these poems are
the same girls who made up the chorus of performers, and one should
repeat that here, as with any piece of choral poetry, interpretation
must take into account all those referents through which the poem is
rooted in social reality, as well as the character of the particular festive
occasion that gives the poetic message its meaning.

It is widely believed that female homosexuality was an institution confined to the island of Lesbos. But the "Sapphic" form of women's community—so-called because it is best known, in a certain sense, through the fragments of Sappho and the ancient testimony relating to her—was not a purely Lesbian phenomenon. We know from Plutarch (*Lyc.* 18, 9) that homoerotic female relationships were also allowed in archaic Sparta, in communities of more or less the same type as the Lesbian ones. And it has been demonstrated—by now conclusively—that the partheneia of Alcman are full of stylemes, metaphors, and typical expressions that derive from the language of love and are extensively paralleled in Sappho.[3] These considerations necessarily open up new perspectives on the interpretation of the Louvre partheneion (1 P. = 3 Calame), which the scholarly literature on the subject has so far failed to consider.[4]

In accordance with customary choral practice, the partheneion is divided into two parts, one concerned with mythic narrative and the other with present reality. Eleven people are named in the course of it, but one of these, Enesimbrota, is not a member of the chorus (assuming that vv. 73ff. have been correctly understood as referring to her as a person of authority and importance, a confidante to whom the girls turn in revealing their desires and their feelings of love).[5]

There are two central figures, Agido and Hagesichora, the second of whom is clearly, as her name itself indicates, the chorus leader (v. 84). Their beauty is the occasion for a series of similes that set them apart from the other girls in the chorus and at the same time make it clear that they function together as a pair. Hence the comparison with the two types of thoroughbred horse, Ibenian and Colaxean, that run one alongside the other (v. 59), or the identification with doves[6] that gleam like the star Sirius (v. 60ff.):

> they are the doves
> which rise
> like the star Sirius
> in the ambrosial night
> and compete with us
> who are taking the plow
> to the goddess of the dawn.
>
> It is neither glut of finest purple cloth
> that can help us,
> nor serpents chased in gold,

nor Lydian miter enhancing
the young girls' melting glance;
not Nanno's tresses,
nor Areta—beautiful like a goddess—
nor Thylakis nor Cleaisitera;
you shall not go to Enesimbrota's
to say "Let Astaphis be mine
and Philylla cast longing glances at me
and Damareta and lovely Ianthemis,"
but, "It is Hagesichora who consumes me."

Is not the lovely
ankled Hagesichora here
alongside Agido and praising the festival?
Oh gods, accept their prayers.
From the gods come end and completion.
I wish to speak, O mistress of our choir:
maiden am I and from the roof beam
like an owl I have chattered to no purpose.
I wish to please Aotis,
who assuages our pains.
But it is only through Hagesichora
that the young girls attain
the peace they long for.[7]

It is these verses that constitute the knot to be unraveled if one is to find the proper clue for interpreting the poem. The girls in the chorus are celebrating the two companions who are the subject of the song, asserting that these two, the doves, "are competing" with them as they carry the *plow* to the goddess of the dawn. Here the plow is a symbol of procreative fecundity—the same sacral symbol to which Plutarch (*Praec. coniug.* 42, 144b) applies the qualifying adjective *gamélios*—and is a votive offering for the maintenance of the tie of marriage.[8]

The type of relationship set up between Agido and Hagesichora seems to exclude the other girls in the community, none of whom will be able to cherish erotic aspirations with regard to either of them. The chorus explicitly proclaims its helplessness when, overcome by a mood of dejection, it asserts that nothing—neither beauty nor precious things—will be able to gain it the love of one of those two.

The address in the second person, which should be understood as directed toward Agido, makes the inescapability of the new tie be-

tween the two girls even more explicit. Agido will no longer turn to
the mistress of the *thíasos* Enesimbrota to reveal her passion for this or
that companion: she will say that it is Hagesichora's love that makes
her suffer. In the succeeding verses a rapid succession of rhetorical
questions describes one moment of a scene in which Agido and Hagesichora appear as if at a distance from the rest, one next to the other, in
an attitude of close and firm union.[9] And the girls of the chorus who
preserve, as they themselves affirm, their *maiden* status, regretfully
acknowledge the ineffectiveness of their every word, their every movement, their every hope. Like owls they have chattered in vain. Hence
the invocation to Aotis, who assuages the pains of love.

But who is this divinity Aotis? Her identity has been a real enigma
both for earlier and more recent critics, once metrical considerations
forced the elimination of the reading *Orthíai* (v. 61), on the basis of
which some scholars had supposed a reference to the Spartan deity
Artemis Orthia.[10] If Aotis is neither Artemis Orthia nor the moon
goddess hypothesized by Page, one must try other means of solution,
and these suggest that she is a goddess of the dawn: "she who rises in
the east," as the Laconian suffix *-tis*, used here in a locative sense, would
indicate. She will thus be the morning–or evening–star, which the
ancient commentary to the *Phaenomena* of Aratus[11] calls the brilliant
star of Aphrodite and which had, already in the archaic period, the
double designation of *Heosphóros* and *Hésperos*.[12] Morning and evening
star played a significant role in the nuptial songs of Sappho (frr. 104a,
b V.), the same one that is well documented for them in the epithalamium of Catullus 62.[13] Moreover, the epithet *Orthría*, which
is applied in v. 61 to the goddess to whom the girls offer the plow,
takes us back to the same idea of morning light which is contained
in Aotis.

Orthría-Aotis is thus none other than the goddess Aphrodite (already mentioned in the fragmentary and more obscure portion of the
poem where the myth of the sons of Hippocoon was told [v. 17]: "let
no one aspire to become the bridegroom of Aphrodite").

The analysis as developed thus far seems to yield a single, unambiguous conclusion. This partheneion is an epithalamium composed for
ritual performance within the community to which the girls belonged.
The reference to Orthría not only confirms this view of its function
but also defines its genre more specifically. It is an epithalamium
chanted to the dawn, at the moment of awakening–the type of composition which, to judge from an ancient commentary on Theocritus,
could be called indifferently an *órthrion* or a *diegertikón*.[14] A. Grif-

fiths[15] deserves the credit for having seen and pointed out this aspect of the poem, though his interpretation should be modified to make the occasion celebrated in the song an initiation within the *thíasos* rather than an ordinary marriage ceremony.[16] Himerius, writing in the fourth century A.D. and interweaving his orations with paraphrases and citations from archaic lyric, particularly that of Sappho and Anacreon, bears witness in one passage to the presence of an internal ceremony of exactly this sort. Drawing on the poetess's own works, he describes how, once the contests are over, Sappho enters the bridal chamber, spreads the marriage couch, has the girls brought into the *nympheîon*, leads in the Graces' chariot bearing Aphrodite and her chorus of Cupids, and finally joins with them in a procession that raises aloft the nuptial torch.[17] In one of his erotic *Epistles*, Aristaenetus uses language that he says is borrowed from Sappho in speaking of the same type of ritual. It was customary on such occasions, he says, for the girls with the most harmonious and melodious voices to be chosen to sing the marriage song.[18]

Himerius's reference to the "rites of Aphrodite" is certainly an allusion to a precise moment in the cult activity of the *thíasos*. Within the women's communities of archaic Lesbos there were liaisons of an "official" character, which could involve a genuinely matrimonial type of relationship, as is shown by Sappho's use (fr. 213, 3 V.) of the term *yokemate* (*sýndygos* [= *sýzyx* or *sýzygos*]). The word, which has not, it seems to me, received the attention it deserves,[19] is a specific, not generic, way of referring to the actual bond of marriage.[20]

A further piece of interesting information comes from the commentary (fr. 213, 4ff. V.) that follows this citation from Sappho's text. There we learn that Pleistodice, along with Gongyla (a girl mentioned several times by Sappho), is the "wife" (*sýzyx*) of Gorgo, the woman who presided over a rival community.[21] This means that the directress of the *thíasos* could be paired with two girls simultaneously.

We are thus supplied with the basic ingredients for understanding the terms in which the discourse of Alcman's chorus of girls is couched and for following it as it moves from agonistic language to reference to precious objects as a means of defeating a rival for the affection of the beloved, to resigned withdrawal from combat, and—finally—to the attainment of "peace" when one of their number accedes to the amorous desires of another at the moment of ritual marriage. First comes the amorous struggle,[22] a part of the girls' final attempt to separate Agido from Hagesichora, then the idea that they are now beyond being helped by any precious object, or even by their own beauty.

Grief and pain and disappointed hopes for Hagesichora's love will soon be assuaged by the goddess Aotis-Aphrodite—though only Agido attains to "peace"; that is, to the state of tranquillity and satisfied erotic passion which Hagesichora provides through the initiatory nuptial bond:

> But it is only through Hagesichora
> that the young girls attain
> the peace they long for.[23]

Experiences of this sort—even if in situations that are, historically and culturally, profoundly different—are still alive in the Far East. Simone de Beauvoir cites the direct testimony of a Chinese friend, the writer Han Suyin, in reference to women's communities whose conventions and cult practices offer interesting analogies to those of Lesbos and archaic Sparta: "She [Han Suyin] tells me that at Singapore and, in spite of the regime, at Canton there are still communities of women (around thirty thousand in Canton) made up of recognized lesbians; *they marry among each other* and adopt children. *They can leave their communities and marry a man.* And in that case they cut their hair. *They have their own patron divinity, their own ceremonies,* etc. [italics mine]."[24]

It hardly needs saying, of course, that Alcman composed his partheneia on commission for the Spartan *thíasoi* of his time, whereas Sappho, being a poet, composed songs for performance in her own *thíasos*. The meager fragments of Sapphic epithalamia do not allow us to determine which ones were composed for nuptial rites of initiation—those of which Himerius speaks—and which for the "true" nuptial ceremonies that took place when girls married outside the community.[25]

References to ornamental objects, clothes, jewels, perfumes, and grace of bearing certainly reveal a distinction of style that separated the girls of Sappho's community from those of rival ones. Splendor, elegance, and gracefulness[26] must have been the distinguishing traits of the group; witness the joke at the expense of the boorish rival Andromeda,[27] who does not know enough to let her long gown fall above the ankle (fr. 57 V.). What was characteristic in the conventions regulating the communal life of the *thíasoi* could not have been confined to externals of dress; it must have pervaded the other aspects of the community's existence, as well as the realm of language and religious cult.

All archaic poets sang of love as an immediate, sensuous emotion—a profound disturbance of the lover's own being. But for Sappho it is also a memory, alive in space and time, of shared feelings of joy in the life of the *thíasos* and one that even at a distance can reawaken feelings of longing and torment—an experience that constantly, and easily, lends itself to modernizing interpretations.[28] The memory is always of something concrete and real, "of lovely things enjoyed together," things that made an impression on the senses and roused the emotions. But this common experience, which lives again in the memory, always registers the ambience of culture and the mediation of divinity through typical situations. Delight in beauty enjoyed together is also delight that the radiance of the flowers of Aphrodite and the goddess's own presence have awakened in the erotic life of the community.

There is no need to raise once again the problem[29] of the character and meaning of divine epiphanies in the Greek world, whether they are to be regarded as pure literary convention, or as records of real personal experiences—true moments of hallucination. The question is an ancient one, to which different answers were already being given in the late Hellenistic period,[30] and the studies of Dodds have made reconsidering it unnecessary. Epiphanies "have ... the same origin and psychological structure as dreams, and like dreams they tend to reflect traditional culture patterns. Among the Greeks, by far the commonest type is the apparition of a god or the hearing of a divine voice which commands or forbids the performance of certain acts."[31] To be understood the phenomenon obviously requires tools of analysis supplied by psychology and anthropology. Can there still be any doubt that in seventh- and sixth-century Greece, and not only there, apparitions of gods and goddesses were felt as real—given the fact that they continue to be a frequent occurrence, even in the most advanced of contemporary societies?[32] Critics have often made the mistake of regarding experiences of this type as allegories or mere literary ornamentation. Yet K. Latte was perfectly correct about this tendency in criticism when he noted, a number of years ago,[33] that the address of the Muses on Mount Helicon which Hesiod records in the *Theogony* was not intended as an allegory of poetic inspiration but as a narrative of what the poet had actually experienced. And it is along such lines that all the direct or indirect references to experiences of this sort which appear in the archaic and classical periods should be interpreted;[34] skepticism and agnosticism with regard to dreams and divine visions were always confined to a few intellectuals and even then do not appear earlier than the second half of the sixth century.[35] With regard to other literary epochs and, in particular, the poetry of Dante, it is worth drawing attention to what T. S. Eliot and Ezra Pound have to say in response to the formalistic type of criticism that considered the visions recorded in Dante conventional and literary:

> Dante's is a *visual* imagination. It is a visual imagination in a different sense from that of a modern painter of still life: it is visual in the sense that he lived in an age in which men still saw visions. It was a psychological habit, the trick of which we have forgotten, but as good as any of our own. We have nothing but dreams, and we have forgotten that seeing visions—a practice now relegated to the aberrant and uneducated—was once a more significant, interesting and disciplined kind of dreaming.[36]

> Anyone who has in any degree the faculty of vision will know that the so-called personifications are real and not artificial. Dante's precision both in the *Vita Nuova* and in the *Commedia* comes from the attempt to reproduce exactly the thing which has been clearly seen.[37]

A striking feature of Sappho's poetry is the frequency of epiphanies and dream visions, particularly those connected with Aphrodite. One such epiphany occurs at the moment of ritual invocation in the spot sacred to the goddess, and her presence reveals itself in the act of her pouring nectar for Sappho (fr. 2, 13ff. V.); more often, however, epiphany is mentioned in the course of remembering a whole situation (fr. 96, 26ff. V.) or an actual[38] or dreamed conversation with the goddess (fr. 134 V.). The ode to Aphrodite (1 V.) gives a precise idea of these "conversations" and of the occasionally disturbing events that provoked them and secured the aid required from her.

The structure of the song reproduces the usual prayer scheme, but, given the very nature of its content and the highly personal mode of address adopted, its intended occasion could not have been a public ceremony in honor of the goddess. It must have been presented before an audience of girls, and one naturally wonders what meaning such prayers would have had in that context. It is begging the question to say that they were purely literary,[39] and not in keeping with what we know about the preeminent role that the cult of the divinity played in archaic communities.

The unusual features of the prayer, such as the extended description of the goddess descending from heaven in her chariot, the remarkable presentation of one's own love in dramatic form, through words spoken by the goddess,[40] and finally the affectionate attitude—totally without precedent—of Aphrodite herself, are not simply derived from real episodes in the life of the *thíasos* or *representative* of amorous ties past and present under the vigilant, sure care of the goddess. They must also mirror a precise ceremonial for which a place was set aside in the area where the private religious rites of the community were performed. Otherwise there would be no way of explaining why Sappho felt it necessary to structure the account of the course of her own love according to the formal scheme of a prayer of invocation.

The occasion for the poem is a new love, which causes Sappho to suffer. She invokes Aphrodite to free her from the harshness of her pain, as she has invoked her on other occasions when the goddess's presence brought relief and persuaded the other girl to love her in return. At this point there follows the address of the goddess, peremptory and elliptical in the manner of one proclaiming an inalterable norm of justice:

> . . . whom must I persuade
> to return (?) to your love, Sappho?[41]
>     Who is wronging you (*adikéei*)?
> If she is fleeing now, soon she will pursue;
> If she is refusing gifts, soon she will give them;
> If she does not love you, soon she will do so,
>     even against her will.

The poem is, in short, Sappho's prayer to Aphrodite to come to her aid, to be her ally in reestablishing the bond of mutual love which the beloved has broken by deserting the Sapphic *thíasos* for the community of a rival.

Several fragments illustrate the dynamics of these amorous crises within the group and the tense competitive relationships between different communities. The fact that Gorgo and Andromeda belonged to aristocratic Mytilenean clans, the Pentilidai[42] in the one case and the Polyanactidai in the other,[43] suggests that the amorous quarrels between the Sapphic community and its rivals[44] were not without their political implications in the context of late seventh- and early sixth-century Mytilene. The Pentilidai were related to Pittacus,[45] to whom Sappho refers, with unmistakable scorn, as "the fellow from Mytilene," so political resentment may well have entered into her aversion for at least one of her rivals. It could have been occasioned by, for example, Pittacus's decree forbidding the importation of clothes and luxury objects from Lydia, of which an echo can be heard in the ode to Cleis.[46]

Even if Sappho, unlike Alcaeus, did not actively participate in the political strife of her city, the traditions concerning her exile in Sicily[47] show that she was in some sense involved in it. Her philo-Lydian attitude and the cult of elegance and splendor (*habrosýne*)* which was to be expected in a *thíasos* that admitted girls from Ionia and sported clothes and jewelry of Asiatic manufacture, could not fail to be in striking contrast with the political orientation of Pittacus. His relations with Lydia were marked by ill-concealed aversion,[48] notwithstanding the riches that Croesus sent him (and that he refused).[49] The hostility is further confirmed by the aid that the Lydians gave to Alcaeus to enable him to return to his city (Alc. fr. 69 V.), probably during the course of his third exile, which coincided with Pittacus's coming to power.[50] Unfortunately, our limited information does not allow us to reconstruct the actual episodes in the interplay of erotic and political motives that must have been behind the tensions within Sappho's group and her open expressions of jealousy toward her rivals. Certain institutional differences notwithstanding, the uniformity of the linguistic code pertaining to crisis, exile, and lovers' wrongs suggests that, like the male clubs that provide Alcaeus and Theognis with their subject matter,[51] the female communities of archaic Lesbos were familiar with the way erotic relationships and political orientation can influence and interfere with each other. One must not, in any case, forget that one of Sappho's two major rivals—we do not know whether it was Gorgo or Andromeda—was, like Pittacus's wife, a Pentilid.

The beautiful Atthis, Sappho's favorite among her girls, was won away from her by the love of Andromeda (frr. 49, 130, 3–4 V.):

Atthis, there was a time when I loved you . . .
you seemed to me a little girl then, without grace.

Atthis, it grieves me to think of you:
you flit away toward Andromeda.

But the persuasiveness of the redoubtable rival did not always have its way in the contest of love. Quite the contrary: the rival's favorite might be seized and spirited away through love for Sappho. This seems to be the background for the mocking exclamation (fr. 133 V.):

Andromeda has got her just deserts.

The situation must have been the same with Gongyla, who deserted Sappho's community to become the mate of the hated Gorgo.[52]

It is thus obvious that the notion of injustice (*adikía*) formulated in the ode to Aphrodite has community, as well as individual, implications.[53] A girl's failure to reciprocate Sappho's love was tantamount to her detachment from the community to which she belonged and her entrance into the sphere of the rival community. This is the background for Sappho's prayer: the irresistible power of the goddess will force the girl, even if she is unwilling, to return the love of the woman who feels love for her.

The prayer's message is applicable both to the present situation and to similar ones experienced in the past or expected in the future. Love must be reciprocated; the girl who fails to do so does wrong to Sappho and to Aphrodite herself. The norm of reciprocity and irrefusability operative here is totally unaffected by the desires of either lover or beloved. "Even against her will," says Aphrodite of the girl, in an effort to soothe Sappho's torment; "albeit reluctantly" repeats Theognis, in an effort to overcome a young man's resistance by citing the mythical paradigm of Atalanta.[54]

This norm of reciprocity and reversibility will be a cardinal principle of courtly love in the twelfth century[55] and will provide medieval theorists with an argument for the love of God (justified as a necessary reciprocation of the love that God cherishes for man).[56] It will then become, in Dante, the symbol for the tragic love of Francesca (*Inf.* V 103). "Amor ch'a nullo amato amar perdona" is love that does not allow the one who is loved not to love in return.

The poems on remembered experience regularly display a pattern that includes the flowers in Aphrodite's garden and an instant of divine epiphany. In one of them, addressed to Atthis, the friend of the moment, Sappho recalls how at one time it was Arignota who especially loved her. Now, however, Arignota is in Sardis—doubtless married—and from Sardis thinks back to Atthis and her life in the *thíasos*. The memory at once invokes the beauty of the distant companion (fr. 96 V.):

> Now amid the women of Lydia she is resplendent
> the way, at sunset,
> the rosy fingered moon,
> outshining every star, sheds
> its light equally
> on the salt sea and the flowering plains.

But suddenly the thought shifts from imagination to reality. The moon simile, which at the start seemed almost symbolic, dissolves into the contemplation of a real moonlit landscape in which are discerned, alongside the chervil and clover, the roses that customarily grow in the gardens of Aphrodite:

> And the lovely dew covers all,
> and the roses bloom and the tender
> chervil and flowers of clover.

The flowers are not decorative elements here.[57] They belong, rather, to a precise spot and take us back to the *thíasos* surroundings—to the very place described at greater length and with detailed realism in the ode preserved on the Florence *óstrakon* (fr. 2 V.).

This interpretation is confirmed by what immediately follows. The original theme, which seemed to all appearances forgotten, is taken up once more in the sixth and seventh strophes (vv. 15–20), with the return to Arignota longing for her distant friend. There is an exaltation of the beauty of Atthis ("it is not easy for us to vie in beauty with goddesses"), and so a point of contact with the second strophe (vv. 3–5), where the present friend is reminded of the praises of her beauty once sung by Arignota ("Arignota [used to think] you the equal of the goddesses").[58] Finally, the ninth strophe (v. 26ff.), with its references to Aphrodite in the act of pouring nectar, takes us back to the blooming garden described earlier and presents the goddess in the same pose and attitude as does the epiphany of the *óstrakon* ode.[59]

The structure of the other memory ode (fr. 94 V.) is simpler. First there is the evocation of the sorrowful parting of the friend, then that of the "beautiful things enjoyed together," which introduces one immediately into the active life of the community. The memory fixes lovingly on the wreaths of roses and violets, the garlands of flowers, the hair soft with unguents, and the actual physical joys of love (v. 21ff.: "on the soft couches you satisfied the strong pangs of desire . . ."). Here, too, are the usual flowers of Aphrodite and, finally, though the last two strophes are, unfortunately, only partly understandable, sacred rites and sacred spots—the holy grove, to be exact (v. 27), with which we are familiar from the *óstrakon* poem.

In their repetition of identical motifs these structures seem to correspond to ritual formulae operating within a system in which the sources of the poet's inspiration—the crises and separations of love, the floral landscapes, the visions of divinity—are *privileged* religious experiences bringing closer communion with the god. In this context the role played by the standard theme of memory[60] is a determining one. Memory is not simply, as in Homer, a means of evoking emotions and sensations:[61] it reactualizes shared experiences in paradigmatic fashion and offers the assurance that the life lived together exists as an absolute *reality* beyond space and time.[62] The religious meaning that attaches to this notion is clear in the surviving lines of an ode directed, as we know from ancient testimony, to a crude or uneducated woman—one excluded, at any rate, from Sappho's circle (fr. 55 V.):

> Dead shall you lie and none shall remember you hereafter,
> for you had no share in the roses of Pieria.
> Even in Hades, once flown from here,[63]
> you shall wander unknown amidst the nameless dead.

If Sappho was able to say to a woman who did not belong to her *thíasos* that death would mean oblivion not only in the world of men but also in the realm of Hades, she evidently thought to reserve sure hopes of a better afterlife to the companions in her own circle.[64] But the entertaining of eschatological hopes of this sort was possible—for the girls in the *thíasos* and for Sappho herself[65]—precisely because of the close bond that linked them to the gods, particularly the Muses. The closeness to the Muses can only be explained by the hypothesis of an actual cult in their honor within the community. Its existence is proven by the presence of *moisopólos,* a word with precise religious meaning, in the fragment in which Sappho addresses her daughter, Cleis, and enjoins against raising "the song of lamentation in the house of the servants of the Muses" (*moisopólon*).[66] To the picture created by these passages of eschatological hope one should add the topological references to death—as something to be longed for as one sadly remembers a distant friend[67] or grieves over desertion by a companion (Gongyla: cf. fr. 95 V.), or to be noted alongside other physical symptoms as a possible outcome of love (fr. 31, 15ff. V.). But death, even if it is an evil,[68] no longer has anything terrible about it. It is not seen as a grim inevitability, but as a natural passing that leads to a longed-for mythical place, beautiful as the garden of the *thíasos* (fr. 95, 11 V.):

> I wish with all my heart to die
> and see the banks of Acheron,
> abloom with lotus, soft with dew.

The recurring debate over the sincerity or nonsincerity of these expressions of longing makes sense in the rationalizing, secularizing context of our own time, but not in an archaic Greek one. When a strong religious personality, living in a closed collective environment, uses ritual formulae, conventions, and shared beliefs for the creation of heightened intensity and tension, the poetry that results is a reflection of the degree and type of *valorization* which those formulae have received. Expressions of a longing for death, repeated with almost schematic rigidity, were evidently ritual formulations—a recurrent aspect of the special language used within the group. It is their repetition that reveals the longing as something sure and durable—as sure as the continuity with life after death which memory assures.

Sappho transfers the divinities of myth—Aphrodite, the Muses, and the Graces—onto a plane more accessible to the daily life of the *thíasos*. Even in epic, of course, the hero has his own gods whom he recognizes as friends. Their friendship and aid constitute a privilege of which he can boast. But their world is still foreign to him, sharply circumscribed in a realm remote from his own activity. This is true even when the man-god relationship reveals itself in gestures and actions that seem to suggest greater intimacy and closer collaboration—for example, the teasing laughter and affectionate banter with which Athena greets the lies of her protégé in *Odyssey* 13, 287ff., or the conversation under an olive tree, in which hero and goddess contemplate the final destruction of the suitors (372ff.). It is the same in the *Iliad* (5, 799ff.) when with a friendly gesture Athena rests her hand on the yoke-beam of the wounded Diomedes' chariot and urges him back into battle. But though the gods may fight side by side with heroes, encouraging, helping, and protecting them, there is always a broad, unbridgeable gap between the two. When Diomedes, in the midst of his warrior's rampage, dares to hurl himself against Apollo, the angry god calls out to him to stop—not to think himself equal to the gods, for unequal is the stock of immortals and mortals (*Il.* 5, 440ff.).

Sappho's goddesses know nothing of such separation and remoteness. Her Aphrodite, like the gods of Homer, assists and protects, but her manner and attitude are more human, more gentle, more intimate— almost, one would say, those of a favorite friend in the *thíasos* rather than of a goddess. In talking to Sappho she uses the affectionate tones of a sister or a mother (1 V.), now calm and serene, now impatient; but her impatience is always kindly,[69] without any trace of anger or remoteness. Such is the Aphrodite of the first ode. Sappho entrusts her sorrows to her without hesitation, confident that the goddess will hear her prayer and turn her anguish into calm (v. 25ff.). And there were other occasions when Aphrodite spoke to Sappho with the same tone of confidence and gentleness: "you and my slave Love" are her words in fragment 159 V.[70] An almost identical attitude of easy familiarity with the goddess appears during the course of a dialogue with a friend (Gongyla?). The friend is stunning in her splendid mantle, "a marvel to the beholder," and also stunning because of the way winged desire "hovers near her." This delights Sappho, for there was a time when "she herself"—the goddess—was in the habit of finding fault with the way Gongyla looked and dressed.[71]

Assiduous companions of Aphrodite, the Graces and the Muses are linked to her in mythical models that are repeated according to fixed, conventional schemata. One of these figures the Graces in the act of bathing and anointing Aphrodite with the immortal oil of the gods[72] or dancing and singing in her company on Mount Ida.[73] In another—found, for example, in the Delphic continuation of the *Hymn to Apollo* (v. 186ff.)—the Muses sing upon Olympus to celebrate the god's arrival, while the Graces, together with the Hours, Harmonia, Hebe, and Aphrodite, join hands and dance. Sappho repeated this model with slight variations in a poem in which Apollo, golden-haired and carrying his lyre, goes forth on Helicon in a chariot drawn by swans to dance with the Graces and the Muses.[74]

The traditional myth patterns live on through the active participation of these divinities in the life of the community, as is clear from the ritual invocations composed for their epiphany.[75] Their presence reveals itself through the special grace of a gesture, a pose, a smile. Having exhorted one of her companions, Dica, to wreathe "your hair with lovely garlands, taking and intertwining sprigs of dill in your soft hands," Sappho concludes with the warning that the Graces avert their gaze from the girls who are not wearing crowns (fr. 81b V.). A habitual ornament in group celebrations becomes in this way a *signifier* for the presence of the Graces or an expression of the loveliness and charm they confer.

Based as it was on a precise ritual bond, the relationship with the Muses was very close. Sappho had entrusted them with her own destiny on earth and with the hopes that she and her friends entertained for a life of equal honor after death. Her attitude is evident in the ostentatious pride with which she proclaims their favor and protection. The Muses have bestowed on her not only the gift of art but also honors[76] and wealth,[77] a privileged combination much sought after by the poet of the archaic age, as we know from the opening prayer in

Solon's elegy to the Muses: "Grant unto me wealth and a good name."[78]

Sappho contemplates the fleetingness of life and the physical decay of old age with serenity and detachment.[79] Her skin is wrinkled; her hair is white; her gait is no longer steady; still, "what is there for me to do about it?" she says. Even Tithonus, beloved of the Dawn, could only obtain immortal life, not eternal youth. The note of nostalgia barely colors the gaze backward into the past. Tithonus, the old man who could not die, became for Mimnermus a paradigm of eternal misfortune worse than death (fr. 1 Gent.-Pr.). Here he is only a symbol of the irreversibility of earthly time. Old age is not, even in its ugliness, a disaster without remedy—a condition of total misery in which everything loved and desired in youth must be abandoned. It is, rather, an unavoidable episode in the passage of biological time, one that has failed to destroy the essence of the reality Sappho has constructed within the circle of her friends: delight in life's splendor, and love "of the brilliant and beautiful."[80] The impulse toward innovation allows Sappho to assign new values to inherited paradigms of divinity, giving them a fresh meaning and importance in relation to the life of the community.

In the famous ode of remembrance for Anactoria[81] Sappho contrasts her own notion of what "the most beautiful thing" in the world is with that of others. It is not an army of cavalry or foot soldiers, or a fleet of ships, but the person one loves. In support of this she adduces the example of Helen: the most beautiful of women abandoned the best of husbands and sailed to Troy, forgetting her daughter and her parents to follow the promptings of Aphrodite in a voyage to distant lands.[82] And now the same goddess rouses in Sappho the memory of the distant Anactoria, whose graceful step and radiantly beautiful face she would rather see than an army of Lydian chariots and foot soldiers in full battle array. Here Sappho is giving an answer to one of the "world-record" items in what might be called the archaic cultural questionnaire ("what is the most beautiful thing?" or "the most just" or "best" or "biggest," etc.). Its querying of the supreme forms of excellence is a familiar part of legends concerning Homer, the Seven Sages, Aesop, Pythagoras,[83] and of archaic poetry in general.[84] Beauty as this supreme value is not tangible—not grand and powerful in the way the spectacle of cavalry or foot soldiery or a fleet of ships could be—but, as the concluding strophe says, an impalpable something in the light step or radiant countenance of the beloved which sends a ripple of emotion through the senses:

For one person it is a host of foot soldiers
for others a host of cavalry, for others ships,
that is the most beautiful thing the dark earth bears;
for me it is what one loves.

And this is something anyone can see:
Helen, who surpassed all mortals
in beauty, abandoned her husband,
noblest of heroes,

and sailed toward Troy, and to daughter
and parents she gave no thought:
it was the goddess Cypris who swept her
away with love.

. . .

and now wakens in me the memory
of Anactoria, who is far away;

I would like to see the lovely way she walks
and the radiance that lights her face
more than the chariots and foot soldiery of the Lydians
armed for battle.

It is easy, however, to accept too modern an interpretation of the affirmation that the most beautiful thing is what one loves, the object of one's own desire in all the grace and sweetness of its loveliest manifestations. To understand this assertion in its proper historical dimensions, one must not forget the paradigmatic significance of the mythic episode that opens the second strophe. Helen abandoned her husband, although he was by virtue of his rank and power the worthiest of men—a known quantity of secure and solid value—and departed for Troy to live with Paris because she thought that the most beautiful thing was the man she loved. But she did not choose love *freely:* she followed the irresistible pull of the same Cypris who has now wakened in Sappho the memory of Anactoria. Here love is not the free personal inclination or inner psychic disposition some critics have supposed—even those who give due emphasis to the intervention of the divinity.[85] It is, rather, an unstayable force exerted from without through the will of a god. The choice of Helen as an example is not accidental, nor is the particular emphasis that is placed on her beauty (she "who surpassed all mortals in beauty"). She is an ultimate and an absolute, and so someone on whom Cypris's gaze fell for the express purpose of overwhelming her with love for a man who was himself famous for his beauty.[86] The myth is reinterpreted without any concession to the traditional schematism, still present in Sappho's contemporary Alcaeus, of Helen the adulteress who causes grievous misfortunes and the final ruin of Troy.[87] She thereby becomes the incarnation of beauty and love, the two cardinal values of a unique shared experience that can never be relived within the confines of matrimony, but that will live on in *memory* as an eternal, inalienable possession.

Alcaeus's apostrophe to "violet-tressed, holy, sweetly smiling Sappho" expresses, as eloquently as one might hope for from a contemporary and a poet, the sacral dignity that linked Sappho to the divinities she worshipped and the grace she conferred on the forms of love.[88] The allusive epithet "sweetly smiling" (*mellichómeide*) repeats in its first part Sappho's own designation for the quality of gentle sweetness to be found in the face and voice of her girls.[89] In it is revealed the Aphrodite of the first ode—not the goddess with the fixed, immobile smile (*philommeidés*) of epic poetry, but the one who "laughs from her immortal countenance" (v. 14 *meidiaísais' athanátoi prosópoi*) in a spirit of human gentleness.

The poetry of Anacreon draws its themes from the festivities of banquet and symposium.* What such occasions meant for the poet can be seen from his programmatic lines:

> come, let us no longer, as before,
> conduct our drinking amid
> shouts and clamor the way the Scythians do,
> but slowly, to the sound of lovely songs.[90]

It is no wild debauch or drunken brawl, but a festive gathering of friends capable of enjoying life fully without exceeding the bounds that civility and urbanity impose on forms and modes of behavior. Convivial propriety does not close the door to social intercourse at a level of greater vitality and intensity.

The bloom of Bathyllos's youthful beauty,[91] the eyes of Cleoboulos,[92] the blond hair of the Thracian Smerdis,[93] and the gentle disposition of Megistes[94] were recurring themes in the erotic poems dedicated to young men. Softness of rhythm and insinuating grace of expression

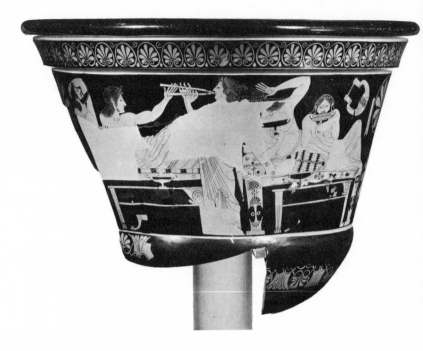

FIGURE TWO. Crater by Euphronios. About 510. Staatliche Antikensammlungen, Munich.

are the genial hallmarks of this poetry. But over and above such formal qualities, there is the problem of evaluating its function in the archaic symposium. The Eros it celebrates is neither superficial hedonism nor devoid of inner moral values; its task had to do with the forms of life and conduct to be encouraged during the course of a boy's erotic relationships. There is a certain symbolic value to the story[95] that the poet, upon being asked why he composed poems for boys and not hymns to the gods, replied: "because it is they who are my gods":

> boys should love me for what I say,
> I know how to speak sweet things and sing sweet songs.
> (fr. 22 Gent.)

> I wish to make love to you, for sweet is your nature.
> (fr. 23 Gent.)

This ethico-aesthetic vision of sweetness and grace takes us back in certain ways to the ideal of love found in Sappho. For Sappho, too, beauty was not merely external beauty: "the beautiful is beautiful as long as it is visible, but if a man is worthy (*agathós*) he will soon be beautiful as well" (fr. 50 V.). Elsewhere in Anacreon the identification of the beautiful and the just (*díkaion*), a general principle also formulated in Greek gnomai,[96] is applied specifically to the relationship between lover and beloved:

the beautiful (in love) is the just.
(fr. 120 Gent.)

And the realization of what is just involves, as has been seen in Sappho, the reciprocity and unrefusability of love.[97]

But Anacreontic love knows nothing of passion, dramatic power, or the tension between desperation and ecstasy, bitterness and sweetness. The profound dissonance of Sapphic Eros—the terrible, bittersweet god (fr. 130 V.)—resolves itself into a single parallelism between affirmation and negation, existence and nonexistence, of the erotic impulse:

I am once again in love—not in love,
mad and not mad.
(fr. 46 Gent.)

An urbane form of love this, one that remaps the polarity of the contrast into a dimension that is emotionally less profound, more worldly wise and nuanced in the way it allows for the free interplay of situations. Love is the fanciful and unpredictable creature symbolically figured in representations drawn sometimes from the practice of a craft (Eros as smith, Eros as boxer), and sometimes from mythico-religious images of the god (winged Eros, Eros-Dionysus-Aphrodite). Such representations serve less to express the intensity of love than to evoke the momentary atmosphere of a symposiastic situation:

Once again Eros the blacksmith
has struck me a blow with his mighty hammer,
has plunged me in his winter torrent.
(fr. 25 Gent.)

The god tempers his victim as a smith tempers iron, first by heating it red-hot, then by chilling it.[98] The finished products are different, but

FIGURE THREE. Kylix by the Brygos painter. Interior. About 480. Ashmolean Museum, Oxford.

the metaphor, in and of itself, is well suited to express the ups and downs of an emotional crisis. A similar action is described in the Cyclops episode of the *Odyssey* (9, 391), where Ulysses is compared to a smith with a red-hot hammer that hisses and sizzles as it is plunged into cold water to be tempered. But Eros's tempering bath is the eddying current of a chill winter torrent, an image that adds the new factors of momentum and violence to the idea of cold.

Elsewhere it is the boxing metaphor that embellishes the theme of the invincibility of Eros. The speaker—probably the poet himself—prefers the serene joys of the symposium to fierce fighting with the god, hence his command to a slave to bring wine and garlands of flowers:

> Bring water, boy, bring wine
> and bring us wreaths of flowers;
> come bring them on, for I do not wish
> to have a fisticuffs with Eros.[99]

On another occasion the fighting has exhausted the poet, but he is able to catch his breath again and find the necessary relief now that he has finally succeeded in freeing himself from the vise in which love holds him:

> Wearily I did battle with my fists.
> Now I can breathe and am almost recovered
>
> . . .
>
> having made good my escape from Love.[100]

In the prayer to Dionysus (fr. 14 Gent.) the Dionysus-Eros-Aphrodite triad is transferred from its divine setting into the atmosphere of an actual banquet. The drunkenness of the gods' erotic sport (*sympaízein*) is to set the tone for the ceremony: this is the purpose of the prayer offered on behalf of all those present. But in the final strophe the mood becomes more intimate and personal: the poet invokes the god to intercede in his favor with his beloved Cleoboulos. The apostrophe "make him, O Dionysus, accept my love" recalls the "be thou my ally" of Sappho's prayer to Aphrodite (fr. 1, 28 V.), but tone and situation are different:

> Lord, with whom the young colt Eros
> and the blue-eyed Nymphs
> and purple Aphrodite
> play together,
> who dwellest on the high mountain peaks,
> to thee I make my supplication: come
> bringing blessing, and let my prayer
> find favor with you; hear me.

Be thou a wise counselor to Cleoboulos,
make him accept,
O Dionysus, my love.[101]

The game of dice, a pastime of boys and girls, symbolizes Eros's play with his victims:

Tumult and madness
are the dice of Love.

The originality of the figure lies in the contrast between the boyishly delighted god and the violent quarrels and frenzied acts of the men who are the instruments of his game.[102] But if love is a humdrum boy's game, its agonies have no significance, and its power, which might appear destructive, is not so in reality. The metaphor seems to reduce the passion of love into a playful to-and-froing during the course of which, through the "I love, I do not love" experience, man attains to a proper tempering of his nature and a full command over himself. This sound mixture of vigor and equilibrium, of Dionysian joy and clear-minded wisdom, is reflected in the Attic vase paintings depicting the poet and his friends in festive *kômos* scenes[103] and finds its clearest formulation in the polemical lines of one of his elegies (fr. 56 Gent.):

I have no liking for one who over the brimming wine bowl
    tells of quarrels, brawls and sorrowful wars;
but rather for him who draws from the splendid store
    of Aphrodite and the Muses to sing of loveliness and joy.

But the theme of love is not exhausted by the poems dealing with ephebic Eros. Female figures of various types and various degrees of importance are vividly depicted in their customary roles and settings. Women of high social status—the Sapphic *thíasos* is an exception—being normally excluded from archaic lyric, it is courtesans, flute-girls, and dancers who appear. They were the regular entertainers of the revelers assembled at a banquet: Callicrite with her imperious ways,[104] the blond Euripile who catches the fancy of the plebeian Artemon,[105] the noisy Gastrodora seen at a characteristically uninhibited moment in the progress of the symposium,[106] the popular Leucippe,[107] the elegant young lady of Lesbos:

A ball of many hues
hurled once again
by golden-haired Eros
invites me to sport
with a girl
in bright-colored sandals.

She, though—she is from Lesbos with its fine houses—
looks with disdain on my hair—which is white—
and stands open-mouthed, gaping after another.

(fr. 13 Gent.)

Here the image brings into precise focus a momentary situation in the course of the symposium. The god's capricious game directs the poet's attention toward an elegant girl from Lesbos, a musician to whom the banqueters are all attracted. But the hope in Anacreon's case is disappointed: he is old, and the girl, disdaining his white hair, stands "open-mouthed, gaping after another."

But how are we to understand "another"—as another head of hair, that of a young man, which is not white like that of the poet, or as "another girl," in more or less explicit reference to the erotic habits of a girl from Lesbos? The latter interpretation, which has found widest acceptance, is only superficially plausible:[108] it is based on the false assumption that a girl from Lesbos was, necessarily and exclusively, a practicer of homosexual or, as it is now termed, Lesbian love. This sense of the word involves, however, a grotesque piece of semantic distortion,[109] heavily influenced by the presence on the island of Sappho and her women's *thíasos* and by the ancient biographical tradition concerning her erotic practices.[110]

The reputation of the women of Lesbos was in fact quite different, linked by the Greeks to the erotic practice of fellatio. This "ancient and well-known" custom was, according to the comic poets, an actual invention of the girls of Lesbos.[111]

Already in the second half of the fifth century then—and the usage is certainly much older—the words *Lesbian* or *girl from Lesbos* had the typical connotation of *fellatrix,* not that of *Lesbian* in the modern sense.[112] *Lesbís* and *lesbiázein* were essentially pieces of social terminology with a specific, unequivocal erotic meaning.

The widespread but erroneous view that female homosexuality was a distinctive feature of the sexual habits of the women of Lesbos is based on a crude generalization that fails to distinguish different levels of love: in the one case, community-oriented, and linked to rites of initiation with well-defined paideutic goals; in the other, a part of the free atmosphere of the symposium, where the partner might be any musician or flute-girl but in general a hetaira, even if she did happen to come from Lesbos.

These sociological considerations are, in the present case, the only means of control which allow us to isolate the true meaning of the parenthesis "she is from Lesbos with its fine houses." Whatever symposiastic audience was present, the phrase was meant to suggest, as the erotic scenes in Attic vase painting show,[113] one particular erotic practice, that of fellatio.

Now that the meaning of the key element in the interpretation of the poem has been clarified, we can see the ambiguity of the phrase "stands open-mouthed." The gesture indicated is only apparently the expression of a mood of ecstatic or stunned bewilderment. It is in fact a movement that corresponds with a specific erotic purpose. The erotic connotations of "stands open-mouthed" (*cháskei*) seem obvious,[114] as long as we proceed on the assumption that, to the extent the context allows, all elements in the strophe must stand to each other in a relation of complementary, reciprocal interdependence. The "other" at which the girl from Lesbos stands gaping with open mouth, rejecting the white hair of the poet, will accordingly be another . . . piece of hair (pubic), presumably black, belonging to another guest. The ironic play of parenthetical thought suspensions and verbal ambiguities has nothing obscene about it. The poet does not say that the girl is a *lesbís*, adept in the practice of fellatio. He tempers the identification by a periphrasis that describes, through an eloquent epic reminiscence, the sophistication and beauty of the island of origin ("Lesbos with its fine houses")[115] and, implicitly, the gracefulness of the girl herself, already indicated by noting the elegance of her footwear—the "bright-colored sandals" of v. 3.

The metaphor of the Thracian filly (fr. 78 Gent.) depicts a girl who conceals beneath the fierce exterior of a woman who is totally unapproachable the soul of a hetaira. The same contrast between appearance and reality comes out, as will be seen, in the characterization of the low-born Artemon. Here, however, it is partially concealed by the ambivalence of the metaphor; there it explodes openly in realistic description of the before and the after: the peasant and the *parvenu* (who for all his riches is still a peasant). There the contrast is externalized in the form of a simultaneous display of boorishness and self-importance; here it is brought into focus by the character of the girl, who is better

FIGURE FOUR. Neck detail of an amphora by Oltos. About 520. Musée du Louvre, Paris.

able to conceal her true courtesan's nature and thus not always compliant with the desires of her admirers:

> Why look at me askance, Thracian filly,
> and pitilessly avoid me, as if I were good for nothing?
> You know that I could skillfully put a bit upon you
> and, reins in hand, guide you around the turning post.

> Now you are pasturing in the meadows, frisking and gamboling
>     lightly;                                                                     5
> you do not yet have an expert mount to mount you.

(fr. 78 Gent.)

The instinctive play of the filly is contrasted with the *Liebesspiel* of the able and expert riding master. A tone of elegance prevails, keeping closely to the developing sense of the metaphorical ambiguities: filly—coy and reluctant girl; able riding master—*maître de plaisir.*

There are other themes and topics as well—not simply love and wine. A lesser world of people of modest means and social status is evoked in a series of rapid portraits, drawn against backgrounds full of life and realism: the perfumer Strattis;[116] bald Alexis, the indefatigable suitor;[117] the typical ladies' man:

> why this fluttering to and fro,
> chest dripping with unguents,
> head emptier than a hollow reed?
>     (fr. 17 Gent.)

the hen-pecked husband:

> and the bridal chamber wherein he did not take, but rather was taken, in
>     marriage;

(fr. 54 Gent.)

the elegant discus-thrower;[118] the laundress;[119] the passionate courtesan in despair and praying for death.[120] The characteristic feature in such passages is the assigning of direct speech to a *persona loquens,* a procedure not completely foreign to archaic lyric,[121] but especially important in the poetry of Anacreon, as we know from ancient tradition.[122] At times the language is appropriate to the speaker; at other times it makes use of elevated style in order to highlight by contrast the seriocomic aspect of the situations and characters involved.

Artemon, the low-born parvenu who conceals beneath his showy golden pendants the true face of a scoundrel and swindler, is characterized with words that belong more exclusively to the *sermo vulgaris*. The mocking humor of the description culminates in the final strophe. There the solemn overtones of words belonging to the high style of the poetic tradition (*satínai*) and the sharp assonance (*skiadísken-elephantínen*) underline the self-important and effeminate ostentatiousness of the parvenu; and the focus on the new but still unchanged Artemon is accentuated both by the opposition *nùn dé* with which the strophe begins and by the sustained and solemn rhythm of the choriambs:[123]

He used to wear a scrubby cap on his head,
cubes of wood in his ears, and around his sides
an untanned piece of ox hide—

the dirty covering of a cheap shield; female bakers and male prostitutes
were the company he kept, scraping together a living by fraud,
god-forsaken Artemon.

His neck was often in the pillory, his body tied to the wheel,
his back striated by the leather whip, his skull
and chin plucked bare of hair.

Now, it is in a chariot that the son of Cica goes abroad,
sporting pendants of gold and an ivory parasol,
like women . . .[124]

The dramatic irony of this mimetic art reveals the inclinations of someone whose poetic vocation does not exclude, but instead welcomes, the realms of human experience associated with the new social classes coming into prominence under the influence of movements associated with the cult of Dionysus. The vital force of the new religion, which was by then, with Pisistratus and the Pisistratids, already established among members of the upper classes in Athens,[125] found in the art of Anacreon its proper measure and its proper style.[126]

In the poetry of Ibycus the theme of love takes on, as H. Fränkel has shown,[127] a new coloring, both stylistically and compositionally. In a decisive departure from traditional compositional modules, the charac-

FIGURE FIVE. Amphora by the Flying Angel Painter. About 480. Musée du Louvre, Paris.

FIGURE SIX.  Amphora by the Flying Angel Painter (reverse).

teristically archaic tripartite structure melts into a precisely defined unity, so that the thematically linked individual sections form part of an organic thought structure, functionally related to the same idea. The result is a closed type of composition, built up out of a concatenation of elements, which prepares the way for the grand strophic architecture of Pindar.

The two erotic encomia addressed to young men belong with other symposium and *kômos* pieces;[128] we probably hear in them the authentic voice of the poet—"most passionate in ephebic love" according to the unanimous testimony of ancient tradition.[129] The subject is here treated in a completely original way, with attention focused exclusively on the negative aspects of erotic passion. It becomes the magic, inescapable power of a god who confuses and terrifies.

Love so conceived has no room for the ecstasy and abandon of the experience described by Sappho, nor does it know the sophisticated delight of Anacreon's game—the polar oscillation between emotional impulse and intellectual control, the tension-resolving parallelism "I love and love not." It consumes the victim with its ever-present fire, at every stage of life:

> In the spring the Cydonian apple trees,
> watered by the rivers' streams,
> where the Maiden Goddesses
> have their unprofaned garden, come to bloom,
> along with the buds of the vine
> that have sprouted beneath its shady leaves.

> But for me there is no season
> of respite from Eros.
> Like the North Wind he blazes with lightning bolts,
> and, hurling himself from Cypris's side
> with withering blasts of madness
> dark, undaunted,
> violently ensconced, he holds control
> over my heart . . .
>
> (fr. 286 P.)

> Eros once again
> from beneath his dark eyelids
> shoots me with a tormenting glance,
> and working all his wiles thrusts me

into the inextricable toils of Cypris.
Truly I shrink back at his approach,
the way a race horse with many victories is unwilling to draw
the swift chariot back into competition as old age draws near.

(fr. 287 P.)

Here the poet offers a precise, organic vision of the more than normal dimensions, the dark and obsessively compelling power, of the
lover's destiny. Love is seen and conceived as a mysterious force that
allows no rest at any stage of life. Its fire ceaselessly consumes the victim, requiring even the unwilling old man to show the prompt vigor
of a youth—hence its depiction as violent and raging like the North
Wind, or languid and enticing like a hunter luring his prey into the
nets of Cypris.[130]

The darkness of the eyelashes (fr. 287, 1ff. P.) is the attribute of the
mature man—someone of an age to command and control.[131] It thus
symbolizes the obscure power that Eros exercises over the soul of the
person who has been the object of his glance (v. 2)—the sharp, uniquely penetrating gaze[132] that radiates from the eyes of the god and acts on
the beloved with devastating force. There is no parallel in Lesbian
poetry, much less in epic, to this exact analysis, forcefully and subtly
presented, of the nature and power of the glance of love. It has seventh-
century Spartan forerunners, however, in the works of Alcman.[133]

The pivotal idea, which gives meaning to the opposed images of the
calm garden of the Nymphs in full bloom and the "dauntless," "dark"
Eros, is that of the *constancy* of the emotional climate that love gener-
ates and maintains. Its relation to the two images makes the idea ambiguous—temporal with respect to the periodic rebirth of nature in
spring, qualitative with respect to the wild passion that Eros shares
with the North Wind. Love grants neither respite in time, nor slackening in intensity.

Structure and arrangement of words in the poem follow a precise
thought scheme. Love is observed: (1) in its basic essence—passionate
and stormy like a force of nature; (2) in its violent and unpredictable
actions ("with withering blasts"); (3) in the quality of its character and
behavior; and (4) in the ways it makes its presence felt ("violently
ensconced, he holds control").

The fourth element brings the arc traced by the poet's thought back
to the personal, passionate note from which it started: the idea of
guarding and controlling completes and reinforces that of the sleepless
presence of Eros.[134] Violent, simultaneous actions and sensations are

symbolically figured here through a reelaboration of Sapphic and Anacreontic images of Eros, but the tone and coloring are different, as is the
notion of love. The searing blasts of "madness" with which Ibycean Eros
hurls itself upon a man are not the same which Anacreon figures in
the form of dice—the boy god's toys in a game for children—but an
elementary force of nature, dark and hostile, which spreads terror and
destruction.

Even when all allowances are made for the role of traditional conventionality in works of this sort, one is struck by the intensely personal character of the poem's tone. It is hard to believe that experiences
presented in so subjective a fashion were actually sung by a chorus;
they seem more appropriate to citharoedic solo performance, as is also
suggested by Pindar's allusion (*Isthm.* 2, 1–3) to citharoedic poems on
erotic subjects, and by the ancient commentary (*Schol. ad loc.*) that
explains the allusion as a precise reference to Alcaeus, Ibycus, and
Anacreon.[135]

The dread divinity that is Ibycean Eros has a parallel, hitherto unnoticed by critics, in Simonides' idea of love as Aphrodite's "gadfly," an
obsessive power that limits the ability of anyone possessed by it to
display what aristocratic ethics defined as the proper virtues of the
man of worth.[136] It is here that ideas of love destined to be popular
later, in the second half of the fifth century, have their point of departure: Eros as the demon destroyer to be feared because of the catas-
trophes brought on by the infatuation he arouses, and love as disease,
something totally negative in man's natural make-up.

PART TWO

. . .
. .
.

# VII

· · ·

# Praise & Blame

*I have observed — from a distance —*
*nasty-tongued Archilochus keeping*
*his misery fat with insult and hatred.*

— *Pindar,* Pythian 2

In *Pythian* 2 (v. 54ff.) Pindar refers explicitly to the poet Archilochus and his ability to flourish, in the midst of poverty, on the fierce hatreds his slanderous attacks aroused. The passage sets up what seems to be an *institutional* relationship between wealth and praise on the one hand and faultfinding and poverty on the other. Praise (*épainos* or *en-kómion*) and blame (*psógos*) are seen as two radically antithetical poetic genres. The best thing for man is wealth in conjunction with poetic ability.[1] And the poet's wealth is in direct proportion to the liberality of the man who has commissioned the poem of praise.

Pindar proclaims on more than one occasion his rejection of the role of faultfinder,[2] but the exact character of the opposition between the two types of poetry remains to be determined. A key to interpretation is the poet's own statement that praise combines with blame when it comes from someone belonging to the same community of citizens as the person praised[3] — evidently because of the tensions and jealousies that inevitably arose within such a community.[4] The foreign guest thus finds himself in a privileged position; his commissioning constitutes the securest guarantee that praise will remain untouched by blame.[5]

In tracing out his general history of poetry, Aristotle[6] draws a basic distinction between the two poetic genres of invective and praise, the first understood as "mimesis" of base actions, the second of noble actions.[7] The classification was a fundamental one in Greek culture, dating back to the archaic period and beyond: it was already a part of the structure of Indo-European society.[8] In Doric-speaking areas, more particularly Sparta (as we learn from Plutarch), the contrast between the two types of discourse was even integrated into the institutional system, functioning specifically to further the greater good of the community by praising the worthy and censuring the unworthy.[9] Elegy 6–7 Gent.-Pr. of Tyrtaeus is in fact a kind of diptych in which praise of the valiant fighter appears alongside excoriation of the coward who runs away.

It is obvious that the *psógos* discussed by Aristotle does not refer exclusively to censure in the narrow sense of personal abuse. Its semantic field embraces the whole realm of the *humorous* (*geloîon*) or *seriocomic*, in the sense the latter term has assumed in M. Bakhtin's theory of the literary text.[10] There are accordingly various nuances and gradations in the relation between a piece of *psógos* and its object. Sometimes it appears as biting, hostile polemic, sometimes as good-humored depiction of ridiculous behavior—even on the part of friends. The mood that it evokes is the gay, vital one of the *kômos*—the festive banquet procession in which friends (*phíloi*) and comrades (*hetaîroi*) took part, members of a single confraternity bound together by a particular set of social and political interests.

Praise poetry (*enkómion*) is also linked to banquet and festive symposiastic procession (*enkómion* is something performed *en kómoi*),[11] but it is a larger category, including every type of poetry dedicated to celebrating the achievement and excellence of worthy men. The variety and complexity of the *psógos* category can be further documented by the vast number of synonyms used in referring to it: *mômos, óneidos, phthónos, éris, neîkos, mémphomai, diasýro, helkýo,*[12] *síllos, sillaíno, échthos, loidoría, geloîon,* and so forth. These all come under the general category of *íambos-iambízein* as well, a notion that Gorgias (82 A 15a D.-K.) and Aristotle—in the same chapter in which he deals with *psógos*—interpret as equivalent to "insult," "jeer," "mock." In this sense the ancients were right in deriving *íambos* etymologically from Iambe,[13] the name of the servant girl of the Eleusinian king Celeus,[14] whose jokes cheered Demeter when she was stricken with grief for the loss of her daughter, Persephone.

There is no point in reopening the old and fruitless debate as to whether the meter in which such poetry was composed came to be called iambic because of the subject matter with which it regularly dealt, or whether seriocomic subject matter came to be called iambic because of the meter used in treating it. For the cultural historian, the important fact is that the iamb was not, in any case, the only meter so

used. As is well known, both the elegiac couplet and the hexameter
were possible alternatives: certain elegiacs of Archilochus are expressly
said by the ancients to be "rather iambic" in character,[15] as were the
hexameters of Democritus of Chios[16] and the *Silloi* of Xenophanes,
composed *for the most part* in hexameters.[17] The very variety of meters
employed (iambs, trochees, elegiacs, hexameters, compound rhythmical structures) was one of the basic characteristics of this poetry, and it
was accompanied by a corresponding multiplicity of styles, tonalities,
and levels of narrative. Within this diversity it is possible to distinguish
certain thematic constants. The world represented is the contemporary one, and the author's relation to it is always direct, immediate,
provocatory—sometimes even, as in Hipponax, intentionally coarse
and vulgar in its language.[18] Everyday reality, always changing from
moment to moment, suggests a variety of topics and formats: political
and social polemic, the occasional anecdote based on some commonplace episode of ordinary life, personal abuse, moralizing invective,
cynical criticism of traditional ideas and the poets who are their spokesmen. Extravagant living and ambition are described, as well as the
grotesque foibles of eccentrics—captured along with what is comic in
the behavior of their profession or social class. The treatment shows a
ready imagination, bold and aggressive, and a variety of stylistic levels,
obtained through the introduction of colloquial slang.

Such is the poetry of Archilochus, Hipponax, Semonides of Amorgos, and of Xenophanes himself—though suggestions of the sort of
theme favored in Solon, the elegies of Theognis, and the political invectives of Alcaeus are also present. But seriocomic mimesis can be
seen at its most brilliant and vital in the poetry of Anacreon, with its
gallery of female figures and character types delineated against a background of both individual and social mores.[19]

A characteristic figure of this poetry is the use of the *persona loquens*—a character who relates some pleasant or disagreeable event in
the first person (like the female figures who appear in certain poems of
Alcaeus [fr. 10 V.] and Anacreon)[20] or presents his own ideas (like the
carpenter Charon, who expounds his views on wealth and power in a
well-known poem of Archilochus [fr. 22 T.]). Sometimes the character's words open the poem directly—a procedure particularly well
suited, according to Aristotle,[21] to defamatory discourse (*psógos*) because the poet could thereby conceal his own identity beneath that of
the *persona loquens* and avoid the resentment his attack would otherwise provoke. Obviously this persona could be totally fictitious, or a
general type, or an actual individual living in the poet's own city.

In this connection an important, but neglected, piece of evidence is that which comes from Evenus of Paros (second half of the fifth century), as reported by Plato (*Phdr.* 267a) in his discussion of the argumentative techniques of famous Sophists and rhetors. Evenus's treatment of praise and blame introduced the two terms *parépainos* (para-encomium) and *parápsogos* (para-invective) as a means of designating "indirect" forms of both procedures.[22]

Here praise and blame are not presented directly, but through various rhetorical ploys. Recourse to a *persona loquens* must have been just such a device, as were aphorisms and gnomic statements. The pentameter of Evenus cited by Hermias (fr. 5 Gent.-Pr.) is an example of the latter: "A son is always sorrow or grief for the father." The elegy in which it appeared must have offered an example of "para-invective"; and Hermias implies as much when he characterizes the tone and function of the line as "iambic" (*íambon*).[23]

Similar devices are mentioned at a later period by Demetrius. He illustrates "covert allusion" in *psógos* (*De eloc.* 288 Rhys Roberts) by citing the incipit of Plato's *Phaedo* (59c)—Phaedo's simple reply: "They were in Aegina," an implicit criticism of Aristippus and Cleombrotos for banqueting at Aegina at a time when Socrates had already been in prison at Athens for several days—and discusses indirect censure of persons in power by suggesting that if outspokenness is unacceptable, criticism should be directed at others who have acted in the same way (*De eloc.* 292).

Plato's discussion is equally important for the light it casts on the use of verse (the elegiac couplet) rather than prose in a piece of praise or blame. More easily memorizable[24] and thus more readily available to anyone who wished to reuse them, such elegiacs were model specimens of para-encomium and para-invective.

Evenus's categories (subsequently ignored by Aristotle) of encomium and invective, para-encomium and para-invective, were set up in reference to the function, occasion, and intended audience of a piece of discourse, and as such were based on poetic practice of long standing.[25] The example provided by the new Archilochus papyrus (see chap. 10) is especially revealing. There the *persona loquens* (probably the poet himself) combines censure of Neoboule with praise for her sister, who is his interlocutor in the dialogue; and praise is bestowed both directly and indirectly, through initial praise of the girl's dead mother. Artifice is skillfully deployed to emphasize the different behavior of the two sisters while avoiding the resentment that direct criticism of Neoboule might arouse.

The eulogistic mode pervades all poetic discourse celebrating the virtues of famous men. Aristotle was right to regard the heroic verse of Homer as one of its earlier manifestations, a companion to the model for *psógos* provided by Homer's *Margites*. He further observes that the origins of both probably antedate that of the epic. Plato also (*Resp.* 10, 607a) speaks of *enkómion*, using the word to refer to the poem in honor of worthy men, by contrast with the hymn in honor of the gods. It was later taken over in this sense by the Alexandrian grammarians in their editions of Simonides, Pindar, and Bacchylides.[26] There the term *epinician* applies in a narrow sense to the particular category of encomiastic song devoted to winners in the Panhellenic games. Typical instances of the "encomium" in praise of a famous man are Ibycus's poem dedicated to the young Polycrates, Simonides' address to Scopas, lord of Crannon, Pindar's compositions for notables such as Theron and Thrasyboulos of Agrigentum, Hieron of Syracuse, Xenophanes of Corinth, and so forth, or those of Bacchylides for Hieron of Syracuse and for Alexander, son of Amyntas of Macedonia. A further category is that of collective encomia, which include both poetic compositions such as Simonides' eulogy of the fallen at Thermopylae (cf. 531 P.) and prose pieces such as the funeral oration, dedicated to the celebration of the civic and military virtues of citizens who had died for their country.[27]

The poetic encomium was occasionally monostrophic in structure, though more often triadic. Its preferred meters were of two types: the more solemn and tonally uniform epitrites *kat' enóplion* (the so-called dactylo-epitrites) represented at their simplest by the encomiologus; and the mixed forms created by the association of iambs, trochees, choriambs, and dochmiacs.[28] The latter were more restless and dynamic, and without clear defining features—a rhythmically heterogeneous genre *par excellence* and open to continuous formal variation.

The poem dealt with the various excellences (*aretaí*) of the person celebrated and of his ancestors: courage, justice, statecraft, wisdom, moderation, and liberality in the use of wealth. This thematic orientation allowed the inclusion of reflections on the basic values of human existence and human achievement, as well as an opportunity for the poet to express his own point of view—sometimes with sharp and subtle polemical implications. In Simonides' encomium to Scopas the author's skeptical and essentially negative views on the problem of human worth are presented by means of characteristically eristic procedures that work in conjunction with litotes to make the poet's tone less personal and more objective.

It is usually assumed that all such hints of polemic are excluded from eulogy, but the whole problem (re-posed by Svenbro 1976, p. 142) should be reevaluated in the context of the biographical tradition relating to Simonides and the themes that recur in his work.[29] All the information available to us suggests that he was constantly involved in the discussion of human ethical and social values and in speculation as to the nature of the gods;[30] and that these topics figured not only in his poems but also in the conversations and casual encounters with persons of importance which are the subject of many Simonidean anecdotes. Hence the choice, surely not accidental, of Simonides as one of the two interlocutors in Xenophon's dialogue *Hieron*, on tyranny and the lot of the tyrant.

The theme of human worth posed in the Scopas poem is only one part of the larger debate that occupied Simonides' attention as a *sophós* and whose ethical presuppositions clearly foreshadowed the most advanced of the positions later maintained by the Sophists. The characteristic polemical tone of the poem is not directed—ostensibly—at Scopas but rather at Pittacus's traditional conception of the "man of worth." The criticism is indirect—an example of Evenus's "para-invective" that skillfully underlines the poet's reluctance to play the role of the faultfinder. (No lover of slander he!) On the contrary, he is inclined to praise anyone who refrains from voluntary wrongdoing. The attitude adopted toward the poet's host and patron is thus didactic rather than polemical.

What emerges from the encomium is not, as Svenbro claims, a poetics of the ideal but rather of the anti-ideal. If exemplary perfection, beyond the reach of all criticism, is a chimera, it will be difficult or impossible to put together a eulogy that does not involve criticism of traditional values and thus a degree of faultfinding, however minimal. This poetics—a poetics of *tempered praise*, we might call it—is what justifies the touches of burlesque and parody found in the Simonidean epinician, though the genre is encomiastic in its basic nature.[31]

At the end of *Pythian* 2 Pindar uses an even subtler, shrewder technique to color praise of Damophilos with a hint of criticism for activities undertaken in the past against the legitimate ruler of Cyrene, Arcesilaus IV. The whole poem is an encomium of the king, during the course of which the poet undertakes to be a peace envoy between him and the exiled Damophilos. He could not help but emphasize the virtues and merits of the man for whom he was seeking a pardon; he could choose, however, between being completely silent about Damophilos's faults and mentioning them explicitly. He solves the dilem-

ma by the mythical exemplar of Zeus pardoning the rebellious Titans
(v. 291), and by vouching for Damophilos's good conduct upon his return: he will neither cause offense to anyone nor suffer it (v. 296).
Shrewd strategy is at work here, well suited both to the difficulties of
the actual situation and to the requirements of a genre that had not
been set up to accommodate a blending of praise and blame.[32]

Poems in celebration of the beauty of young men were called *paidiká* and also classed among encomia. Athenaeus (13, 564f) cites a poem
of Ibycus for the youthful Euryalos (fr. 288 P.) as an example of a praise
piece (*épainos*); and the category would also include the encomium in
which Ibycus praised Polycrates by comparing him to the beautiful
heroes of myth,[33] the *paidiká* of Stesichorus mentioned by Athenaeus
(13, 601a), and the partheneia of Alcman.[34] In Pindar's poem for Theoxenos (fr. 123 Sn.-Maehl.), eulogistic motifs blend with those of a
more strictly erotic character.

The dividing line between praise and blame was not always so clearly marked as to exclude reciprocal influences. Timocreon of Rhodes'
poem on Themistocles (fr. 727 P.) achieves a curious marriage of the
two genres when he develops his personal attack on Themistocles in a
rhythm customarily used for encomium.[35] The result is a true "parody" in that its *kat' enóplion* epitrites function improperly to couch
the sarcasm and indignation of an attack on an important person in
the rhythmical accents of a song of praise. The violation of "generic"
norm is brilliantly preannounced by the poet himself when he links
the praise of Aristides to the censure of Themistocles; and the censure
itself, in the indirect manner of "para-invective," only mentions its
target after noting how he was especially hated by the goddess Latona:

> You may praise Pausanias, if you like, or Xanthippos
> or Leutychidas; but I praise Aristides,
> who of all those who came from holy Athens
> is excellent beyond compare—for Leto detests Themistocles.

*Psógos* here takes the form of a parody of *épainos*. The procedure, a
piece of burlesque *contaminatio*, is typical of the seriocomic mode.

The praise-blame antithesis finds its first explicit mention in Pindar
and its definitive theoretical formulation in Aristotle; but it pervades
Greek culture from the beginning, and ultimately becomes prescrip-
tive for biography and history as well as poetry. Polybius regards biography and history as closely related; but the former is encomiastic in
its basic character, dedicated to celebrating some individual, whereas

the latter requires, even when recording biographical data, an impartial presentation that links praise to blame and admits any hypothesis or set of considerations which can further the objective evaluation of the facts.[36]

This theory of how to compose biography is obviously the one that is the basis of Isocrates' *Evagoras*, a biographical eulogy that leaves no room for critical reservation or dissent.[37] To the extent that it takes shape as a literary genre through Isocrates' activities as publicist and propagandist, biography descends directly from the archaic and late-archaic format for the poetic encomium.

# VIII

. . .

# Poet-Patron-Public
## *The Norm of the Polyp*

*A work that shows itself incapable of dominating the world of events and cannot make its audience capable of dominating such a world is not a work of art.*

—*B. Brecht,* Schriften zur Literatur und Kunst, *III*

There was nothing in the monodic lyric poet's relation to his audience to compare with the official, public aspects of choral lyric. Sappho and Alcaeus composed for a restricted circle of hearers, all from the same social group and members of the same political faction. Whether in a *thíasos* of girls or a fraternity of *hetaîroi,* they were bound together by absolute, mutual loyalty to a particular set of ethico-political goals, different from those of other associations.

Choral poetry, however, had a celebratory, religious function, which made conditions of performance very different. It was premised on a direct relationship between patron and poet, which saw its period of greatest development in the late sixth and early fifth centuries—a result of the advent of a monetary economy based on commerce. The new wealth favored the arts in general, painting and sculpture as well as poetry, though not so much for their own sake as out of a desire for prestige and power. For the rich nobleman or city aristocrat and, above all, for the tyrant, the artist's work was a means of increasing status and consolidating political position. The poet accordingly becomes the intellectual professional who works for a patron and receives in return some valuable gift—an "honorarium" in the true sense of the word, and one capable if need be of being increased.

According to the traditional account, Simonides was once asked by Anaxilas, tyrant of Rhegium, to celebrate a victory in a mule-cart race, but refused on the amusing pretext that mules were not a suitable subject for a song of praise.[1] The fee was thereupon raised, and he composed the epinician, which began ingeniously with the line "Hail, ye daughters of storm-footed mares" (fr. 515 P.).[2]

Professional credentials and celebratory function made it inevitable that the poet's subject be from mythology—that complex and varied repertory of divine and heroic tradition and legend which provided the aristocracies of archaic Greece with both an inherited set of precedents and an inherited claim to power. Out of this vast storehouse the poet would periodically choose the legends most suited to the occasion he was to celebrate. Whether from traditional epic or local folklore, they were the web on which he wove his song, now varying the details of the myth for ethico-political ends, now highlighting the particular enterprise in a heroic saga that met the needs of the occasion and suppressing what was inopportune or practically and poetically "unsuitable," now impressing the stamp of new artistic and moral vigor on a mythical hero, especially when a real harmony of spirit—or, more particularly, a bond of common ideology—animated the relationship between the poet's own "intent" and the terms of the commission or "program" he received from his patron. Choosing a myth suited to the occasion meant connecting the person to be praised with a traditional story in such a way that he could be glorified through the deeds of a mythical prototype. And the audience had to see the connection—otherwise the actual significance and paradigmatic value of the myth would be lost.

The practical function and purpose of choral lyric are reflected in other ways as well. The nature of the ceremonial occasion determined the particular form a poet chose to use: for example, the encomium, a eulogy of a patron-host sung by professionals; the paean, sung by a chorus during a religious ceremony in honor of Apollo; the epinician for an athlete victorious in the Panhellenic games. Such victory celebrations took place in the athlete's native city or in that of his ancestors or where the contest itself had taken place. Pindar's sixth *Olympian*, for the Syracusan Hagesias's mule-car victory in 468, was sung at a victory celebration in the Arcadian town of Stymphalos, the home of the family of the victor's mother, and the poet directed the performance himself. The man who trained the chorus was also a Stymphalian, and his name is mentioned in the poem. On other occasions a sudden and unexpected invitation to compose a poem on the spot, immediately following the victory, would require the omission of its most crucial and essential part, the myth. This is the only possible explanation for the provisional and conventional—though, in its own way, quite charming—character of certain short poems of Bacchylides (*Epin.* 2, 4; 6 Sn.-Maehl.) and Pindar (cf. *Pyth.* 7). These temporary pieces were meant to be soon superseded by a second poem, longer and containing the customary myth. Bacchylides 2, composed in 456, for the Isthmian victory of a boy who came, like the poet himself, from the island of Ceos, contains only fourteen verses—less a celebration than an announcement of victory, sent from the Isthmus to the victor's homeland. The celebration proper came later, in the form of the poem now known as Bacchylides 1.

The internal structure of the epinician—to consider only this particular genre—was also determined to some degree by ceremonial necessity. An epinician without certain elements is inconceivable: praise of the victor, reference—more or less explicit—to the athletic event, indication of the athlete's earlier victories and notable achievements on the part of his family, and, finally, gnomic maxims that help to create a link between mythical narrative and present reality. What is not determined is the way the linkage would be achieved. Particular circumstances in the victor's own life or that of his family could offer a direct avenue into the heroic past, especially when the myth was connected with his own ancestors. In *Olympian 6*, for example, the fact that a paternal ancestor of the victor was Iamos, the founder of a race of distinguished seers, provides the grounds for telling a splendid myth and, through it, praising the double excellence of the victor—in military arms and in the art of prophecy. In the absence of such a simple and direct road, the point of contact with the present might be the place where the contest was held, or the victor's homeland and local legends of heroes acting with exemplary valor in enterprises blessed by the gods.[3]

In *Olympian 13*, for Xenophon of Corinth, the mention of the victor's family—"thrice blessed with Olympic triumph"—leads into a praise of his city as well: its past and more recent glories, its customs, its oligarchic institutions, its technological inventions, and its noble families and the divine lineage of the heroes they claimed as ancestors. A fairly transparent poetic device blends into this context the myth of Bellerophon, heroic symbol of the Corinthian aristocracy. The Corinthians were distinguished for intelligence and military prowess; they were famed at one time for the brilliance of their inventors, and among the greatest of them was Bellerophon: to him goes the credit for the domestication of the wild horse Pegasus. The other exploits of the hero are barely mentioned; they held no interest for a Corinthian audience. The "appropriate" enterprise—the one exemplary of intelligence and boldness—was the domestication of the horse.

The variety of transitions back and forth between the worlds of myth and present reality is matched by the variety of ways in which myth may function as example. Ethical and artistic justification for its presence—as well as explanation and confirmation of its message—is provided by a third epinician ingredient, the one that is usually, and too generically, described as gnomic. Here the treatment is also varied and complex, a function of the diversity of subject matter and tone: personal and subjective at times, at other times more in keeping with aphoristic conventionality; occasionally inspired by a rigidly narrow class ethic, but always coherent with the exemplary role assigned to the myth. The relation between myth and maxim brings the personality of the poet into vivid relief, as well as the differences of nuance and degree that give his ethico-political thought and artistic message their character.

Anyone who views the position of the choral poet in this way will be skeptical about the sort of approach that tends to conventionalize a poem's message, reducing it to the level of mere panegyric or entertainment. The result is a criticism content to discover habits of style, commonplaces, and clichés, and inattentive to the specific function and meaning a myth may have in relation to the situation that produced the poem: a kind of ahistorical structuralism whose preoccupation with the synchronic leads it to forget the different diachronic levels of which the interpreter must be aware. His task is always to transform text into the oral or written message sent by author to audience, and this message is not only a linguistic communication but also a transmission of emotions, thoughts, and visual impressions pertaining to the worlds of nature and art. The "competence" required in order to understand it involves mastery of a number of codes—linguistic, anthropological, sociological—and this in turn requires careful research into mental attitudes, patterns of behavior, modes of communication, and the mental and cultural phenomena, whether political, philosophical, artistic, or literary, which are the poet's referents. One may well wonder, therefore, whether jettisoning these referents—which were the mainstay of poetic activity among the Greeks—does not run the risk of turning the text into a mere form without historical structure or reality.[4]

A simple case in point is the diversity with which Bacchylides (*Epin.* 5 Sn.-Maehl.) and Pindar (*Dith.* 2, fr. 249a Sn.-Maehl.) treat the same story of Heracles' descent into Hades to bind Cerberus, and his chance meeting there with the ghost of Meleager, who asks him to marry his sister, Deianira. In the Bacchylidean scene Heracles is about to draw his bow and shoot when Meleager appears to tell him not to waste his arrows on the shades of the dead. Struck by the beauty and vigor of the young hero, Heracles asks who killed him. Meleager weeps and begins the story of his own death with a grim maxim on the unbendable will of the gods. Then comes the bitter memory of the anger of Artemis and its sequel, the terrible boar that the goddess sent against the beautiful land of Calydon. The narrative takes on a more openly epic color as the hunt is described: the wild rage of the animal, the fearless valor of the Aetolians, the death of Meleager's brother, Agelaos, and, finally, the fight with the impetuous Curetes come vividly to life as links in a fated chain. Even Meleager's own indomitable heroism was brief and vain. He and his companions fought vigorously and unrelentingly, but to no purpose. There is a pathetic insistence in the way the young man here remembers the fierceness of the epic battle waged with equal courage against the boar and against the Curetes. But the blind fury of that battle was ultimately his undoing: he killed, without wishing to do so, his mother Althea's two brothers. A god willed their death. The phrase is like a prelude to the final episode in Meleager's life, marking as it does a stopping point in the epic battle narrative. It is followed by a mention—nothing more—of the mad act of Althea, with only a hint of blame as he recalls it. Even his remorse over the uncles is dimmed as he thinks of the ineluctable necessity that snuffed out his life in the full vigor of its powers. In the epilogue to the battle the heroic note returns, but only for a moment. Resignation and re-evocation give way to a style of tense drama: the brand thrust pitilessly into the fire by Althea, Clymenos dead at the hands of the hero, the enemies in flight toward Pleuron, and, finally, the sudden languor of death and Meleager's lament for the ebbing away of his youth (vv. 136–54):

Heedless of this,

the pitiless daughter of Thestius
resolved in her anguish
that I, her son, should die;
shrinking from nothing,
she drew from its finely worked chest
the brief-fated brand and burnt it,
for so destiny had decided:
in that very instant
my life was to be at its end.
I was stripping Clymenos of his arms,

beautiful Clymenos,
the valiant son of Daipylos,
overtaken beneath the towered wall;
the rest were in flight toward the ancient city,
the fair town of Pleuron.

One instant more of life's sweetness,
and I felt my strength go slack, alas,
as with my final breath
I wept for the youth and beauty I would see no more.

As if to comment on Meleager's sad death, Heracles, who has never been known to weep, repeats amid his tears the melancholy wisdom of Silenus: "Better for man not to have been born and never to behold the light of the sun." Still stunned at the sight of the young man, he asks if Oeneus has a daughter in his house who resembles his son, Meleager; he would gladly marry her. And so Meleager speaks of his sister, Deianira, whose gentle beauty lights up for an instant the gloomy scene in the underworld. Here the heroic world of epic goes slack and dies, like the hero in the story, leaving behind it a sad, pensive Meleager, but also one who is resigned to his destiny and to relinquishing a world that no longer belongs to him and was always a fleeting one. The external aspect of epic heroism is all that remains to him—beauty and the gleam of arms. Bacchylides chooses the more dramatic, less heroic of the two traditional versions of the death of Meleager, bringing out its most strongly pathetic aspects and making the brand the tragic symbol of fate—not only that of the hero but also that of Althea, who is presented elsewhere by the poet (fr. 20D Sn.-Maehl.) in close association with Niobe, another symbolic destroyer of her sons.

The destiny that hangs over the unvanquished Heracles is equally blind. His lament is practically an unconscious premonition of his own ruin. Meleager's undoing was his killing of his uncles in a blind moment of warrior fury; Heracles' is his asking for the beautiful Deianira in marriage—in a moment of pity and, above all, passion, inspired by the sight of her unfortunate brother's beauty. Two figures, two characters linked by a common destiny.[5]

In Pindar (*Dith.* 2, fr. 249a Sn.-Maehl.), Heracles descends to Hades and there encounters Meleager, who begs him to marry his sister, Deianira. Upon his return Heracles goes speedily to Aetolia, where he obtains Oeneus's consent for the marriage and frees Deianira from her current suitor, the bull-formed river god, Achelous. The character and meaning of the scene are different in the two poets, each of whom gives his own version of the reasons for the meeting, which may itself be derived from the tradition used later by Apollodorus (2, 7, 6ff.) and Diodorus (4, 36ff.).

As has been observed,[6] the Pindaric scene fits better with the spirit of the myth. It contraposes two great heroes, the living and the dead, one of whom asks the other to marry his sister, as he is the only one who can save her from her hateful suitor and be a worthy husband for her. As in other Pindaric odes, Heracles—the true hero—is the protagonist of the mythic episode in which he appears, not Meleager. Thus the main line of the story—as is clear from the ancient testimony containing a summary of the poem's content—turns on the motifs of Deianira's marriage and liberation from Achelous: Meleager entrusts to a hero whose greatness equals his own the enterprise that will constitute the proof of his prowess.

In the Bacchylidean version the relationship is reversed. The poet was not interested in the Heracles of heroic tradition or in a Meleager who is dominated by the thought of his past greatness and still concerned with the world of the living. His Heracles is a stylized figure in the archaic manner, but less crude and violent as a hero, more gentle and human. What impels him to ask for Deianira as a wife has less to do with heroic prowess than with the beauty that shines from the shade of Meleager. The figures are no longer created on the epic model but in accordance with a more skeptical and pessimistic vision of the world—that which was also, as we have seen, the vision of Simonides. The pathos of their exchange gives it a new psychological reality, no longer heroic but dramatic.[7]

It makes little sense, given the basic perspective adopted here, to raise once again the problem of the "unity" of the epinician and of choral lyric in general, which has obsessed critics for more than a century, from Boeckh's day down to our own.[8] Unity can only be denied if one looks at the problem abstractly, as those critics did, using modern criteria in their desperate search for some unifying logic and aesthetic. What does exist is, as has been observed, a unity in the world of values for which the poet was a spokesman insofar as those values had to do with his public and the social function of his poetry.[9] He was fully aware of the public's ability to understand and appreciate what he had to say, even if he could not expect everyone to agree with it.

The differences between the character and occasion of epic and choral performances do not affect the basic continuity of function between the two genres. This was secured, at the rhythmical level, through the major role assigned in choral lyric structures to dactylo-epitrites, two of whose base patterns, the *hemiepes* and the enoplion, were constituents of the epic hexameter itself; and at the level of theme by the traditional mythical setting of the choral poet's message—a celebration, through retelling of heroic legend, of the family of a patron or the ancient "history" of a community. Among such legends, composed for public performance, were the grand mythical narratives of the Sicilian poet Stesichorus, roughly contemporary with Sappho.[10] These were lyric productions and used the triadic stanza structure characteristic of choral poetry and, presumably, citharoedic singing as well.[11] One can get an idea of their importance in the history of citharoedic and choral performance from the fragments (*SLG* frr. 7–87 P.) of the *Geryoneïs*, a long poem of at least thirteen hundred verses, whose recent discovery and publication allow us to view the earliest lyric poetry of the archaic age in a new light.[12] Although the poem survives only in fragments, it is possible to see its dactylo-anapestic metrical structure[13] and the general outlines of its retelling of the Geryon myth (one of the most popular in the archaic period, depicted on numerous vases beginning with the seventh century and treated by Pisander of Rhodes in his epic poem on the exploits of Heracles).[14]

The most interesting aspect of the new text is the heroic dimension it gives to the myth, transforming the three-headed monster, Geryon, into a "tragic" figure modeled on the protagonists of Homeric epic.[15] The stages in the presentation of the story are as follows: Heracles' voyage in the cup of the Sun, council of the gods (? *SLG* fr. 14 P.), arrival of the hero at the island of Erytheia,[16] Callirhoe's speech to her son, Geryon, urging him not to fight against Heracles, Geryon's reply, and, finally, the hero-monster's death.[17] Epic vocabulary and stylistic features (already noted by the first editor, Lobel) mark the narrative as epico-lyric in character; but even more important is the chronological organization of the individual episodes and the presence of epic motifs such as the simultaneous intervention of two gods, Athena and Poseidon, in favor of one or the other of the two heroes, and the passionate address of mother to son, the immediate parallel to which is the analogous scene between Hector and Hecuba in book 22 of the *Iliad* (vv. 79–89).

The elaboration of material is not a selective one centered around the pivotal episode, which is taken up as exemplary and paradigmatic—a way of proceeding that will become typical in Pindar—but rather a gradual succession of episodes drawn from the saga that moves toward

FIGURE SEVEN. Bronze pectoral. Last quarter of the seventh century. Archaeological Museum, Vathy, Samos.

a culmination of drama and pathos in the brutal, realistic description of the defeated warrior's death (*SLG* fr. 15, col. II, 6–17 P.):

> Silently, unseen,
> the dart pierced his forehead
> and tore asunder his flesh and bones
> —so the god decreed.
> It passed straight through
> to the crown of the head
> and stained with crimson blood
> his helm and limbs.
>
> His head drooped to one side
> as when a poppy
> losing its soft beauty
> stripped bare of its petals . . .

In spite of his gigantic strength and fierce heroism, Geryon is brought low by the will of a god, succumbing to a *ruse de guerre* on the part of Heracles—the better hero by virtue of his cleverness and resourcefulness.[18] The note of grandeur and elevation struck at the end is clear from the fragments that come from this part of the poem, as is the decisiveness of the conclusion of the myth for its reinterpretation. Geryon dies like the Trojan hero the flawless Gorgythion, whose head drooped to one side as he was struck by Teucer's arrow (*Il.* 8, 306ff.)— like a garden poppy "heavy with its seed and the rains of springtime." The "temporal linearity" of the poem's structure must be borne in mind when one considers the outcome of the Stesichorean tradition in the choral lyric of the fifth century. Its influence can be seen in the narrative patterns of the poetry of Bacchylides,[19] and—so far as ethical presuppositions are concerned—in Pindar's version (discussed later in this chapter) of the Geryon saga as well. Ancient critics were thus correct in seeing Stesichorus as heir to the epic tradition: he "sustained with his lyre" the whole weight of Homeric epos (Quintilian, *Inst. Or.* 10, 1, 62). The legacy manifests itself even in precise elements of narrative technique such as long speeches put in the mouths of dying heroes.[20]

Further confirmation for the stylistic affinity of epic and Stesichorean narrative is provided by Lille Papyrus 76abc, which contains the longest surviving fragment of the poet, a narrative of the division of

the kingdom of the Labdacids between Eteocles and Polyneices following the death (or exile) of Oedipus.[21]

These affinities should not, of course, obscure those aspects of Stesichorean epic which link it, not directly to Homer, but to the earliest,
pre-Homeric citharoedic traditions. This connection was already recognized in antiquity. Heraclides Ponticus[22] says that the most ancient
citharoedic poets (Thamyris of Thrace, who narrated the war of the
Titans with the gods; Demodocus of Corcyra in his poems on the fall
of Troy and the marriage of Aphrodite and Hephaestus; and also
Phemius of Ithaca in his *Homecomings* of the Greek heroes) did not
write their poems in "free" rhythms without any "regular measure,"
but in structures identical to those of Stesichorus and other ancient
composers of lyric (*melopoioí*), who composed epic verses to melodic
accompaniment. This line of interpretation, which establishes a continuity of poetic tradition between the songs of pre-Homeric citharoedes and those of Stesichorus, has a degree of historical validity, and
it is applicable to both content and compositional form.

The new fragments of Stesichorus allow us to reconsider the origin
of one such form, the hexameter, in a new light. The old notion, still
deeply rooted in traditional classical studies, of Homer as the beginning of all Greek literature is destined to disappear. And this is as true
in metrics as elsewhere. Some of the most vital metrical structures of
choral and citharoedic lyric, the so-called "dactylic *cola*" of dactylo-
epitritic, continue to be regarded as derived from the hexameter—in
accordance with the stubborn preconception of Stesichorus as exclusively indebted, like all other archaic poets, to Homer. However, Homeric epic was merely one such tradition among many that flourished
in the earliest period of Greek history—as the Greeks themselves were
perfectly aware. In his *Poetics* (1448b 25) Aristotle says explicitly that
even though he is unable to cite any of Homer's predecessors in the composition of epic poems by name it is still probable that they existed.[23]
The continuity of citharoedic tradition from Demodocus to Stesichorus postulated by Heraclides involves not only modes of execution
but also common preferences in themes chosen from the Trojan cycle.

No less important than the problem of theme and execution in relation to earlier tradition is that of the position and function of the poet,
especially when he was composing on commission from princes, noble
families, and cities for celebrations and festive occasions. Granted that
choral song was composed for public performance, what were the
limits within which the poet was able to operate? What procedures

were open to him? What sort of meaning did his words have for an audience? And, finally, what social and artistic value was assigned to his poet's calling? Audience reaction is a practical consideration—"a kind of fertilizer around the roots of every healthy artistic plant."[24] As has often been reiterated, art without a public is art without meaning and purpose. In epinician poetry (see above) the presence of patron—hence public—at the celebration for the victorious athlete imposed on the author precise terms having to do with what myth he chose and what elements of the myth were deemed "appropriate" to the occasion; acceptable, that is, to the patron and to the community of which he was a member—sometimes the most important member or at any rate a leading political figure. And similar terms must have governed every other type of choral composition—whether dithyramb or paean or encomium.

Reinterpretation of heroic themes and reproduction of occasionally contradictory versions of the same myth are explicable in terms of the poet-patron-public relationship. A typical instance is the treatment of the Helen myth, which Stesichorus presented in three different versions. Having first followed the epic tradition of an adulterous Helen who abandoned her husband and family to follow Paris to Troy (fr. 190 P., cf. 223 P.), he later came back to the story with the purpose of removing this stain on Helen's reputation. It was only an image of Helen that went to Troy with Paris; Helen herself left Sparta with Paris but remained behind with Proteus in Egypt.[25] But this palinode was followed by another, in which the poet, evidently in response to audiences' dissatisfaction with the first one, went further, to the point of insisting that his earlier account had not been "true": Helen had never gone on board ship and never arrived at Troy.[26] Only by eliminating altogether the stretch of sea which would have taken her to Egypt was Stesichorus able to allay the suspicion that Helen might have had time, even during that much briefer voyage, to sleep with Paris.[27] This attitude toward traditional mythological subject matter seems to anticipate the intellectual iconoclasm with which Simonides pursued his poet's profession and presupposes a composer completely open to the desires and suggestions of his audience—in his case a Locrian[28] rather than Spartan[29] one, if we are to believe the traditions preserved both by Pausanias (3, 19, 11) and the historian Conon. From them we learn that the leader of the Crotonian forces, Autoleon (Conon) or Leonymos (Pausanias), was wounded in the battle at the river Sagras[30] by the apparition of Ajax Oileus, which was fighting in the ranks of the Locrians. He was thereupon advised by the Delphic oracle to go to the island of

Leuce at the mouth of the Danube in order to be cured by Ajax himself. On his arrival there Helen told him to sail to Himera and tell Stesichorus that he would recover from the blindness her wrath had inflicted upon him if he would compose a *Palinode* (Pausanias) or poems in her honor (Conon)—if, that is, he would issue a retraction of the first song in which he had outraged her memory. There are a few minor divergences, but the essence of the account is the same in both authors, who draw ultimately, as Pausanias says explicitly in his own case, on local Crotonian and Himeran tradition.[31]

Both recantations were composed after the battle of the river Sagras, for an audience in Italian Locri. The cult of Helen's brothers, the twins Castor and Pollux, was especially important there, and it is certainly not accidental that ancient tradition attributes the restoration of the poet's sight to their agency as well as Helen's.[32]

For a complete picture of the structure and function of the sort of eulogy that was sung for a patron at a banquet ceremony the best source is Ibycus's poem to the young Polycrates, later to be tyrant of Samos:[33]

ant.  They came from Argos and destroyed
      the great city, glorious and opulent,
      of Priam, son of Dardanus,
4     pursuant to Zeus's mighty decree.

ep.   For the beauty of fair-haired Helen
      they did battle storied in song,
      and woe and punishment were the lot of wretched Troy
      through the sad years of war,
9     with golden-tressed Cypris the cause.

str.  But now I have no mind to sing
      of Paris the treacherous guest
      or slim-ankled Cassandra
13    or the other children of Priam

ant.  and the ignominious day
      when lofty-gated Troy was sacked,
      nor to tell
17    of the overbearing prowess of the heroes

ep.    who were borne in strong-nailed hollow ships
        to be a bane to Troy,
        the noble heroes whom mighty Agamemnon led,
        warrior king of the stock of Pleisthenes,
22    son of glorious Atreus.

str.   These exploits the Muses of Helicon,
        skilled in song, might tell,
        but a man of flesh and blood, a mortal,
26    cannot say how each thing occurred,

ant.  how many ships, having set forth at Aulis
        and crossing the Aegean, made their way
        from Argos to Troy,
30    the nourisher of horses, and on board them the heroes

ep.    with their brazen shields, sons of the Achaeans;
        among them, skilled in hurling the javelin,
        ... swift-footed Achilles
        and the grand and mighty Telamonian Ajax
35    ...

str.   [and there also came] to Troy
        from Argos [the beautiful Cyanippos]
        ...

ant.  [and Zeuxippos]
        whom golden-sashed Hyllis bore;
        Troilus was likened to him
43    in beauty by the Trojans and by the Danaans—

ep.    likened the way fine gold is to orichalch.
        Alongside of these, for your beauty,
        you also shall have undying fame, Polycrates,
        just as, through song,
48    my fame too shall be undying.

The initial portion of the poem divides itself into two triads narrating the high points of the story of the Trojan War: the conquest of the city by the Achaeans, the celebrated beauty of Helen that caused the war, and the ensuing disasters that descended on the Trojans. Then comes the list, introduced at the beginning of the second triad, of what the poet does not want to sing—neither "treacherous" Paris, nor Cassandra, nor the ignominious day of Troy's fall, nor the arrogance of the chieftains, nor the ships that were the bringers of ruin, nor Agamemnon, the warrior lord of the Danaans. Another refusal opens the third triad: these events cannot be told by the poet, who is a "mortal man." Only the Muses have the poetic expertise to tell each thing as it happened—the number of ships that departed from Troy and the heroes who sailed in them: glorious Achilles, brave Ajax, and Cyanippos and Zeuxippos, the most beautiful men in the Greek army. And so to the eulogy that concludes the poem: Polycrates will be accounted among the foremost of heroes for his beauty, and he will have undying fame by virtue of the same song that confers fame upon the poet.[34]

The initial reference to the Trojan War presents it in a decidedly negative light. There is a subtle selection of those epic epithets that emphasize what is violent, painful, and overbearing in the exploits of the mythical age, and thus a sharp contrast with the tonality of the concluding references to heroes distinguished for courage and beauty.

This negative perspective is closely connected with the refusal to sing of certain themes, here presented as a formal *recusatio*. The topos has strikingly close parallels in Horace's ode to Agrippa,[35] for there, too, the center of the poem is a contrast between the narration of military episodes, whether contemporary or mythical, and songs on lighter themes of an erotic or convivial character. Horace's reference to the thematic repertory of the banquet, with the precise selections and exclusions of poetic subject matter it imposed, is of special interest here, quite apart from any particular reasons he may have had for using the device of the *recusatio*. It suggests how Ibycus's own refusal should be understood in relation to archaic norms of banquet poetry, which exclude all talk of war, tumult, and violence.[36] Ibycus does not have a program in the fullest sense of the word—one that would exclude heroic themes from the poet's own repertory as it does in Horace; but he does adhere to a rigorous selection of subject matter related to the occasion of the song in praise of beauty.

It has often been suggested[37] that these verses of Ibycus mark a point of transition in the poet's career, from a period in which he wrote epic and lyric to one in which he wrote love poetry. But they are better seen in a purely synchronistic perspective—as a fitting of treatment and theme to the norms of convivial encomium in honor of a young man.[38]

This does not exclude, however, a specific reference in the mention of the great fleet that sailed against Troy: any mythical material included in an encomium had to have a function in relation to the person being celebrated. In this case the poet's intention must have been to call attention, through mythical allusion, to the nautical power[39] of the family of Polycrates, a power they enjoyed even before he became tyrant of Samos. The discreet, allusive form that the compliment takes is typical; and the *recusatio* formula has significant parallels in the Homeric proem to the Catalogue of Ships in *Iliad* 2 (v. 484ff.).[40] There, too, the poet exalts the omniscience and omnipresence of the Muses—because they are goddesses and as such see and know all things—by contrast with the helplessness of mankind, who must base their knowledge on hearsay; that is, on repute (*kléos*) or the memory of distant happenings that they did not witness. Even if he had ten tongues and ten mouths and a voice of steel, a man would never be able, without the help of the Muses, to enumerate and name one by one all the warriors who set sail for Troy. The poet will only tell—he goes on to say—"the leaders of the ships and the ships' numbers." Ibycus is equally unable to say—unless, of course, the Muses come to his aid—how each event in the war took place, he being a mere mortal.[41] Hence the focusing of attention on the heroes who were distinguished not only for their prowess as warriors—Achilles and Ajax—but also for the beauty that is the special quality of Polycrates, now in the flower of his youth. Alongside the heroes celebrated in myth there is now also Polycrates, rising in the immediacy of the present and with a poet among his guests to entrust his renown (*kléos*) to the "truth" of undying song.

What is formally a refusal to speak of things that would not have contributed to the festive mood of the occasion becomes first the poet's subtle device for glorifying the maritime might of his patron and then a means of concluding—in conformity with the occasion—with praise of the young Polycrates' beauty.

In difficult situations the poet might well be constrained to adopt intellectual attitudes that were not always consistent with his own basic ideas. But this did not mean that he had to adopt a disguise, or abandon all attempt at moral consistency, or—most important—be hesitant about revealing his own personality.

The skeptical and substantially negative solution to the problem of *areté* envisioned by Simonides in the closing years of the sixth century (see chap. 5) was certainly not in harmony with the aristocratic creed of the powerful ruler of Crannon, nor was it, in general, ideally suited to satisfy the ambitious pretentions of a Thessalian prince. A poet, as Ibycus's encomium shows, could be proudly aware of the value of his social mission and of his own powers as a poet; otherwise he would never have ventured to tell his patron that a man's glory depends on the enduring fame of a work of art.

Awareness of one's own poetic talents acquires a new dimension in Pindar and Bacchylides and is expressed with new vigor and pride. Pindar becomes the "melodious prophet of the Pierides," in *Paean 6*, composed for the Delphians, or even a "prophet-priest" (*Parthen.* 1, 5 Sn.-Maehl.). Bacchylides' epithets go further still: he is the "divine prophet of the Muses" (*Epin.* 9, 3). And conviction of one's own worth is inseparable from the conviction of the sublime mission of one's art. Bacchylides ends his third epinician, for Hieron, with a solemn affirmation in which he actually defines the quality of his own poetry:

> ... Oh Hieron,
> you have shown to mankind
> the utmost that fortune's bloom can bring:
> success is not enhanced by silence.
> Your true renown shall be celebrated
> alongside the grace of the sweet poet who sings of it—
> the nightingale of Ceos.

In *Nemean 7*, for Sogenes of Aegina, Pindar affirms poetry's claim to the lofty role of immortalizing actions inspired by great valor (v. 11ff.):

> The man who succeeds in his exploits
> pours sweet material for song
> into the streams of the Muses;
> black darkness shrouds
> great prowess that has no song.

It is no accident that these verses appear here. The poem was composed for citizens of Aegina, an oligarchical city whose lofty aristocratic tradition was an embodiment of Pindar's own political ideal. He could thus count on an audience ready and able to appreciate his thought. The sequel develops an idea that reappears with minor variations in *Isthmian 3* (v. 7), composed for his fellow citizen Melissos of Thebes: poetry as reward for the labor of achievement, and a reward that also had the further property (cf. *Nemean 8*, v. 50) of soothing or even laying to rest the athlete's toil and weariness, like a ritual sacrifice. This idea is symbolically expressed in the famous cup metaphor of *Olympian 7* (vv. 1–12):

> Like one who, raising a cup
> frothing with the dew of the vine,
> and reaching out with bounteous hand to the young bridegroom,
> offers it to him,
> drinking a toast from home to home, a cup all of gold,
> pride of one's store, delight
> of the banquet and honor
> to the new kinsman, whose perfect match
> has made him the envy of his assembled friends.
>
> So I too, offering a present of flowing nectar
> to those who have triumphed—sweet fruit
> of my spirit, gift of the Muses—
> bring satisfaction to
> the victors at Delphi and Olympia.
> Happy the man who has glorious fame;
> the grace of life-nourishing song
> enfolds now one man, now another,
> with the sweet sound of the lyre and the echoing flutes.

The ritual value of the song is brought out by the key word in the metaphor—*hiláskomai*, "bring satisfaction"—a sacral term referring to the process by which the worshipper placated the gods and made them gracious by sacrifice. There was good reason for Pindar's calling himself a "prophet-priest."[42]

This secure conviction of one's own poetic talent, a profoundly aristocratic conviction deeply rooted in ideas of a "Delphic" character,[43] cannot be ignored if one is to understand the occasionally puzzling features of certain poems, where the difficult external circumstances in which Pindar's professional duties have placed him are a visible source of embarrassment. It is as if the poet were unable to conceal completely his efforts to follow the precept of Amphiaraus and imitate the polyp that assumes the color of the rock to which it clings. Amphiaraus's well-known advice to his son on the point of departing for Thebes is mentioned by Pindar in a hymn (fr. 43 Sn.-Maehl.):

Let your mind, my son, behave like the skin
of the rock-clinging beast of the sea
and consort with men of all nations;
go along willingly with those around you,
change your thoughts to suit the season.

Today we would call it the precept of *savoir-faire,* which requires
adroitness and mastery of protocol in the behavior of the aristocrat. In
his collection of aristocratic maxims, Theognis (v. 213ff.) had already
enunciated this principle through the metaphor of the polyp: the
nobleman's ability—his *sophía*—lies precisely in his capacity to adjust
himself to the situation at hand and not to lose his inbred, intuitive
sense for what is opportune to say or not say in the presence of a given
audience. Without such vigilant attention to the social context in
which he is moving, the nobleman falls into an obtuse inflexibility—a
true condition of *atropía,* dulled perceptions, and inability to extricate
himself adroitly in difficult situations.[44]

The difficulties of interpretation offered by *Pythian* 2, which was
composed for Hieron once Pindar had returned to his own city from
Sicily[45] and following what were for him fairly bitter experiences at
the court of the tyrant, are the result of the peculiar position in which
he finds himself. He must try to reconcile his aristocratic ideology and
his resentment over court intrigues against him with the necessity of
eulogizing the ruler of a city for which he had no great affection.[46]
The style accordingly shifts back and forth between the ceremonious
and the didactic, persuasiveness and arrogant assertiveness. Metaphors
follow each other in quick succession (monkey, fox, cork, dog, wolf);
and an effort is required to maintain coherence within the accompanying series of clear injunctions to Hieron to follow the norm of the true
*agathós* (v. 86ff.):

The man of straight speech carries authority
in every regime—in a tyranny,
and when the obstreperous crowd holds sway,
and when there is government by the wise.
But one must not fight with God,

who now raises up one group, now to another
concedes fullness of glory.

Here the impersonal reference to tyranny contrasts with the explicit expression of sympathy for oligarchy (government by the wise—that is, by wise aristocrats) and antipathy toward democracy, evident in the pejorative epithet *lábros*, suggesting the violence and noisy unruliness of the crowd. Pindar could not, for obvious reasons, express the same negative judgment on tyranny that he was to proclaim slightly later in his ode for Thrasydaios of Thebes;[47] but his aversion is subtly suggested through the praise of oligarchy. Its inclusion is not likely to be accidental, given Hieron's attempt to found a new tyrannical regime under the rule of his son Deinomenes in the town of Aetna, a regime "founded on the god-given liberty" of the Dorian aristocracy, as Pindar solemnly proclaims in *Pythian* 1 (v. 61), written for Hieron six years after the foundation occurred. Pindar's scorn for the noisy crowd must also have carried special meaning for the tyrant, because at the time of writing there were already ominous indications of the popular movements that were to break out in insurrection after Hieron's death.

In the encomium for Xenophon of Corinth (fr. 122 Sn.-Maehl.) the right coloration for the polyp was gallantry and light irony. This allowed the poet to extricate himself from the difficulties caused by the scandalous nature of his topic: a eulogy addressed to the public prostitutes whom the commissioner of the poem had dedicated to Aphrodite in celebration of a double Olympian victory (cf. *Ol.* 13). "Your thoughts," he says, "take flight toward the celestial mother of desires; to you it is granted to harvest blamelessly in beds of delight the fruit of tender youth. When they are unavoidable, all things are fair"; and later, after a lacuna of several verses, "But I wonder in amazement what the lords of the Isthmus will say of me for having devised such a prelude to a sweet song of escort for public women." With wit and elegance Pindar exculpates the ministrants to the goddess on the ground that their hospitable labors are imposed upon them by divine will, just as he too is acting out of necessity in praising them—a favor owed both to Xenophanes and the goddess herself, to whom the girls had been promised before the contest as a fulfillment of the victor's vow in the event of success. The modern reader, on the other hand, will be as surprised as the lords of Corinth when he compares this eulogy with the verses of the encomium to Theoxenos, which faithfully reflect the aristocratic idea of ephebic love (fr. 123 Sn.-Maehl.):

At the proper time, when you were young,
my heart, you should have plucked the fruits of love;
but anyone who sees the rays

that shoot forth from the eyes of Theoxenos
and does not seethe with desire
has a black heart of steel or iron
tempered in an icy flame;

he is one who pays no honor to gleaming-eyed Aphrodite
or toils ruthlessly for profit
or is slave to a woman's effrontery,
dragging himself along a cold path.[48]
But I, at the goddess's command,
go soft when pierced by those rays
like the wax of sacred bees,

beholding in the fresh limbs
of young men the grace of love.

"At times the paths of silence are much more reliable" (fr. 180 Sn.-Maehl.). *Olympian* 13, for Xenophon of Corinth, has nothing to say about the death of Bellerophon, which should have concluded the account of his deeds. "Of his end I shall be silent" is Pindar's firm and forceful comment (v. 91). Practical considerations suggested passing over an episode that would not have pleased a Corinthian audience. Bellerophon dies for having dared too much, for having aspired to immortality, for transgressing the limits imposed by the gods: his impious action was the cause of his ruin. In the *Isthmian* 7, however, which celebrates the victory of a Theban athlete, the end of the Corinthian hero will be pointed to (v. 44ff.) as exemplary punishment meted out to one who in an ill-considered quest for pleasure set his sights on things too far removed from the straight and narrow path.[49]

Elsewhere, to illustrate the principle that *nómos*, "king of mortals and immortals, makes violence just," Pindar enumerates several enterprises of Heracles, such as the theft of the cows of Geryon and the episode involving the horses of the Thracian king Diomedes: two instances of naked and open violence.[50] Diomedes resists the hero's aggression, not out of arrogance but because of his *areté* (v. 15), for it is better to die to defend one's property against a marauder than be revealed as base and cowardly (vv. 15–17). At this point the ancient commentary (*Schol.* v. 15) justly observes that Heracles was in the wrong for having stolen Diomedes' horses. Geryon behaves just as Diomedes did in the dithyramb entitled the *Cerberus* or *Katábasis* (Descent to Hell) of Heracles, composed for the Thebans (fr. 81 Sn.-Maehl.). There the poet claims to be praising Geryon, but adds immediately the phrase "May I be completely silent about that which is not pleasing to Zeus." Even if an action proceeds, like that of Diomedes, from *areté* rather than arrogant pride, it may still be displeasing to the gods—not in accordance with the order of things sanctioned by divine will. We must admit, therefore, the existence of a deep schism, an irreducible inconsistency in Pindar's ethics.[51] In at least two instances the principle of divine law is invoked to justify an outrageous act of arrogance. Ability and effectiveness, no matter how violently and insolently displayed, are just if in accordance with divine will; and the courage of the nonviolent is unjust when not inspired by a god and not confined within properly ordained limits.

If we knew the whole context of the poem, the audience and purpose for which it was intended and the historical circumstances out of which it arose, we would certainly be in a better position to understand the reasons for this apparent antinomy and to define the precise value of *nómos* and *bía* as they apply to the actions of the hero. This much however is clear. The aggression of Heracles and the fierce resistance of Diomedes and Geryon are expressions of two distinct and contrasting types of *areté*. One of these is the true *areté* of the perfect man of valor who displays his might, violence, and headstrong daring in accordance with his god-given nature[52] and for whom just measure is in proportion to the measure of his own valor. The other is the negative *areté* of the man whom success eludes and who must, because he operates outside the limits of the just order sanctioned by Zeus, succumb to the stronger, to the true *agathós*. And this negative and unreliable prowess is essentially the same as that which in a dark hour impelled Bellerophon to stray from the proper path: it is an *areté* that sought the occasion for acting outside the moment of *kairós*—the particular instant of god-given assistance for man.[53]

The Pindaric hero functions as a paradigm in two ways—both through the positive qualities that make him like the gods and the negative ones that distance him from them. Man's destiny may be defined in terms of this relationship. It is possible, therefore, that the antinomies discussed above are more apparent than real, and the sentence that opens the fragment, though it may seem ambiguous and inconsistent with the ethico-political ideology of the poet,[54] may well be tantamount to a serious injunction not to resist the just violence of the stronger—of the aristocrat who operates under the sign of the will of the gods.

Heracles was the civilizer-hero *par excellence*, the one who explored

FIGURE EIGHT. Bronze statue from Riace. About 450. National Museum, Reggio Calabria.

the whole earth, plumbed the depths of the seas, and made maritime routes safe for sailors. There were no mishaps to his career, no dark aspects.[55] To understand completely his position in Pindar one must consider his specific role as a culture hero[56] or, to use a modern notion that seems relevant here, an acculturization symbol.[57] The *Heracles* of Euripides, a tragedy whose cultural implications have yet to be explored in their entirety, contains the most significant eulogy of the hero from this point of view. When Iris urges the goddess Lyssa to fill Heracles' mind with homicidal madness, Lyssa refuses to carry out the order, enumerating the hero's services to mankind. He has opened up inaccessible regions, tamed the savage sea, and by his own unaided efforts reestablished the worship of the gods, which had collapsed because of the deeds of impious men (v. 849ff.). The figure of the hero-civilizer finally emerges in its full grandeur in the second stanza: "The son of Zeus, who through his prowess in the course of many labors was able to surpass the loftiness of even his own origins, made human life civilized and eliminated the fear of the monsters that beset it." Heracles here figures as founder of cults and civil institutions, domesticator of wild beasts and slayer of monsters—those prodigious beings whom the Greeks envisioned as a form of barbaric otherness with respect to their own nature as civilized men. The concept is a Hellenocentric one, paralleled in the Eurocentric ideology on which modern colonialism was founded.[58]

Traces of it are already to be found in the *Geryoneís* of Stesichorus, in the contrast drawn there between a monstrous Geryon who nevertheless wears a helmet and cuirass and fights with the prowess of an Iliadic hero, and a Heracles who obeys the higher will of a god (*daímonos aísai*) in assaulting Geryon and draws on his own skill and cunning to conquer the brute force of his adversary. The nature of the *nómos* whose dominion is apodictically proclaimed at the beginning of Pindar's poem becomes clear in the light of the acculturizing role of Heracles. *Nómos* is the norm of civilized "culture"—as Herodotus had the anthropological acumen to see (3, 38, 20). It is a system with its own religious and social institutions imposing its control on a wild state of nature, such as that represented by Geryon and the Thracian Diomedes, and also by the monstrous Centaurs of whom Heracles himself says in the *Trachiniae* of Sophocles that their overweening might knows neither law nor limit (v. 1096: *ánomon, hypérochon bían*). It makes little sense to seek, as critics usually do, some sort of reconciliation between the law of "culture" and the use of force and violence: the necessity of violence within the just scheme of things willed by the gods is exactly Pindar's point. What he has done, essentially, is to pose the problem that lies at the heart of the whole civilizing process, emphasizing the paradoxical character injustice assumes when violent actions are the means for the creation of a stable system of civil equity and order. Herodotus's position was different, in spite of his explicit harking back to the Pindaric asssertion that "*nómos* is the king of all things." As an anthropologist, he was inclined to place Indians and Greeks on the same level, assigning equal value to the *nómos* of both nations.

The problematic character of Heracles' role as a culture hero had been noted as early as Pisander of Rhodes, who called him "the *most just* of murderers."[59] Pindar was taking up and developing a theme that continued to be important much later, in the propagandistic literature of the fourth century. Isocrates calls war against barbarians most necessary and most *just* and links it as such to the wars that free mankind from the ferocity of wild beasts (*Panath.* 163). He also (*Phil.* 110) presents Heracles as the paradigm for all such war and violence on the part of Greeks against barbarians—a hero who surpassed his predecessors not so much in physical strength as "in intelligence, loftiness of purpose, and *justice.*"

Another Pindaric instance of fluctuation in the treatment of a single mythical episode is encountered in *Paean* 6 and *Nemean* 7. The paean was composed first,[60] to be performed at a Delphian theoxeny—a festival in which the gods were invited to share a banquet with their worshippers. After a solemn initial invocation to Delphi, the poet says that, because a Delphian choir was unavailable at the time, he brought with him a choir of his own—to prove himself worthy of the honor that was being conferred upon him.[61] There follows, in the second triad, a reference to a famine that had afflicted all of Greece and to the prayers of the Delphians which brought it to an end, an event specifically recalled by the annual rite of the theoxeny.[62]

Transition to the myth seems to be marked by a reference to Panthoos,[63] the priest of Apollo who, according to a tradition, had gone to Troy to report the god's oracle to Priam and then settled permanently there;[64] here Delphic Apollo is clearly linked to the Apollo who was Troy's defender and who, disguised as Paris, slew Achilles, thereby delaying the fall of the city. The mention of Achilles introduces the story of his son Neoptolemus (v. 98ff.):

> Once they had laid to rest in its tomb with much lamentation
> the glorious panoply of the son of Peleus,

the sea's waves brought back the heralds
from Sciros and with them
valiant Neoptolemus,

who sacked the city of Troy.
But he did not live to see again his dear mother
or his ancestral fields
and the horses of the Myrmidons,
marshaling the brazen-helmeted host.
He reached the land of the Molossians
near the Tomaros, unable to avoid
the winds and the far-shooter
god of the mighty quiver.
Apollo swore that the man
who had slain old Priam
as he leapt for safety to the altar of his house
would never return to the peace of his own home

or live to old age.
And when in a question of due honors to be paid
he fell to quarreling with Apollo's priests,
the god slew him in his temple
near the earth's great navel stone.

The ode concludes with a praise of Aegina, "glorious island that holds dominion over the Dorian sea, gleaming star of Zeus Hellanios," and a fleeting reference to the god's affair with Asopos's daughter, the nymph Aegina from whom the island got its name. From her sprang Aeacus and "the infinite virtues of the Aeacids."[65]

It is not hard to see the reasons for the final apostrophe to Aegina— not, of course, those suggested by some critics, who would have it that the chorus was composed of Aeginetan citizens,[66]—but more fundamental ones, solidly built into the structure of the song. Aeacus, son of Zeus, was the very hero whom the Greeks, following an oracular response from Delphi, urged to intercede with his father to save them from famine. Zeus hearkened to his request and put an end to a period of drought.[67] This fully justifies the reference (v. 125) to the Zeus Hellanios who is worshipped on the island. The institutional reasons for his cult were closely connected with those behind the theoxeny; both rites originated in the same happy event that had freed Greece from a calamitous famine.[68]

The central figure of the poem is Neoptolemus, a hero who expiates
the impiety he committed when, during the sack of Troy, he killed the
suppliant Priam at his household altar. He paid for the act with his
own death during a fight with the priests in Apollo's temple at Delphi
over the proper apportioning of honors; it was the god himself who
slew him.[69]

In *Nemean 7*, composed for the victory of Sogenes of Aegina in the
boys' pentathlon, Pindar presents the same myth and an almost identical narrative structure, but from a different perspective, in which the
less positive aspects of Neoptolemus's venture have been completely
suppressed (v. 34ff.):

> And Neoptolemus lies buried in the soil of Delphi,
> having destroyed the city of Priam,
> object of much suffering for the Danaans.
> On the return voyage
> he missed the route for Scyros;
> his men touched in at Ephyra in their wanderings.
>
> For a short time he ruled in Molossia,
> but his race kept control of kingship there.
> Then he came to the god of Delphi bringing
> as rich offerings the first fruits of Trojan spoils.
> Here in a fight over the sacrificial meats
> a man killed him with a knife.
>
> Deep was the grief of his Delphian hosts.
> But what was fated for him came to pass;
> it was necessary that one of the mighty Aeacids
> remain in the primeval grove
> beside the god's strong-built temple,
> overseeing with straight justice
> rites and rich offerings for heroes.

There emerges in the course of the epinician a set of subtle, closely
cohering allusions to the earlier poem on Neoptolemus. This fact was
already noted in antiquity, by Aristarchus of Samothrace and his pupil
Aristodemos, who say that the content of that poem disturbed the
Aeginetans once it was known, with the result that Pindar became the
object of criticism in the very city to which he was most closely linked
by professional connections and by political and ideological affinity.[70]

The epinician begins with a brief preamble on the victor's family, followed by an apparent digression introducing the topic of poetry's proper function: the celebration of the excellence of famous men. The topos is so familiar that it may even seem banal at first sight. However, it brings Pindar to the point where he can confront the problem that his theme poses. Poetry is sometimes lying and deceptive: the reputation that Homer's verses won for Odysseus exceeds his merits, whereas Ajax, a man "brief in speech, but strong in heart,"[71] found no adequate recognition of his "true" merit through poetry and was forced to suicide. But death comes equally to all, whether expectedly or unexpectedly, and posthumous fame is in accordance with the will of the god.[72] This pronouncement is also a topos, but it performs the specific function of introducing the theme of the misfortunes of the Aeacids, whether exemplified by the fate of Ajax or that of Neoptolemus, who was slain by the unexpected stab of a knife. The ambiguous reference to death which comes both expectedly and unexpectedly, to obscure and famous alike, is an implicit allusion, as was noted by ancient commentators, to the accidental, unforeseeable character of the hero's death,[73] a death, moreover, whose very accidentalness makes it ultimately an inglorious one as well.

This is the starting point for retelling the myth of Neoptolemus, who came as a friend[74] to Delphi to dedicate the first fruits of the booty acquired at Troy. But an unforeseeable quarrel with the priest of Delphi over the distribution of the meat of the sacrificial victims led to his death. His end was a destined one because it was the will of the god that he oversee with straight "justice" the annual rites of the Delphic hero cult, applying the same standard of distributive justice which the temple priests had not accorded to him in the final moments of his life.

Comparative analysis of the two mythical narratives in *Paean* 6 and *Nemean* 7 shows that the second is not a true palinode[75] like that of Stesichorus, but rather has the function of reinterpreting the earlier narrative, *not changing in any way its factual content* but highlighting its positive aspects and passing over the negative ones. In both versions the death of Neoptolemus is willed by the god, in the paean in order that the hero expiate an injustice, his impious murder of Priam; in the epinician in order that he become the "just" protector of the cult (v. 47 *themiskópos*) as a result of an action that was, ethically and religiously, ambivalent: just in that he had asked for an equitable division of the sacrificial victims, unjust in that he had quarreled with the priests of Apollo. The objective fact of the existence of the cult, which was certainly already in operation at Delphi at the time Pindar composed the *Paean*,[76] plays a cardinal role in the *Nemean,* giving the poet a means of attenuating the degree of impiety attributed to Neoptolemus in the earlier poem. Because the god accorded him the honor of a cult, it could be assumed that he had already expiated not only the crime against the Delphic priesthood but also that against Priam.

There seems now little basis for the recent attempts to deny all connection between the content of the two odes. The argument rests on the idea of a "program" of conventional norms automatically determining the content and form of all epinicians, and so eliminating the possibility of any specific reference or allusion to historical or biographical reality.[77] In general, however, this approach is questionable methodologically and flies in the face of the most reliable interpretative tradition in ancient criticism.

More particularly, a careful and unprejudiced reading establishes the undeniable presence of references to *Paean 6* in at least two places in *Nemean 7* where explanation in terms of conventional motifs will simply not work. At the opening of the fourth triad Pindar is explicit in defending his own work. He says that even an Achaean citizen living on the coast of the Ionian Sea in Epirus (the land of Neoptolemus) would have no grounds for complaint against him if he were present and goes on to appeal to his own official role as proxenos for the Epirotes and to his position among his fellow citizens. He is a man who walks with head held high, without arrogance and refraining from all insults and violence (vv. 66–67).

These words have the flavor and tone of refutation and protest in the face of accusations stemming from a previous telling of the same myth. They would make no sense outside the situational context analyzed and elucidated—already in antiquity—by earlier criticism.

The same may be said of the statements with which the poem concludes: the poet will never admit to "having put down" (*helkýsai*) Neoptolemus—that is, to having offended him with words that were unsuitable and inappropriate (*atrópoisi*); but he is now past the point of wanting to repeat the same thing three and four times. It would merely be taken as a sign of lack of ability or resourcefulness.[78]

The word *átropos* is in itself an indication of Pindar's awareness of his own ways of proceeding and of the Protean temperament that led him to fit his poetry to occasion,[79] patron, and audience—the temperament described elsewhere through the metaphor of the polyp.[80] It is a skillful and fluid adroitness in manipulating language and attitudes in such a way that a solid core of basic "truthfulness" continues to be maintained—the ethical ideal that the nobleman's absolute loyalty does not allow him to betray. A rule of life is thus transformed into an orienting norm of the artist's profession. The rehandling of the Neoptolemus myth in *Nemean* 1 was a response to the Aeginetan public's insistence on playing down the negative elements in the portrayal of a hero who belonged to the stock of Aeacus, the founder of their race. Audience requirements were quite different at Delphi, where there were no ties of kinship with the Aeacids. It was precisely there, at the scene of a cult in Neoptolemus's honor, that it was possible to develop at length a paradigmatic tale of bloody violence, which was punished by the god of Delphi but did not detract in any way from the perpetrator's stature as a hero. The coexistence of piety and impiety, worthy and unworthy deeds in one's biographical dossier was a distinguishing and defining trait of the hero as conceived by the Greeks.[81]

The Janus-faced character of Pindaric heroes and the contrasting areas of light and shade in their portrayal provide a key for understanding the occasion-oriented attitude of the poet. They are what allow him to remain true to his basic vision of man. Depending on the circumstances he shows the "beautiful" to be imitated, or the "base" to be avoided, in human conduct. And the "base" is what is lacking in measure and proportion, what fails to find that "proper moment" (*kairós*) in which the perfection of all things lies (*Pyth.* 9, 78ff.).

Hence the value accorded to the Delphic maxim "know thyself"— that is, "know your human limits"—which becomes Pindar's moral safeguard against all desires that are inaccessible (*Nem.* 11, 44ff.) or show no regard for measure or proper place and time. Against the background of the divided character of men's actions, the Delphic maxim acquired the status of a prudent norm of political behavior for the various communities that patronized his art. For the people it meant not challenging the true *agathoí*, men of noble birth and political prominence; for the aristocrats it meant maintaining, within an oligarchical political context, the equilibrium of forces which guarantees justice and peace. The personifications of Eunomia and her sisters, Justice and Peace, twin dispensers of wealth, assume, like all Pindaric personifications, an almost corporeal form when they appear in the proem to *Olympian* 13. But the meaning of the invocation is clear. Pindar is emphasizing, for an oligarchical Corinthian audience, the high ethical value of a "right ordering" of political affairs founded on equal division of power between the individual members of the oligarchy, an ordering that encourages due measure and discourages violence.[82]

Truth, like the hero's dossier, also shows a double aspect in Pindaric ideology. Good and evil, beautiful and base, just and unjust, pious and impious are equally a part of her message. She reveals unerringly the worth of man,[83] but she also bears witness to his unjust and overweening violence.

As recent studies have shown, *alétheia* in fifth-century Greek refers to truth as opposed to lying[84]—a faithful representation in thought or words of a person or thing as it is; its function is to communicate messages that correspond to the reality of events, not false and erroneous ones. Such is the notion of truth which emerges at *Olympian* 1, 28ff.: there are many prodigious occurrences, but there are also times when the talk of man goes beyond what is true and deceives us with an elaborate embroidery of lies.

In *Pythian* 3, addressed to an ailing Hieron, knowledge of truth (v. 103ff.) is the necessary prerequisite for enjoying the happiness that the gods grant to man. The poem is a piece of consolation, urging the ruler to bear his suffering courageously, secure in his awareness of the large share of good fortune that has befallen him as leader of his people. Complete and absolute prosperity is an unattainable goal (v. 105ff.). Even Cadmus and Peleus, heroes who knew at one time the height of happiness, were later deprived of it through the misfortunes of their children. This is the "way of truth" that Hieron must travel to enjoy the measure of good that has been granted him. Moreover, it is a way that he is capable of traveling: the gods inflict two evils for every good they bestow on mankind; and a man of Hieron's worth will know how to display the one and conceal the others with good grace.[85] Sovereign power and incurable illness are the two sides of the face of truth that Hieron must recognize—a truth that presents its double aspect of good and evil to all mankind.

In *Nemean* 5 (v. 16ff.), for Pytheas of Aegina, Pindar says that "it is not always profitable for truth to show its face," truth being in this case the "mettle" of the hero, which, like gold, can be tested by contact with the pure touchstone (fr. 122, 16 Sn.-Maehl.). In such situations "silence is the best piece of advice one can give." At a point where following the story of the Aeacids would have forced Pindar to mention a disagreeable episode, the murder by Peleus and Telamon of their stepbrother, Phocos, he protests (v. 14) that he is "ashamed to tell of a heavy deed, ventured upon unjustly," which would have caused offence to his Aeginetan audience. The injunction to Hieron to hide the bad and show only the beautiful and the good is thus a norm of poetics as well as a norm of conduct.

On the other hand, "negative" truth has its own paradigmatic function to perform when occasion and the needs of the audience allow, as is shown by the different treatments of the end of Bellerophon found in *Olympian* 13 and *Isthmian* 7 (cf. above).

No one before Pindar had given expression to the idea that the dimensions of a man's mind may make him equal to God. Yet in *Nemean* 6, for Alcimidas of Aegina, we read (v. 1ff.):

> One is the race of men,
> one and the same of gods,
> and from a single mother we draw our breath.
> But disparate might divides us,
> for we are nothing, and the brazen heaven
> an abode that endures unshakeable through all eternity.
> Yet mind and nature
> make us equal to the immortals,
> ignorant though we be of what limit
> to the course of our journey from day to day
> and in the night destiny has set.

The polarity of the image lies in the dual affirmation of a profound diversity between human and divine prerogative, and at the same time of an equality that may obtain within certain limits. Man is both celestial and terrestrial in his basic nature,[86] and as such has within him both the mind that can make his worth equal to God (v. 4ff.) and the ephemeral transience whose nonworth radically distances him from God (v. 3). Hölderlin was perhaps never so Pindaric as when he wrote of himself:

> Men's words I have never understood . . .
> it is in the arms of the gods that I grew strong.[87]

This notion of the human mind's innate transcendence looms large on Pindar's intellectual horizon. It illuminates the frequent programmatic formulations and metaphors with which he proclaims to his audience the exceptional character and exalted thrust of his inspired words,[88] the lofty evocative power of the new paths traveled by his Muse (*Pae.* 7b, 9ff. Sn.-Maehl.), and the authentic validity of the high moral function of his art.

Developing further the idea of the union of human and divine which opens *Nemean* 6, Pindar's last poems seek to create a sense of the nature of human existence as a kind of escape from the historically

determined character of the present, a present that in his case coincided with the decline of the old oligarchies and the destruction of the
values that they represented. It is, significantly, in his last poem, an
Aeginetan ode composed in 446, a year before his death, that he pointed in the direction of a solution to the contradictory dualities of life,
at a time when the "right ordering" of the island's affairs according to
the aristocratic principles in which he had believed was already a thing
of the past, shattered eleven years earlier under the assault of Athenian
democracy. Addressing himself to Aristomenes, the scion of an illus-
trious family of athletes, and composing for the benefit of the aristocratic groups who constituted the audience best able to understand the
value of his words, he says (vv. 92–97):

> Brief is the time for the joy of men to grow
> and equally to fall to earth
> if shaken by an opposing will.
>
> Creatures of the day—
> what is someone, what is no one?
> Man is the dream of a shadow:
> but when radiance descends from God,
> splendid is the light that gleams on men
> and sweet their life.[89]

An awareness of the tentative day-to-dayness of man, always changing
in respect to the situation at hand (*epámeros*), was not completely foreign to archaic thought before Pindar. Joy and sorrow, the two poles
of human life, are extremes with which one is always confronted in a
to and fro of fluctuating opinion or alternating good and ill will. To
the question of what meaning existence can have in the volatile, day-to-
day tentativeness that is man, Pindar's answer is that in the flux of
changing phenomena the only certainty is the day itself—the moment
of radiance from the gods which illuminates human action.

Extratextual inference lies beyond the scope of the present discussion, but one ambiguity needs to be eliminated if it is not to stand in
the way of understanding a type of celebrative poetry such as the
epinician, which was extremely conventionalized in its structure and
gnomic repertory. Ancient interpreters of Pindar often detected what
they thought, with good reason, were traces of biography and polemic
in the fabric of Pindar's discourse. And modern criticism proceeded
further in this direction, multiplying the number of biographical

references: I am referring in particular to Wilamowitz's *Pindaros*.[90] It is not necessary to ignore the relevance and value of this approach to see that some of its speculative excesses provoked a justified reaction on the part of those more recent critics who have sought to emphasize the conventional aspects of the epinician and its use of recurring thematic motifs linked to the celebratory character of the occasion.[91] The result has been a welcome contribution to the establishment of the traditional character of the genre at the level of structure and topological phraseology. But it has also been an almost exclusively formalistic type of analysis, directed toward finding intertextual constants without regard for the internal articulation of particular passages or the shaping ideological concerns of their various authors. Traditional language does not and cannot mean eternal tautology.

D. C. Young's analysis[92] of *Pythian* 11 may stand as a case in point. It exemplifies a type of verbal criticism which tends to reduce the poetry of Pindar to a repertory of ideas and topoi whose only link to each other is the tenuous thread of encomium.

In *Pythian* 11, for Thrasydaios of Thebes, Pindar passes a completely unfavorable judgment on tyranny (v. 50ff.), asserting his own preference, in the realm of civic life, for the "prosperous" condition of the just mean (*tá mésa*). Here Young may well be right in rejecting the interpretation of Wilamowitz,[93] who sees in these verses a sort of *apologia* presented by Pindar on his return from his first voyage to Sicily, excusing himself, as it were, to his Theban public for having been required to sing the praise of Hieron, the "tyrant" of Syracuse. Once this hypothesis has been set aside, however, Young apparently wants to make the Pindaric formulation a totally trivial and harmless topos—a simple gnomic corollary to the myth of the sons of Atreus. His reading of the poem creates the impression of a Pindar who repeats commonplaces to construct a song of celebration and, in the present case, to praise what is assumed to have been the victorious athlete's simple life style. But certain objections arise almost immediately: (1) Why, out of a vast available repertory, did the poet's choice fall on the particular myth of the sons of Atreus? (2) What is the actual meaning of the reference to tyranny, a reference that is not a Pindaric "topos" at all? (It appears in only one other place [*Pythian* 2, 86ff.] in the poet's extensive body of works.)

It is difficult in such a context to eschew ideological interpretation completely and insist on ignoring the extratextual considerations which offer the only possible explanation for the rapid allusions to hatred of tyranny and the condition of the just mean. The political history of Thebes from the time of the Persian wars down to 474, the date of composition of *Pythian* 11, contains episodes that may offer a legitimate key to interpretation. We learn from Thucydides (3, 62, 3) that at the time of the second Persian war a "nonegalitarian" oligarchy gained control of the city. It numbered only a handful of men in its ranks and they exercised their *tyrannical* power to align the city alongside the Persians. After the battle of Plataea (479), however, the Medizers among the aristocracy were eliminated, and a different regime took control, probably a democratic one.[94] It should be noted that Pindar must have sided on that occasion with those aristocratic circles who were urging on their fellow citizens a policy of unity and peace. This is clear from a fragment of a hyporcheme he composed for the Thebans (109 Sn.-Maehl.).

These facts suggest that in *Pythian* 11 Pindar was giving expression to his own deep-seated aversion to tyranny, personified in the figure of Atreus, with an implicit reference, immediately comprehensible to his Theban audience, to the unfortunate oligarchico-tyrannical experiment that had forced the city into alliance with Persia. His political convictions here are the same ones that he had had to play down when he composed *Pythian* 2 for Hieron (see above), presenting them in language suited to the identity of his patron.

The parallel passages assembled by Young, from Archilochus (fr. 22 T.), Anacreon (fr. 4 Gent.), and Simonides, to which may be added Solon's tetrameters to Phocos (fr. 29 Gent.-Pr.), are evidence for the traditional character of Pindar's phraseology, but at the same time they point the way to an individualizing interpretation of the political thought of their authors. Solon, for example, alludes polemically to the positive connotations that the idea of tyranny carried for most people. He was unwilling to have anything to do with tyrannical policies and is not ashamed of the fact, even though the citizens of Athens think differently and call him a fool for not seizing the chance to become tyrant when he had it. Like Solon, Pindar defends the "true," aristocratic view of the situation against the common opinion held by the many. Simonides, on the other hand, recognizing as he did the tendency of opinion to prevail over truth (fr. 598 P.), pointed to the tyrant's lot as one of the most desirable for man, provided it did not interfere with one's enjoyment of life (fr. 584 P.):

What mode of life should a man seek,
what tyranny, if it fails to bring pleasure?
Without pleasure even the life
of the gods would not be one to envy.

Although convincing as pure verbal analysis, Young's interpretation neglects the real meaning that these passages have in their contexts. The ultimate goal of the interpreter should be to bring together the synchronic and diachronic planes—poetry as structure and poetry as development and growth—integrating the results of both levels of his investigation. This is the perspective that gives the myth of the house of Atreus inserted into Pindar's epinician its historical referent. The bloody and violent quarrels over the dynastic succession that it relates thereby become paradigmatic in relation to the recent experience of tyrannical oligarchy at Thebes. The exaltation of the just mean and "ordinary virtues" was a precise response to the new political regime—democracy or moderate oligarchy—in power at Thebes in the year in which Pindar saw his song for Thrasydaios performed.

The narrative movement of Pindar's epinicians is characterized by rapid transitions, passing allusions, and ambiguous phrasing (sometimes signifying a multiplicity of things, sometimes made up of signs to which a multiplicity of cultural referents are attached), as well as by a structure that often seems discontinuous—a matter of fits and starts. It only becomes intelligible with the aid of a historical and ideological exegesis that opens the way to a range of meanings beyond those suggested by purely formal analysis. This sort of exegesis is less urgent for the reader of the epinicians of Bacchylides, where narrative syntax is more linear, more clear, and more uniform, both rhythmically and semantically. Unlike Pindar, Bacchylides always adheres to the tripartite movement from the present to the mythical past back to the present. There is only one instance (*Epin.* II Sn.-Maehl.) where the *explicit* of the poem coincides with the end of a myth. Even the gnomic element functions unambiguously as a means of transition from the world of the present to that of myth. In the fifth epinician, the statement that no mortal man is happy in all things (v. 53ff.) introduces the mythical narrative and applies with special significance to the human tragedy of Meleager, the unfortunate hero who died in the flower of his youth.

The gnomic element may also appear, as it does in this same poem, within the fabric of a narrative as a means of linking its individual episodes; but the poem's narrative reveals the profound difference be-

tween the Pindaric and the Bacchylidean epinician, which is conspicuous for psychological analysis of character and for the pathetic
and dramatic aspects of its action. The myth does not serve as an exemplar for heroic prowess: it operates within a context that humanizes
the hero and brings out the fragility and transience of his destiny. The
poet's style is more concerned with formal values, with the effects of
sound and coloring to be obtained from a careful collocation of epithets and from a quest for neologisms whose function is primarily
psychological and descriptive. It is an aural poetry, more immediately
appealing than its Pindaric counterpart and requiring emotional rather
than intellectual involvement from its audience.[95] The poet's characterization of his own work which appears in the *explicit* of the third
epinician (see above) seems very appropriate. The two brief poems
without a myth, composed for Argeos (2) and Lacon (6) immediately
following their victories, show a design of clearly Anacreontic derivation, both in its terse clarity and in its diction—studied and stylized,
yet graceful and elegant at the same time.[96] This technical solution to
the problem of the epinician was undoubtedly original, using as it did
the refined stylization of certain odes of Anacreon as a means of narrowing and tightening a lyric form destined for the celebration of triumph in contests. It is easy to see why the epinicians of Bacchylides do
not raise the complex and difficult problems of poet-patron relationship that confront the reader in some of the odes of Pindar.

The distance between the epinician techniques of Pindar and Simonides must have been greater still, having to do with the skeptical,
secularizing attitude that Simonides displayed toward his activity as an
artist (see chap. 9). Even success and fame, which are the cornerstones
of Pindar's poetics,[97] are regarded as passing phenomena in Simonides,
durable only in a relative sense. Fr. 581 P. is a brief attack on Cleoboulos, tyrant of Lindos:

> Who in his right mind would praise Cleoboulos of Lindos,
> who against the ever-flowing rivers
> and the flowers that return in the spring
> and the gleam of the sun and the golden moon
> and the eddying sea
> set up as a match the enduring power
> of a tombstone?
> Such things cannot withstand the gods; a stone
> can be shattered even by mortal hands.
> This is the conceit of a fool.

The lines set firm limits to everything that is the work of man. It is ridiculous and absurd to claim for any such product the vital energy of what is immortal. Even fame, the most enduring of all human things, like a "fair ornament for a tomb" is destined "in the end to sink beneath the earth" (fr. 594 P.).

Hence the traces of burlesque and parody which can be seen in the few surviving fragments of his epinicians.[98] In the poem for the champion wrestler Crios of Aegina (fr. 507 P.) there is a subtle play on the athlete's name (*Kriós* = ram) and the word *pékein*, "shear" (the animal's fleece), used with the additional meaning of "beat":[99] "Not discreditably was Crios shorn when he came to the glorious, shady sanctuary of Zeus." Crios won, but only after taking a pounding, which he bore in a way that did not do him discredit. The "comic" point lies in the litotes, which Simonides emphasizes for expressive purposes. In the epinician for the boxer Glaucos of Carystos there is a demystifying reference to Heracles and Pollux, the patron heroes of the games (fr. 509 P.): "Neither the might of Pollux would have been a match for his [Glaucos's] hands, nor Alcmena's iron-fisted son." In reproducing the fragment Lucian shrewdly notes that the exaggerated character of the eulogy did not arouse the ire of Glaucos or the two gods, who punished neither the athlete nor the poet himself for his *impiety.* Agonistic prowess is praised in very different fashion when there is occasion to describe the extraordinary power and energy of an athlete in Pindar. In *Isthmian* 3/4 (vv. 63ff.) the pancratiast Melissos of Thebes is praised for his lion's daring and for the cleverness of the fox who checks the attack of the eagle. He does not have the build of Orion, the giant huntsman; on the contrary, his stocky figure is not much to look at. But his strength in a fight is formidable. Hence the comparison with Heracles, a hero squat in build but invincible in spirit, who defeated the giant Antaeus in battle. Here too there is exaggerated praise but it does not pass over, as in Simonides, into the assertion—not without a touch of burlesque humor—that the athlete was superior to Heracles himself.

The traces of fable which appear in Simonides are equally indicative. Fr. 514 P. is from a poem for Orillas, victor with the four-horse chariot in a minor contest held at Pellene in Achaea. The games were held in winter, and the prize was a characteristic local product, a woolen cloak. Simonides parodies the whole procedure by comparing Orillas, who had braved the rigors of winter to win himself a mere cloak, to the fisherman in the Carian fable who, upon catching sight of a polyp in the icy winter waters, exclaimed, "If I don't dive in to

catch him I will die of hunger." The friendly, detached irony with
which Simonides views the victorious athlete contrasts strikingly with
Pindar's lack of generosity toward the defeated ones. In *Pythian* 8 (vv.
81ff.) he has this to say of them:

> Four bodies felt the force of your blows
> raining down on them from above.
> No sweet homecoming like yours
> was ordained for them at Delphi;
> no sweet smile of joy embraced them
> when they came back to their mothers' side;
> they skulk along the back alleys out of sight of rivals,
> bitten to the quick by their ill luck.

This panorama of the opposing artistic and ideological tendencies at
work in the late archaic period contains indications of a profound cultural crisis, during the course of which poetry served as an instrument
in the evolution of the Greek consciousness of reality.

Poetry of absolute values and human perfection on the one hand
and, on the other, poetry of relative values and human imperfection—
these are the two opposed positions taken up by Pindar and Simonides.
Pindar sought a conservative solution to the crisis in the old order
created by the rise of the new artisan and mercantile class—a solution
calling for a renovation of the aristocratic ethic through a new conception of the relation between human and divine and "new highways of
song" appropriate to it. The alternative was to follow Simonides in
assuming a more progressive position, one that would replace the old
aristocratic absolutism with a new relativism better suited to the
changed social situation and the views of those who had worked with
success to replace an oligarchy of lineage and innate excellence[100] with
a meritocracy of acquired wealth. The aristocratic idea of man operating under the illumination of divine guidance gives way to that of
human frailty; the ethic of absolute value is countered by an ethic
oriented toward practical reality with all its risks and misadventures.
There are no more highways of song setting forth anew, as in Pindar,
the "truth" of the mythical hero acting in accordance with divine law,
but rather, as in Simonides, poetic footpaths where the pace is more
relaxed and discursive, less stately and portentous, more in keeping
with the multiform, Odyssean nature of man.

The divergence in points of view is present even with regard to the
notion of *polytropía:* ability and adroitness in seizing upon the essen-

tial psychological aspects of a situation and adapting oneself to them with flexibility and intelligence. For Pindar this *polytropía* is a kind of *souplesse* and sense of discretion which insures that quarrels and hard feelings, professional or otherwise, will not be provoked unnecessarily. It never calls for abandoning basic ethical and political beliefs, and thus has nothing to do with the slippery and uninhibited changeability personified in the figure of Ulysses,[101] a hero whom Pindar repeatedly condemns as lying and untrustworthy.[102] Simonides, on the other hand, takes the inexhaustible inventiveness and resourcefulness of the "man of many counsels" (*polýmetis*) and projects it onto a larger plane when he describes divinity as *pammêtis* (fr. 526, 3 P.), a kind of "Super-Ulysses"[103] which knows, sees, and is capable of everything. The conception has its perfect counterpart, on the human level, in the Simonidean ideal of the man who is never embarrassed or at a loss, even in the most difficult circumstances of life.

This basic cultural dichotomy provides a background against which to understand the lively polemics attested in the ancient tradition, echoes of which can be detected on more than one occasion in the work of the three leading composers of choral lyric in the late sixth and early fifth centuries.[104] Professional rivalry was obviously a factor here, but a less important one than the real gap that separated two different visions of the world and society. Simonides replaces the utopian monologue of Truth with a true-to-life dialogue of Opinion, a dialogue that is based on critical observation of practical reality and sets up the new truth of becoming and flux. Hypostasized as personification, this truth becomes the new god Tomorrow.[105]

# Intellectual Activity
# & Socioeconomic Situation

Book 8 of the *Odyssey* (v. 62ff.) offers in the figure of Demodocus the earliest surviving representation of a poet at work—an epic singer (*aoidós*) who accompanies himself on the lyre (*kítharis, phórminx*) as he improvises narratives of the deeds of gods and heroes.

It is clear from the passages relating to Demodocus and his Ithacan counterpart, Phemius (*Od.* 1, 325-59), that this type of performance was reserved for bards, but we know from other precise pieces of evidence that the term *bard* was associated with another one, *rhapsode*.[1]

The singer lives at the court of a prince (Alcinoos, Odysseus) from whom he receives food, lodging, and honors. His importance is evident from the words with which Odysseus accompanies the gift of a plate of meat, tasted in advance by him as a visible sign of respect: "Take this meat, herald, and carry it to Demodocus, so that he may eat: stricken with grief though I am, this tribute comes from my heart; singers should have honor and respect from all men who dwell on the earth, for the Muse has taught them the ways of song and shown love for the race of singers" (*Od.* 8, 477ff.).

Demodocus is the prototype of the singer integrated into a homogeneous society dedicated to agriculture, navigation, and the pursuit of pleasure in its various forms: athletic contests, banquets, music, dance, exercise and bodily adornment, the joys of love. His function was to entertain his audience, treating it to stories of gods and heroes which reinforced its own sense of social and cultural identity, in return for which he received both appreciation and concrete rewards. At a later period, however, the singer ceases to be employed steadily and exclusively by a single court:[2] his profession takes him from place to place and doubtlessly leads to wider experience and freer contact with men and ideas.

With the rise of the polis the singer's audience comes to consist, above all, of the populace assembled on the occasion of public festivals. These also provide rhapsodes with the opportunity to compete with each other in recitations from their own repertory. Hesiod himself tells (*Op.* 654ff.) how he crossed the sea from Aulis to Chalchis for the funeral games in honor of Amphidamas and there won as his prize a bronze tripod that he dedicated to the Muses. Such competitions were numerous and much frequented by Greeks in the archaic period. One need only think of the Pythian contests at Delphi, the Carnean ones at Sparta, and those at Delos known from Hesiod (fr. 357 Merk.-West) and the Homeric hymn to Apollo (vv. 149–50). At Dodona, too, seat of the famous oracle, there were poetic contests, as we learn from an inscription found *in situ* on a bronze tripod dedicated to Zeus by the rhapsode Terpsicles.[3] Sicyon (Herod. 5, 67) and Epidaurus[4] were the scene of other rhapsodic competitions, though less famous than those at the Panathenaea, where recitations from Homer were presented.[5]

The importance of the contests and the prestige of the rhapsodes themselves were in direct proportion not only to the pleasure provided by the spectacle but also to its educational and political utility. Epic poetry served as an instrument for cultural indoctrination and at the same time as a repertory of models for behavior.[6] By moulding character, it contributed to the education of the members of the governing class; by assimilating the figure of the contemporary aristocrat to that of his heroic forebears, it tended to create among the lower classes a certain predisposition toward social integration into the order of the polis. It was only in isolated instances and for particular reasons, linked to local political situations, that these rhapsodic performances failed to meet with official approval. This is what occurred at Sicyon, where they were actually forbidden, under orders from the tyrant Cleisthenes.[7] Anticonformist positions in the face of general moral beliefs and practice do not begin to be encountered until later. What has often been explained, from the time of Burckhardt on, as the product of emerging individualism and subjectivism is better connected with the actual circumstances of poetic composition—the poet's own social situation and the concrete forms that his activity took.

A particularly sharp stand against prevailing ethical and religious ideas is taken by Xenophanes, whose activity as an itinerant rhapsode (fr. 7 Gent.-Pr.) doubtless made for a richer experience of men and ideas than was allowed by constant, exclusive relationship with a single patron. This is one source of his attack on the polytheism, anthropomorphism, and amorality of Homeric religion and his monotheistic assertion of the existence of a god who is all-seing, -perceiving, and -hearing.[8] It is also a source of his attack on the agono-centric view of life and his proud exaltation of the activity of the poet. Poetry is more useful to the community than anything the athlete has to offer (fr. 2 Gent.-Pr.) and so ranked—here for the first time—on a higher level than feats of physical strength. The function of poetic *sophía* has to do with the contribution it can make to political equilibrium and stability (*eunomía*), hence to the peace and well-being of the city. This helps explain Xenophanes' explicit rejection (fr. 1 Gent.-Pr.) of the sort of poetry that introduces into the symposium mythical tales of titanomachies and gigantomachies; that is, tales of internal dissension and seditious insubordination within the council of the gods.[9] The reference to *eunomía* suggests that Xenophanes' critique, refusing as it does any epic narrative that could offer a model of social behavior harmful to the city, was basically compatible, for all its iconoclasm, with maintenance of the status quo in a stable, harmonious oligarchy. It is obvious, however, that his polemic could not hope to meet with unanimous audience approval, much less with that of those oligarchical groups who were sporadic promoters of discord and sedition in a period when the crisis of the aristocratic order was already at hand.

With his downgrading of the contribution of the athlete in favor of the superior wisdom of poetry, Xenophanes was also assigning to the exercise of a craft a higher position in the traditional scale of values than that given to agonistic activity. The latter was reserved to the aristocracy as part of a system of education devoted primarily to the creation of warriors. This untraditional approach could appeal for support to the role of social and political advisor which famous poets of the past had played within their communities.[10] Thaletas of Gortyn is a significant figure in this respect. One of the most representative contributors to the culture of archaic Sparta, he was an author of paeans and processional hymns, as well as an able statesman and lawgiver. His poems, as we learn from Plutarch, were, quite literally, exhortations to civic obedience and concord, and thus instruments for the creating and maintaining of a social order. The very sound of his rhythms and melodies is said to have exercised a fascination on the audience, leading to an unconscious predisposition toward love of the good and the beautiful.[11] Terpander of Lesbos, also active at Sparta in the first half of the seventh century, combined the activity of mediator and pacifier with that of poet in the same way. He founded a school of music, and his prestige allowed him to contribute to the settling of civic strife. Anyone who went to consult an oracle was given the response that he should heed the words of the poet.[12] Stesichorus of Himera was equally influential with the contending factions in the city of Locri.[13] Moreover, the whole anecdotal tradition concerning the Seven Sages, some of whom also composed elegies (Periander, Pittacus, Chilon), presupposes the existence of a kind of political wisdom which combines the skills of lawgiver and poet.

It is hard to imagine the ideas of Xenophanes finding acceptance among the varied audiences of the cities that were the scene of his activity.[14] The later notice (see below) concerning the poor pay he received for his public performances is against such a supposition, and to assume that his polemic had a democratic message and appeal would be to make an anachronistic generalization on the basis of forms and situations typical of political life in the Athens of Cleisthenes. It was precisely his polemical stance toward the tradition which ultimately caused economic difficulties for Xenophanes, as may be inferred from an anecdote preserved by Plutarch.[15] Having heard Xenophanes complain that he had barely enough to support a household with two slaves, the tyrant Hieron of Syracuse commented, "Homer—whom you are always pillorying—is able to support ten thousand people, even though he's dead." Hieron is here alluding to the fees the rhapsode received for his Homeric recitations. Xenophanes' habit of finding fault with Homer was the very thing that offended the sensibilities of his audience, with the result that he was paid less well than those who esteemed Homer and praised him highly. It is also clear, however, that Xenophanes was himself a rhapsode, one who, like Theagenes of Rhegium, appended his own commentary to his recitations of passages from Homer. Theagenes' commentary was allegorical; that of Xenophanes, critical and polemical.[16] Herein lay the wit of Hieron's comment. He linked Xenophanes' economic difficulties directly to his acerbic criticism of the poet who was the great cultural repertory on which all his contemporaries drew.

A complete picture of the activity of the rhapsode is provided by Plato's *Ion*. Like Xenophanes and Theagenes at an earlier period, Ion did not limit himself to Homeric recitations but added his own interpretations (*Ion* 530cd). The degree of success of the entire rhapsodic performance—closely linked to the degree of emotional involvement on the part of the audience—determined the amount of pay the poet received. "I must be especially attentive," Ion says, "to the spectators, because if I make them weep I shall laugh for the money that I will take in, and if I make them laugh, I shall weep for the money I lose" (*Ion* 535e). Xenophanes, as we have seen, complained about his poverty; Plato has Ion boast of his prosperity – the results of the prizes he has won in poetic competitions (*Ion* 503ab).

The financial situation of the person involved in this sort of intellectual activity did not depend on a regular, fixed salary but on the irregular income derived, above all, from prizes. Herodotus's story of Arion (1, 23–24) gives an idea of the possibilities open to a singer, which might include very large profits. From the court of Periander, the poet decided to go to Italy and Sicily, whence "having accumulated great riches" (*chrémata*) he set forth on the return trip to Corinth. The sailors formed a plan to "seize his wealth" but allowed him to sing one last song, dressed in his performance attire and lyre in hand, before flinging himself into the sea. The story of the death of the poet Ibycus at the hand of robbers who wanted to get possession of his belongings[17] is another instance of anecdotal tradition linking poets to a reputation for wealth.[18]

Elegiac and iambic poets composed with a greater variety of purposes and occasions in mind and without the prospect of direct, immediate reward, a fact reflected in their different socioeconomic status. Solon's ideology is of a piece with his aristocratic social origins. It is based on the economic values generally recognized by the aristocratic circles to which he belongs, as is his prayer to the Muses to see to it that he has good fortune and prosperity (*ólbos*)[19] from the gods and a good reputation (*dóxa*) among men, and to make him sweet to his friends and bitter to his enemies, respected by the former and feared by the latter (1, 1–6 Gent.-Pr.). In other words, he is aware that a poet directly involved in political affairs will acquire enemies as well as friends, thus endangering the very foundations of his social and economic security. This is why he asks the Muses in their capacity as goddesses of poetry to protect him against loss of the prosperity that legitimately belongs to him.[20] But he categorically rejects the illegitimate wealth (*chrémata*) that comes from neglect of the norm of just dealing (*díke*) (v. 7ff.). The prosperity to which Solon refers is fairly clearly landed wealth (*ploûtos*), legitimized and guaranteed by passage from father to son in accordance with the will of the gods (v. 9ff.). It is safe and secure, not precarious and uncertain like the moveable wealth (cf. *kérdos*, v. 44) that comes through the risky ventures of commerce and trade.[21] The Muses are thus called upon to do more than help the poet in composing his song: their task is to insure him against the risks to which his poetry exposes him, intimately bound up as it was with his political program. It is here that one can see the clear contrast between a poet who, like Solon, works in conditions of complete economic independence, putting his poetry to work for a political goal, and the poet who pursues his calling—as the itinerant rhapsode must have done—to gain a living (v. 51ff.). The latter's activity is like that of any other professional (v. 43ff.)—the merchant, the farmer, the artisan, the diviner, or the doctor.[22] The poem is clearly an indispensable point of reference for what it tells us about the ideology of labor in the archaic age, an ideology that emerges, as has been pointed out,[23] in its classification of various professions (v. 43ff.), in its idea of causality linking labor to need (v. 41), and in its awareness of the risk, present in every calling (v. 65), of there being no adequate compensation for a given piece of labor, or no compensation at all.

With Solon begins the long debate on the source and legitimacy of material goods in relation to their proper use by the wise man. The rejection of unjustly acquired wealth and uncontrolled greed in general found a concrete application in his activity as a lawgiver. With the specific goal in mind of limiting both expenditures and citizen incomes, he issued regulations that placed a precise maximum on the cost of funerals and fixed the prize for Olympian and Isthmian victors at five hundred and one hundred drachmas, respectively.[24]

The ambition of the archaic poet was that his works should win him the honors and social and economic prestige necessary to sustain a position as sage—"master of truth."[25] This is the situation of which Sappho boasts when she declares that the Muses themselves have presented her with all their honors, enabling her to be truly rich and an object of envy.[26] In her case, however, the honors and riches came specifically from her role as educator in the female community to which she belonged and which included the daughters of Lesbian and, above all, Ionian aristocrats.[27]

The rise of the tyrants and their cultural programs brings in a new type of relation between poet and patron. Anacreon was one of the first to conform to the model of the courtier poet, first with Polycrates at Samos and later with the Pisistratids at Athens. The Herodotean account (3, 121) of how Anacreon was present when the envoy from the Persian satrap Oroetes was first introduced to Polycrates shows clearly the extent to which he enjoyed the confidence and esteem of the tyrant. The talent of gold which Polycrates offered him and which he refused[28] suggests that prestige was accompanied by adequate economic inducements. The splendid court of the tyrant offered an ideal scene for the various activities of a courtier poet, whether he was looking, like Anacreon, for festive themes to entertain friends assembled to enjoy a symposium,[29] or, like Ibycus, for motifs more specifically suited to celebrations.[30]

Fully conscious by now of the dignity and importance of his role, the poet also becomes aware of its "commercial" value. He puts his own *sophía* at the disposal of the highest bidder, thereby creating a basis for the tendency to regard wealth and poetic "wisdom" as interchangeable moral equivalents.[31] This attitude is reflected in a set of anecdotes whose central figure is Simonides, the prototype of the intellectual[32] as now conceived and the poet whose reputation for greediness (*philokérdeia*) is unanimously attested to by later tradition. The prevalent monetary and mercantile economy of the time furthered the new type of contractual relationship linked to the name of Simonides. The unsentimental attitude toward the profession of poet and toward competitive athletics itself which is evident elsewhere in his work was also reflected in his willingness to accept commissions from people of less distinguished social backgrounds or from victors in less prestigious contests.[33] Such was the epinician for Glaucos of Carystos, a peasant's son, over seven feet tall and with a powerful and murderous pair of fists, who was to become, thanks to his strength and his fame, a person of importance in Sicily, first as the tyrant Gelon's bodyguard, then as ruler of the city of Camarina. He paid dearly for this unexpected rise to power, however, being finally put to death on orders from Gelon himself.[34]

Simonides' greed is further attested by several bits of repartee attributed to him. When asked which he preferred, wealth or the *sophía* of the poet, he replied, "I do not know, but I observe the *sophoí* waiting in attendance at the doors of the rich."[35] On another occasion he was asked whether everything grew old, and said, "Yes, everything—except insatiable profit."[36] The traces of parody or burlesque which appear in his epinicians reveal a less serious evaluation of the figure of the athlete, but also a tendency to measure his own calling by the same criteria as the activities of other craftsmen. Hence the charge of avarice directed at him by Xenophanes (fr. 21 Gent.-Pr.) and taken up by the biographical tradition. Closely connected with this accusation is that of "petty greed" (*aischrokérdeia*)[37] and "love of money" (*philargyría*).[38] Simonides' venality in the practice of his calling was neither an isolated case nor without later imitators. Witness Trygaios's reply to Hermes (Aristophanes, *Peace*, v. 695ff.) when asked how Sophocles is doing:

"Very well indeed . . . he used to be Sophocles, now he's turned into Simonides: old and decrepit though he is, he would go to sea in a sieve provided it netted him a profit."

In breaking away from the traditional mold of the inspired poet and the model of the poet as master of truth, Simonides inaugurates a process of secularization that replaces a special, privileged type of knowledge with what is essentially a lay person's knowledge, more accessible and political.[39] Its potential social role was seen by Hipparchus when he induced Simonides to come to Athens through the offer of spectacular fees and gifts.[40]

The eulogistic, celebrative role of poetry and its value as propaganda conferred social prestige on the poet, which is reflected in the scale of the rewards disbursed to him by his patrons. We know that Pindar requested a fee of three thousand drachmas from Pytheas of Aegina for the composition of Nemean 5[41] and received ten thousand drachmas, plus the post of proxenos, for his dithyramb in honor of the Athenians.[42] Fees paid to other types of craftsmen in the same period were considerably lower. Herodotus (3, 131) reports that the physician Democedes received an annual salary of six thousand drachmas from the Aeginetans, whereas the Athenians paid him ten thousand and the tyrant Polycrates of Samos, twelve thousand. Other figures are even more indicative: Phidias worked at the chryselephantine statue of Athena for eight years at an annual salary of one talent—forty thousand drachmas for the whole period.[43] The amount was certainly not large, given that it had to pay the salaries of the highly skilled équipe of craftsmen working under him, not to mention the actual production costs. What Pindar received for the two odes just mentioned seems much greater in comparison.

According to Plato (Men. 91d), Protagoras "earned more money through his expertise than Phidias, with so many undisputed masterworks to his credit, and ten other sculptors combined." Herodotus is said to have received from the Athenians, on the motion of a certain Anytus, the immense sum of ten talents,[44] the occasion being a public recitation of his Histories.[45] These notices seem to confirm the existence of a gap between pay for artist-craftsmen and that for professions of the spoken word. However, certain activities that we would now call "intellectual" did not bring remuneration on the same scale. Such is the case of the Cretan Spensitios, who lived around 500. He was a scribe and secretary-archivist (mnámon), ranking on a level with the chief magistrates and receiving from the community maintenance at public expense, an annual salary of twenty drachmas, exemption for both himself and his family from certain taxes, and, finally, the income from several pieces of sacred land.[46] His duties occupy an unusual middle position between those of a simple craftsman (writing is a *téchne*) and those of an expert in political and religious matters. His high social position stems partly from his ability as a scribe—fairly rare in a semiliterate society—and partly from the fact that he was a public official.

The proud proclamation of one's own poetic talent—a recurring motif in the choral songs of Pindar and Bacchylides—reflects a clear awareness of the prestige and social function that attach to the art, and it is reinforced by the notion of the superiority of verbal to visual representation. As Pindar asserts with pride in the proem to *Nemean* 5:

> I am no maker of statues,
> no producer of figures who stand
> motionless on their pedestal;
> rather, on every ship, every bark
> set sail, sweet song, going from Aegina
> to say that Pytheas,
> the mighty son of Lampon,
> won the victor's crown in the pancration at Nemea.

The metaphor of the ship or bark that will carry the praise of Pytheas of Aegina far and wide is the same one with which Theognis describes the growing fame of Cyrnos, spread by the poet's praise through all of Greece and across the sea to the islands as well. Poetry is a continually widening patrimony of song which comes alive again on the lips of men during various community and social occasions, both present and future.[47] The poet's superiority to the sculptor lies precisely in his greater communicative effectiveness. Rigidly fixed on their pedestals, statues only convey a message to the immediate observer (reproduction and diffusion through xylography, lithography, and photography were as yet unknown);[48] but the poet's word, to use Theognis's image (v. 237ff.),[49] flies swiftly over all the seas and all the lands. This primacy of words over marble will be discussed at greater length by Isocrates in his eulogistic biography of Evagoras (73–74): figurative representations are static, he explains, whereas the content of verbal discourse circulates in the talk of all those who are interested in fame and glory. This hierarchy of range by which the various means of communication are ordered gives the poet a very concrete reason for emphasizing the value of his own artistic mission, a mission whose claim to superiority is economically vindicated by the greater remuneration he receives.

Judging from available evidence, artistic patronage at the court of Archelaus of Macedonia in the final years of the fifth century operated with a similar pay scale. The great painter Zeuxis is said to have received four hundred minas (forty thousand drachmas) as a fee fixed in advance for frescoing the king's palace,[50] whereas the poet Choerilos of Samos got a salary of four minas (four hundred drachmas) per day.[51] And at a later period in Macedonian history, the poet Choerilos of Iasos is said to have received a piece of gold for every encomiastic verse he produced.[52]

The social and economic position of the figurative artist—relative to those of both the verbal artist and the ordinary artisan—has been the subject of extended discussion in the last several decades. Few definite conclusions have emerged, however, largely owing to the fragmentary character of the available documentation.[53] There are three general schools of thought on the subject. One of them adheres to what we may call the traditional view that the artist was seen as an artisan practicing a manual craft—hence as a person of low social status.[54] A second school holds an exactly opposite view. Despite some differences in critical approach, its proponents are agreed in seeking to rehabilitate the figure of the artist and his status within the Greek social context.[55] N. Himmelmann[56] argues for a more dialectical position, a kind of equilibrium between these two extremes. While agreeing in general with the first view as developed by Schweitzer and Bianchi Bandinelli, he acknowledges that the works of exceptional artists such as Phidias, Parrhasius, and Zeuxis were viewed in a different light from the rest and esteemed more highly. But Himmelmann's most important contribution is his insistence on a more rigorous reexamination of the ancient evidence, which, when salaries are documented, has been too often used without sufficient attention to the skill level and duration of the work performed.

Pindar draws analogies, replete with transferred architectural and sculptural terminology, between the structure of a poem and that of a building.[57] He must, therefore, have conceived of his own work as a craft—as existing, technically, on the same level as one of the figurative arts; and this is exactly the sense of the Simonidean definition of poetry as speaking painting and of the word as "image" of the thing.[58] Such comparisons certainly reveal, as Philipp has pointed out, a high evaluation of the figurative arts as craft and technique.[59] It is equally certain, however, that, once this objective resemblance has been acknowledged, Pindar exalts poetry as the necessary mediator between deeds worthy of remembrance and the glory that is their due, thereby according it a communicative function superior to those of architecture and statuary.[60] Consciousness of the high quality of one's own work and of technical achievements at a level that would be hard to surpass was certainly an established phenomenon in the second half of the fifth century—as true of figurative artists such as Parrhasius and Zeuxis as it was of poets.[61] But all this does not change the nature of the problem. The gap between poetry and the figurative arts is communicational, not technical or intellectual—the result of greater spatial mobility and temporal durability. The poet's words "live longer than deeds when touched by inspiration through the favor of the Muses and the Graces" (*Nem.* 4, 1ff.). The phrase is an incisive synthesis of Pindar's whole conception of the enduring value of his own art.

The discussion of the relationship between language and the figurative arts did not end with Pindar. It was developed further, and in an interesting way, to the point of becoming a true theory of communication, many aspects of which continue to be important today. Having followed Pindar in contrasting the mobility of the word with the immobility of the figurative arts, Isocrates supplements the analysis by arguing that it is only the word, not the image, that can convey the behavior and thought of the person who is the subject of a eulogy. Similarly, words themselves can become in their turn an ethical model, so that there is a mutual mimesis between speech and action.[62] In the later formulation of Aristides Quintilianus this theory of psychological mimesis is completed by a discussion, borrowed from Plato, of music and dance as component parts of poetry.[63]

Pindar's view of poetry as communication is what lies behind his recurring references to the patron's liberality toward the poet who is his guarantor of fame. The expense involved in commissioning a song of praise from a poet is above all a means of securing permanent fame for athletic success, which would otherwise be passed over in silence and remain unknown. Wealth must be spent in an intelligent way: hoarded treasures do not secure a man good repute (*Isthm.* 1, 67). Sometimes explicit mention of the terms of the poet's contract is included along with references to reward—by way of introducing or returning to the praise of the victor.

The relationship between patron and poet was a difficult one, involving a posing and accepting of conditions on both sides:

Foundation of great excellence,
sovereign Truth,
grant that the agreement I make
not stumble on the rough terrain of falsehood.[64]

These verses, which contain Pindar's most effective formulation of the principle governing the relationship, probably come from a situational context similar to one that appears in *Pythian* 11 and *Nemean* 4.[65] They are not simply an additional instance of reference to the contract, but, above all, a categorical affirmation of a professional ethics that gives priority to absolute respect for truth. The agreement with the patron must not allow deviations from this supreme standard, which is the essential precondition of human and heroic worth. If one is unwilling to speak an unpleasant truth, it is better to follow the path of silence than that of falsehood.

With the passing, in the course of the fifth century, of the great public occasions for which choral lyric was designed, a new type of paid performance begins to be popular. The performers were masters of encyclopedic knowledge and the art of eloquence—genuine intellectuals, or, in the terminology of the time, "Sophists." The knowledge that they transmitted to their young students was intended to produce citizens capable of active participation in the life of the city. Their lectures were open to anyone able to pay, and thus to members of the new social classes whose influence was on the rise. Earlier education, by contrast, had been restricted to a select circle of young aristocrats, the recipients of a *paideía* that took place in the institutionalized exclusiveness of symposium or initiation rite. The success and popularity of these intellectual professionals in a city such as Athens cannot help but be linked to the democratic character of the city's political life, which was making access to power possible for classes traditionally excluded from it.

In his dialogues Plato gives a vivid, detailed portrait of the figure of the Sophist, self-proclaimed master of all the arts and, above all, the art of verbal persuasion. In his highly negative picture one can see the hostility of the aristocrat, who saw these intellectuals as creating, through the persuasive power of speech, an insidious challenge to his own preeminence.

The success of the Sophists was matched by the size of the fees they received. Protagoras was the first to set a fee of one hundred minas (ten thousand drachmas) per student,[66] and he established an unusual system for payment: the student could pay the stipulated amount directly if he was satisfied with the instruction he had received; if not, he was to go to a temple and place on deposit there the amount of money which—according to his own sworn statement—he believed the instruction to have been worth.[67] Gorgias also received a hundred minas from each student for instruction in rhetoric,[68] thereby accumulating such a large fortune that he was able to pay for the erecting of a solid gold statue of himself in the precinct of Apollo at Delphi.[69] His earnings must have been the most significant realized by any Sophist.[70] Those of Evenos of Pros, who asked only five minas per student,[71] were more modest. Prodicus became quite wealthy, discharging official duties for his fellow citizens on the island of Ceos[72] and setting various levels of remuneration according to the type of instruction offered.[73] A visit to Sicily earned Hippias 150 minas in a very short period.[74] Isocrates, who follows the lead of the Sophists in the educational importance he assigns to the art of speaking, earned a truly exceptional fee for his trio of encomia (*Evagoras, To Nicocles, Nicocles*) dedicated to the rulers of Cyprus—thirty talents for the first and twenty for the second, if the figures are correct as transmitted.[75]

The practice of instruction for pay came under vigorous attack from defenders of the strict aristocratic tradition of elitist instruction given free of charge. Hence the fierce scorn for the Sophists manifested on more than one occasion by Aristophanes, especially in the *Clouds*,[76] and the harsh criticism of Plato, who accuses them of prostituting knowledge. They are "paid hunters of the young and the wealthy," "merchants of wisdom," "retail sellers" (*Soph.* 231d).

Not all the Sophists were so successful, however. We learn from Plato (*Hipp. mai.* 282b), for example, that the best-paid were Gorgias, Prodicus, and Hippias. As for the evidence of Isocrates, he seems to undercut his own argument when he says (*Antid.* 155ff.) that Gorgias was the richest of the Sophists, having dedicated his entire life to making money out of his profession, yet left barely a thousand staters (twenty thousand drachmas) when he died. Isocrates further points out that Gorgias did not have the burden of maintaining a house, a family, and children when he was alive, and that his continual touring from city to city freed him from having to pay taxes. The argument fails to take into account, of course, that there were countless other ways in which Gorgias could have spent large sums of money for his own private use: for example, on the statue of solid gold just mentioned. Here Isocrates is less concerned with reasoning cogently than with defending himself against the charge of having become rich through the practice of his profession. He had actually been prosecuted in court three years earlier (354), when a certain Megaclides challenged his refusal to assume the financial burden of a trierarchy. Isocrates was convicted and remembered the affair when he came to write, in the *Antidosis*, a general vindication of his career as a rhetorician. The work is cast in the form of a defendant's plea, and insists that, far from having enriched himself through his profession, he had actually done a service to the Athenian state by educating its youth to the practice of civic virtue. Isocrates was certainly correct in denying that his earnings matched those of the most successful Sophists of the past—though the fees he received from the royal family of Salamis in Cyprus were anything but negligible. On the other hand, it is clear that this did not prevent him from being among the twelve hundred richest Athenians, those whose capital was large enough (at least three talents) to put them under the obligation to perform public liturgies.[77]

Isocrates' speech is interesting for the way it reflects not only the immediate facts of the case but a basic and widely encountered phenomenon of social psychology. Once valued above everything else, riches had almost become, as Clause Mossé has shown,[78] a thing to be ashamed of. Or as Isocrates himself incisively puts it (*Antid.* 160), "it has become more dangerous to be a reputed person of wealth than a known criminal." This phenomenon might seem at first sight inconsistent with the consolidation, toward the middle years of the fourth century, of a moderately well-to-do middle class, which tended to bridge the traditional gap between the rich and the poor—that is, those whose livelihood came from manual labor.[79] But it is in the very nature of democracy that rising standards of living among the less well-to-do should accentuate rather than diminish their hostility to the very rich. The latter felt an increased sense of unease, not only because of the precariousness of their own prosperity but also because of the many liturgies imposed upon them by what we would now call the Athenian welfare state.

The period witnessed its share of ideologies preaching the rejection of excessive wealth or even the cultivation of absolute poverty. The ideal becomes one of self-sufficiency (*autárkeia*)—a freedom from bondage to pleasure or passion which vindicates the superiority of wisdom to wealth. The Platonic philosopher Xenocrates, who succeeded Speusippus as head of the Academy, values wealth only to the extent that it contributes to satisfying the essential needs of life. When offered fifty talents by Alexander the Great, he kept only half a talent for himself and gave the rest back, saying that the king had more need for the money, given the enormousness of his expenses.[80] The Cynics took an even more radical stand, preaching the ideal of true poverty—a hard life that rejected all material needs.

These changes are a reflection of the larger transformations, political, economic, social, and cultural, that had taken place in the Greek world in the late fifth and early fourth centuries. A crisis in cultural development had led to the gradual obsolescence of a coherent system based on two apparently different but in fact closely correlated and complementary things: oral communication and the institutional structure of the city-state. The most obvious innovation was the advent of the book and the book trade as primary instruments for the diffusion of knowledge. Their increasing importance went hand in hand with the declining importance of democratic institutions, or of popular assemblies at any rate, in the political life of the city. The act of writing was felt for the first time as a true literary process—as literature *tout court*. Thucydides, Plato, Isocrates, and Aristotle are the vanguard of the new book culture, access to which was only through a process of attentive, solitary reading. And discourse produced with the written page in mind requires, obviously, a transformation in communicative structures and compositional norms—basically, to use Aristotle's formulation, the replacement of an "agonistic" manner with a "graphic" one.[81] Hence the impulse toward the specialization of knowledge and the rise of scientific as well as literary prose. In this way a new culture comes into being, one that could not help but limit the size of its intended audience, no longer identical with an entire community, but confined to those individuals possessed of the necessary skills for deciphering a written text. Both the perspectives and the dimensions of discourse are profoundly changed, its functions as well as its meanings; there is a narrowing in range but, as has been pointed out, a compensating gain in depth.[82]

Poetry's more restricted social horizon leads to elitist isolation and increasingly private modes of expression. It conceives of itself as addressed to a select, learned audience, one capable of understanding subtle and elaborate messages.[83] It is no accident that the poet is sometimes himself a philologian or literary critic. A gulf opens between the poetic experience and the larger problems of life in the human community. The latter become the province of philosophy and historiography.

The different laws under which poetry now operates could not help but involve profound changes in the system of pay and patronage. Once removed from direct and immediate contact with an audience, and hence from the musical accompaniment that was an inseparable part of performance, the poetic text loses its economic value, just as its

FIGURE NINE. Funerary stele. Beginning of the fourth century. Abbey, Grottaferrata.

author loses his ability to obtain commissions once he has ceased to compose for particular civil and religious occasions and to meet the needs of a particular audience or private individual.

The passing of the old system coincides with the opening up of new perspectives for poetic activity in the closing years of the fourth century. The rise of the Hellenistic monarchies and the establishment of royal courts at Alexandria, Pergamum, and Antioch provided a situation that was favorable for the creation of literary circles, such as those of Samos and Cos. And now that the poet is no longer bound by the expectations of an audience, he is able to seek financial support from a private patron or from rulers willing to take care of his material needs in return for court eulogies of an increasingly adulatory character. Hence the rise, on the one hand, of poets such as Asclepiades, Poseidippos of Pella, and Hedylos of Samos, who made up the Samian poetic circle, or of Philetas, who gathered around himself poets and scholars belonging to the local nobility at Cos. These were men with the independent economic means to dedicate themselves to love and banqueting, but also to erudition and to poetry, which were seen both as a form of cultural refinement and as a means for artistic elaboration of one's own personal experience. On the other hand, poets such as Callimachus and Theocritus sought protection and pay for their services at the courts of the sovereigns of Alexandria and Syracuse.

Callimachus complains on more than one occasion of his poverty: his indigence even excludes him from the joys of love.[84] One of his youthful compositions, the *Hymn to Zeus* (c. 280?), is an adroit request to Ptolemy Philadelphus to be allowed to come to his court and enjoy the bounty of his patronage. The least religious of Callimachus's hymns, it takes the form of a direct encomium of the king. The king's own patron is Zeus, who is praised with an account of his birth and youth; but this gives way at the end of the poem to praise of the sovereign: Zeus is the granter of riches and well-being to deserving rulers, as is evident from the good fortune of Ptolemy, who incorporates in himself the royal virtues of success and prosperity. There follows an invocation to Zeus in which Callimachus asks for virtue and wealth (v. 94 *aretèn t'áphenós te*)—that is, excellence and success combined with wealth—the complementary and inseparable gifts that Zeus confers on meritorious rulers (v. 84). This leads immediately into the *explicit* of the poem, which consists of the same prayer, "grant virtue and wealth," in the form (*dídou d'aretén te kaì ólbon*) in which it closed the hymns that were regularly sung as proems to the performances of rhapsodes (cf. *Hymn. Hom.* 15; 20). But the very act of alluding to the rhapsodic formula makes it clear that this time the poet is making the request for himself as well: the specific *areté* for which he asks is ability and effectiveness as a poet and the success to which this leads; only thus will he be able to obtain an adequate reward for his labor. Callimachus here claims the same entitlement to wealth and fortune which was, as we have seen, regularly claimed by poets of the past such as Solon and Sappho. He is still uncertain of his position at the court, and this explains his wish that Zeus stand guard not only over the fortune of the king but also over that of the poet who celebrates him.[85]

It is remarkable that in one of his *Iambs* Callimachus denies that he is a poet who writes for pay: "I do not nourish the mercenary Muse, like the poet of Ceos (Simonides) of the race of Ilicos."[86] This mercenary (*ergátis*) and greedy (*philokerdés*) Muse is the one whom Pindar (*Isthm.* 2, v. 6ff.) equates with the new poetic practice of his own day, alluding implicitly, according to the ancient critics, to Simonides.[87]

Against this unanimous ancient view, evidently shared by Callimachus, some scholars[88] raise the objection that Pindar himself composed on commission, for pay, so that the "greedy" and "mercenary" Muse (*Moîsa . . . philokerdés . . . ergátis*)[89] is unlikely to be a reference to Simonides as the institutor of the custom—contrary to earlier practice—of a stipulation of fees between poet and patron. As has been pointed out, however, Pindar tends to emphasize that his contract does not require that the poet prostitute himself. He does not abandon ideological consistency, "trip himself up on a lie," or abandon the truth. This attitude is completely different from Simonides' uninhibited readiness, if his greed should so require, to go to the point of praising mules as "daughters of storm-footed mares" (fr. 515 P.). Allusion to Simonides is all the more likely in that Simonides himself had already sung the same victory of Xenocrates of Acragas to which Pindar refers in this poem[90]—not, strictly speaking, an epinician but a poetic epistle to Xenocrates' son, Thrasyboulos.[91] In the context of the ode the meaning of the passage is precise and unmistakable: Pindar harks back to the practice of earlier poets to emphasize that he is not sending Thrasyboulos—to whom he was bound by ties of friendship[92]—a eulogy whose fee had been agreed upon in advance. The passage contains a praise of liberality and the good sense of Thrasyboulos: he is wise (v. 12) and will know the meaning of the poet's words.

In what sense are we to take Callimachus's rejection of the mercenary Muse? His was obviously a deliberate choice in favor of "indigent," unremunerative poetry: he was determined to maintain a position of independence which would allow him to write in accordance with the canons of his new poetics. It is significant that on more than one occasion he touches on the theme of poverty and the scorn for wealth in tones that are reminiscent in some ways of the preaching of the Cynics.[93] And one should also note that it is in the *Iambs* that this theme recurs insistently, most particularly in *Iamb* I, with its evocation of the figure of Hipponax.[94] It is thus linked to a type of poetry whose pedigree goes back directly to the seriocomic genre of the *psógos*—the domain of the indigent Muse *par excellence* in the archaic period. Callimachus's entry into the entourage of Ptolemy Philadelphus, an enlightened monarch whose efforts to encourage the arts were at the center of his political program, did not confine him within the narrow limits of purely court poetry. On the contrary, it opened the way to his participation in the organization of culture around the activities of new institutions such as the Museum and the Library. Hence his undertaking to produce that archetypal catalogue of authors and their works (*Pínakes*) which was to become the model for all future literary histories.

Theocritus's story was a similar one. He was Callimachus's contemporary and is on record, like Callimachus, as seeking at the very beginning of his poetic career an entrée into contemporary court circles.[95] The poem (16) called *The Graces or Hieron* is his earliest effort along this line, addressed to the ruler of his own city. Hieron II of Syracuse was a tyrant whose very real power did not prevent him from having to deal with the delicate problem of the double threat to the autonomy of the city posed by Carthage and Rome. As a result he was not readily available for the sort of cultural role taken at a much earlier period by his predecessor in the tyranny, Hieron I. It is no accident that Theocritus's poem combines traditional motifs belonging to both eulogy and exhortation in an evident attempt to move the sovereign to make good use of his wealth by honoring and protecting poets, thereby securing both present and posthumous glory. There is a paradigmatic recall of the early kings of Thessaly, couched in terms reminiscent of Pindar's views on the function of poetry: the greatest gain that their wealth brought those kings was the glory secured for them by the songs of Simonides. And the poem is rich in allusions to those two masters of choral lyric, both of whom had graced the court of Hieron I. The allusions have the further purpose of reminding Hieron II of the remunerative aspects of traditional poetic eulogy. Hence the metaphor of the Graces, who, having failed in their attempt to be properly rewarded for their services, return downcast and barefooted to the poet and sit "in the bottom of his empty money box" (v. 8ff.) with their heads buried between their knees. The metaphor contains a subtle allusion to two anecdotes about Simonides and his views on poetry and pay. One of them is mentioned by the ancient commentators on this passage.[96] Simonides said that he kept two boxes, the one "for favors" (or "for the Graces": *tôn charíton*), the one "for him who pays" (*tôn didónton*). When someone came to him to ask for a favor (*cháris*) he would have both boxes brought. The first was empty; the second was full. The other anecdote, neglected by the commentators, concerns Simonides' caustic definition of poets (*sophoí*) as those who wait in attendance at the doors of the rich.[97] By a skillful art of combination, fully worthy of a Hellenistic poet, Theocritus personifies the "favors" of the Simonidean passage as the "Graces" worshipped by Pindar. But these same Pindaric Graces—a symbol for poetry—then become women soliciting at the doors of a man of wealth—like the *sophoí* in the other Simonidean anecdote.

The answer that the poet was waiting for from Hieron turned out to be negative. But not yet knowing what the reply will be, he ends his poem on a properly dignified note: "If no one invites me I will remain where I am; but I am confident that my Graces will attend me wherever someone does invite me" (v. 106ff.). Whatever his relationship to the ruler, there remains the other bond, firm and lasting, between the poet and the Graces.

Theocritus's poem to Ptolemy (17) has the character of true and proper encomium. In the process of glorifying the power, wealth, generosity, and divine favor enjoyed by the king, he gives a vivid picture of his kingdom: the number and variety of its peoples, the opulence of its rites and festivals, the splendor of its temples. This panorama provides the background for talk of the liberality of the sovereign and the Dionysian contests where munificent awards, commensurate with their talents, are bestowed on poets. The spokesmen of the Muses reply in kind, celebrating the king for his deeds and his generosity. Ptolemy's lavish patronage provided Theocritus with the reception that he had sought in vain from Hieron.

The culture with which we are dealing flourished in the narrow world of courts and coteries, exclusively reserved for an intellectual elite. Alongside it, however, there was another type of culture, not learned or literary in the proper sense of the terms, but what we would now call a *popular* or *mass* culture. It was designed to be accessible to broad sectors of the population and was orally transmitted by reciters, singers (*rhapsoidoí, kitharoidoí, auloidoí*), and itinerant actors (*tragoidoí,*[98] *komoidoí,* etc.). These artists gave public performances and were rewarded with fees and honors in the contests and festivals that were a well-established institution in various Hellenistic cities. Addressing themselves to large audiences, they functioned as a source of information on Panhellenic and local myths—those that provided the traditional beginnings of the history of individual cities. But their repertory was not confined to poetry, whether epic, lyric, or dramatic: history, grammatical exegesis, philosophy, and medicine were also the subject for public lectures, especially in gymnasiums.

This lively and varied itinerant culture, persisting over the course of several centuries, would be completely unknown to us were it not for the extensive documentation provided by a large number of honorary inscriptions. Here we learn the names of poets, poetesses, lecturers, and a host of other performers otherwise largely unknown, and get an idea of the subjects of their renditions and the—at times—quite remarkable honors and fees they received from the communities in which they performed.[99] The dimensions of the phenomenon were shown by a representative collection of texts published in the 1920s by a distinguished student of Greek epigraphy, Margherita Guarducci.[100] The research done since then by Sifakis[101] and by me[102] is focused more specifically on the theater and the new forms of dramatic spectacle, but it provides a comprehensive overview of the various aspects and basic social function of the phenomenon.

The pseudo-Aristotelian *Problems* (19, 15) allow us to see what is new in this theater—a theater of entertainment, basically expressionistic and centered around musical mimesis. It was the mimetic possibilities of the solo aria, now more varied rhythmically and melodically, and more expressive musically, which required the technical abilities of a new type of professional performer, the virtuoso singer of tragic (*tragoidós*) or comic (*komoidós*) parts. The nature of their role is documented in the inscriptions of the Delphic *Soteria*,[103] which concern the organization of companies of artists (*technîtai*) operating in the first half of the third century. The types of dramatic spectacle involved belong to an era in which the theater had acquired forms and functions fundamentally different from those it had originally, in the fifth century. In addition to tragic and comic actors, chorus leaders, and flute players for comedy, the companies were composed of rhapsodes, citharoedes, lyre players, chorus leaders, and flute players for dithyramb. The spectacle (called *epídeixis* or *akróasis*) was a heterogeneous one, performed by virtuosos who usually sang early epic, lyric,[104] or dramatic texts to the accompaniment of lyre or flute. The selection of texts indicates a preference for themes having to do with manners and mores;[105] divine and heroic exploits; or passages of pure entertainment. In 194, for example, the flute player Satyros of Samos presented a selection from the *Bacchae* of Euripides in the stadium at Delphi, performing the part of Dionysus to the accompaniment of the lyre and with the participation of a chorus.[106] Also at Delphi, in 160, two Achaean brothers, Thrason and Socrates of Aegyra, performed ancient texts celebrating the god and the city.[107] At times original epic or lyric texts, usually those having to do with local themes, might be performed. The mixture of original productions with revivals and reelaborations of archaic and classical material is the same as that found in performances of a more specifically dramatic character.[108]

One completely new element was the presence of female poets and child prodigies—figures that were absent from earlier dramatic performances and that only began to reappear in fairly recent times, especially in eighteenth-century Italy, with its multitude of poetic improvisers of both sexes.[109] In or around 218–217 the poetess Aristodama of Smyrna went with her brother to Lamia in Aetolia to give a recitation of epic poetry celebrating the Aetolians and their ancestors.[110] And a boy poet, Ariston of Phocaea, gave a series of performances in the Council Hall and theater of Delos, singing of Apollo and the island's other patron deities.[111] Very few of the numerous texts that contained the libretti for these performances are preserved in the epigraphic tradition. The exceptions are certain *Hymns* and *Paeans* composed for cult purposes.[112] Some of these are accompanied by musical notation: for example, the two Delphic *Paeans,* one by Limenios, the other anonymous.[113]

The Hellenistic period presents the spectacle of a culture with two totally different aspects, moving along distinct but parallel lines— learned poetry, libraries, and erudition on the one hand; and, on the other, festive performances, popular education, and entertainment, which still operate within the oral institutional framework provided by theaters and public competitions. One should not underestimate the importance of the latter type of activity, for there was no other way in which large sectors of society could become familiar, orally, with the poetry of the past—the poetry that elite culture knew mainly through books and libraries. From our point of view the phenomenon was a transient and passing one, linked to the here and now of particular occasions, but it played an essential role in the formation of what we would now call middlebrow culture. Hence the honors, the prestige, and the frequently immense fees enjoyed by the virtuosos of the day, men famous among their contemporaries but now no more than a set of obscure names.*

# PART THREE

# X

# Archilochus & the Levels of Reality

*In a work of literature various levels of reality can meet and still remain sep-*
*arate and distinct—or they can fuse, meld and mingle, bringing their contra-*
*dictions into some sort of harmony, or creating an explosive mixture.*

—*I. Calvino,* Una pietra sopra

The first half of the seventh century, the age of Archilochus, marks a
turning point of major importance in the history of Greek society and
culture. The determining factor here was the widespread phenomenon
of colonization, one of whose focal points, in the Aegean area, was the
island of Thasos.[1] "The misery of the whole Greek world has con-
verged on Thasos"[2] is Archilochus's vivid comment on the character of
and reasons for this event. French excavations conducted on the island
in recent years have unearthed pottery of both Cycladic and Aeolic
manufacture from the first half of the seventh century[3]—a simultaneous presence of different techniques which suggests the Panhellenic
aspect of the colony described by Archilochus. It is clear that what
principally attracted the Greeks were the deposits of gold found not
only on the island itself, where they had been mined by earlier colonists, the Phoenicians, but, most important, on the stretch of Thracian coast which lay opposite it.[4] Archilochus's fellow Parians were the
ones in charge of the colonization, and the poet himself seems to have
held positions of responsibility in the direction of the enterprise. This
is a natural inference from several pieces of evidence which point to
the existence of a hero cult, either at Paros or Thasos, honoring him
not only as a poet but also as a warrior.*

A marble relief (figure 10) discovered in the Archilocheion of Paros
and datable to 520–510 depicts a hero reclining on a *klíne* in the center,
a woman seated on a throne at the left, an ephebe pouring wine
(*oinochóos*) next to a mixing bowl at the right, and, at the top, above

FIGURE TEN.   Relief from Archilocheion. About 510. Museum, Paros.

the human figures, a lyre on the right and a shield on the left.[5] What we have here is thought to come[6] from the hero shrine (*heróion*) of Archilochus, emblematically presented in his double character of warrior and poet. The same iconographic scheme reappears on another marble slab, datable to around 470 and found on the island of Thasos, though without the musical instrument. Symptomatically, the only emblems present are arms—the shield and the helmet.[7] In his native city, Paros, the figure of Archilochus was evidently associated with the arts of both poetry and war, whereas at Thasos there was specific emphasis on his role as hero-colonizer.

It has been correctly pointed out that the biographical testimony is not in itself sufficient to justify assuming that Archilochus was the original oecist for the colony. Still, one should not underestimate the intrinsic significance of the two marble pieces found on Paros and Thasos, which clearly imply the ancient tradition, already accepted in the fifth century, of heroic honors accorded Archilochus. This does not exclude the possibility of earlier Parian settlements in Thasos, which need not have amounted to a real act of colonization, however. We learn from Pausanias, for example,[8] that in the *lesche* of the Cnid-

ians at Delphi Polygnotus of Thasos depicted two youthful figures riding in the bark of Charon: Tellis, the grandfather of Archilochus, and Cleobeia, the girl who was said to have brought the rites of Demeter from Paros to Thasos. The sanctuary of Demeter and Kore—the Thesmophorion—has been discovered outside the walls of the city, along with the altars of its ancestral gods, and this bears out the historicity of a tradition with which Polygnotus, as a native of Thasos, must have been very familiar.[9] There is also the story of an oracle given at Delphi to Telesicles, the father of Archilochus, concerning the foundation of a city on the island of Eeria (Foggy)—that is, Thasos.[10] This need not mean that Telesicles was the oecist of the colony, but it does suggest that, already in the generation before Archilochus, the Parians were beginning to be interested in Thasos.[11]

As for the personal reasons that might have induced Archilochus to leave Paros, the ancient biographical tradition is fairly unanimous and, precisely for that reason, worth serious consideration. Writing at the end of the fifth century, the Athenian intellectual and statesman Critias says that the poet himself, in his verses, gave poverty and the desire for a better life as the reason for his going to Thasos.[12] However, we also know that this poverty was the result of a certain lack of political discretion on his own part, the source, according to the tradition, of no small amount of grief and bitterness. His decision to solve his problems by emigration is even said to have been prompted by an oracle.[13] It is probable that this notice, like the one reported by Critias, also found its way into the biographical tradition from something said in the poet's own works. The same aspect of his life is what Pindar is referring to when, in *Pythian* 2 (v. 54ff.), he speaks of Archilochus fattening himself on hate-filled songs in the midst of the economic straits into which his slanderous tongue had got him. But Pindar broadens his perspective so that the facts of Archilochus's life provide a confirmation of an actual theory linking wealth and poverty to, respectively, praise and slander, seen as the subject matter of radically antithetical poetic genres.[14]

Critias's report bears out something that was already apparent in the Archilochean verse cited at the beginning of the chapter and will continue to be so in the verses considered later. Archilochean poetry was a poetry genuinely concerned with real life and everyday experience. Seen as part of an autobiographical record, direct and concrete, of the poet's relation to his fellow citizens in alternating episodes of party strife and colonial adventure, the famous "poet-soldier" distich takes on added meaning:

> I am the servant of Ares, lord of battle,
> and I know the lovely gift of the Muses.
>
> (fr. 1 T.)

The lines reflect an awareness of one's own ability to guide and control, whether directly or through words. What they assert is not so much a double professional competence as a double role in the life of the community.

Amid the pieces of biographical information contained in the inscription of Mnesiepes (middle of the third century)[15] is a highly instructive account of poetic initiation. When Archilochus was still a boy he was sent to the country by his father, Telesicles, to get a cow to bring to market. The particular spot was in the area known as the *Meadows (Leimônes)*. As he was returning, by the light of the moon, through a region called the *Rocks (Lissídes)*, he encountered a group of women who seemed to be coming back from work in the fields. He went up and started to make fun of them (*skóptein*); they replied with laughter and jokes, asking him if he were going to sell the cow. When he said yes, they promised that they "would pay him due honor," and with that women and cow both disappeared. Where they had been, before his feet, the young man saw a lyre (*lýra*). After his initial surprise, he realized upon reflection that the women he had seen were the Muses and the lyre was their gift.

The episode has an immediate parallel in Hesiod's story, from the proem to the *Theogony*, of having as a boy encountered the Muses while he was pasturing his sheep on Mount Helicon. They addressed him and bade him sing the generations of the blessed gods. It is curious that there is a touch of mockery—even if not the same kind or to the same extent—in Hesiod's verses as well: the Muses begin with the apostrophe "Ye shepherds of the fields, a disgrace and an outrage, you are nothing but bellies" (v. 26).

Both accounts contain a typical initiation episode centering around the apparition of an appropriate divinity, who intervenes, as is usual in archaic theophanies, to bring about a crucial decision in human affairs. But their difference is more important than their similarity. In Hesiod the Muses' function is to contrast true telling of divine genealogies with the false telling that has only the appearance of truth, and their symbolic gift of a scepter is an implicit promise to make the songs with which they inspire the future poet truthful.[16] In the Archilochus inscription, on the other hand, divine solemnity has given way to the playfulness of a group of girls. And their proneness to mockery symbolizes Archilochus's own inclination for a certain type of poetry in which humor, mockery, and bitter attack did in fact play a major role.

The lyre that was given in exchange for the cow[17] also has symbolic importance. It is an allusion to the specifically "lyric" aspect of Archilochus's work, the rhythmical and musical inventiveness that it displayed and that was destined to be highly influential both on contemporary and later poetry. Ancient metricians are unanimous in attesting to the presence in his work of meters typical of citharoedic and choral lyric;[18] and Glaucos of Rhegium (fifth century)[19] reports, in a passage that has not received the attention it deserves, that Thaletas of Gortyn, one of the leading composers of choral lyric in seventh-century Sparta, imitated the melodies of Archilochus, only departing from his model in the use of cretic and paeonic rhythms and meters.

Although the initiation story narrated in the inscription of Mnesiepes may be a tradition of Archilochean or, at any rate, Parian origin,[20] one cannot exclude the possibility that it arose later, the invention of someone familiar with the conventions current in the poet's time. It would then be of a piece with the oracular responses that punctuate

the inscriptional account and even establish specific connections between Archilochus and certain divinities. But whichever of the possible hypotheses is the correct one, it is certain that the initial scene
points to the double character of Archilochean poetry, which consisted both of "lyric" pieces and recited, auloedic iambs. The division
reappears in an epigram of Theocritus (*Ep.* 21), in which the fame of
the poet is linked to his iambs, and his position as the favorite of Apollo and the Muses is attributed to his talent in composing verses (*épea*)
and singing them to lyre accompaniment. In this context *épea* is a
generic term that obviously, given the mention of the lyre, does not
refer to hexameter poetry but to all types of "lyric" verse.[21] It must
have included, of course, citharoedic treatment of heroic themes such
as the adventures of Lynceos, who made war against Danaos, depriving
him of both his kingdom and his daughter (fr. 283 T.), or the episode
involving Achilles' son Pyrrhus and his dance of joy over the death of
Eurypylos (fr. 282 T.). But hexameter epic was sharply distinguished
from citharoedic epic, which is lyric poetry even when it has a narrative theme.[22] Its direct forerunners are the songs of the pre-Homeric
bards such as Demodocus and Phemius, and it is continued in the
work of Stesichorus.[23]

That Archilochus belongs to this tradition is further shown by the
explicit statement of Dio Chrysostomus, who in comparing him with
Stesichorus says that both were imitators of Homer, even though
neither composed in Homer's meter.[24] The references to heroic themes
treated in his work can be explained in various ways without recourse
to the specious hypothesis of Archilochean hexameters. They might
have appeared in citharoedic or choral compositions[25] or even in
iambic ones, where mythic narrative could very easily have played a
paradigmatic role in marking acts and situations as ridiculous or repre-
hensible. The episode involving Heracles, Deianira, and Nessus at the
river Evenos (fr. 280 T.), in which Deianira's willingness to go along
with the wishes of the Centaur surprised ancient critics, may well be
from such a poem. The trimeter "We shall not transport you without
a fee"[26] certainly fits well with the episode of crossing the river.[27] The
Archilochean Deianira, who distracts Heracles with the tale of her
earlier wooing by the river god Achelous so that Nessus can have the
time and the means to make love to her as he ferries her across, could
easily have served as a clever parallel for the duplicity of Neoboule,
who was the constant object of the poet's polemic.[28]

For a proper understanding of the scope and meaning of much of
the surviving work of Archilochus, Aristotle's summary account of

the history of poetic genres remains essential. In that fundamental passage of the *Poetics* he draws a distinction[29] between poetry of invective
(*psógos*) and poetry of praise (*épainos*), understanding the first as mimesis of base actions and the second as mimesis of noble actions. The
first of Aristotle's two categories corresponds essentially to the notion
of the seriocomic as it has been developed in modern theories of the
literary text. Its general character and the characteristic role it assigns
to the device of the *persona loquens* have already been discussed.[30]

The recently published Cologne papyrus,[31] which contains the
longest fragment of Archilochus presently available to us, provides one
of the most representative examples of the poet's seriocomic technique:

> . . .
> "but if you are too eager to wait,
>   we have here with us
>   a lovely, tender girl,                                5
> longing for marriage and beautiful—
>   no one, I think, will deny it—
>   take her for your wife."
> She said this, and I replied,
>   "Daughter of the wise and noble                 10
>   Amphimedó,
> whose body the moist earth holds in its bosom,
>   many are the joys
>   which the goddess grants to young men
> other than the marriage bed: one of those will suffice.     15
>   We shall give calm thought to the matter
>   when . . .
> you and I with the help of the god.
>   I shall do as you say,
>   many . . .                                      20
> from beneath the frieze and the doors . . .
>   do not refuse me, my darling,
>   I shall proceed to the flowering garden.
> Be assured then of this: someone else can
>   marry Neoboule for all I care;                  25
>   she is spent and done with already,
> and her virgin's bloom is gone
>   and the grace that once was hers;
>   she could never have enough of love:
> madwoman—she has let the full measure       30

of her youth be taken;
to hell with her—perish the thought
that I through marrying such a wife
    should be a laughingstock for my neighbors.
    You are the one I would marry,                                    35
for you are neither faithless nor deceitful,
    whereas she is full of wiles
    and a weaver of tricks;
I fear lest I beget in my haste
    a blind and premature brood,                                     40
    like the proverbial bitch."
All this I said, and taking hold of the girl
    I laid her down amid the blossoming flowers
    and wrapped her in my soft
cloak, putting my arms around her neck.                              45
    She had ceased (fleeing me?)
    trembling like a fawn,
and I stroked her breast softly
    where the fresh skin—
    youth's enchantment—was laid bare.                              50
Fondling the whole of her lovely body
    I discharged my white seed,
    just touching her tawny hair.[32]

The dialogue, presented in the usual narrative manner of Homeric epos, probably takes place in a temple precinct,[33] which is the abode of a community of girls. Critics have not, in general, emphasized this fact sufficiently, though it is very important for understanding the course of the action. Because the beginning of the poem is missing, we cannot reconstruct the narrative in detail, but its essential elements are clear. The protagonists are a girl, referred to by her interlocutor as "Daughter of the wise and noble Amphimedó" (v. 10ff.), and a man who has gone to the sanctuary to satisfy an immediate sexual urge. His request is taken as an indication of a desire to find a wife (vv. 3–5), and it is suggested that he marry a certain tender young girl: her beauty is faultless (v. 6ff.). But the young man refuses, making clear what he really wants, which is satisfaction of his sexual desires in a way other than the usual one of marriage:

many are the joys
which the goddess grants to young men
other than the marriage bed: one of those will suffice.[34]

But the rejection of marriage is not final. In reality the young man merely seeks to postpone that important decision; all he wants from the girl in the meantime is sexual satisfaction. There is one thing he wishes to make perfectly clear immediately, however: he will never marry the person suggested to him, who is Neoboule (v. 25), evidently the sister of his interlocutor. The reason given is the immorality of the girl, whose charms are also withered and past their prime (v. 26ff.): to marry her would be to risk having blind offspring—like the hasty bitch (v. 40ff.).

The conversation ends; and the young man in his eagerness seizes the girl, takes her to the flowering meadow of the sanctuary, lays her down on the grass, and fondles and caresses her until he has an orgasm. The scene is the same "flowering garden" where the young man had suggested taking the girl earlier (vv. 21-23).

The episode belongs to the world of the everyday—a typical encounter between a young man and a young girl near a sanctuary, one of the few places where it was possible, given the constraints of Greek society, for affairs, initial overtures between adolescents, and proposals of marriage to occur. This sort of scene recurs in Greek romances from the *Ephesian Tales* of Xenophon down to the *Ethiopica* of Heliodorus, as it does in Musaeus's epyllion on Hero and Leander, not to mention the myths and rituals, attested even in earliest times, to which scholarship has rightly drawn attention.[35]

It seems obvious that in this instance the *persona loquens* is the poet himself, whose affair, and subsequent break, with Neoboule is well documented in the biographical tradition and in a number of fragments. The situation presented in the poem should thus be linked to typical happenings in the poet's own life; it is not pure literary creation without any specific reference to reality. Such a procedure would not be in keeping with the basic thought configurations encountered in seventh-century poetry. This is not equivalent to assuming that every detail in the poet's narrative is a description of what actually occurred. The important thing to emphasize is that the episode corresponds to something real in the poet's biography, even if reality has been modified by a certain talent for inventing slander—probably, as we shall see, with a specific point and specific ends in mind. The slander had the appearance of truth, of course: this was what made it credible.

In an epigram of the Hellenistic poet Dioscourides,[36] Neoboule and her sister, the two daughters of Lycambes, insist that they never disgraced their own good name, or their father, or the island of Paros; Archilochus, a man whom they had never met either in the streets or in the sanctuary of Hera, was responsible for the slander against them. If they had been unchaste, Archilochus would never have aspired to marry them and have them bear his children—an obvious reference to our poem and its talk of the hasty bitch and blind offspring. But Dioscourides' epigram contains additional material that is useful in determining the context of the episode. The sanctuary in which the action takes place is that of Hera, and the girls were evidently her devotees.

Probably composed for a circle of friends (*phíloi*)—the usual audience at a symposium or *kômos*—the poem derives its narrative structure from what may be called the constants of seriocomic form and content. Such are the playful misunderstanding in the initial dialogue between the girl and the young man; the sudden scurrilous attack on Neoboule (cf. Dioscourides' reference to *óneidos*), which also flatters the girl addressed by favorably contrasting her morals with those of her sister; and the unexpected turn of events in the concluding seduction. The language is clearly Archilochean in its manner: realistic but metaphorical, categorical and aggressive but not without a certain delicacy in its tone and imagery, narrative and dramatic at the same time—a tissue of epicisms and neologisms[37] whose seriocomic character is appropriately reflected, at the formal level, in the combination of dactylic (*hemíepes*) and iambic (dimeter) which constitutes the second part of the epodic verse structure.

The individuality of the poem stems partly from the identification of its *persona loquens* with the poet himself, who must achieve his purpose by contriving an attack on Lycambes' daughter Neoboule in the course of a conversation with her sister. The normal *psógos* pattern as formulated by Aristotle—partially on the basis of Archilochean examples—involved the attribution of such attacks to a third person, whether real or invented. This is exactly the situation with the carpenter Charon, who delivers a critique of the power and riches of Gyges (fr. 22 T.), or with the father, perhaps Lycambes himself, who expresses his outrage at the unexpected and incredible behavior of his daughter (fr. 114 T.). The passage just examined deviates from the norm, in keeping with the requirements of the situation, but does not reject the indirect method entirely. There is indirect praise for the dead mother of both girls and for the sister who is being addressed. The latter's virtues are

relative—underlined by comparison with the other sister and the litotes "you are neither faithless nor deceitful." Mention of them has the
effect of setting one sister against the other and, by an appeal to her
vanity, achieving the double goal of minimizing her indignation on
Neoboule's account and predisposing her for the amorous overtures to
follow. It is the character of the situation which allows the poet to attack his victim in the very presence of one of the victim's closest
relatives.

The problem of how to compose a piece of *psógos* obviously admits
of various solutions. The most common was to put the speech of censure into the mouth of a third person and to have it delivered before
an audience of *phíloi*, in the absence of the person being censured; but
there were particular situations in which another technique might be
more effective. If a reproach was spoken as a joke, it could easily be
directed at someone present at the symposium, like Archilochus's
good-humored address to Charilaos, like the son of Erasmon, dearest
of his *phíloi*. "I want to tell you," he says, "something funny. You'll
enjoy hearing about it" (fr. 162 T.). And the funny thing probably
turned out to be *polyphagía*, his dearest friend's voracious appetite.[38]
Even a polemic inspired by real bitterness might take the form of
direct, immediate address to someone present, with recourse, if need
be, to the usual expedient of the *persona loquens*. This is the situation
that Aristotle appropriately illustrates from Sophocles' *Antigone*. The
series of objections (v. 683ff.) which Haemon raises on Antigone's behalf in addressing his father, Creon, are presented, not as his own
views, but as what everybody in the city is saying.

Whether the shape of the narrative in the Cologne epode owes more
to the nature of the actual events recounted or to the functioning of
the canons of iambic composition[39] is a question that can only be dealt
with on the basis of certain very definite pieces of information whose
relevance to the interpretation of the poem has not hitherto been
noticed.

We have seen that Dioscourides' epigram touches upon the subject
of the epode at a whole series of points. If the place of the encounter
is in fact a temple, as is fairly clear in light of the reference to architrave
and doors, it is certainly the temple of Hera—the same one to which
the girls refer in the verses of Dioscourides. In which case the goddess
who, according to the protagonist, allows many and varied pleasures
beyond those of the marriage bed, is not, as has seemed obvious up to
now, Aphrodite, but rather Hera, the goddess who presides over the
legitimacy of marriage. Archaeological excavations as well as Dioscour-

ides' epigram seem to confirm the presence of a sanctuary dedicated to her on Paros.[40] The daughters of Lycambes, like their mother as well, whose memory is so solemnly invoked in the poem, must have been ministrants in her cult—a cult with which, presumably, Lycambes' entire family had close connections. Significantly, Hera is not a goddess mentioned elsewhere in Archilochus's work, and she was not even among those honored in the island's Archilocheion.

Such a failure to participate in the cult of Hera would be in harmony with the absence of a sanctuary, or even so much as a single altar, dedicated to her on Thasos, an island in whose colonization the family of Archilochus had played a decisive role (see above).[41] All this makes it quite clear that the erotic act described in the poem must have been presented as an illicit one—performed in a precinct sacred to the goddess of lawful marriage and involving the seduction of one of her priestesses. But whereas for Archilochus the act was in some sense a transgression, for the girl it was nothing less than a sacrilegious betrayal of her duties and sufficient to bring her entire family into disgrace.

In the light of these considerations the language of Dioscourides' epigram becomes fully understandable: the emphasis on the dishonor that the "outrageous insults" (v. 5) of Archilochus brought not only on the girls but also on their parents, their family, and the entire island of Paros and, in conjunction with it, the specific reference to holy places: "We swear by the gods and all that is sacred," the daughters of Lycambes say, "that we never saw Archilochus in Hera's holy precinct or even in the streets"—streets (*agyiaí*) being especially associated with festive and religious celebrations.[42]

A passage in the Mnesiepes inscription,[43] where it is said that the father of Archilochus, along with Lycambes, was sent by the city as an official envoy (*theoprópos*) to consult the Delphic oracle, suggests that there was once harmony and collaboration between the two families. The subsequent falling out can only be understood through the information supplied by another epode, the famous one that opens with a direct address to Lycambes:

> Father Lycambes, what can you have been thinking of?
> Who has addled your wits,
> which once were whole and sound? Now you are a great cause
> for laughter throughout the city.
>
> (fr. 166 T.)

The poet is probably speaking in his own person and mounting a direct attack—justified in this case by the state of open hostilities between him and Lycambes. The two had once been friends, to the point of concluding a sworn agreement complete with a betrothal to Lycambes' daughter,[44] subsequently broken off by the father:

> You went back on your solemn oath,
> the bread and the salt we shared together.
>
> (fr. 179 T.)

Lycambes' behavior, laughable and contemptible at the same time (fr. 166, 3ff. T.), was then illustrated by an animal fable—the story of the fox and the eagle. They also had been joined by a pact of mutual friendship (fr. 168 T.), subsequently broken by the eagle, who was justly punished for his betrayal. The fox herself was the one who called on Zeus to bring the offender to justice:

> Oh Zeus, father Zeus, yours is the dominion of heaven,
> you behold men's works,
> impious and pious, and the outrageous and just acts
> which animals do are your concern.
>
> (fr. 174 T.)

The evidence is too scanty to allow us to see all the ins and outs of the episode. But there are immediate points of parallel between the oath that cemented the alliance and the similar oath that, at a later date, was to provide Alcaeus with grounds for assailing the faithless, perjured Pittacus (fr. 129 V.). The marriage contract was merely a necessary corollary to a larger agreement that was part of the common ties created by the fellowship of the symposium and the political club. The Cologne epode takes its place within the evolving dynamics of the episode as an immediate sequel to the breakup of the alliance. It is a polemical message that cleverly combines outrage with irony, ridicule, and possibly slander as well. And at this point the question of whether or not the seduction inside the temple precincts actually occurred ceases to be relevant for the interpretation of the text.

Abuse and invective, whether based on fact or invention, are a way of life and a way of art for Archilochus, the outgrowth of an ethic of reprisal and retaliation that he formulates explicitly on more than one occasion:

I know how to be a friend to him who is a friend to me,
but to hate and abuse my enemy.*

(fr. 54, 14ff. T.)

Or:


I know one thing only, a crucial thing,
to do terrible wrong in return to him who wrongs me.

(fr. 104 T.)

It is *díke* once again—the archaic notion of justice as a norm of equilibrium and reciprocity pervading all manifestations of human society and the natural universe, down to and including the most complex cultural developments encountered in the fifth and fourth centuries.

It is no wonder that Archilochus, basing his career on these assumptions, became renowned in later tradition as the incarnation of *psógos*. Upon reading Plato's *Gorgias*, the famous Sophist is said to have exclaimed, "How well Plato knows the art of producing iambs (*iambízein*)";[45] and the reference to Archilochus becomes explicit in Gorgias's judgment on Plato as reported by the biographer Hermippus: "What a handsome new Archilochus Athens has produced."[46] Besides pinpointing Archilochus as the exemplary figure in the tradition of poetic *psógos*, Gorgias's sarcastic comment strikingly anticipates, by many centuries, M. Bakhtin's view[47] of the Platonic dialogue as one of the highest manifestations of the seriocomic mode. Gorgias's attitude is emblematic, as is the expression "Thasian seasoning" used by the comic poet Cratinus in speaking of the human and poetic personality of Archilochus.[48]

Dioscourides' use of the verb *phlýo* in reference to Archilochus's spiteful outpourings against Lycambes underlines his attitude toward unrestrained abusiveness in language, and it may well be intended to recall the political *phlyaría* of which our sources speak.[49] One may well wonder, therefore, whether there were not sociopolitical motives and undercurrents, connected either with religious practices or the conduct of public duties, in the feud between the families of Archilochus and Lycambes.[50] The phrase "Lycambean magistracy," which Cratinus uses in criticizing an Athenian polemarch in his comedy *The Laws*, makes it clear that Lycambes was an officeholder, thereby exposing himself to the assaults of Archilochus.[51]

The repeated attacks on the daughters of Lycambes, documented in most striking fashion by the Cologne epode, are typical of a sort of conflict whose incidence was much more widespread, though its character, unfortunately, can no longer be known in any detail. A related incident, recounted by Aristotle in his work *On Constitutions* (fr. 551 Rose), is that which, toward the middle of the next century, brought Lygdamis to power as tyrant of Naxos. Before then the island had been ruled, not altogether harmoniously, by an oligarchy. The occasion that caused its fall was a quarrel over food prices. The local farmers and fishermen were in the habit of telling anyone who tried to bargain with them that, rather than lower their prices, they would prefer to give their products to Telestagoras (a nobleman of the day who lived in the country and was well liked by the populace). Exasperated at always hearing the same reply, a group of city youths, evidently from oligarchical families, decided to pay a visit to Telestagoras on the pretext of celebrating a *kômos*. He gave them a friendly welcome, expecting to hear an encomium. But the young men produced a *psógos* instead, heaping abuse on Telestagoras and his young daughters, who were of an age to marry. Their insults cannot have been too different from what we read in Archilochus, and the incident sparked the popular revolt that put Lygdamis in power.

Aristotle's account shows in exemplary fashion that slanderous attacks on the reputation of noblemen's daughters did occur during the course of Greek *kômoi* and might often have had political implications. And it cannot help but dissipate some of the cloud of uncertainty that surrounds the presence of the daughters of Lycambes in so much of Archilochus's poetry. At the same time, the Naxos episode bears out the truth of our earlier generalization: direct abuse delivered in the presence of the person attacked was the exception rather than the rule. It could too easily be the prelude to dangerous reactions, even to the point of endangering the stability of a political system. Archilochus's *psógos* was not disruptive of public order in Paros to the same degree, but its results for the two parties to the feud were certainly catastrophic. Lycambes' family had been fatally compromised in both its civic and religious identity, and the suicide, by hanging, of the father and his two daughters remained with good reason a cause célèbre throughout antiquity. But Archilochus's completely uninhibited practice of the art of defamation—a matter on which the ancient tradition is unanimous—ultimately brought discredit on him as well, both with his fellow islanders and with posterity. This was the source of the loss of standing which put him in economic difficulties—difficulties that made it necessary for him to emigrate to Thasos and of which he himself, according to Critias (Test. 46 T.), spoke in his poetry. In the light of all this, it is even easier to believe the report preserved by the philosopher Oinomaos, according to which Archilochus was reduced to poverty because of the unrestrained character of his verbal attacks on political opponents.[52]

The checkered character of the poet's career and later reputation is remarkable, though not unique or completely unparalleled by the changing fortunes of other famous names in human history. There is a sharp dichotomy of traditions—one that recognizes the greatness of his poetry while finding the slanderous, ill-tempered character of its subject matter morally objectionable; and another, indigenous to his native island, that glorifies him to the point of making him a local hero to whom cult honors are paid. This position among his fellow citizens was one that he recovered, following a brief period of adversity, by successfully carrying on the colonization of Thasos which his family had already begun. His connection with the cult of Demeter, which his grandfather, Tellis, had introduced into Thasos, may provide a partial explanation for the iconoclastic, anticonformist aspects of his iambic poetry. For the "iambic" mode is already, through the familiar figure of Iambe, a part of the traditional version of the Demeter myth.[53]

The poetic activities of Archilochus as described thus far are sharply distinguished from the traditional ones associated either with the Homeric bard, who remains attached to the royal court where he is protected and maintained, or with the itinerant rhapsode who derives his income from the various audiences whom he entertains with stories of heroic deeds. His role in the community is most closely paralleled by that of his contemporaries Terpander and Thaletas, whose poetry allowed them to fulfill an important function as mediators in the political and social life of Sparta. There is one very clear difference, however. Whereas Terpander and Thaletas were called in to settle disputes in their specific capacity as professional poets,[54] Archilochus was totally immersed in political events and made poetry his chosen instrument for representing and commenting upon a world in which he participated as a protagonist. This is the context that determines the character of most of his surviving work, whether it is concerned with the internal politics of the island of Paros or, on a different but related plane, with the dramatic colonial venture on Thasos. A specific tone of epic history can be detected in all the fragments that seem to belong to this second level in the poet's work, and they represent a new departure in the history of archaic literature.[55] This new epic no longer deals with mythical wars fought in the remote past but with armed skirmishes between Greek settlers and the indigenous populations (largely

Thracian) whom they encountered, and with their various other adventures on land and sea. The proper meter for it is no longer the
hexameter, but the two-line elegiac strophe, or the tetrameter, with its
insistent, pressing trochaic rhythm.[56] Some fragments allude to particular episodes or details of everyday human behavior in such a way that
they almost sound like a war diary, where the occasional, unheroic
aspects of the soldier's life are described along with everything else.
Others are brief, humorous jottings—another outlet for the poet's seriocomic vocation: he may describe himself stretched out on the deck of
a ship, eating his bread and drinking the good wine of Ismaros;[57] or tell
how he was forced, against his will, to abandon his shield beside a bush
as he fled from the scene of battle (fr. 8 T.); or, again, how the enemy
dead add up to seven and the number of their slayers to a thousand (97
T.). And alongside such touches of humor there are moments when
the narrative is intensely emotional—in keeping with the dramatic
character of the events being related.

Archilochus's adoption of the elegiac meter as a vehicle for narrating
recent or contemporary events places him at the point of confluence
between seventh-century Spartan and Ionian traditions. Tyrtaeus at
Sparta and Callinus at Ephesus composed elegies of exhortation in
which evocations of the past achievements of their cities were included
by way of inspiration and example. At a later date Mimnermus's elegiacs narrated at length the history of Smyrna, beginning with its
foundation.[58] But Archilochus did not confine such subject matter to
elegiacs; he extended it to the trochaic tetrameter as well, setting up a
type of presentation which was historical and exhortatory by turns.
His direct heir in the use of this mode was Solon—witness the tetrameters to Phocos, in which the poet's own defense is linked to scornful
attacks on his fellow citizens for their behavior.[59] The tetrameter apostrophe in fr. 86 T., "You wretched men of this city, try to understand
my words," is strikingly paralleled in the passages of Solonian invective
against the political foolishness of the Athenians: the verse to Phocos
just cited and those verses found in the elegy on the coming to power
of Pisistratus (fr. 15 Gent.-Pr.).

It has become a commonplace of criticism to suggest that in the
poetry of Archilochus human individuality has been discovered and
given a proper mode of expression for the first time in the history of
Greece or, for that matter, of the West.[60] Methodologically, however,
it would be better to speak in terms of a functional opposition between the narrative genre of heroic epic and the "pragmatic" genre
represented by the compound of personal, political, and historical ele-

ments which is Archilochean poetry. This formulation also permits easy explanation of the absence of the traditional pattern by which the Muse speaks through the voice of the poet, a pattern correlated with the special role played in bardic and rhapsodic performance by the divine gift of memory and impersonal evocation of the mythic past. Archilochus's emphasis on his own words (*rhémata*) has been taken as a sign of an emerging notion of individual personality,[61] but it is better explained in terms of the allocutory character of his poetry. What is involved is an institutional difference between different types of discourse. Recognition of this fact is already implicit in Giorgio Pasquali's only apparently paradoxical observation[62] that poets such as Archilochus, Callinus, and Tyrtaeus do not share Homer's illocutory mode, but rather transfer into a different meter the speeches of Homer's heroes, men immersed in the practical world of action. Hence the continuity (and discontinuity) between Archilochean and epic diction: formulaic technique is the technique of lexical and semantic adaptation to fit the perpetually changing requirements of the referents at hand. It is a technique of variation, but variation that does not upset the basic syntactic structures handed down by tradition.[63]

A typical piece of Archilochean variational technique is the beast fable. As in Hesiod, it functions as a source of examples; but it now has the structural form of an agon,[64] and may even proceed in the manner of a lively human conversation. Its use in the polemical attacks on Lycambes has already been noted. Some critics have gone further and seen Archilochus as first and foremost an author of fables,[65] but this is surely to overvalue the importance of what is only one among a number of expressive techniques. They are, moreover, techniques encountered wherever there is seriocomic language and realistic representation of life and human experience.

# XI

. . .

# The Ship of State
## *Allegory & Its Workings*

*To attribute a cognitive function to metaphor is not to lay down conditions for its truth content. . . . It is obvious that speaking metaphorically is, literally, lying—and everyone is aware of the fact. But this problem is connected to the larger one of the fundamental modalities of* pretending—*how one merely pretends to make assertions and still wishes seriously to assert the truth of something over and above what is literally true.*

*—U. Eco, s.v. "Metafora,"* Enciclopedia Einaudi

The poetry of Alcaeus, born out of and for action, bears the unmistakable marks of participation—lively, direct, immediate—in the events that inspired it. It mirrors the varied, turbulent life of an archaic political club deeply committed to the contest for power in the city of Mytilene in the years around 600. The stylistic and moral unity it displays is the unity of a world perceived from a single perspective, a world in which realism is blended with idealism, but an idealism strictly limited by the political program of the poet's own faction.[1]

If we were to ask what was the highest good recognized by this poetry directed toward a narrow circle of aristocrats bound together by their oath of loyalty, we would have to reply, with Alcaeus, that the highest good was the genuine sincerity of a "friend"—sincerity, that is, of ethical and political commitment, and of unambiguous dedication to action. Within the fraternity of the symposium, the great spyglass or "speculum" of the friend's sincerity and loyalty is wine.[2]

The link between action and expression, both on a physical and psychological level, is an indispensable element in the coherence of Alcaean poetry: the poet and the political partisan pursue one and the same path, which is also one and the same with that of the confraternity of the "Alcaeans" in their pursuit of power. Whatever procedures—narrative, didactic, figurative—are being used for the implementation of the poet's discourse, there is always complete reciprocity of mood and emotion with the audience and the subject matter—the dramatic events of civil war. Dionysius of Halicarnassus was exactly on target when he noted that one has only to strip the poems of Alcaeus of their meter in order to have a political oration.[3]

Allegory—the "extended metaphor" of the ancients[4]—was a means of signifying ideas or events through images selected from a different, independent area of existence on the basis of some analogical relationship between the two semantic levels.[5] It provided Alcaeus with a symbolic projection for a profound crisis in the affairs of his city and his party, one in which the insistent immediacy and "truth" of the allegorical representations allow a feeling for the dramatic character of events to emerge—as if the poet were presenting them to his audience at the very moment of actually living them. Heraclitus says as much in his *Homeric Allegories* (5, 5) when he discusses the famous poem about a ship in a storm.[6] While citing the text as an allegorical depiction of the city of Mitylene threatened by a conspiracy to make Myrsilos tyrant, he admits that the description of the travails of the ship sounds like a reevocation of things that the poet and his friends actually experienced at sea. This is why the traditional interpretation of the poem has aroused skepticism in some modern scholars, skepticism that still persists and extends to several fragments which, there is reason to believe, come from poems of the same type.[7] Heraclitus himself provides evidence for the frequency of sea images and their symbolic meaning.[8] It is the poet's habit, he says, "to compare the disastrous consequences of tyranny to storms at sea." And a papyrus commentary to Alcaeus supports Heraclitus's allegorical interpretation of the particular poem in question and its central image.[9] The reference is to the conspiracy of Myrsilos, a conspiracy that took place after he had returned from exile on a boat supplied for the occasion by a certain Mnamon:[10]

I do not understand the direction of the winds,
one wave rolls in from this side
and another from that, and we are in between,
carried along with the dark ship                                    4

and worn down by the violent storm;
bilge fills the mast box,
you can see right through the sail,
a rag furrowed with great rips,                                      8

the shrouds give way, the steering paddles
. . .
. . .                              tied
to their sheets, may the two feet (of the sail) hold fast.          12

only this can save me as well;
the cargo is destroyed, one part
set adrift, the other (?) . . .[11]

Interpreted according to this symbolic key, the storm that assaults the ship becomes an overall emblem for the civil discord that wracks the city of Mitylene. If allegory is an extended metaphor—or metaphorical narrative—it is obvious that every element must convey a piece of information; and comprehensibility is a prerequisite for credibility within the circle of *hetaîroi*. The winds, the waves, the bilge water, the shrouds, the rudders, the sheets, the ship's cargo are all sensory images through which the audience is made to perceive the extreme gravity of a situation, the ferociousness of an encounter that it will be difficult to survive.

The wave figures the movement and shouting of warriors: in the *Iliad* (15, 381ff.) the Trojans hurling themselves against the wall are like a vast wave (*méga kŷma*) hurling itself against the side of a boat (*neòs hypèr toíchon*); in Aeschylus's *Seven against Thebes*[12] the messenger urges that the city be defended "before Ares releases his blasts, for the land wave (*kŷma*) of the army is roaring." The chorus of maidens uses the same image, this time modeled directly on Alcaeus, to describe the disaster of war that is descending on the Thebans (v. 758ff.): "a sea of evils drives on the waves (of warriors); one breaks, another raises its triple crest and roars about the city's stern."

The water that penetrates into the bilge (*ántlos*) of the ship also refers to the wave of armed warriors bursting into the city: in the *Seven against Thebes* (v. 795ff.) the messenger exultingly tells the chorus that their city has now escaped the yoke of slavery. It enjoys calm weather and "does not take in bilge water (*ántlos*) from the many blows of the waves"; that is, their buffeting opened no cracks in the hold and, at a nonmetaphorical level, the assault of the enemies failed to breach the walls.

The steering paddles (v. 9 *oéia*) and the sail (v. 7 *laîphos*) are further aspects of the ship/city symbolism: in the *Seven against Thebes* (v. 3) the guardian of the commonwealth is the one who guides the rudder (*oíaka*) on the poop deck of the city. In the *Rhesus* of Euripides (v.

323ff.) the violence and disasters of war are expressed by the image of Ares blowing furiously and rending the sails of the city of Troy.

Even in the case of the much-discussed phrase "tied to their sheets, may the two feet (of the sail) hold fast," it is hard to see how the poet could be stepping outside the allegory and describing the actual situation of sailors in a storm compelled to keep their feet firmly tied to the sheets—a strange way to avoid being swept overboard by the waves.[13] What a sailor can do in such circumstances is described in a similar piece of allegorical description from an anonymous comedy: grab hold of the ropes and pull hard on the corners or "feet" (*pódas*) of the sail.[14] If the description is metaphorical, it is obvious that what I. A. Richards would call the "tenor" is not the sailors in danger of being swept overboard but the members of Alcaeus's faction in danger of being swept away by their rivals. The word *feet* has the double function of denoting the two lower corners of the sail which are tautened or loosened by ropes[15] and, figuratively, as has been shown through a comparison with Tyrtaeus, the feet of the warrior.[16] The Tyrtaean description of the soldier "standing steady on his legs" who must hold firm (*menéto*) in battle, "with both feet planted solidly on the ground," presents the same image and the same nexus of ideas as does Alcaeus's metaphor.[17] The lower extremities, or "feet," of both sail and combatant are the tangible and visible means for all-out resistance to the fury of wind and waves or, figuratively, to the spread of civil war and, in particular, the attacks from the opposing faction which will come with Myrsilos's return. It is in them that Alcaeus places his hopes for safety. The appropriateness of the term *save* (*sóizein*) to both nautical and political contexts is well documented.[18] One immediate parallel is found in the Theognidean version of the ship-of-state theme (v. 671ff.):

> Now, with our white sails lowered, we are adrift
>     beyond the sea of Melos, in the dark night;
> they are unwilling to bail out the hold; the sea washes over
>     both gunwales; safety is a slim hope.
> They are the ones responsible; the skilled helmsman          675
>     who kept careful watch has been removed;
> they are seizing the cargo; discipline is dead;
>     there is no more of fair and equal sharing;*
> stevedores are in command: bad men over good;
>     I fear that the waves will engulf the ship.          680

What we have here might be called an "impure" allegory: the ship/ city analogy is made explicit through the brief reference to the members of the emerging class (*kakoí*) who have seized power from the nobles (*agathoí*). But the allegory is not so impure as to be clear to just any audience. As the poet's concluding observation shows, only the person familiar with his symbolic language will be able to understand it:

> these dark, riddling words of mine are for noblemen:
> if a man has the key, he will know also the ill (they portend).[19]

The allegory turns on certain structural elements identical to those found in Alcaeus:[20] the ship is adrift (v. 671 *pherómestha*) on a stormy sea; the waves are pouring over its sides;[21] the crew refuses to bail out the hold[22] and plunders the cargo; rescue is impossible. There is a veritable insurrection in the ship/city on the part of the bad (*kakoí*)— the riffraff—against the men of worth (*agathoí*)—the nobles—who have scant chance of saving themselves. The insurrection of the *kakoí* is envisaged as a series of acts of insubordination: (1) elimination of the helmsman (i.e., the governing class);[23] (2) pillaging of the cargo (i.e., the wealth of the city);[24] and (3) undermining of the discipline (*kósmos*) of the ship (i.e., of the equilibrium of powers and equitable division of goods [ship's cargo] on which the oligarchy's position rested).[25]

*Chrémata* is a general word designating possessions, goods, and money as well,[26] or, on a literal level, the merchandise that constitutes the cargo of the ship. The use is well documented in epic,[27] though *phortíon*, a word found in another Alcaean allegory,[28] would have been the more proper term.[29] The idea of cargo becomes explicit with the later reference to stevedores (*phortegoí*), the lowest element in the crew. The pejorative character of the word is underlined: "stevedores are in command: bad men over good."[30]

We are now able to see the ultimate referent, in Alcaeus's ship-of-state poem, of the image of the ship's cargo laid waste by the waves: it is the material substance, the goods and possessions of the poet's faction.

Once the historical circumstances surrounding its delivery are taken into consideration, the informative message conveyed by Alcaeus's allegory becomes clear. It is a description, orally transmitted to his companions at arms, of an imminent danger requiring all-out resistance if they are to survive. The visual images are charged with emotional and moral overtones, which deepen the meaning of the poet's words as he moves from the "I" perspective with which he begins to a "we" per-

Comparative Table

| | Alc. 208a Voigt | Alc. 6 Voigt | Alc. 73 Voigt | Alc. 249 Voigt |
|---|---|---|---|---|
| v. | 1 ἀσυν(ν)έτημμι<br>τὼν ἀνέμων<br>στάσιν | | | 11 ἄν]εμος φέρ[ |
| v. | 2 κῦμα κυλίνδεται | 1 sg. τόδ᾽αὖτε κῦμα<br>τὼ προτέρω ᾽νέμω<br>στείχει | 3 κύματι πλάγεισ[αν | |
| v. | 4 νᾶϊ φορήμεθα<br>σὺν μελαίνᾳ | | | 3 νᾶα φ[ερ]έσδυγον |
| v. | 5 χείμωνι μόχθεντες<br>μεγάλῳ | | 4 ὄμβρῳ μάχεσθαι | |
| v. | 6 πὲρ μὲν γὰρ<br>ἄντλος ἰστοπέδαν<br>ἔχει | 2 sg. παρέξει δ᾽ἄμμι<br>πόνον πόλυν<br>ἄντλην, ἐπεί κε<br>νᾶος ἔμβᾳ | | |
| v. | 7 λαῖφος δὲ πὰν<br>ζάδηλον | | | |
| v. | 12 sg. πόδες<br>ἀμφότεροι<br>μένο[ιεν ἐν<br>βιμβλίδεσσι | 12 νῦν τις ἄνηρ<br>δόκιμος γε[νέσθω | | |
| v. | 13 sg. τοῦτό με καὶ<br>σ[άοι μόνον | | | |
| v. | 14 sg. τα δ᾽ἄχματ᾽<br>ἐκπεπ[α]τάχμενα<br>. . ]μεν φ[ό]ρηντ᾽<br>ἔπερθα | | 1 πὰν φόρτι[ο]ν | |
| v. | | 8 ἐς δ᾽ἔχυρον λιμένα<br>δρό[μωμεν | | |
| v. | | 9 sg. καὶ μή τιν᾽<br>ὄκνος μόλθ[ακος<br>λάβῃ | | |
| v. | | 13 sg. καὶ μὴ<br>καταισχύνωμεν<br>[ἀνανδρίᾳ ἔσλοις<br>τόκηας<br>17 ἄπ πατέρω[ν μάθος<br>(suppl. Gall.) | | |
| v. | | | | 5 ἀνέμ]ω κατέχην<br>ἀήταις |
| v. | | | | 6 ἐ]κ γᾶς χρῆ<br>προίδην πλό[ον |
| v. | | | | |

| Alc. 302c V. | Alc. 306i col. II V. | Archil. 91 Tarditi | Archil. °92 Tarditi | Theogn. |
|---|---|---|---|---|
| | 2 sg. ψόμμος . . . ὀστείχει | 1 sg. κύμασιν ταράσσεται πόντος | 6 κῦμα . . .]ν ἵσταται κυκώμενον | 673 sg. ὑπερβάλλει δὲ θάλασσα\| ἀμφοτέρων τοίχων 680 ναῦν κατὰ κῦμα πίῃ |
| | | | 1 φέρο]νται νῆες (ἐ)ν πόντῳ | 671 φερόμεσθα |
| | | 3 σῆμα χειμῶνος | | |
| | | | | 673 ἀντλεῖν δ᾽οὐκ ἐθέλουσιν |
| | | | 2 ἱστίων ὑφώμεθα | 671 καθ᾽ἱστία λευκὰ βαλόντες |
| | | | | |
| | | | | 674 sg. μάλα τις χαλεπῶς σῴζεται |
| | | | | 677 χρήματα δ᾽ἁρπάζουσι βίῃ (cfr. 679 φορτηγοί) |
| | 16 sg. πόλλ]α (suppl. Gall.) τε καὶ θάμε[α δρομ[οίσᾳ cfr. 24 sg. (schol.) καθορμισθῆναι | | | |
| 1 τάρβημι[ | | 3 κιχάνει δ᾽ἐξ ἀελπτίης φόβος | 5 φόβον δ᾽]ἄπισχε | |
| | | | 4 ὄφρα σέο μαμνεώμεθα | |
| | | | 3 οὐρίην δ᾽ἔχε | |
| | | | 7 ἀλλὰ σὺ προμήθεσαι | |
| 5 νέφος κα.[ | | 2 ὀρθὸν ἵσταται νέφος | 6 κῦμα . . .]ν ἵσταται κυκώμενον | |

spective and back again to "I." The speaker plays a double role, addressing his interlocutor and at the same time experiencing events along with him. The poet is confused and disoriented, no longer able to comprehend which way the winds are blowing;[31] one wave breaks over the ship from one direction, another from another, and he and his comrades are caught in the middle.[32] The figure suggests an assault on the city by two armed factions, so that Alcaeus and his men are surrounded, with no way of escape. If this interpretation is correct, it is natural to assume an allusion to the faction of Myrsilos,[33] which was seeking (see above) to come back to Mytilene from exile, and to that of Pittacus, which allied itself with Myrsilos after breaking its pact with Alcaeus.[34] The impossibility of carrying on a battle on two fronts makes the enemy's victory very likely: if the water from the hold is already on the point of coming into the ship and the ship's gear is unable to stand up against the fury of wind and waves, the assaults of the enemy must have already achieved a certain success. Life has become precarious for the city and the Alcaeans—weakened as they were by an earlier series of dangerous events which had broken down their capacity to resist. The sail, which is essential for the ship's voyages, is here pictured as a threadbare "rag."[35] The metaphor suggests a life worn down by ceaseless war, a situation expressed elsewhere with the usual sea image: there will be no end to war, no more than there will be to "draining the white sea."[36] The sad state of the sail is a secure indication of other stormy crossings the boat has endured. Their historical counterpart is the series of violent events which took place at Mytilene in the years preceding the coming to power of Myrsilos. It is highly probable that Alcaeus himself was still on the island at the time of the crisis he describes.[37]

Poem 6 V. has a similar allegorical theme:

Here comes another wave from the preceding wind;
bailing out the hold will be hard
if water comes into the ship
. . .                                                                                      4


. . .

. . .
Let us firm up the sides as quickly as we can . . .
let us run to a safe haven;                                                       8

weariness and hesitation must not overcome (you);
great (danger) is in sight ahead;
remember past (toils);
let every man now show his courage,                                    12

and let us not dishonor (by baseness)
our glorious ancestors
who lie buried in earth's bosom . . .[38]

There follows a reference to the teaching of earlier generations[39] and then, in the final, very fragmentary verses, the mention of one-man rule (*monarchían*)—that is, the tyranny of Myrsilos, whose actions were, as we know from Heraclitus's citation of the first three verses,[40] the subject of the whole poem. The threat of a new enemy attack, just as violent as its predecessor,[41] is in the offing; it will be a hard task to free the city if the enemies invade; the walls must be reinforced immediately and some secure means of protection found.

The linguistic presentation has been enriched by the addition of new elements: (1) the verb *steíchein* is not an appropriate word for the movement of waves. It is an "intruder" in the context of the allegory,[42] a term used elsewhere in archaic poetry in connection with animate things alone:[43] for example, the advance of marching soldiers (*Iliad* 2, 833).[44] In thus "animating the inanimate"[45] Alcaeus gives tension and vigor to his image, focusing on the aggressive hostility of the wave at the expense of its mere movement: it advances in threatening fashion like a battalion of armed men; (2) the double reference of the verb *phrássein* to firming up the sides of a ship or erecting fortifications along a wall is part of the traditional poetic diction of epic;[46] and (3) the term *limén* (harbor, haven) in the injunction "let us run to a safe haven" fits a maritime context, but *tréchein*, in Alcaeus's time, is less appropriate for the motion of a ship. It may be applied to the revolving movement of inanimate objects such as a top[47] or a drill,[48] but there the catachrestic extension of meaning is an inherently obvious one. Here, as in the earlier reference to the "onward march" of the wave, the result is a tension in the imagery—a bold and unprecedented animation of the ship/city called upon to run with its entire complement of crew/political partisans to a strong and secure harbor/place of refuge,[49] where it can hold out against the onslaught of the wave/enemy faction. This piece of semantic boldness can only be accepted by a community that knows the referential code. As Umberto Eco observes, "among the practical considerations that determine the acceptability of metaphors (and the decision as to whether or not to proceed to interpret them) are also sociocultural laws establishing certain taboos, limits *quos ultra citraque nequit consistere rectum.*"[50] At a distance of several decades Theognis (v. 856) was to present once again to gatherings of banqueting aristocrats the image of the ship adrift,[51] and with explicit reference to misgovernment of the city. In the *Ajax* of Sophocles (v. 1083), Menelaus uses the same image in warning of the fate of a city that, if subjected to a regime of insolence and outrage, will fall sooner or later into the abyss, "after having run for a time before favoring winds." By then, however, in the fifth century, the metaphor had come to the point of being acceptable to any type of audience.

It is inconceivable that this new message was originally meant for exiles. The injunctions to "fortify the walls" and "run to a secure place of refuge," and the exhortation not to grow soft and slack in the face of the coming crisis, indicate that Alcaeus is still in Mytilene involved in a desperate last attempt to beat back the new attack from Myrsilos and keep him from gaining absolute power (v. 27 *monarchían*) in the city.[52]

This line of interpretation fits with the notice in Heraclitus[53] which places the two poems in the tumultuous period of Myrsilos's conspiracy. The plot must have involved more than one piece of subversive activity, given what Heraclitus says concerning the first of Alcaeus's allegories, "The poem is about Myrsilos and the conspiracy that he organized to impose a tyranny on Mitylene," and what immediately follows, by way of introduction to the three verses cited from the second allegory, "The poet alludes elsewhere to the actions of Myrsilos in the same way."[54] There is no reason to doubt notices of this sort, which must derive directly from ancient commentaries on Alcaeus, even though only a tiny portion of them are now known to us, through papyrus fragments.

Two further allegories[55] belong to the period of exile or, more precisely, to that of the second exile. Only a few bits of the second of these poems have been preserved, embedded in a piece of analysis that is preserved in the same papyrus[56] as a commentary on the first of the two.[57] Here the ship theme undergoes a sudden change of tone. The spirit of combat which had once animated her adventurous voyages is gone (fr. 73 V.):

all the cargo (is lost?)

· · ·

and, battered by the waves, . . .
refuses to carry on a struggle . . .                                         4
with the rain, but (is wrecked)
through having struck a treacherous rock.

As for her, (the devil take her) if that is the state she is in;
abandoning any thought of return, (my friend,)                              8
(I wish) to be happy in your company and enjoy myself,
and with Bucchis . . .[58]

It is obvious that the poet is no longer on board the ship/city (v. 7
*kéna*); he is in exile and in despair by now of ever returning to Mytilene; beaten down by the blows of the waves/enemy faction, the ship/
city refuses to continue the struggle; the hidden rock that she struck
has done serious damage; the cargo swept away by the waves is a metaphor for the property or possessions of the Alcaean faction, which
have fallen into the hands of their rivals.

But what are the referents of the new signifiers, "rain" (*ómbros*) and
"rock" (*hérma*)? Pindar seems to have favored the metaphorical use of
*ómbros* to designate revolution (*stásis*)[59] or war:[60] in *Pythian* 5, 10, he
alludes to the revolt that broke out against Arcesilaus IV as a "winter
rain," by contrast with the "calm" (*eudía*)—that is, peace—which Castor has brought back to the city for the benefit of his protégé the king;
in *Isthmian* 5, 49, the battle of Salamis is presented as a "death-bearing
rain of blood," which caused countless warriors to perish.[61] Doubtless
these metaphorical uses were modeled on Alcaeus, at a time when
pieces of his poetry were part of the standard repertory of Athenian
banquet songs.[62]

It follows that the "rain" against which the ship will no longer struggle is the ongoing sedition promoted by one of the poet's rivals. To say
that the "ship/city refuses" is essentially the same as saying that the
"crew/citizens refuse"—out of weariness with civil war, as is clear from
the image of the rock against which the ship has foundered.[63] The rock
is invisible—concealed beneath the surface of the water—hence unexpected and insidious.[64] But the use of the word *hérma* to mean *rock* is a
metaphorical reduction for which Alcaeus himself is responsible—
followed later by Anacreon, as the commentary cited earlier notes,[65]
and Aeschylus (*Ag.* 1006).[66] In Homer it means a *prop* or *support* for a
ship drawn up on the shore[67] and, metaphorically, a person who is the
*support* or *mainstay* of his city.[68] *Rock* is a meaning that becomes prevalent only in the fifth century,[69] the archaic term for *rock* being *pétre* or

*choirás.*[70] Alcaeus's metaphor involves rhetorical substitution in a situation where there is semantic equivalence (props of wood or stone = rock) but divergence of effect: not support but destruction. The figure is a "deviant metaphor" or, rather, metonymy,[71] whose meaning must lie in the relationship to referent: what seems to be support is in fact destruction. The metaphor cuts two ways—not without a touch of irony, as we shall see. The rock is presumably a person as well, one whom the original audience would have had no difficulty in identifying. Who is he? After the death of Myrsilos, which Alcaeus greeted with a shout of joy,[72] the poet returned to Mytilene from the exile into which he had gone after the failure of a conspiracy against the tyrant.[73] During the ensuing interregnum period, Pittacus, who had collaborated with Myrsilos, sought to consolidate his own position, which was still insecure and uncertain.[74] This is the background for the poet's call to the people of Mytilene to dissociate themselves from the man (Pittacus) who is seeking supreme power: he will soon subvert the delicate balance on which the city's safety depends.[75] Elsewhere the tone is even more peremptory:

> you remain silent . . . incapable of resisting the tyrant; now is the time, citizens of Mitylene, now while the log is giving forth only smoke (that is, as the ancient commentary explains, while he has yet to make himself tyrant) douse it quickly, so that it does not burst into brighter flame.[76]

In this crisis Alcaeus had to have recourse to armed violence against his opponents in his effort to keep them from gaining power, but without success. Evidently he was unable to find the needed support and consensus among his fellow citizens. In the end nothing remained but to go into exile once again. We learn from Aristotle[77] that the Mytilenians unanimously elected Pittacus as dictator with full powers (*aisymnétes*) in order to conduct the fight against the exiles led by Alcaeus and his brother Antimenides. Through shrewd and able policies, he succeeded in soothing tempers and reestablishing order in the city.[78] Of course, from the point of view of Alcaeus, the great loser in the struggle, Pittacus was nothing but a petty political manipulator who made himself "tyrant." This explains the hatred and venom behind the charges of corruption and immorality,[79] the opprobrious epithets,[80] and also the sense of bitter disappointment which pervades his admonitions to his fellow citizens. Too compliant to offer any resistance to Pittacus's unlimited ambitions, they showered him with praise instead, making him "tyrant of an inert and passive city, doomed to misfortune."[81]

The event described in the allegory can thus be located with precision. Pittacus is in the process of eliminating Alcaeus's faction, who are fleeing into exile,[82] and the people have tacitly endorsed his rule. Political reality is thus slightly different from what the allegory suggests. The refusal of the ship/city to carry on the struggle did not stem from inertia or incompetence: it was the consensus and approval Pittacus enjoyed that induced her to lay down her arms. The political truth that lies behind the metaphorical context is Alcaeus's truth, not the truth of history. The hidden, hence insidious and treacherous, rock is Pittacus, the "sly fox" attacked in another poem from Alcaeus's exile,[83] but a particular type of "rock" in that it can help as well as harm. In the context of the poem its connotations are strongly negative—like the effect it produces. But Alcaeus has distorted the meaning of a word that in the poetic tradition referred to the *prop* of a ship and metaphorically, to the *support, rock of refuge,* of a city—an epithet that the Mytileneans would have been perfectly happy to include in the accolades they were showering on Pittacus. The metaphor is especially significant in the light of what immediately follows: "As for *her* [the ship], the devil take her if that is the state she is in." The use of the pronoun at the opening of the verse has the same negative connotation that it is made to carry elsewhere in reference to Pittacus, "As for *him*, the inlaw of the descendants of Atreus."[84] The indignant, contemptuous expression conceals a piece of sarcastic irony, as if the ship/city had sought out the rock on purpose for protection and support—as in fact occurred. For the poet and his companions there is nothing left but to drown all thought of return in the joys of the banquet—the usual Alcaean remedy for misfortunes.[85]

We now come to the fourth allegory, the one that can be recovered (see above) from the commentary in *P. Oxy.* 2307, fr. 14, col. II = fr. 306i col. II V.:

"sand" (*psómmos* = *psámmos*) as far as "rises" (*osteíchei* = *anasteíchei*). . . it refers to impurities (*akatharsía*); because she (i.e., the ship) is compressed and penetrated (?), there rises a great quantity of white impurity (or much impurity and white sickness?); the word "white" refers to the swelling[86] . . . "its sides have already yielded": even her sides have become old; "she has completed many and frequent voyages": allegorically . . . because of her having voyaged they (i.e., the sides) have become old through many and frequent sea voyages[87] . . . (she says) that it is not because of being old that she is at a mooring place or (has ceased) from gatherings; . . . the old ship ceases from (further) sailing.[88]

The subject is once again the ship, now decrepit from its many voyages and stranded in a bank of sand, which as it rises (*anasteíchei*) presses around the ship and works its way inside, presumably through the cracks and rents produced by the collision with the "hidden rock." It is clear that the situation of wreck and decaying idleness presented here presupposes the events described in the preceding allegory (fr. 73 V.).[89] The damage done to the ship has caused it to be grounded on the sand. It is old and worn-out, its legs/sides slack and disjointed.[90] *Psómmos* and *skélea* are the new metaphorical elements, conveying the idea of ruin and decay. The *skélea* or "legs" (of men or animals) are figuratively "masonry work" or "walls," a meaning already attested before the fifth century.[91] The ambivalence of *toîchos*—"city wall" and "sides of a ship"—has already been noted.[92] It is thus very probable that here, too, Alcaeus has animated the inanimate. The "legs" are thus the wooden structures that support the ship—that is, as Merkelbach[93] interprets the passage, "the lateral axis pieces that join to form a V at bow and stern," creating the two sides of the ship.[94] The same sort of procedure leads to the metaphorical reference to "sand" as the putrescent matter or "impurities" in a diseased body.[95] Here the whiteness of sand mixed with sea foam suggests the whiteness of pus in a swelling or abscess.[96] It is significant that the terms used by the author of the commentary in his exegesis—"impurity," "swelling," tumescence—belong properly to the vocabulary of medicine.[97]

The allegorical structure that emerges seems to exist at several levels: the sand covers or presses against the ship, rises on all sides of it,[98] is washed into it by the waves through the cracks and holes in its sides;[99] full of sand, the ship looks like a white swelling, full of pus.[100] At the same time, given the passive participle *perainoménes* (penetrated), with its exclusively sexual connotation,[101] there are some grounds for supposing that the metaphor is that of an old prostitute (*pórne*).[102] Three considerations support this line of interpretation: (*a*) the ambivalence of the word *skélea* (line 13); (*b*) the parallel with the lacunose fr. 117 V., where the occurrence of the words "ship" (v. 21), "prostitute," and "prostitutes" (v. 26 *pórnai;* v. 29 *p[órn]aisin*) have suggested a "mixing" of allegories;[103] and (*c*) the recurrence of the same ship/prostitute metaphor in Meleager and Philip of Thessalonika.[104]

In spite of these arguments, a number of points remain obscure. It is hard to get any plausible sense out of the statement "Being pressed in and penetrated" (i.e., "finding herself in the condition of being, etc.," or even "if she is pressed in and penetrated")[105] "there rises a great quantity of impurity," as applied to a prostitute who is (as the analogy with the ship would require) old and ill. Why should this take place when she is performing the sexual act? And why, during the sexual act, at the very moment of being embraced and penetrated by the man?[106] Because only two things are being compared in the metaphor, ship and prostitute, their relationship must be plausible and coherent at every point.

(These objections stand even if *leúke* is taken as a substantive, the technical term ["white sickness"][107] for the cutaneous disease that Celsus describes as vitiligo.[108] Its characteristic symptom is a whitening of the skin and of head and body hair. The reference cannot be, as usually assumed,[109] to "leprosy," which is also a cutaneous disease but one characterized by the appearance of eruptions on the skin.[110] Page seems to have considered these very objections himself, seeking to eliminate them by altering the text of line 12.[111] He renders his emended version of lines 12–14 as, "The leprosy [sic!] has gone right through her legs," explaining the commentary's subsequent statement that her legs have grown old as a reference to the fact that "they are rotten with disease and decay." But there remains the problem why the white sickness—which, moreover, does not involve swellings—should *rise* at the moment of embrace and penetration. If one interprets the text closely, the pronouns *autês* [line 8ff.], *aútai* [line 14], *autês* [line 15], and *autê⟨i⟩* [line 19] can only refer to the ship that is mentioned explicitly in line 27. On the other hand, there remains the problem why the author of the commentary used a word, *perainoménes*, whose connotations are exclusively sexual. No answer is possible here, given the meagerness of the available documentation on the use of *peraíno* to mean "penetrate.")

It is best to stick to the hypothesis—the most acceptable one—of the semantic nexus *ship-inflammation-city.* The rotting condition of the old ship "that has seen many voyages"[112] is a figure for the squalid, ruinous condition of the city of Mytilene, voluntarily fallen under the sway of the idolized Pittacus.[113] One cannot help but be struck by how many of the epithets that Alcaeus fastens onto his rival[114] elsewhere in his poetry are in keeping with the sense of this allegory: *gaúrex* (bloated, arrogant); *phýskon* or *gástron* (paunchy, potbellied); *agásyrtos* (impure, dirty, corrupt), also explained by the ancients as equivalent to *akáthartos*.[115] The words *akatharsía* and *éparma,* which refer literally to the decay of the ship, have the figurative meanings of, respectively, "viciousness," "corruption"[116] and "vanity," "empty pride."[117]

This is the context in which the reference to inflammation and swelling takes on its symbolic overtones, allowing us to see the figure of Pittacus as a physical and moral emblem: Pittacus the bloated, the pot-bellied, the polluted scoundrel who contaminates and oppresses[118] an entire city with his own corruption, to the point of making it a gross, swollen piece of putrescence like himself. The ship/city is unwilling to entrust quarreling helmsmen with her safety in a sea where storms are a normal occurrence; so she refuses to sail—not "because she is old" (line 23ff.) but because she seeks the harbor of peace, acquiescing in the sole guidance of a single helmsman who is an overbearing tyrant.[119] But this peace means the end of all political activity. We learn from Aristotle that tyrants' means for securing themselves in power include the elimination of citizens who are prominent as individuals and the abolition of the practice of common meals (*syssítia*), political clubs (*hetairíai*), and every sort of educational activity.[120] Alcaeus's reference in the present poem to the ship's having ceased "from gatherings" (i.e., aristocratic symposia)[121] looks like a specific reference to a ban on such meetings issued by Pittacus. The poet is still in exile and resumes in violent and vivid fashion his attacks on the city that has betrayed him—ignoring his insistent call to action, to resistance, to quenching the tyrant's burning desire for power.[122]

His present message to his *hetaîroi* is a gloomy one: condemnation and indictment of the Mytilenians for the moral and political degradation of their city—but also, indirectly, of the main architect of this degradation.

The four "principal" allegories examined here (principal in the sense that they are the ones that the tradition has preserved in most legible form) offer a vivid cross section of Mytilenian history in the years around 600. The poetry of Alcaeus can be called the swan song of the island's old aristocracy. The political picture he sketches has a kind of truth to it, but it is truth as seen by Alcaeus's own confraternity—at the point of no return for the disintegrating oligarchical equilibrium, which he was later to recall, with bitterness and nostalgia, in a poem from the years of exile.[123]

In such a situation, with armed encounters between members of opposing factions a frequent occurrence, allegory becomes the favored instrument of communication within a group of companions at arms bound to each other by an oath of loyalty. It serves to convey messages in a veiled and allusive language understandable *only* to members of the group, and its effectiveness, on both the informative and emotional level, is in direct proportion to the novelty of the message transmitted and the originality of its allegorical representation. The semantic "scandal" provoked by unprecedented metaphors such as rain = sedition, rock = support, and sand = impurity, pus could not have been understood outside the narrow circle of the *hetairía.*

To ask whether or when the ship in these poems is a figure for the city or merely for a single faction within it is to address oneself to a false problem. Our analysis has shown that the constant meaning is *city,* and this is the sense in which the allegory was understood and imitated by Theognis and Aeschylus. The question to ask is what did *pólis,* a term that recurs several times in his poetry, mean for Alcaeus. Was it the geographical entity made up of urban center and surrounding country; or was it the city-state, its complex of civic institutions, and the particular set of social, cultural, and political conditions of which they were the expression? Both senses of the word were common throughout antiquity,[124] but it is obvious that Alcaeus's allegory involves the latter: his ship is the oligarchically steered ship of state. The analogical relationship between ship and city is grounded in the very structure of the former, with its internal spaces apportioned according to the same criteria that lie behind the political organization of urban space. It was on the basis of just this analogy that Ennius,[125] several centuries later, could call the passageway that runs from bow to stern between banks of rowers a "street" (*agea*), and the poop deck a "piazza" (*forus*).[126] And later still, in the famous ode (1, 14) inspired by Alcaeus's allegories, Horace was being completely faithful to the technique of his model when he symbolized the Roman state by a ship, the civil wars by storms and waves, and peace by a safe harbor (cf. the discussion in Quintilian 8, 6, 44).[127]

Even before Alcaeus, however, Archilochus had used allegory as a means of conveying military messages to his companions in the conquest of Thasos. In speaking to his friend and fellow citizen Glaucos he refers to the threat of imminent battle with the Thracians through the metaphor of a storm at sea:[128]

> Look, Glaucos, at how the waves are churning up the sea from deep below;
> a cloud is rising high over the tops of the Gyrai,
> sign of storm ahead; all of a sudden we are afraid.[129]

Waves (*kýmata*) = soldiers, storm (*cheimón*) = war are, as has been seen, metaphorical signifiers that can be paralleled in epic similes; and the same is true of the word *cloud* (*néphos*) = soldiers or war,[130] which reappears in this sense in Alcaeus as well.[131]

In another fragment, probably from the same poem, the allegory takes the form of an excited, dramatic description of ships at the mercy of the waves, as if the poet were actually living the episode at the moment of narrating it:[132]

> ... the swift ships are adrift on the waves
> ... let us slacken up on the sails
> ... loosen the ship's ropes so you can catch a good wind
> ... (save) your crew if you want us to remember you
> ... away with (fear?) and don't hurl                                    5
> ... the wave is churned up to a crest
> ... but you provide (*prométhesai*).

Description and second-person address—perhaps directed at the same Glaucos—are here blended with features of style and imagery which recur in almost identical form in the allegorical odes of Alcaeus.[133] The concrete visual image of a storm at sea and ships in imminent danger of being wrecked is a symbolic announcement of a military action led by foreign enemies against the members of the poet's *hetairía*. This explains the insistence with which the captain is urged to keep the ship on course, look to the great danger ahead, and make immediate provision for the safety of his men. The injunction to "provide," lest the worst befall, means that the captain, given his experience and ability, is responsible for seeing to it that incalculable risks are avoided: his own reputation turns on the outcome of his actions—the degree to which he will be remembered by his companions (cf. v. 4) as an example of ability and courage.[134]

The idea of "providing," in the double sense of nautical expertise and political ability and shrewdness, becomes an essential norm of action in Alcaeus's ship-of-state poems. The man of ability and capacity, he says, must foresee the ship's course before embarking; and once at sea he must sail with the wind at hand: the wind cannot be changed— you go where it takes you.[135] This is sage and expert advice from a man of understanding (*synetós*); the man without understanding (*asýnetos*) is the one who cannot comprehend events and thus cannot foresee the course they will take. His situation is that described in the first allegory by the verb *asynnétemmi* ("I do not understand").[136] In the war of conflicting winds/factions, the poet does not have the capacity to foresee what will happen; he has become disoriented in the storm. We read in Diogenes Laertius (1, 78) that Pittacus was in the habit of saying that a man was intelligent by virtue of his ability to foresee (*pronoêsai*) difficult situations beforehand in order to prevent them from occurring, and brave by virtue of his ability to deal with them once they did occur. He had learned to his cost the validity of this sage rule through his experiences in the darkest moments of the civil war; but in the end, unlike his rival, he enjoyed a success to match the acuteness of his political vision. At a later period the norm of foresight was to assume in Solon the value of a general moral precept—a rule for action and behavior amid the risks that all human activity involves. A man who seeks to do good without foreseeing the danger that threatens him falls into a state of total blindness, whereas even if he does evil the gods may grant another man the success that saves him from the consequences of his folly.[137]

A final point to be considered in connection with Archilochus is the meaning of the reference to "ships" in the plural. If the image of the storm is an allegory, every element in it should have a precise reference—as the analysis of Alcaeus's allegories has shown. But it is hard to see what cities Archilochus could be referring to. The historical background for the allegory is the war against the Thracians, of which a vivid echo survives in the surviving fragments of the poet's work.[138] Even granting that the allusion is to an attack of the Thracians against Thasos, it was still not several cities but a single city—the Parian settlement on the island—that was threatened. A possible hypothesis is that the ships are the Parian factions or military detachments involved in the war with the Thracians.

Whatever Alcaeus may have owed to predecessors such as Archilochus, it is legitimate to conclude that the true matrix for the ship as symbol of the city-state in the many vicissitudes of its civil existence is to be found in his poetry. It is to him that the image owes its long and successful history in both ancient[139] and modern literature.

# XII

· · ·

# Holy Sappho

*Violet-tressed, holy, sweetly smiling Sappho.*

*—Alcaeus, fr. 384 V.*

This famous verse of Alcaeus[1] has a place of its own in the history of Sapphic criticism—more particularly in all the speculative myths that have arisen about the purity of Sappho's loves and in all idealizing modern interpretations of her poetry. A contemporary poet's apostrophe—"violet-tressed, *chaste* (or *pure*), sweetly smiling Sappho," according to the usual rendering—offered a good argument for defenders of Sappho's virtue against the accusations of immorality and base love (*aischrà philía*) found in the ancient biographers.[2] But the text itself, as was decisively shown by W. Ferrari,[3] contains no basis for such an inference. The epithet "holy" (*ágna*) applies only to the realm of the sacred in archaic usage; the semantic shift toward the meaning "chaste," "virginal," in a secular, moral sense cannot be documented earlier than the fifth century, and even then there is usually some other word in the context to make clear wherein the purity or chastity lies.[4]

In spite of the authoritative endorsement Ferrari's study has received,[5] it is less persuasive when it concludes that Alcaeus's apostrophe to Sappho reveals the same type of attitude which would be found in the invocation to a deity—as if the poet felt in her "the purity of a divine presence," feasting his thoughts on "the inspired qualities of a poetry of supreme passion and sweetness." Essentially, then, Alcaeus anticipated by several centuries what would later become a commonplace in antiquity and in the idealizing Hellenism of our own day: the celebration of Sappho as the tenth Muse and of her poetry as a supreme and unique instance of divine inspiration. The logical leap required to arrive at these conclusions from the analysis of the archaic meaning of *hagnós* which precedes them is far too great; they are part and parcel of the author's whole critical orientation, which is of a strictly Crocean cast. The most authoritative statement of this point of view, from a classicist, is Gennaro Perrotta's study of Sappho, published in 1935, barely five years before Ferrari's. Against the moralizing interpretation of Alcaeus's line, it set up an aestheticizing one. Both positions are equally abstract, equally extreme, and equally unconcerned with what should be the determinants of any interpreter's perspective: the actual content of Sapphic poetry and the function and meaning it had within its social context.

There are other difficulties as well, stemming from too generic an understanding of *hagnós* as equivalent in archaic usage to "sacred, divine"—almost, in certain cases, a synonym of *hierós* as applied to things and objects pertaining to divinity.[6] In order to see that Ferrari is wrong in making *hagnós* an epithet interchangeable on occasion with *hierós,* one need only think of the words with which the chorus in the *Agamemnon* (vv. 219ff.) stigmatizes the impiety of the king's decision at Aulis. Three adjectives follow one another in solemn succession, each singling out one characteristic and essential aspect of those actions and attitudes that are unnatural and against the will of the gods: the impious (*dyssebê*), the impure (*ánagnon*), the sacrilegious (*aníeron*).[7] It is methodologically incorrect to maintain the synonymy of *hagnós* and *hierós* or *hagnós* and *semnós* simply because the three adjectives appear, in different authors, in reference to the same object or thing. If Sappho calls the marriage song for Hector and Andromache *ágnon* (fr. 44, 26 V.) and Theognis (v. 761) uses the word *hierón* for song in honor of the gods, or if the water of the Muses is *hagnón* for Simonides and the waters of Pirene, at a later date, *semná* for Euripides; this does not mean that the three epithets could be felt as synonymous. One can only say that they designated different aspects of the sacred or (should textual connotations and other aspects of the context justify such a hypothesis) that they had sunk to the level of being merely ornamental.

Semantic studies done over the past several decades, from those of E. Williger[8] to the more recent ones of Rudhardt,[9] have shown the substantial difference in meaning between *hagnós* and *hierós.*[10] The Greek language was particularly rich in the religious vocabulary that it put at the poet's disposal—a vocabulary reflecting not only the variety of meanings and nuances attached to the basically ambivalent notion of the sacred but also the evolution of Greek religious thought from

Homer's time to the fourth century. It is by now generally agreed that
*hagnós* has to do with one typical aspect of the sacred: the deep reverence and religious awe that it inspires. The word designates everything
in the sacred which is disturbing and forbidden or taboo to man. This
sense is documented by the use of the word, from Homer to the tragedians, either in reference to a divinity (Artemis, Athena, Persephone),
or a religious rite, or sacred places and sacred things.[11] The other
meaning of *hagnós, ritually pure,*[12] is not clearly detectable in archaic
poetry, even though its development has been regarded, since Williger,
as yielding a meaning complementary to the first: the sacred as something forbidden to man on the one hand, and, on the other, the sacred
as something proper to the gods—their purity and immunity from all
human contact.[13]

Gerber's analysis[14] of passages in Bacchylides (*Dith.* 17, 8–10) and
Pindar (*Pyth.* 1, 21) has added further confirmation to the primary
meaning of *hagnós* ("that which inspires fear or veneration"). But some
additional observations are still in order, if only to complete and, in
certain instances, correct what has been said thus far on the use of the
epithet in Greek lyric.

In his dialogue on the oracular responses of the Pythia (*Pyth. orac.*
17, 402c), Plutarch discusses the spring of the Muses which rose near
the ancient Delphic sanctuary of the goddess Earth, citing fragment
577a of Simonides[15] to confirm the tradition concerning the sacral use
of its water for ablutions and libations to the gods. Further on, in at-
tacking the views of Eudoxus of Cnidus, Plutarch adds that the water
was not, as erroneously believed, that of the river Styx, but rather, like
the art of prophecy itself, under the special protection of the Muses.
The opinion endorsed by Eudoxus and rejected by Plutarch was evidently based on the early chthonic character of the oracle. Before the
advent of Apollo the Earth had been the source of prophecies at Delphi; and one may infer from Plutarch's account that this chthonic cult
is responsible for the association of the Muses, ancient deities of foun-
tains and springs, with the oracle.[16] All this is clearly indicative of the
original meaning of *hagnós* as an attribute of the water of the Muses.
It is holy to mortals in the sense that its use is forbidden for any but
sacral purposes and that it sprang from a fountain in what was once
the scene of a chthonic cult. Although the secondary and more recent
meaning of *pure*[17] might seem obvious in the case of spring water used
for lustral purposes, it is not the predominant one here, as is shown by
the cult character of the spot and the traditions that arose concerning
it.[18] The polemical fragment on *areté* (579 P.) shows that Simonides was

still acutely conscious of the force of the epithet in its primary sense. There the poet's personification of *areté* as a supreme ideal, abstract and practically unattainable, leads him to picture her as dwelling in solitary and inaccessible places.[19] His point of departure is a passage in Hesiod (*Op.* 286ff.), but the parallel itself provides a measure of the distance that separates man from this mythical "virtue," solitary inhabitant of a holy spot (*chôron hagnón*), invisible, not to be approached by mortals at all, or at any rate only accessible to those few stalwarts—if any there be—who have given proof of truly exceptional capacities. This is a more than human "virtue," which inspires reverence just as a goddess would, and requires extreme sacrifice and trials of anyone who approaches her. The particular aspect of the sacred involved here is essential for the structure and meaning of the personification as conceived by the poet; it is what gives his divinity her exceptional character and puts the mark of the inaccessible and forbidden on the spot that she inhabits.

In Pindar's reference (*Ol.* 3, 21) to the *hagnàn krísin* of "mighty contests" the epithet has generally been taken in the "secular" sense of "just, impartial"—an immediate and obvious reference, from the modern interpreter's point of view, to the verdict (*krísis*) of the judges at the games, and so, it has been suggested, the earliest attested example of a shift in meaning from a religious concept to a definitely ethical one.[20] This interpretation, however, is inconsistent with several details both external and internal to the text: first, the sacral character of the acts of Heracles described in the poem—importation of the sacred olive from the land of the Hyperboreans, institution of the Olympic games and, earlier, altars in honor of Zeus; and second, the sacral office of the judges at the games, who were bound by religious oath to the proper fulfilling of their duties. Their verdict was a verdict pronounced by persons invested with a religious office and, as such, sacred and inviolable. It is worth noting that the religious connotations of the epithet are reinforced by the appearance, two lines earlier in the same context (v. 19), of the rare verb *hagízo*, not elsewhere attested in Pindar.

These passages from Simonides and Pindar provide further confirmation for what is now more or less acknowledged, that *hagnós* in the complementary, secondary sense of "pure" is not "clearly perceivable" before the tragedians.[21] The usage of Sappho and Alcaeus, at least in those few cases where context allows certain interpretation, shows no deviation from the word's primary meaning.

The epithet is applied in Sappho to a temple (fr. 2, 2 V.), to a song (fr. 44, 26 V.), and to the Graces.[22] In the first passage the object is such as to be in and of itself *hagnós*. It is mentioned in a typical context, one that doubtless suggests a precise spot sacred to the cult of Aphrodite and frequented by a select group of participants, Sappho and her companions, with their own ceremonies and their own rites (ritual epiphany of the goddess, etc.).[23] Here the epithet emphasizes the sacral exclusiveness of a place forbidden to all those who were not part of the cult—that is, not members of Sappho's community. The second case might seem more difficult: the *mélos ágnon* for the marriage of Hector and Andromache in the suggestive scene of the arrival of the bridal pair at Troy. To the music of the flutes and the rattle of the castanets, a chorus of maidens raise their voice in "holy" song, and the sky re-echoes to mighty sound (*ácho thespesía*). The common *hierón* would have been the obvious epithet to use here. Theognis, as we have seen,[24] uses it in reference to a song in honor of the gods; and Alcaeus describes the ritual cry of the women during a ceremonial beauty contest as *íras ololýgas* (fr. 130b, 20 V.). The choice of *ágnon* cannot be explained in terms of linguistic Homerisms. These are more noticeable here than elsewhere in Sappho,[25] but appeal to them is not a real alternative to the theory of interchangeable and hence, as Ferrari maintains, equivalent epithets.

Even admitting the presence of an extension of Homeric usage (*Od.* 21, 259), it is difficult to account for the epithet without falling back on the simplistic *hagnós* = *hierós* equation.[26] In the Homeric context the adjective refers not so much to the "sacred" character of a festival as to what is mentioned in the line immediately following, the prohibition against shooting a bow, which the sacrality of the occasion imposes.[27] And this is an aspect of the notion of the "sacred" which the Sapphic context excludes. The poem's final scene (vv. 21–34) is highly suggestive, but the feeling it creates has less to do with the visual splendor and festive joy that surrounds the bridal pair than with the pervasive solemnity of a grand ceremony described during its culminating moments, from the arrival of the bride and groom until the hymn to Apollo and the song in their honor. Ignoring all those things that connect the poem to its period and social milieu[28] and concentrating on the way in which the content is structured, it is possible to see the scene developing step by step through stages that emphasize first the auditory sphere (vv. 24–27; 31–33) and then the olfactory (v. 30), but always through words that have some sacral resonance.[29] An expressive blending of sounds and perfumes is highly effective in marking the sacred ceremony as an extraordinary event, one that raises real events to the superhuman level of a mythic rite in honor of a bride and groom "like unto gods" (vv. 21; 34).[30] It is not only "old and new"–traditional language and the individual character of the whole scene[31]–but also human and divine that merge with each other in an atmosphere of grand solemnity. These are the *signifying* elements whose association makes precise the meaning of *ágnon* and the ensuing epithet *thespesía* (already applied in Homer to mighty events to indicate both their exceptional character and the awe and fear they inspire in listener and beholder).[32] The underlying idea is not the faded "ritually ordained" (*hierón*) attested in Alcaeus,[33] but one coherent with the connotations of the whole context–the sacred as a set of emotional resonances, as the frisson communicated to participants in a solemn rite. It is an "arcane and mysterious"[34] song that the high-pitched maiden voices float out over the notes of the flutes and the rattle of the castanets.

In the third instance the absence of a *signifying* context, not only in Sappho but also in Alcaeus's one reference (fr. 386 V.) to *ágnai Chárites*, makes the problem of meaning an insoluble one. One should not assume, however, that the Graces are *ágnai* simply because they are "daughters of Zeus" (Sappho fr. 53 V.) and accordingly "pure." It is more likely that the epithet has something to do with the chthonic origin of ancient vegetation deities–a hypothesis that also provides a plausible explanation for the application of the same epithet to the Muses.[35]

A final passage to be considered uses *ágnos* as an epithet of Athena in Alcaeus's account of the sacrilege committed by Ajax Oileus when he dragged Cassandra away from the statue of the goddess.[36] Athena was so infuriated by the outrage that she sent a storm, which wrecked the Achaean fleet. Here the epithet seems appropriate enough in view of the goddess's role as avenger and destroyer. The emotional dimensions of the sacred are evident not only in her action but also in the external appearance that she presents: the livid face and the dread gaze that inspire terror (vv. 23–25).

Having proceded thus far in our semantic analysis of *hagnós* we are at last in a position to get at the true meaning of Alcaeus's apostrophe. The verse is a series of three epithets followed by a proper name (*Sápphoi*) as a clausula. Neither structure nor choice of epithets is accidental. The order in which the adjectives appear is perhaps that imposed by the metrical form of the dodecasyllable, but it may also be the expression of an inner necessity. The third attribute appears in the place determined for it by the fact that it is a necessary complement to the second and even the two disyllables, *ágna* and *Sápphoi*, are underlined by occupying the two emphatic positions in the line. Metrical necessity is here identical with semantic necessity. Hence the presence of certain features of morphology and phonology which seem "abnormal" in the context of normal Lesbian usage but cease to be so once the greater conventionality of the language of Alcaeus as against that of Sappho is taken into account.[37] The component elements in the first epithet (*ióplok'*) and the third (*mellichómeide*) are linked by their allusive connotation and sacral provenance. "Sweetly laughing" is an Alcaic compound not elsewhere attested which links the second element of the Homeric epithet for Aphrodite (*philommeidés*)[38] with a typically Sapphic piece of erotic vocabulary.[39] "Violet-tressed" (or "violet-crowned"), with its unmistakably Aphrodisian use of flower symbolism,[40] is also a calque of a similar Sapphic compound (*iókolpos*) applicable to a goddess[41] or to a bride (fr. 30, 5 V.). The first and third epithets are thus the necessary complements to the second: they locate the idea of the sacred within the realm of the cult of Aphrodite or, more precisely, make the sacral reference of *ágna* apply specifically to her.

What then is the meaning of the whole apostrophe, with its three structuring religious epithets, and, in particular, what is the meaning of *ágna* when applied to a person, a usage not elsewhere attested until the fifth century? It may still be possible to believe that this apparently affectionate greeting from a contemporary poet was intended as a tribute to the unique greatness of Sappho's poetry. But if we confine ourselves to the actual meaning of the Alcaean context, the greeting presents itself as a reverent tribute to the sacral dignity of the poetess as ministrant of Aphrodite and to the grace and beauty that her role as love's priestess conferred upon her.

# APPENDIX

. . .

# The Art of Philology

*Philology is that venerable art which demands of its votaries one thing above all: to go aside, to take time, to become still, to become slow—it is a goldsmith's art and connoisseurship of the* word *which has nothing but delicate cautious work to do and achieves nothing if it does not achieve it* lento. *But for precisely this reason it is more necessary than ever today; by precisely this means does it entice and enchant us the most, in the midst of an age of "work," that is to say, of hurry, of indecent and perspiring haste, which wants to "get everything done" at once, including every old or new book: —this art does not easily get anything done, it teaches to read* well, *that is to say, to read slowly, deeply, looking cautiously before and aft, with reservations, with doors left open, with delicate eyes and fingers.*

— F. *Nietzsche,* Daybreak: Thoughts on the Prejudices of Morality
*(trans. R. J. Hollingdale)*

*Philology* in the narrow sense of the term refers to the "discipline that, through textual criticism, seeks to reproduce or reconstruct and interpret correctly literary documents and texts."[1] In other contexts it may mean the "study of the origin and structure of a language."[2] The latter use of the word is largely confined to English-speaking countries and distinguishes *philology,* which is above all the science of language, from *scholarship,* which is the general term for activity having to do with disciplines called philological.[3]

In a broader sense the word has also been understood as the study of a civilization in all of its aspects. Wilamowitz, one of the greatest of German classical philologians, defines the range and purposes of his discipline as follows:

The nature of classical philology—as it is still called, though it no longer claims the primacy the epithet implies—is defined by its subject-matter: Graeco-Roman civilization in its essence and in every facet of its existence.

223

This civilization is a unity, though we are unable to state precisely when it began and ended; and the task of philology is to bring that dead world to life by the power of science—to recreate the poet's song, the thought of the philosopher and the lawgiver, the sanctity of the temple and the feelings of believers and unbelievers, the bustling life of market and port, the physical appearance of land and sea, mankind at work and play. . . . Because the life we strive to fathom is a single whole, our science too is a single whole. Its division into the separate disciplines of language and literature, archaeology, ancient history, epigraphy, numismatics and, latterly, papyrology, can be justified only as a concession to the limitations of human capacity and must not be allowed to stifle awareness of the whole, even in the specialist.[4]

In thus promoting philology to the rank of an "all-embracing science of language and history," Wilamowitz was seeking to bring the study of antiquity out of its aristocratic isolation into the active mainstream of historical investigation. But from the moment philology is identified with *Kulturgeschichte* it begins to lose its specific character, and this cannot help but raise problems touching on its very existence as a discipline. The aims and tasks of philology had already been extensively discussed in nineteenth-century Germany. The debate pitted the strict formalism represented by Gottfried Hermann against the historical and philological orientation of August Boeckh, who saw philology's task as the reconstruction of the life of antiquity through knowledge and understanding of all the concrete data pertaining to it. In Italy, Giorgio Pasquali was a representative of this tradition, regarding philology as essentially historical in its aims and methods. At the same time he refused to make it an exact discipline on a level with mathematics and physical and natural science: intuition and imagination were, he insisted, indispensable for the activity of the philologian:

Philology is neither an exact or natural science but—essentially, if not uniquely—historical in its character. Any serious philologian who has thought a little about his own profession knows that this is true. And unless a philologian is totally devoid of all culture, all acquaintance with the methods of other disciplines, and all ability to think clearly, he knows perfectly well that this applies not only to the study of classical antiquity but also, and to an even greater degree, to other disciplines as well. Before they were ever demonstrated, the most important truths have been intuited through an act of imagination. The mathematician especially must show a much greater power of imagination than the philologian, from whose discipline scientific philologians acting in the interest of science would, we are told, have the imagination totally excluded. Without imagination one cannot represent even three-dimensional solids, much less $n$-dimensional ones; without imagination it is impossible to understand even the simplest theorem in solid geometry.[5]

What seems to me an essentially correct mean between these two extremes—and one still relevant to contemporary critical discussions—was struck by Hermann Usener's distinction between two special fields of research, a philological one devoted to the criticism and reconstruction of texts, and a historical one dedicated to the interpretation of the ancient world in its totality.[6]

The Greek and Roman counterpart to the philologian was, of course, the grammarian, whose task included the criticism and editing of texts—philology in the narrow sense of the term as now understood. The modern debate on the nature, function, and limits of philology is essentially a recapitulation of ancient discussions of the definition of grammar. The school of Crates made grammar a separate discipline, distinct from, and subordinate to, history and literary criticism; whereas Dionysius Thrax and, following him, Asclepiades of Mirlea (first century) preferred to make grammar include the wider as well as narrower tasks of interpretation, defining them as "greater" and "lesser" versions of the discipline,[7] or, in the case of Asclepiades, distinguishing two different aspects of grammar, one "technical," the other "historical."[8]

In the preparation of editions—the art of *ecdotics*, to use H. Quentin's convenient term[9]—the Alexandrian philologians had already attained a high level of technical and theoretical expertise, which included both textual criticism and linguistic and critical exegesis. Aristarchus of Samothrace, perhaps the greatest of the Alexandrian philologians, had already applied to Homeric criticism an anthropological method that insisted on "interpreting Homer with Homer";[10] that is, in the light of the customs and social structure of the heroic age that the poet describes.

Even today the debate on philology hinges on whether or to what degree the spheres of philology and literary criticism, broadly defined, are separate and distinct. Scholars are clearly of two minds as to the character of the relationship, to judge from the actual attitudes displayed in their research. On the one hand, ecdotics has moved beyond the procedures established by Lachmann in the first half of the last century[11] to become a scientific technique based on mathematics and statistics;[12] on the other hand, there is a tendency to posit a close interdependence between the actual act of reconstructing a particular text and a far-reaching process of interpretation that takes into account the concerns and epistemological tools of modern humanistic disciplines as varied as semiotics and cultural anthropology.[13] Thus the distinction posited explicitly by Bense[14] between two levels of investigation does not in any way exclude close interdependence between them. His contrast is between text and literature, of which the former may be described in statistical and structural terms and the latter in terms of logic and the phenomenology of the text. Ultimately all of the possible perspectives proposed by Bense—statistical, logical, phenomenological, and aesthetic—are capable of combining to produce a total understanding of the internal and external world of the text, even when they exist autonomously as successive phases in the process of analysis.

The text is a complex structure of linguistic materials with metricorhythmical, practical, and referential implications. A number of disciplines are thus involved in its interpretation—beginning with the initial act of constituting or establishing it.

Textual criticism is a method that has its own rules governing the systematic analysis of the tradition; but the application of these rules must be combined at every level with interpretation. The constraints they impose on the editor need not be strictly observed when context and extratextual references known to the philological reader clearly require the choice of one particular reading rather than another. Statistical data on phrase and word occurrence are interesting and useful, if one does not lose sight of the role that rare or unique expressions play within the general relational system of a linguistic structure. Quantification is essentially a means of determining the density or range of information in a message; it tells nothing about its character or specific contents.

Interpretation is equally indispensable in the case of "equivalent" variants. Fränkel[15] offers an unsatisfactory method for dealing with them when he recommends that editors "select consistently on the basis of the quality of the witnesses, or else completely arbitrarily" as soon as the choice between variants makes so little difference that the readings are in effect interchangeable. The criterion is, as has been observed,[16] "too objective, hence inexact," and it is open to two different types of objection. The first brings us back to the distinction between *codices superiores* and *deteriores:* it is now generally agreed that there are no manuscripts that are absolutely "good" (i.e., free from errors); and even bad manuscripts can contain correct readings. The second objection has to do with the very notion of "equivalence" of variants, a notion that a full understanding of the text sometimes shows to be inadequate.

I would like to illustrate this point with a fragment of Anacreon (81 Gent.). It comes to us by indirect transmission, reported in two late sources, the *Etymologicum Magnum* (714, 38) and the *Orthographia* of Johannes Charax, a grammarian of the sixth century A.D.[17] The citations are identical except for their initial word: Θρηϊκίην σίοντα χαίτην in the *Etymologicum;* ὡρικὴν σίοντα χαίτην[18] in Charax's *Orthographia.*

Both readings yield satisfactory sense: "shaking his Thracian locks," on the assumption that the subject is a person from Thrace, as Smerdis, one of the boys celebrated in the poet's verse, in fact was; or "shaking his youthful locks." And either line is acceptable metrically: a trochaic dimeter if one reads *horikén,* a combination of choriamb and reizianum well documented elsewhere in Anacreon[19] if one reads *Threïkíen,* and scans it as a tetrasyllable. Trisyllabic scansion is equally possible, in which case the line will be, as with the reading *horikén,* a trochaic dimeter.

Editors regularly choose Θρηκίην, following paleographical criteria: ὁπικήν, the erroneous reading of *Codex Haunensis* 1965 (Charax), is explained as an obvious corruption of Θρηκίην. Egenolff,[20] on the other hand, was of the opinion that the original reading was ὡρικήν, subsequently corrupted into ὁρικήν and, ultimately, Θρηκίην. A more solid basis for discussion is provided by context, which in this case, because a fragment is involved, consists of the complex of testimony relating to Anacreon's entire poetic *oeuvre,* as well as such indications as can be found in the late imitations known as the *Anacreontica.* It is this macrocontext of relevant data which contains several pieces of information that can help determine the textual critic's choice. The first of these is the presence of praise for Bathyllos's youth and beauty as a recurrent motif in Anacreon's poetry, for *hóra* was, as can be seen from a reference in Maximus of Tyre,[21] the descriptive word used in this connection. The second piece of information is an easy inference from the late imitation in *Anacr.* 17.18 Bergk[4] where Bathyllos's locks are praised through the image of a tree "with soft, quivering leaves" (v. 12 ἁπαλὰς δ' ἔσεισε χαίτας). Our fragment has evidently served as a model here, as its use of the phrase σείειν χαίτας shows. One should add that some of our information concerning Bathyllos comes from Herodian,[22] who is Charax's source.[23]

All this evidence seems to confirm the reading *horikén*, especially if we take into account that the adjective, as is clear from Aristophanes,[24] was a characteristic part of *sermo amatorius*.

What seemed equivalent variants at first turn out not to be so in reality. Although it is hard to accept literally Waszink's somewhat categorical assertion that perfect equivalence is "extremely rare,"[25] it is still true that, as he points out, its occurrence is destined to become less and less frequent in direct proportion to the broadening and deepening of our knowledge.

But even if *horikén* is accepted, for the reasons indicated, as a true reading, the alternative represented by *Threïkíen* is a significant one and suggests important considerations as to its possible origins. Praise of the locks of the Thracian boy Smerdis was also, as has been pointed out, a favorite theme with Anacreon; and their cutting is a motif for which there is papyrus attestation as well.[26] It was a genuine Anacreontic reminiscence that led to the replacing of "youthful locks" by "Thracian locks"–a variant that is not necessarily late but more likely, in my opinion, a very early one, perhaps already mentioned in the Alexandrian editions by Aristarchus and Aristophanes of Byzantium.

One further hypothesis is in order, however–having to do with the earliest (i.e., oral and symposiastic) phase in the history of our text. It was constant practice among the Greeks to reuse poetic texts, both epic and lyric, at banquets,[27] rhapsodic recitations, and public occasions whose character was always changing. One must also remember that, until a very late period, it was usual for itinerant rhapsodes to alternate performances of epic and lyric texts.[28] So far as Anacreon is concerned, we know from the later testimony of Aristophanes[29] that he, like Alcaeus, was one of the favorite sources in the fifth century for the texts that were sung at Athenian banquets. It is thus legitimate to ask whether on some particular occasion a professional singer or one of the guests did not deliberately introduce the variant *Threïkíen* as a compliment to some Thracian boy actually present at the banquet. Reuse of expressions from famous poems of the past here takes the form of adaptation to the particular facts of a new situation, as it did regularly at this stage in Greek literary development.

The textual problem is worth dwelling upon because it illustrates the complexities that can arise with a text that has passed through a phase of oral transmission. In this particular instance we were in a position to determine the genuine reading with some degree of probability, but it is precisely in connection with the rhapsodic epic tradition that the phenomenon of interchangeable or equivalent variants is encountered with systemic frequency. This was duly pointed out as early as the first century A.D. by Flavius Josephus, when he linked the frequent variants (*diaphoníai*) found in the Homeric poems to the fact that they were memorized texts, orally transmitted.[30] The tradition is a highly fluid one, as can be seen from the variants in the papyri and citations in other authors which go back either to the creative phase of bardic improvisation or to the more exclusively repetitive one of rhapsodic recitation. The variants are not always accidental: often they are determined by the requirements of the particular location or occasion of performance. And the phenomenon is not confined to epic. Among many lyric instances, one of the most striking is the complex of variants in several couplets of Mimnermus and Solon which were included in the Theognidean collection of verses for use at symposia.

An exemplary case for anyone interested in textual critical theory as applied to problems of oral transmission is the Homeric Hymn to Apollo, the Delian section of which contains several lines (vv. 146-50, 165-72) transmitted both directly and indirectly, through citations in Thucydides (3, 104, 4-5) and Aelius Aristides (34, 35).

The Thucydidean version offers a series of readings that are interchangeable with their counterparts in the medieval manuscripts—competing variants, involving formulaic expressions for the most part, which do not compromise the formal correctness of the poetic style. We are thus presented with two equally valid redactions—two parallel outcomes of the oral rhapsodic tradition. The only thing an editor can do is recognize that he is dealing with a polymorphous text and offer an open edition of the text which presents the Thucydidean version in an appropriate section of the apparatus.[31] Traditions of this sort are those to which it is most legitimate to apply the skepticism of J. Bédier and his principle of the individuality of each separate witness.

What justifies this ecdotic practice are the concrete dynamics of the rhapsodic tradition, within which oral-mnemonic transmission and written transmission—when it existed—were in a state of continuous interchange and interdependence.

As far as the Delian hymn is concerned, we know that there were two written redactions in the archaic period. The older, on a whitewashed tablet (*leúkoma*), was preserved on the island of Delos itself, in the temple of Artemis. According to the *Contest of Homer and Hesiod*,[32] its transcription was a result of the enthusiasm produced by Homer's performance of the hymn on the occasion of the solemn festival of the Ionians at Delos. The other version, which goes back to the second half of the sixth century, was the work of a Chian rhapsode,

Kynaithos, who wrote down the hymn and then claimed to be its author.[33] The divergences between the Thucydidean text and that found in the medieval codices show, however, that sporadic written transcription did not save the text from the fluctuation that is normal in the rhapsodic tradition.

Analogous fluctuations affect the linguistic coloration of such texts. I am referring here to the overall tendency for poetic texts originating in a particular area of the Greek world to appear in a different dialectical dress when reused in a different area. The phenomenon is a natural one, given the propensity of scribes and performers to follow the linguistic habits most congenial to them, and it is paralleled, as has been pointed out (chap. 4), in other literary cultures. The best-known instances involve a strophe of Alcaeus (fr. 249 V.), now available in its original version thanks to a papyrus discovery, but also transmitted by Athenaeus (15, 695a) in Iono-Attic form as an anonymous banquet song; the Ionicized elegies of Tyrtaeus, which contain secure instances of Dorisms (the future ἀλοιησεῦμεν, the comparative μάλιον [= μᾶλλον], and -α stem accusative plurals in -ας) that cannot be explained if one accepts the *communis opinio* that the original language of elegy was always Ionic; and the inscription for the Corinthian dead at Salamis (7 Peek = 7 Pfohl), which appears in Iono-Attic in Plutarch's citation (*De Herodt. malign.* 870e) but in Doric on the stone. The only non–Iono-Attic form preserved by Plutarch is the short -α accusative plural Πέρσας, which, for metrical reasons, could not be changed. The text of Tyrtaeus was clearly subjected to the same sort of treatment during the period of its greatest popularity in Attica (fifth and fourth centuries), the non-Ionic forms it contains being those that could not have been changed without damaging the meter.[34]

The phenomenon was well understood by the Alexandrian editors who, to the extent that it was possible, sought to reestablish the original dialect of the works of poets such as Alcman, Stesichorus, Sappho, and Alcaeus. In many instances, however, not having sufficient epigraphical evidence to guide us, we do not know to what extent this restoration managed to stick to genuinely archaic dialectical forms, as opposed to those current in the editors' own day.

The linguistic term *diasystem* has been applied to the concrete study of textual tradition by Segre,[35] and it provides the most useful conceptual tool for understanding the complex of phenomena discussed here. A *diasystem* is, in the dialectology of Weinreich,[36] either a compromise between two linguistic systems in contact with each other or the supersystem that includes, or is presupposed by, two related subsystems.

In the study of texts the term may apply either to linguistic coloring—
what Segre calls a *linguistic diasystem*—or, more generally, to a *stylistic
diasystem*—the system of variants which characterizes an individual
witness to the tradition of a particular text as a direct expression of the
culture and taste of its period. However, insofar as the system of variants which distinguishes one witness to a tradition is not simply
dialectological, it tends not to be simply stylistic either. At times it
may involve genuine reelaboration of the text within the context of a
particular setting and in response to various requirements, not the
least of which are those of the audience. The reuse of epic and lyric
texts in rhapsodic recitations and banquets offers as convincing a
demonstration of this as any. The text of the *Iliad* transmitted in the
medieval codices is the result of a long process of reelaboration and
normalization (affecting, among other things, the metrical structure of
the hexameter itself), which extends from the age of bardic citharoedes
such as Demodocus and Phemius down to the Hellenistic period. One
need only think of the exordium to the *Ancient Iliad* (Ἀρχαία Ἰλιάς)
mentioned by Aristoxenus (fr. 91, 1 Wehrli), whose content and metrical structure are completely different from the exordium to our edition
of the *Iliad,* not to mention further variants, such as those recorded by
the grammarians Crates (second century) and Nicanor (second century A.D.).[37]

The notion of diasystem can certainly play a clarifying role in the
debate between neo-Lachmannians and Béderians, removing some of
the dogmatic certainties involved in postulating mechanically recon-
structable texts and final, definitive critical editions. It is by now generally recognized that a given recension is rarely the result of a purely
mechanical process; thus reconstruction of an archetype is always
problematic and not always legitimate. The innovatory views of Giorgio Pasquali on this subject have won increasing endorsement in recent
decades, culminating in the radical, if at times questionable, position
of the latest editor of Sophocles, R. D. Dawe.[38] Obviously the notion
of diasystem must be adjusted to the different forms that a textual tradition may take depending on the character of the period, the literary
system involved, and also the individual literary work.

In studying the phenomenology of a text in which orality has been
a determining factor, one should take into account certain important
analogies between the earliest phase in the transmission of archaic
Greek poetry and the eighteenth-century tradition of poetic improvisation discussed earlier.[39] Several of these eighteenth-century texts have
survived in the transcriptions of scribes and stenographers. These were

sometimes made without the improviser's knowledge and never revised by him. The few printed editions were seen through the press by friends and admirers. When asked by the audience to repeat a theme already treated in an earlier performance, the improviser would present it in a version that was completely different, even in metrical structure. The result was a new song with only a thematic link to the earlier one. The practice of the Yugoslavian poet-improvisers discussed by Lord in his comparative study of ancient and modern oral epic[40] is exactly the same. Transcriptions of the same performance made by several scribes show obvious errors resulting from mishearing, but also lexical, phonological, and orthographic variants of which the only thing that can be said is that, for whatever reason, they go back to the scribe or the first editor. Thus for Perfetti's *Lament of Adam* we have three transcriptions from different hands, all preserved in the Biblioteca Comunale of Siena, the poet's birthplace. But the printed edition, published one year after the poet's death by his friend Domenico Cianfogni,[41] also shows a number of variants, though at times all three manuscripts agree with each other against Cianfogni.[42]

One does not need to go into the complicated problem of explaining and correlating such variants to see that any future editor of these improvised texts must adhere to the Béderian criterion, weighting manuscripts and printed text equally, even though Cianfogni in his preface insists on the greater fidelity of his version vis-à-vis the other, in his view, less conscientious ones.

It is obvious from everything said thus far that, so far as critical theory is concerned, the chapter on the ecdotics of the oral text has yet to be written. Medievalists and students of folklore have demonstrated, up to now, a far greater sensitivity to this problem than classicists. A comprehensive theory must, however, be based on a typology of oral texts which takes full account of the different ways in which a particular composition can be oral and of the different levels—cultivated and popular—on which orality may operate. Plotting the eighteenth-century tradition mentioned above on these two axes allows us to characterize it as learned and extemporaneous at the same time—an almost unique combination among the cases recorded by literary and anthropological research.

The prospect of an open edition is not, however, confined to texts whose transmission has gone through an oral phase. It should be, with appropriate modifications, the ideal objective of textual criticism in general. I am not, of course, proposing a revival of the views of Bédier, whose neutrality in the face of alternative possibilities is only valid in particular cases. What I do propose is an "open" edition, open in that, through a full collection of documentary and critical material, it provides the reader with basic orientation on the problematic aspects of the text and on their possible interpretations and solutions. This will also be an edition that is aware of diasystems, both ancient and modern—that is, of the way differences in place and time determine the reception of a text. Editorial choice should always be offered as part of a dialectic, directed toward creating an audience of active rather than passive readers. For a critical edition is by its very nature provisional, never definitive. It is never so scientific that it ceases to be a part of history.

To penetrate into the structures of the text and determine its meanings, the philological reader must use a multileveled interpretative technique, oriented toward considerations that are syntactic, semantic, and pragmatic (i.e., concerned with reception by an audience). His perspective calls for a close interaction between formal analysis and socio-anthropological analysis, directed toward as complete a recovery as possible of the textual code; that is, of the system of ideas and conventions for which the text is a correlate. The result is a state of tension in which it is all too easy to lose sight of the fact that there always remains a margin of arbitrariness, a margin produced by the unconscious interference of the contemporary codes of interpretation that are familiar to the reader and are capable of being artificially expanded through dogmatic application of a priori ideological formulae. There is a thin line between the art of interpretation and what has been called "interpretative cooperation."[43] The latter involves what is certainly a legitimate reuse of a text for personal purposes or as documentation, but it is not an activity on the same level as the effort to recover a work in its historical totality and uniqueness.

In threading his way through the diasystemic web, the philologian must achieve simultaneous mastery of three closely linked operations: technical *recensio;* interpretation aimed at historical reconstruction in all its aspects; and, finally, that art of knowing how to read which Friedrich Nietzsche saw as the identifying mark of the whole discipline.[44]

. . .

# Notes

1. See "L'interpretazione dei lirici greci arcaici nella dimensione del nostro tempo," *Quad. Urb.* 8 (1969): 7-21 (translated into English as "The Interpretation of the Greek Lyric Poets in Our Time," in *Contemporary Literary Hermeneutics and the Interpretation of Classical Texts,* ed. S. Kresic [Ottawa, 1981], pp. 109-20).

2. (The author's addenda appear either as new paragraphs added to the notes of the original edition, or as separate notes referred to in the text by asterisks rather than numbers [translator's note].)

3. (Also omitted are a long note on the meters of Archilochus [pp. 255-56 in the Italian edition], two paragraphs on the interpretation of Simonides 542 P. [pp. 89-90], and several brief passages where it seemed better to replace summary and recapitulation of arguments developed elsewhere in the text by a simple cross-reference [translator's note].)

## ONE: ORALITY AND ARCHAIC CULTURE

1. Burckhardt 1900, pp. 185ff.

2. On oral literature and culture in general see Innis 1950; Vansina 1961; Ong 1967; Stanford 1967, pp. 1-26 (on the predominance of the oral over the written word in Greek culture); J. J. Duggan, ed., *Oral Literature: Seven Essays* (Edinburgh and London, 1975); B. A. Stolz-R. S. Shannon, eds., *Oral Literature and the Formula* (Ann Arbor, 1976); Finnegan 1970; Finnegan 1977; H. Jason-D. Segal, eds., *Patterns in Oral Literature* (The Hague and Paris, 1977); Gasparov

1977; Lotman 1978; Zumthor 1979; Goody 1980; Detienne 1980; Havelock 1982; B. Gentili–G. Paioni, eds., *Oralità: Cultura, letteratura, discorso* (Atti del Convegno Internazionale, Urbino, 21–25 July 1980), Rome, 1985. Cf. also *Alfabetismo e cultura scritta nella storia della società italiana* (Atti del Seminario, Perugia, 29–30 March 1977), Perugia, 1978, and the journals *Quaderni storici* 35 (1977) (*Oral History: Fra antropologia e storia*); *New Literary History*, especially no. 8 (1977) (*Oral Cultures and Oral Performances*); and *Cahiers de littérature orale* (Publications Orientalistes de France). For an introduction to the bibliography of Homeric epic see J. Latacz, ed., *Homer* (Darmstadt, 1979); and Broccia 1979, to which should be added Durante 1971; Durante 1976; J. Russo 1971; Nagler 1974; E. A. Havelock–J. P. Hershbell, eds., *Communication Arts in the Ancient World* (New York, 1978); Tsagarakis 1979; Skafte Jensen 1980; Fantuzzi 1980a; *I poemi epici rapsodici non omerici e la tradizione orale* (Atti del Convegno di Venezia, 28–30 September 1977), Padova, 1981; and Cantilena 1983. The list of general works should also include I. Okpewho, *The Epic in Africa: Toward a Poetics of Oral Performance* (New York, 1979); M. Detienne, *L'invention de la mythologie* (Paris, 1981), pp. 50–86; A. Assmann–J. Assmann–C. Hardmeier, eds., *Schrift und Gedächtnis: Archäologie der literarischen Kommunikation*, I (Munich, 1983). For interesting new contributions on various aspects of oral culture and the methods of investigation to be used in studying it, see D. G. Miller, *Improvisation, Typology, Culture and "the New Orthodoxy": How "Oral" Is Homer?* (Washington, D.C., 1982); W. J. Ong, *Orality and Literacy: The Technologizing of the Word* (London, 1982); P. Zumthor, *Introduction à la poésie orale* (Paris, 1983); W. Kullmann, "Oral Poetry Theory and Neoanalysis in Homeric Research," *Gr. Rom. Byz. Studies* 25 (1984): 307–23; G. Cerri, ed., *Scrivere e recitare: Modelli di trasmissione del testo poetico nell'antichità e nel medioevo* (Rome, 1986); I. Morris, "The Use and Abuse of Homer," *Class. Antiquity* 5 (1986): 83–94; R. Whitaker–E. Sienaert, eds., *Oral Tradition and Literacy: Changing Visions of the World* (Durban, 1986). A new journal devoted specifically to the subject, *Oral Tradition*, began appearing in 1986. See, for a general bibliographical survey, J. M. Foley, *Oral-Formulaic Theory and Research: An Introduction and Annotated Bibliography* (New York, 1984).

3. See, most recently, Finnegan 1977, pp. 16ff.

4. It is now generally believed that in the earliest period the activity of the bard was not placed in the same category as that of the craftsman (Svenbro 1976, pp. 194ff.); and E. A. Havelock (1978a, pp. 18ff.) would make the notion of the poet as craftsman a product of the growth of literacy. Hence the numerous metaphors taken from the realm of the arts and crafts that can be found in the choral lyric of the fifth century. What an analysis of terms relating to the activity of the poet already in use in Homer does show is that effective narrative, like effective speech in general, was felt as a technical capacity for the construction of discourse. This is the sense of the epithet *artiepés* in Homer (used of Achilles at *Il.* 22, 281; cf. Calame 1977b); and the same applies to other

terms used with reference to poetic composition: *thésis, sýnthesis, syntíthemi, kósmos epéon,* and the like. Cf. chap. 4.

5. 90, 9, 1 D.-K. This and all subsequent classical dates are B.C., unless otherwise noted.

6. *Marmor Parium, FGrHist* 239 A 54; Cic. *De finib.* 2, 32; Quint. 11, 2, 11-14; Longin. *Rhet.* 1, 2, 201 Hammer; *Suda,* s.v. "Σιμωνίδης"; cf. also Christ 1941, pp. 75ff.; Detienne 1967, pp. 110ff., 123; and Blum 1969, pp. 41-46.

7. Plut. *De glor. Ath.* 3, 346f; cf. Lanata 1963, pp. 68ff.

8. Yates 1966, p. 43. On the conception and its relation to the forms of memory and the various aspects of the mnemonic process, see Le Goff 1979, especially pp. 1068-81.

9. Goody 1977.

10. R. Mastromattei (letter to the author, 2 April 1980).

11. Havelock 1978a, pp. 11-14.

12. Durante 1976, pp. 177ff.; C. O. Pavese 1972, p. 215; C. O. Pavese 1974, pp. 15-22. The word *rhapsoidós* occurs for the first time in Herodotus 5, 67, where it is told how Cleisthenes of Sicyon, being at war with Argos, forbade rhapsodic competitions, because of the constant celebration of Argos and the Argives contained in the Homeric poems that they were in the habit of reciting. But the use of the term may well be earlier—at least as early as Cleisthenes himself (shortly after 600). One thing, at any rate, is certain: the notion of *rháptein aoidén* was already familiar to Hesiod (see below). On *rhapsoidós* with reference to the Sphinx (Soph. *O. R.* 391), see Ritoók 1962.

13. West (1966a, p. 164) observes, quite sensibly, that "if Hesiod bore a staff instead of a lyre, then it was not because this was typical at his date, or in his area or for his genre, but rather because he could not obtain a lyre or could not play one—he had had no professional training."

14. For the meaning of *rháptein* cf. the analysis of Durante 1976, pp. 176ff.

15. Philoch. *FGrHist* 328 F 212.

16. The *rhaptà épe* of Pind. *Nem.* 2, 1ff. should be understood in the same way.

17. Svenbro 1976 (pp. 44ff.), arguing from the episode narrated at Herodotus 5, 67 (cf. n.12), maintains that the rhapsodes in the time of Cleisthenes of Sicyon were no longer masters of a formulaic technique but reduced by now to the simple delivery of rigidly fixed texts: otherwise Cleisthenes would not have been forced to exclude renditions of Homer from public competitions. (Rhapsodes who still possessed the creative ability of bards would have been able to adapt their Homeric material to the political situation, eliminating all those references to Argos and the Argives which the tyrant found unacceptable.) But can we be really certain that by *Homéreia épe* Herodotus intended a reference to the poems of the Trojan rather than the Theban Cycle (the *Thebais* and the *Epigonoi*)? Elsewhere (4, 32) he attributes the latter, albeit with some hesitation, to Homer. (Cf. the commentary ad loc. of How-Wells 1928, p. 34; Rossi 1981.) It would have been very difficult, even for a bard, to eliminate

all references to Argos and the Argives from a poem that began with the words *Árgos áeide, theá.*

In support of my hypothesis concerning the content of the rhapsodic poems recited at Sicyon, see E. Cingano, "Clistene di Sicione, Erodoto e i poemi del Ciclo tebano," *Quad. Urb.,* n.s. 20 [49] (1985): 31–40.

18. *Schol.* Pind. *Nem.* 2, 1c, III p. 29 Drachm.

19. Athen. 14, 620bc, a notice derived from the Peripatetics Chamaeleon (fr. 28 Wehrli) and Clearchos (fr. 92 Wehrli). For rhapsodic performances of the poems of Archilochus in the sixth century, cf. Heraclitus, 22 B 42 D.-K. = Archil. Test. 75 T., and, for a later period, Plat. *Ion* 531a.

20. Plat. *Leg.* 2, 658b.

21. Plat. *Ion* 533b.

22. Aristot. *Poet.* 1447b 20.

23. Cf. Lord 1960; Lord 1985.

24. Cf. J. Russo–Simon 1968, now revised and expanded in Simon 1978, pp. 53–88.

25. See, for documentation, Gentili 1980.

26. Cianfogni 1748, pp. 51–83.

27. Tommaso Sgricci of Arezzo (cf. Gentili 1980, pp. 25ff., nn. 15, 16, 17; 38n.44) was accustomed to treat only three types of subject matter in his improvisations: heroic, elegiac, and tragic, setting them to, respectively, blank verse, terza rima, and "in the tragic mode"–a combination of blank verse (for dialogue) and (where the chorus was supposed to be speaking) a medley of various meters, mostly heptasyllables and octosyllables.

28. Fernow 1806, pp. 315ff.

29. Cf. chap. 2.

30. On the technical aspect of the musical accompaniment to this extemporaneous poetry, see Franchi 1985.

31. Cianfogni 1748, p. 31.

32. Fernow 1806, p. 312.

33. Bettinelli 1799, pp. 47–50. I must cite from the edition prepared by the author himself, the more recent ones being, as is well known, mere anthologies.

34. C. De Brosses, *Lettres d'Italie* I, Dijon, 1928, letter 28 (21 October 1739), pp. 229ff.

35. See Gianni 1807-8 (vol. V in the Silvestri ed.), pp. 17–24 (poem improvised on the occasion of the battle of Marengo); 35–44 (capture of Vienna); 45–54 (battle of Austerlitz); 55–67 (battle of Jena); 71–84 (battle of Friedland); and the preface by the friend of the poet responsible for collecting his works (vol. II, pp. 5–16).

36. Fabi Montani 1843, p. 22.

37. Cf. Vitagliano 1905, p. 83.

38. Strab. 14, 5, 15 = Snell, *Tr.G.F.* 144.

39. For poetic *manía* and an analysis of the relevant Platonic passages, see the observations of Dodds 1951, pp. 80ff., and, above all, Massenzio 1985.

40. B 17 and 18 D.-K.; cf. Lanata 1963, pp. 254ff.

41. Cf. Havelock 1963, especially chaps. 1–3.

42. P. Metastasio, *Tutte le opere*, III, ed. B. Brunelli (Milan, 1951), letter 492, pp. 659ff.

43. Isocr. *Panath.* 10–11; *Ad. Nicocl.* 48; cf. Gentili-Cerri 1983, p. 13.

44. Cf. Vitagliano 1905, p. 141.

45. Cf. chap. 4.

46. Cf. Nagler 1974, p. xxiii.

47. Cf., in this connection, the detailed observations of Pfeiffer 1968, p. 25.

48. Gentili 1977b.

49. Cf., for the meaning of *oíme*, Durante 1976, pp. 176ff. It is interesting how closely—down to minute particulars—the vocal and instrumental renditions of B. Perfetti described by De Brosses in his book of travels recall the Demodocus scenes of the *Odyssey*, the oldest travel book in the literature of the West.

For a profile of Demodocus and the type of singer he represents, see A. Gostoli, "La figura dell'aedo preomerico nella filologia peripatetica ed ellenistica: Demodoco tra mito e storia," in *Scrivere e recitare: Modelli di trasmissione del testo poetico nell'antichità e nel medioevo*, ed. G. Cerri (Rome, 1986), pp. 103–26.

50. In that it involves rendition of a song to the accompaniment of a silent chorus of dancers, Demodocus's bardic performance conforms exactly to the citharoedic pattern; see Calame 1977a, I, p. 104n.126, with the bibliography given there.

51. *Ap.* Ps.-Plut. *De mus.* 3, 1132bc = Heraclid. Pont. fr 157 Wehrli.

52. Gentili 1977b, pp. 24ff.

53. Jeffery 1961, p. 21; Guarducci 1967, pp. 70–73. For a discussion of the various lines of approach to the problem see "Dal sillabario minoico all'alfabeto greco," *Parola d. passato* 31 (1976): 5–128.

54. See Havelock 1978a, p. 17 (= Havelock 1982, p. 180).

55. See, for the first of these hypotheses, Burr 1944, who would have the Catalogue of Ships, in its present form, go back to a catalogue of Mycenaean date containing a list of the ships and warriors participating in the expedition against Troy; and, for the second, Svenbro (1976, p. 43n.131), who accepts Jeffery's dating of the earliest alphabet. Kirk, by contrast (1962, chap. 14), tends to assign composition (which he places in the eighth century) and fixing in written form to different phases in the history of the Homeric poems.

56. Havelock 1978a, p. 5 (= Havelock 1982, p. 168).

57. See Finley 1957; Finley 1977a; the introduction in Maddoli 1977; Carandini 1979 (cf. Lanza 1981); Musti 1981, pp. 23ff., with extensive bibliography.

58. See Brillante 1981.

59. Cf. Taylour 1958; Biancofiore 1967; Vagnetti 1970; Vagnetti 1980; Marazzi-Tusa 1976; "L'isola di Vivara: Nuove ricerche," *Parola d. passato* 33 (1978): 197ff.

60. See, in this connection, the pertinent observations of Kontoleon 1963,

pp. 175ff. (on the problem of writing in the time of Archilochus).

61. Wolf 1795, p. 76 (Eng. trans., pp. 94–95).

62. For analysis of these and other pieces of evidence, see Davison 1962, pp. 219ff.

63. Taken probably from Asclepiades of Mirlea (c. 100); cf. Kaibel 1898, p. 26.

64. Davison 1962, p. 220.

65. Xenoph. *Mem.* 4, 2, 10.

66. Xenoph. *Symp.* 3, 5.

67. Plut. *Alc.* 7, 2.

68. The available evidence is too familiar to require illustration at this point. On the fluctuations to which treatments of traditional subject matter are subject cf. Van Groningen 1953; Finley 1965; Brillante 1981, pp. 45–77.

69. Turner 1952 (revised and updated in Turner 1975).

70. See, especially, Aesch. *Suppl.* (463?) 946ff.: ταῦτ' οὐ πίναξίν ἐστιν ἐγγεγραμμένα / οὐδ' ἐν πτυχαῖς βίβλων κατεσφραγισμένα, Pind. *Ol.* 10, 1ff. (474): ἀνάγνωτε . . . πόθι φρενὸς / ἐμᾶς γέγραπται, Crit. fr. 1, 9 Gent.-Pr.: Φοίνικες δ' εὗρον γράμματ' ἀλεξίλογα. Cf., for further documentation, Pfeiffer 1968, p. 26. The very rare references before the fifth century involve either an epistolary text (*Il.* 6, 169), the written recording of laws (Sol. fr. 30, 20 Gent.-Pr.), or the reading of a sepulchral inscription (Peek 1210, 2 Eretria sixth to fifth centuries).

71. Immerwahr 1964.

72. Cf. chap. 4.

73. Havelock 1980; Segal 1982.

74. Page 1963.

75. Cf. chap. 10.

76. The practice is attested to by Heraclitus; cf. n.19.

77. The *skytále* used by the Spartans consisted of a stick and, wound obliquely around it, a strip of hide on which the message to be transmitted was written. If the strip was removed from the stick the message became undecipherable. It was thus necessary for the recipient to have a stick of the same thickness. This means of communication was devised by the Spartans for the purpose of sending military despatches to commanders in the field; cf. Thuc. 1, 131; *Schol. Pind. Ol.* 6, 91 (154d, I p. 190 Drachm.); Hershbell in Havelock 1978a, p. 86. In the fragment of Archilochus ("I shall tell you a story, Kerykides, grim messenger" [*achyméne skytále*]) one should note the wordplay between *Kerykíde* (son of herald) and *skytále* ("messenger stick" with grim tidings). It is unclear whether *skytále* refers to the speaker, to the poet (Lasserre-Bonnard) or to Kerykides (Bonanno 1980a, p. 78); one may infer, however, from the metaphorical way in which the word is used, that the message was one that only the recipient could understand.

78. Thus Jeffery 1961, pp. 57ff.

79. C. O. Pavese 1972, pp. 111–96; Cantilena 1981; Mureddu 1983.

80. On the use of the *Theognidea* at banquets, cf. Vetta 1980, pp. xvii ff.

81. Cf. Finnegan 1977, pp. 82ff.

82. See Calame 1977a, I, pp. 394 and 398ff.

83. Cf. chap. 2, n.4.

84. Cf. n.38.

85. Gentili 1980, p. 38n.44.

86. G. B. Vico, *La scienza nuova seconda, giusta l'edizione del 1744*, ed. F. Nicolini (Bari, 1953)[4], III, "Della discoverta del vero Omero"; cf. Cerri 1985.

87. Bettinelli 1799, p. 209.

88. See, for example, Blackwell 1735, pp. 188ff.; R. Wood 1769, p. 49; Barthélemy 1788, chap. 80; Schlegel 1798, p. 154; Rochette 1817 and 1818; Welcker 1845, pp. lxxxvii–ci.

The historian and anthropologist A. H. L. Heeren occupies a position of special importance among Homeric oralists – far in advance of that of any of his late eighteenth- and early nineteenth-century contemporaries. Drawing attention to the figure of Demodocus as depicted in the *Odyssey* (*Ideen über die Politik, den Verkehr und den Handel der vornehmsten Völker der alten Welt*, pt. 1, sec. 1. Vienna, 1817 [1812], pp. 113ff.), he developed a thesis whose essential novelty lay in the realization that the Homeric singer could either improvise extemporaneously or use songs that had been memorized (or even committed to writing in advance). Improvisation thus allowed the singer to vary preexisting epic material at will. See R. Thiel, "Arnold Heeren und Johann Gottfried Herder: Ergänzungen zur Vorgeschichte der Oral-Poetry-Theorie," *Quad. Urb.*, n.s. 21 [50] (1985): 139–44.

89. Wolf 1795, p. 102 (Eng. trans., p. 78): "Neque enim nobis opus est afferre singularia specimina validioris memoriae, ut Hortensii oratoris, quem Cicero narrat ea, quae secum commentatus esset, sine scripto omnia reddere potuisse iisdem verbis, quibus cogitavisset, sive poëtarum, tum αὐτοσχεδιαζόντων, qui Italis *improvisatores* vocantur, tum aliorum multorum, quos constat, praesertim interdictos usu scripturae, plura milia versuum et fecisse in animo, et memoriae infixa saepius repetiisse."

90. I find it quite impossible to agree with Latacz's categorical assertion (1979, p. 39) that "Milman Parry in 1928 and the years following said nothing of importance that Homeric criticism did not already know in 1850. Parry, to be sure, said it more precisely and was able to do so because he supported his theory with minute statistical analyses. But the theory itself was not new."

91. Frye 1969, pp. 15–16.

92. G. Quasha, D. Antin, J. Rotenberg, R. Kelly, R. Gross, D. Tedlock, and C. Stein, for example. The journal *New Literary History* now functions as an organ for the elaboration and diffusion of their ideas: see Quasha 1977, p. 491.

## Two: Poetry and Music

1. Plut. *Quaest. symp.* 9, 748a. On the character of the hyporcheme, a dance typical of lyric poetry, see the exhaustive study of Di Marco 1973–74.

2. *Rep.* 10, 601ab; 606ab ff.

3. *Pol.* 8, 1340a 12; 1341b 32ff.; cf. *Poet.* 1449b 24ff.

4. Evidence from the figurative arts seems to show that musical notation began in the second half of the fifth century (Pöhlmann 1960, pp. 10ff.; Pöhlmann 1976). The most ancient explicit testimony to the (by then well-established) practice is from the fourth century (Aristoxenos *Harm.* 2.39ff., p. 49 Da Rios). On the thesis (Bataille 1961) that would make the notational system known from the tables in Alypios no earlier than the third century, see Hemmerdinger 1982.

5. Cf. Winnington-Ingram 1936; Comotti 1979, pp. 26ff., 63.

6. Ps.-Plut. *De mus.* 6, 1133b.

7. *Aiólios, Boiótios* (Ps.-Plut. *De mus.* 4, 1132d; Poll. *Onom.* 4, 65).

8. *Orthios, Trochaîos, Oxýs, Tetraoídios* (Ps.-Plut. loc. cit. and 7, 1133f); *Trimelés* or *Trimerés* (Ps.-Plut. *De mus.* 4, 1132d; 8, 1134b).

9. *Diós, Athenâs, Apóllonos* (Poll. *Onom.* 4, 66), *Pythikós* (Poll. *Onom.* 4, 84).

10. Eupol. fr. 148 K.-A. = 139 Kock; Cratin. fr. 276 K.-A. = 256 Kock.

11. Cf. Taillardat 1965, pp. 456ff.

12. On the dithyramb, see Privitera 1965; Privitera 1972a.

13. Xenoph. *Mem.* 1, 4, 3 = Test. 6 Del Grande.

14. Aristot. *Rhet.* 3, 1409a 26ff. = Test. 3 Del Grande.

15. Ps.-Plut. *De mus.* 30, 1141d = Test. 4 Del Grande.

16. Pherecr. fr. 145, 8ff. Kock (in Ps.-Plut. *De mus.* 30, 1141e) = Test. 8 Del Grande; cf. Lasserre 1954, p. 173.

17. Pherecr. fr. 145, 14 Kock = Test. 3 Del Grande; cf. Düring 1945, p. 186.

18. Procl. *Chrest.* 46, II p. 45 Severyns = Test. 4 Del Grande.

19. Ps.-Plut. *De mus.* 28, 1141ab.

20. Ps.-Plut. *De mus.* 30, 1142a = Test. 15 Del Grande: I read, with Westphal, «μονῳδικὰ» μέλη; the «προβατίων αἰγῶν τε» μέλη of Weil and Reinach is much less probable. For a discussion of the passage, see Pickard-Cambridge 1962, p. 46.

21. Cf. Ferrin Sutton 1983.

22. Cf. Düring 1945, pp. 181ff.

23. Dion. Hal. *De comp. verb.* 29 (pp. 85ff. Us.-Rad.); cf. Ps.-Plut. *De mus.* 4, 1132de.

24. Pherecr. fr. 145, 19 Kock (*ap.* Ps.-Plut. *De mus.* 30, 1141f) = Test. 10 Del Grande.

25. Cf., in addition to the passages cited above, Aristoph. *Nub.* 969ff.; *Thesm.* 100; *Ran.* 1250ff.

26. *Resp.* 3, 397c.

27. "Measures" is my translation of the term βάσεις. The word means *thésis*

(strong beat) in the terminology of the rhythmicians, but here it refers to a metrico-rhythmic *measure;* cf. Aristot. *Metaph.* 14, 1087b (*en rhythmoîs básis he syllabé*). In ancient metrical terminology the word has the meaning "foot" or "dipody."

28. Cf. Gentili 1977a, pp. 13ff. (Eng. trans., pp. 22ff.).

## THREE: MODES AND FORMS OF COMMUNICATION

1. The most ancient attestation of *lyrikós-lyrikoí* is from the first century (Philodemus, π. ποιημ. II 35, 28, ed. Hausrath 1890, p. 255). The term was also taken over by Roman writers: Cicero, *Or.* 55, 183; Horace, *Carm.* 1, 1, 35; Seneca, *Epist.* 49, 5. In the second half of the first century a treatise on lyric poets was written by Didymus of Alexandria (Schmidt 1854, p. 386; Färber 1936). The term is certainly not pre-Alexandrian, the ordinary word in use at an earlier period being *melopoiós* (Aristoph. *Ran.* 1250; Plat. *Ion* 533e, 534a; *Prot.* 326a, etc.).

2. The Alexandrian canonical list of lyric poets is preserved in two anonymous epigrams (*Anth. Pal.* 9, 184; 9, 571), the first of which was probably written a century after Aristophanes of Byzantium. It contained nine names, as follows: Pindar, Bacchylides, Sappho, Anacreon, Stesichorus, Simonides, Ibycus, Alcaeus, Alcman (*Anth. Pal.* 9, 184); or Pindar, Simonides, Stesichorus, Ibycus, Alcman, Bacchylides, Anacreon, Alcaeus, Sappho (*Anth. Pal.* 9, 571). The selection, like those pertaining to iambic, epic, tragic, and comic poetry, could not have been made without the use of certain traditional judgmental criteria, but the internal ordering of the two lists was not according to merit. Pindar's position at the head of both of them might suggest a judgment as to primacy (cf. Quintilian 10, 1, 61: *novem vero lyricorum longe Pindarus princeps*); but there is an anonymous epigram on the nine lyric poets, composed probably in the first or second century A.D. (Labarbe 1968; Gallo 1974, p. 104) and transmitted in certain Pindar manuscripts (Drachmann 1903, pp. 10ff.), which arranges the individual poets in a different order: Alcaeus, Sappho, Stesichorus, Ibycus, Anacreon, Pindar, Simonides, Bacchylides, and Alcman. Aside from dialectical criteria (two Aeolic poets, two Doric, the Ionic Anacreon, then four more Doric ones), geographical considerations seem to be at work here: first Alcaeus and Sappho, from Lesbos; followed by Stesichorus and Ibycus, from Magna Graecia; and then Simonides and Bacchylides, from Ceos. The last criterion, though in connection with a somewhat different ordering, recurs in the second of the two canons in prose which are also transmitted in our Pindar manuscripts (Drachmann 1903, p. 11). There the sequence is Alcaeus, Sappho, Stesichorus, Ibycus, Bacchylides, Simonides, Alcman, Anacreon, and Pindar. Contrast the chronological arrangement in the first prose list: Alcman, Alcaeus, Sappho, Stesichorus, Ibycus, Anacreon, Simonides, Bacchylides, and Pindar. On the much discussed problem of the genesis of the lyric canon see,

in addition to Wilamowitz 1900, Pfeiffer 1968, p. 205; Kirkwood 1974, pp. 2ff.; Gallo 1974, pp. 91ff.

3. For ancient etymologies and modern hypotheses relating to the word *élegos,* see Wilhelm Schmid 1929, p. 353n.7; Frisk 1960 and 1972 s.v.; Chantraine 1970 s.v. The ancients hypothesized a derivation from ἒ ἒ λέγειν (*Etym. Magn.* 326, 49); but the word is probably Asiatic and, more specifically, Phrygian in origin. It is already attested in fifth-century tragedy and comedy in the technical sense of lament performed to the notes of the flute, synonymous with *oîktos* and *thrênos.* Cf. Gentili 1967a; Rosenmeyer 1968.

4. Cf. Crit. fr. 2, 3 Gent.-Pr.; Hephaest. p. 51, 21 Consbr.

5. The last meaning is already attested in the fifth century; in the fourth the noun *elegeía* also begins to appear.

6. See the references in Reitzenstein 1907.

7. Cf., in addition to Reitzenstein 1907, Reitzenstein 1893.

8. Friedländer 1948, pp. 55ff.

9. Cf., for example, Peek 1955, nos. 53 (Corinth, 600), 137 (Tanagra, 600–575) = Pfohl 1967, nos. 5 and 19.

10. Page 1936, p. 214.

11. Cf. Huchzermeyer 1931; Wegner 1949, pp. 185ff.

12. Ps.-Plut. *De mus.,* passim.

13. This is the general line taken by Bowra 1960, p. 5, and Luck 1961, p. 20.

14. Cf. *Schol.* Eur. *Andr.* 103.

15. Cf. Ps.-Plut. *De mus.* 3, 1132c; 8, 1134a; 9, 1134b.

16. Eur. *Andr.* 103; cf. *Schol. ad loc.*

17. Ps.-Plut. *De mus.* 8, 1134a = Mimnermus, Test. 5 Gent.-Pr.

18. Hesych. s.v. "*kradías nómos.*" Cf. Gebhard 1926 and Burkert 1979, pp. 64–66.

19. Cf. Lasserre 1954, pp. 23; 158.

20. Friedländer 1948, pp. 65–69, and Harvey 1955, p. 171, have detected the character of funeral lamentation in Archilochus's elegy to Pericles as well. But it is difficult to conceive of a *thrênos* in which it is said, resolutely and explicitly, "I shall not make anything better by weeping, or worse by giving myself over to celebration and feasting" (fr. 13 T.; cf. Gentili 1967a, pp. 59ff.).

21. Mazzarino 1966, pp. 38ff.

22. It has been proposed afresh by Dover 1963.

23. 7 Peek (7 Pfohl).

24. Plut. *De Herodt. malign.* 870e. For a fuller discussion of the problem, see Gentili 1969b, pp. 536ff.

25. Dover 1963, p. 189—though the nature of the problem had already been clearly set forth by Della Corte 1940, p. 90 = 1971, p. 4.

26. Cf. chap. 7.

27. Archil. Test. 4, $E_1$ col. III, 38 T.

28. There is thus no reason to try to impose an iambic metrical structure on fr. 24 Gent.-Pr. of Mimnermus because of the licentious character of its con-

tents and their presumed inappropriateness for elegy; cf. Gentili 1965b, p. 386.

29. Vv. 241, 533, 825, 1041; cf. Bowra 1960, p. 6. The Archilochean phrase *áidon hyp' auletêros* (fr. 65, 12 T.) cited by Bowra need not refer to the singing of elegy, given the iambic character of the (fairly lacunose) context as restored from *P. Oxy.* 2312, fr. 65. A reference to sung performances of iambic is thus not excluded: see chap. 10.

30. Chamaeleon fr. 28 Wehrli (Athen. 14, 620c) = Mimnermus, Test. 22 Gent.-Pr.; Ps.-Plut. *De mus.* 8, 1134a = Mimnermus, Test. 5 Gent.-Pr.

31. Fr. 7, 37ff. Powell = Mimnermus, Test. 2 Gent.-Pr. The expression Hermesianax uses, *polioî d' epì polláki lotôi kemotheís,* suggests that Mimnermus did not always limit himself to the flute but performed alternately as *auletés* and *auloidós.* This would have meant, in the latter instance, singing his own elegies—perhaps accompanied by an attendant flute-girl. I do not find convincing Campbell's hypothesis (1964, p. 63) of an elegy intended primarily for recitation and only sung on special occasions.

32. Cf. chap. 10, n.81.

33. The most famous of these glosses *iambízein* as "insult, jeer, mock"; cf. Gorg. 82 A 15a D.-K., Aristot. *Poet.* 1448b 32. Another etymology, attested in Proclus (*Chrest.* 29 Severyns), derives *íambos* from Iambe, the servant girl of the Eleusinian king Celeus whose jokes cheered Demeter when she was grieving for the loss of her daughter, Kore (*Hymn. Dem.* 195). Both explanations adduce characteristic features that are proper to the seriocomic mode of all places and periods. The earliest attestation of *íambos* in the sense of "iambic element" is in Archilochus, fr. 20 T.: see chap. 7.

34. Note the extensive use, in Aristotle (*Rhet.* 3, 1418b 24) and the Peripatetics, of the term *iambic* to refer to Archilochus's trochaics—a rhetorical usage obviously based on the affinity between the subject matters of iambic and trochaic poetry (cf. Tarditi 1968, p. 13*).

35. Tarditi 1958.

36. See chap. 10.

37. On the problem of the origins of archaic Greek lyric, see Adrados 1976; cf. Cerri 1980.

38. On the *nómos,* see chap. 2.

39. The use of the term is amply documented throughout archaic poetry. For hymn in the sense of *thrênos,* cf. Anacr. fr. 168 Gent., Aesch. *Pers.* 620, 625, *Ag.* 709, and so forth; for the general meaning of "symposiastic song," cf., especially, Anacr. fr. 33, 11 Gent., Xenophan. fr. 1, 13 Gent.-Pr., Theogn. 993. "Song of celebration for athletic victory" is a sense frequently attested in Bacchylides and Pindar.

40. Cf. chap. 2.

41. *Gramm. Lat.* I, pp. 482ff. Keil.

42. *Schol.* Bacchyl. *Carm.* 22–23, pp. 127ff. Sn.-Maehl.

43. The fundamental documentation concerning poetic genres in ancient Greece is to be found in the work of Färber 1936 and the article of Harvey 1955.

Noteworthy attempts to place the evidence in a theoretical context are those of Gentili 1967a, Gentili 1972b; Rossi 1971; Calame 1974; Fantuzzi 1980b; Lanza 1983. On the link between cult occasions and the genesis of literary genres, see Adrados 1976.

44. Cf. *Gorg.* 502c.

45. Cf. *Leg.* 7, 801c-802a.

46. The essential character of Plato's polemic against poetry—epic poetry in particular—and its relationship to the decisive moment at the point of transition between oral and written culture, was first isolated and described by Havelock 1963, pp. 3ff.; cf. Cerri, 1969b. For the contradictory character of Plato's attitudes toward writing, cf. Muth 1966. It is clear that Plato, in spite of his announced preference for oral discourse and the more living, intimate human rapport that it made possible, was, without realizing it, deeply influenced by the new technology of writing. He was, as has been observed (Turner 1952, p. 24), fighting a rear-guard action.

47. See, for example, on characteristic features of theatrical communication, Prato 1978; Havelock 1980; Segal 1982.

48. Pseudo-Gadda 1969. On the criteria for distinguishing written and oral communicational systems, see McLuhan 1962; cf. Dorson 1964 and Sebeok 1964 (with full bibliography).

49. Cf. chap. 4.

50. K. Kraus 1955, p. 111.

51. See Detienne 1967, passim; cf. Cerri 1968; Pucci 1980, pp. 25ff.

52. No completely satisfactory interpretation of these verses has, in my opinion, yet been offered. Euripides is not referring exclusively to either banquet poetry (Page 1952, ad loc.) or bardic poetry (Ed. Fraenkel *ap.* Page 1952), but rather, as the use of the word *hýmnos* (v. 192) shows, to the whole poetic tradition of the archaic and classical age (cf. n.39). The very presence in the context of the words *thalíai* and *eilapínai* alongside *deîpnon*—words that designated a solemn banquet even in festival ceremonies of the public type described by Bacchylides (3, 15ff. Sn.-Maehl.; cf. 14, 15)—shows that Euripides' argument extends to choral poetry sung on the occasion of public festivities. The explanations hitherto offered for Euripides' criticism of poetry fail to touch the heart of the problem. Cunningham (1954, p. 154) has isolated, at least in general terms, the ethical premises on which the judgment is based. G. Paduano (1968, pp. 343ff.) has justly emphasized "the poet's rejection of a hedonistic conception of poetry," but thinks that he can detect in this rejection the requirement that poetry show a "sympathetic" rapport with the feelings of the sufferer. It would perhaps be more appropriate to talk of poetry with a eudaimonistic purpose—a purpose that, in Euripides' view, Greek lyric had been unable to realize, relying exclusively, as it did, on the immediate pleasure of song.

53. 1, 21; cf. Longo 1978; Gentili-Cerri 1983, p. 10.

54. Cf. Snell 1975, pp. 13-29.

55. Cf. chap. 1, n.24. On the phenomenology of the human character and

personality conceived as an open force field rather than as a compact, closed entity, the acute observations of Fränkel 1939 are still valid.

56. Havelock 1963, pp. 145–60.

57. See chap. 11.

58. Bonanno 1976 imagines a temple of Ares as the setting for the poem, in which case the arms would have constituted votive offerings. But the armor described is new and shiny (v. 8), whereas arms presented as votive offerings to a god were those taken from the enemy—a part of the booty of war. For the form Ἄρει in v. 1 (instead of the Lesbian Ἄρευι), see Gallavotti 1957b, p. 229.

59. For a different view, see Mazzarino 1943, p. 46.

60. Aristoph. fr. 235 K.-A. (= 223 Kock, 30 Cassio).

61. Athen. 15, 695a = Alc. fr. 249, 6–9 V.

62. Ταῦτά μοι ἠνιχθήτω κεκρυμμένα is not a generic expression but, rather, pinpoints the ambiguity and deliberate obscurity of the metaphorical language, directed toward persons of worth (*agathoí*); that is, aristocrats. It should be noted that Heraclitus (*Alleg. Hom.* 5, 7) applies the verb *ainíttomai* to the analysis of Alcaean metaphor. At v. 682 *sophós*, as always in archaic usage, designates the person expert in the practice of an art—in this case the art of politics and the language it uses. In v. 682 I read *kakón;* cf. chap. 11, n.19.

63. *Ol.* 2, 92ff.; cf. Gentili 1958b, pp. 26ff.

64. On the notion of *díke* as reciprocity and equilibrium, see Gentili 1972a; cf. Privitera 1967, p. 152; Bonanno 1973; Bernardini 1979; Vetta 1979.

65. Vernant 1968, p. 21; cf. Sambursky 1956, pp. 30ff.

66. Cf. Cic. *Acad.* II (fr. 3): *quid tam planum videtur quam mare? e quo etiam aequor illud poetae vocant.*

67. 7, 23, p. 259 Traglia.

68. The reference is to Pisistratus; cf. *ad* fr. 12 Gent.-Pr.

69. See the examples collected in Marx, *Lucili carminum reliquiae,* II, p. 21 *ad* v. 40; Diehl's edition of Solon, *ad* fr. 11; and Masaracchia 1958, pp. 300ff.

70. See especially *Com. ad.* fr. 1324 Kock; Polybius 11, 29, 9; Cic. *Pro Cluent.* 49; Liv. 28, 27, 11.

71. Cf. frr. 3; 4; 5; 6 Gent.-Pr.

72. In the critical investigation of metaphors from nature used in erotic contexts the comparison with the erotic poetry of "primitive" people is a relevant one. See, for confirmation, the useful collection of Di Nola 1971, which offers parallels with the language of Sappho, Anacreon, and Ibycus: the wind image as a symbol of love's impetuous desire (p. 105), the girl as filly (p. 19), the metaphor of "mutual play" (p. 92; cf. *paízein* and *sympaízein*). For comparative analysis using material drawn from other cultures (Arabo-Hispanic, Egyptian, Sumero-Accadian), see Gangutia Elícegui 1972, pp. 329ff.

73. 1969, pp. 86ff.; cf. Lloyd-Jones 1968, p. 132; Gentili 1976d, pp. 743ff.

74. West 1974, pp. 165ff.; cf. Vetta 1980, pp. 80ff.

For further arguments against West's interpretation, see also R. Renehan, "The Early Greek Poets: Some Interpretations," *Harv. Stud. Class. Philol.* 87

(1983): 24–27; G. L. Koniaris, *Am. Journ. Philol.* 105 (1984): 104ff.

75. Giampiera Arrigoni notes correctly (letter to author, 11 May 1983) that the mythological example constitutes a "double pole of reference," one that points both to the ultimate vengeance of the poet *erastés* and to the boy's coy refusal.

76. V. 1290: ζωσαμένη δ' ἔργ' ἀτέλεστα τέλει. Detienne 1977, p. 84, has shown the ambiguity of *télos* and *atélestos*, words that recur here with a certain frequency. The first means "end" but also "fulfillment" (in parallel relations to *gámos*, vv. 1289, 1293), the second, "without end" but also "without purpose, futile." The *gámos* alluded to is not a specific denotation for institutional marriage, but refers rather to the act of love—as does on occasion the verb *gaméo* (cf. Chantraine 1968, s.v.); see, in addition, the use of *dígamos* and *trígamos* of the daughters of Tyndaros in Stesichorus fr. 223 P. As Miss Arrigoni points out to me (letter to the author), Atalanta "never attains, strictly speaking, to marriage according to the rules, not even with Hippomenes and Melanion." "Far from her father's house" at v. 1291 is a reference to the exposing of the infant Atalanta by her father, who had wanted a male offspring (cf. Vetta 1980, pp. 83ff.). For *titrósko* as an erotic metaphor, cf. Vetta 1980, pp. 81ff. *Nikáo* (v. 1286) should also be understood in a metaphorical sense; cf., for example, Aesch. *Suppl.* 1005; Soph. *Ant.* 795.

On Theognis 1283ff. see J. M. Lewis, "Eros and the *Polis* in Theognis Book II," in *Theognis of Megara: Poetry and the Polis*, ed. T. J. Figueira–G. Nagy (Baltimore, 1985), pp. 214ff. His translation of *gámos* as "marriage" is implausible, however.

77. Cf. chap. 6.

78. The credit for singling out parataxis as a leitmotif in the archaic cultural context should go to several synchronically oriented investigations of phenomena belonging to this period: Notopoulos 1949 (on epic parataxis); Van Groningen 1960b, pp. 29–99.

79. Simon. fr. 541, 3–5 P.

80. This mode of thought follows the categories of the logic of real opposites, which was central to Greek speculation down to the time of Plato. The most clear and incisive discussion of this logic of opposites in its relation to dialectical logic is, to my mind, that found in Colletti 1974, pp. 1–62. On the linguistic structures favored by archaic philosophical thought, see the investigation of Lloyd 1966; cf. also Prier 1976.

81. Van Groningen 1960b, loc. cit.

82. The phenomenon was first noted by Müller 1908, pp. 56ff., then treated by Fränkel, "Eine Stileigenheit der frühgriechischen Literatur, I und II," *Gött. Nachr.* (1924): 63ff. = Fränkel 1960, pp. 40ff., and, finally, Van Otterlo 1944, pp. 131ff.

83. Hephaest. *perì poiem.*, p. 70, 11 Consbr.; cf. Sapph. fr. 111, 2 and 4 V.

84. Hephaest. *perì poiem.*, pp. 71, 16ff. Consbr.; cf. Bacchyl. frr. 18; 19, 1 and 8 Sn.-Maehl.

85. Tyrtaeus is discussed in chap. 7, and by Prato 1968, pp. 8ff. On the fruit-lessly debated question of the unity and authenticity of Solon's elegy to the Muses, see Van Groningen 1960b, pp. 94ff. As for the Theognidean collection, the recurring effort on the part of critics to decide whether a given set of verses constitutes one or more poems is largely otiose, given the character of archaic elegy. Every distich, every group of verses, is always potentially autonomous, while allowing for easy juxtaposition with other distichs to form a fuller piece of exposition. The singer at a symposium availed himself freely of whatever elegiac material he could remember; the present ordering of elegies reflects, by and large, the chance arrangement of an ancient anthology put together for use on such banquet occasions.

## FOUR: THE POETICS OF MIMESIS

1. Lucilius 343 Marx (381 Krenkel) testifies to the continued vitality of *thésis* = *poíesis* in the vocabulary of ancient poetics; cf. Ardizzoni 1953, p. 33n.4 and, for compounds of *thésis*, Morpurgo-Tagliabue 1967.

2. Cf. chap. 1.

3. Pind. *Pyth.* 3, 113: ἐξ ἐπέων κελαδεννῶν, τέκτονες οἷα σοφοί / ἅρμο-σαν; fr. 194, 2 Sn.-Maehl. εἷα τειχίζωμεν ἤδη ποικίλον / κόσμον αὐδάεντα λόγων; cf. *Pyth.* 6, 9; Democr. 68 B 21 D.-K.: Ὅμηρος . . . ἐπέων κόσμον ἐτεκτήνατο παντοίων.

4. Cf. Democritus, loc. cit., and Parmen. 28 B 8, 52 D.-K.

5. 2, 2 Gent.-Pr.: κόσμον ἐπέων ᾠδὴν ἀντ' ἀγορῆς θέμενος.

6. Stesich. fr. 212, 2 P.: Φρύγιον μέλος ἐξευρόντας; Pind. *Ol.* 1, 110: εὑρὼν ὁδὸν λόγων; *Ol.* 3, 4ff.; *Pyth.* 12, 6–7; *Nem.* 6, 53ff.

7. Pind. fr. 122, 14 Sn.-Maehl.: ἀρχὰν / εὑρόμενον σκολίου.

8. Webster 1939, pp. 166ff.; Else 1958, pp. 73ff.

9. *Mimeîsthai, mímema,* and *mímesis* are polysemous words in the archaic and late-archaic periods. For a comprehensive picture of their pre-Platonic range of meaning one must, I believe, combine the perspectives of Koller 1954, Else 1958, and Havelock 1963, pp. 57ff. Imitation is expressive re-creation involving identification with the original (Koller, Havelock), but also – from the fifth century on – "representation," "replica" (for *eikón,* cf. Webster 1939, p. 166; for *mímema* in Aeschylus, Else 1958, p. 77; and, for *mímesis* applied to a statue, Herodt. 3, 37, 2). I do not agree with Havelock's contention that Plato himself invented the notion of mimesis as imitation of the moral character of an original. In *Resp.* 3, 400ab the discussion of rhythms as an imitation of life is illustrated by reference to the theories of Damon, and the expression *bíou mimémata* must have the same origin as the certainly Damonian ones that follow in the text: *enóplion . . . xýntheton kaì dáktylon kaì heróion;* cf., most recently, Lasserre 1967, pp. 245ff. The term *xýnthetos,* one may note, provides further fifth-century

confirmation for the by then well-established use of words referring simultaneously to linguistic and metrico-rhythmical composition.

10. V. 161: *thélgousi dè phŷl' anthrópon.*

11. Else 1958, pp. 74ff.; 88n.9.

12. I follow Else (1958, p. 75) in interpreting ταυρόφθογγοι μῖμοι as equivalent to ταύρων φθεγγομένων μιμήσεις. The ancient evidence seems to exclude the generally accepted translation *mîmoi* as "actors." Also incorrect is Mette's "das Echo des Tympanon" (1963, p. 137) for τυμπάνου εἰκών. The "image of the drum" is, rather, the *rhómbos* itself: see Harrison 1912, p. 61n.3.

13. Fr. 39 P. = 91 Calame; cf. the interpretation in Gentili 1971, pp. 59ff.; and, for a different view, Gallavotti 1972.

14. Cf. Maehler 1963, p. 72.

15. 68 B 154 D.-K.

16. The expression *katà mímesin* which concludes the list of the arts that men have learned from the animals refers to everything in the preceding catalogue—not simply, as Else would have it (1958, p. 83), to music, the last item on the list (*en oidèi katà mímesin*). Else's contention rests on the fact that the imitative relationship between the construction of houses by men and the construction of nests by swallows is an analogical one, whereas human songs are an actual copy of those of birds. But this subtle distinction is illusory: what Democritus is concerned with is *téchne* as imitative process. It is the operation of weaving, mending, house-constructing, and singing that man learns through imitating animals, not the finished product that results from one of those operations; cf. Koller 1954, p. 58, and Lanata 1963, p. 268 (with bibliography).

17. In Athen. 9, 389f = Chamael. fr. 24 Wehrli.

18. Cf. chap. 3.

19. *Resp.* 2, 373b.

20. Cf. chap. 2.

21. Plut. *De glor. Athen.* 3, 346f = Lanata 1963, p. 68.

Fr. 190b Bergk: κατὰ Σιμωνίδην ὁ λόγος τῶν πραγμάτων εἰκών ἐστι. (The latter formulation seems to go back to an analogous definition by Solon—if one can believe the testimony of Diogenes Laertius 1, 58: ἔλεγε [scil. Σόλων] δὲ τὸν μὲν λόγον εἴδωλον εἶναι τῶν ἔργων.)

22. *De sublim.* 15, 7 = fr. 557 P.

23. Cf. above.

24. Here *mimeîsthai* has nothing to do with imitation in the moral sense (so most interpreters, including even Else 1958, p. 77). The word *ásophos* shows that the reference is to the unskilled—those without expertise in the art of composing poetry. In choral lyric, elegy, and, on more than one occasion, Theognis himself, *sophós* designates the poet; cf. W. Kraus 1955, p. 78, and Havelock 1963, p. 57n.22.

25. For a systematic collection of the material, see Bernardini 1967; Svenbro 1976, pp. 188ff.

26. On the notions of "devising" and "searching out" in choral lyric, see Maehler 1963, pp. 73ff.; 95ff.

27. See the studies of Kristeva 1969, especially pp. 143ff.

28. See Zumthor 1972, pp. 100ff; 118.

29. Fr. 14 P. = 4 Calame: Μῶσ᾽ἄγε, Μῶσα λίγηα, πολυμμελὲς αἰὲν ἀοιδέ, μέλος / νεοχμὸν ἄρχε παρσένοις ἀείδην. Cf. *Od.* 1, 351, where the "novelty" of the song refers exclusively to content—that is, to the mythical episode that is being narrated.

30. Cf. Aristot. *Hist. an.* 536 b14.

31. *Il.* 14, 92; *Od.* 8, 240.

32. *Il.* 22, 281 (in a pejorative sense); Hesiod *Theog.* 29 (the Muses); cf. *synáreren aoidé* in the *Hymn to Apollo* 164, cited above. See chap. 1.

33. Cf. Diller 1956, p. 57.

34. Attestations in our surviving texts are too numerous to allow a full documentation. One must be content with a reference to Latacz 1966 and, more generally, Havelock 1963, pp. 152ff.

35. 82 B 11, 9ff. D.-K.

36. 82 B 23 D.-K.

37. Cf. chap. 3 and Gentili 1972a.

38. This interpretation, already advanced in the first edition (1975) of Gentili-Cerri 1983, is also that of Taplin 1978, pp. 167ff., one of the scholars most attentive to the problems of oral communication as they present themselves in tragedy.

39. *Poet.* 1453b; cf. also Plato *Resp.* 10, 602–608a.
The emotional aspects of tragic performances are documented, with full reference to ancient testimony, by W. B. Stanford, *Greek Tragedy and the Emotions* (London, 1983).

40. I use the expression "horizon of expectation" in the sense posited by H. R. Jauss 1967, p. 31: "Literature situates itself within a context of events, the medium for whose transmission is, first and foremost, the horizon of expectation determined by the literary experience of contemporary and subsequent readers, critics and authors. The possibility of objectifying such a horizon of expectation is a precondition for the possibility of giving to one's conception and presentation of literary history the specific form of historicity that is appropriate to it."

41. The results of the systematic study of Führer 1967 are useful here, showing as they do a substantial continuity between epic and lyric in the employment of formulaic introductions and conclusions to directly reported speech. See, for Archilochus and epic language, Page 1963, pp. 119ff.; for an overview of structural and verbal parallels between archaic elegy and elegiac inscriptions, Gentili 1967a; for similar parallels between epic poetry and hexameter and elegiac inscriptions, Di Tillio 1969; and, within the genre of elegy itself, Giannini 1973. Cf. also Gallavotti 1977b; Gentili 1977b, pp. 19ff.; Bernardini 1977, p. 149; Veneri 1977; Gallavotti 1979.

42. Cf., for the earliest forms of choral lyric, antedating or contemporary with Homeric epic, Pagliaro 1953, pp. 6ff.; Koller 1963, pp. 79ff.

43. C. O. Pavese 1967a; C. O. Pavese 1974, pp. 63ff.; Grinbaum 1968.

44. For an essentially similar assessment, see Gallavotti 1979.

45. Beazley 1963, p. 431, no. 48.

46. Alc. fr. 249 V. = *carm. conv.* fr. 891 P.; cf. Nicosia 1976, pp. 71ff.

47. See the introductions to his editions of Sappho (Oxford, 1925) and Alcaeus (Oxford, 1927).

48. Marzullo 1958, p. 200.

49. I exclude, for obvious reasons, the isolated and problematic Alcaean forms βλήχρος (fr. 319 V.) and Ἀλλιήνων (*P. Oxy.* 2506, fr. 77, 22 = fr. 306 A b V.). To attribute βλήχρος, as has hitherto been done (Hamm 1958 p. 54), to the influence of Homeric usage (cf. ἄβληχρος *Il.* 5, 337; 8, 178; *Od.* 11, 135) is a dubious explanation at best; cf. Chantraine 1968, s.v. If one accepts the hypothesis—in itself doubtful—of an Ionic βληχρός (with -*e* vocalism) related to βλάξ, it is certainly strange to find βλάξ recurring even in Heraclitus (22 B 87 D.-K.) and Attic authors of the fifth and fourth centuries and βληχρός, by contrast, in Pindar, Bacchylides, and Hippocrates. "Homeric influence" seems no more than a convenient out in attempting to account for a phenomenon that is very obscure. Nor can one exclude the possibility of an error in the indirect tradition: βλήχρων written in place of βλάχρων. The case of Ἀλλιήνων (the Allienoi) is also a complex one. The hypothesis of an Ionic form corresponding to Ἀλλιάνων (Treu 1966, p. 28n.19) seems improbable; for other, more likely explanations, see Barner 1967b, pp. 12ff. In fr. 34, 7 V. ῥῆα is an apparent instance of borrowing from Ionic epic (i.e., ῥεῖα with the Lesbian transcription -ηα for Homeric -εια [cf. Risch 1946, p. 253]); but the same cannot be said of ζακρυόεντος (cf. Risch 1946), where ζα- is the Lesbian outcome of δια-: see Wilamowitz 1914, p. 241. Ἄρη in place of the expected Ἄρευι in fr. 140, 3 V. is problematic; a solution is offered by Fränkel's suggestion (1969, p. 214n.1 [Eng. trans., p. 189n.1]), Ἄρευι κόσμηται. But Ἄρη is not, in any case, an Ionicism as has been sometimes supposed: the dative *Arei* is already attested in Mycenaean; cf. Gallavotti 1957b; Chadwick-Baumbach 1963, s.v. "Ἄρης."

50. Cf. Ruijgh 1967, p. 74.

51. The objection is well put by Hoekstra 1957, p. 223. Cf., along the same line, the interesting new methodological confirmation provided by C. O. Pavese 1967a.

52. Snell 1952, pp. 15ff. interprets poem 20A as an invective in encomium form inspired by Archilochus's invective against Lycambes. The Archilochean content would, in this case, explain the presence of non-Doric -*e*. Formally, however, both in choice of meters and in vocabulary (cf. the adjectives χρυσόλοφος v. 13 and εὐέθειρα v. 26), the fragment is Anacreontic in inspiration, and the Anacreontic model may be the source of the Ionic coloring of its language as well; cf. Gentili 1958b, pp. 119ff.

53. Forssman 1966.

54. The -αο genitive appears in the famous Corcyrean inscription for the tomb of Menecrates (42 Peek, 10 Pfohl: v. 1 τλασίαϝο), where it is inevitably explained as an epic—that is, Homeric—reminiscence. But if -αο is already present in Mycenaean, why think of it as a borrowing from the Homeric poems rather than as a relic of the Mycenaean substratum preserved in the poetic language of a non-Ionic region? The form is preserved in Arcado-Cypriot, with the phonetic outcome -αυ. One must not underestimate the importance of the fact that in Pindar and other choral poets there survive portions of Mycenaean vocabulary not attested in Homeric epic. Cf., for Pindar, ἐπέτας, λαγέτας, ἀνίαι, βουβότας, ἀνδριάς, ὁλκάς (Gallavotti 1967, pp. 852ff., and Doria 1967, pp. 859ff.). Presumably these belong to a very ancient, pre-Homeric, stratum in the poetic and linguistic tradition.

55. Ὀδυνηρὰ γήραος in the papyrus text of *Paean* 1, 1 (as against the ὀδυναρόν, with -α vocalism, of *Pyth.* 2, 91) is explained by Forssman 1966, p. 150, as an echo of the combination ὀδυνηρόν . . . γῆρας of Mimnermus fr. 7, 5ff. Gent.-Pr. (for echoes between Mimnermus and Pindar, cf. also Segal 1976a). One might object, however, that the reminiscence is less likely to be Pindar's than that of the copyist of the papyrus. A similar explanation is in order for the five instances of -η vocalism in *Pythian* 4 (v. 22 Εὔφημος [but Εὔφαμος in cod. B ed. Turyn], v. 49 Μυκηνᾶν, v. 95 παπτήνας, v. 119 προσηύδα, v. 205 Θρηϊκίων) where Snell, except in vv. 49 and 205, rightly restores the form with long alpha. In my opinion, however, even these two lines should read Μυκανᾶν (the epichoric form which is, moreover, attested also in Simonides 608, fr. 1a + 2, 21 P.) and Θραϊκίαν (which recurs in Pind. *Pae.* 2, 25).

To the objections, already formulated in Gentili 1972b, to the thesis of Forssman one should now add those of B. K. Braswell, "*Color epicus* in Pindar: A Falsely Assumed Type," in *Greek Poetry and Philosophy: Studies in Honour of Leonard Woodbury*, ed. D. E. Gerber (Chico, Calif., 1984), pp. 33-36.

56. Grinbaum 1968, p. 876.

A similar position on the linguistic aspects of choral lyric is now taken by C. Trümpy (*Vergleich des Mykenischen mit der Sprache der Chorlyrik* [Bern, Frankfurt am Main, and New York, 1986]), who tends to isolate the phenomenon both from the Doric dialect and the influence of Homeric epic; cf. the review of C. Brillante, *Quad. Urb.*, n.s. 27 [56] (1987).

57. Georgiev 1966, pp. 55ff., and C. O. Pavese 1972, who distinguishes two linguistic areas for archaic Greek poetry, a northern and a southern (Iono-Homeric).

58. To the -αο and -οιο genitives already noted one should perhaps add the -ι outcome for the group -νσ (as seen in φέροισι[ν], φέροισα, etc.). Cf., most recently, Arena 1967.

59. For the alterations of the Pindaric text attributable to the phenomenon of *metagrammatismós*, see Irigoin 1952, pp. 21ff.

60. Cf. Monteverdi 1954; Quaglio 1970 (with full bibliography).

## FIVE: THE SOCIOLOGY OF MEANING

1. Cf. Treu 1955, passim; Snell 1965, passim.

2. Cf. Nida 1964.

3. Cf. Page 1963.

4. Cf. Snell 1963, pp. 113ff., 169; Treu 1963b, p. 115.

5. Cf. Gentili 1970, p. 118.

6. On the reuse of epic material in Mimnermus, see Gentili 1965b, pp. 383ff., and Dawson 1966; for Tyrtaeus, in addition to Dawson 1966, pp. 50ff., Prato 1968, Snell 1969, and most recently Giannini 1973.

7. Ong 1967, p. 33.

8. The referential code used by the two poets thus points to a substantial difference between poetic contexts. Whoever the "citizens" (*astoí*) referred to by Solon are, they are one with the *démou hegemónes* in their greed for wealth, which is the cause of the city's *dysnomíe* (Masaracchia 1958, pp. 253ff., 267ff.).

9. See the studies of Becker 1937; Bernardini 1967, pp. 87ff., Péron 1974b, pp. 23ff., and passim.

10. *Ol.* 2, 91ff.; for Bacchylides, cf. chap. 4.

11. Text and arguments for Simonidean attribution in Gentili 1961, p. 339; Gentili 1964, p. 302; and Gentili 1981b, p. 102. For commentary, see Gentili 1965a, pp. 315ff., and, for vv. 6–7 in particular, Pretagostini 1980, pp. 134ff.

12. Fränkel (1969, p. 357n.32 [Eng. trans., p. 313n.22]) conjectured *chrónos* as the subject of the sentence, while Pfeiffer (1968, p. 33n.1) and Pellizer 1978 suggest, with equal probability, *kairós*. My own preference for *chrónos* is based on Simplicius, *Comm. in Aristot. gr.* 9, 754, 7 Diels (= fr. 645 P.), where we learn that Simonides celebrated time as the most wise of all things.

13. That is, the man of true worth.

14. The subject continues to be the man of worth.

15. Smoke designates what is groundless, empty, and, in general, worthless—hence trivial and insignificant talk. "There is nothing certain, nothing more than smoke's shadow," is a phrase in Aeschylus (fr. 399, 2 Radt = 677, 2 Mette); and *perì kapnoû stenolescheîn* is Aristophanes' way of referring to empty talk or inane chatter; cf. Plato, *Resp.* 9, 581d. Pindar, *Nem.* 1, 24ff., provides an instructive parallel for the worth-nonworth contraposition. There the excellence of water and the insubstantiality of smoke are set in opposition as concrete parallels to both the excellence of the *esthloí*, who favor the magnanimous Chromios and the maliciousness of wagging tongues: "He [Chromios] has achieved the opposing of noble men to detractors, water to smoke"; other interpretations (cf. Farnell 1932, pp. 245ff.) are unpersuasive. I do not believe,

however, that *kapnós* in the Pindar passage refers primarily to "envy" (the usual explanation: cf., for example, L. S. J. s.v. and, most recently, Stoneman 1979, p. 66). "Water against smoke" is a means of signifying eternal, unchanging value (water, sky, and the like are common in this sense in the literature of the period: cf. Pindar, *Ol.* 1, 1, and Bacchylides 3, 86) by contrast with the evanescent, ephemeral character of that which is devoid of value. The excellence of men of worth is a solid thing of value, with which Chromios can counter the insubstantial allegations of malicious gossip.

16. The word, with metaphorical meaning and specific reference to the incessant longing of love, recurs in Herodt. 2, 93, and Eur. *Hipp.* 1300 (Phaedra's disastrous passion).

17. In spite of numerous lacunae in what follows v. 15 in the text, the presence of the word *díkaios* (v. 16) suggests that here too, as in the encomium to Scopas (cf. below), the discussion must have come around to the theme of justice.

18. For the convenience of the reader the fragment is translated in full here, according to the text in Gentili 1964 (pp. 297ff., with full apparatus criticus); for commentary, see Gentili 1965a, pp. 305ff.

19. The interpretation offered in Adkins 1960, pp. 355–59, which tends to locate the encomium to Scopas within the mainstream of traditional ethical ideas, seems implausible; but Adkins could not have known the new Oxyrhynchus fragment, published barely a year before the appearance of his own book (fr. 541 P., cf. above). The subsequent study of H. Parry 1965 is limited by its exclusive focus on the synchronic aspects of the poem's language. Donlan's critical approach (1969) is more persuasive.

20. In the phrase χερσίν τε καὶ ποσὶ καὶ νόῳ τετράγωνος the datives are to be taken as datives of relation—assuming that τετράγωνος has the meaning "square," with a precise reference to the canon of symmetry of archaic statuary (cf., for the argument, Svenbro 1976, pp. 154ff.). The so-called dative of relation, like the accusative of relation, designates the thing within which a certain condition comes to exist (cf. Kühner-Gerth 1955, p. 440). In this instance the limbs of the body are the physical structure within which there exists a symmetrical structure of a sort to exclude the presence of faults (ἄνευ ψόγου τετυγμένον)—hence a square (or symmetrical) structure that is perfect.

21. The word is connected with *paláme*, "palm," which designates the hand's dexterity and skillfulness; *palámai* in Homer are the hands of an expert craftsman (cf. the analysis of Frontisi-Ducroux 1975, p. 91); hence, by metaphorical extension, a person's ability in general (Alc. fr. 249, 7 V.). *Apálamnos* thus means "unresourceful," "powerless," "incompetent" (cf. Hesych. s.v.), like Diomedes in the simile of *Il.* 5, 597ff., with its image of a man who stops helplessly before a raging river, knowing that he cannot cross it. Alcaeus (fr. 360, 1 V.) tells us that Aristodamus, king of Sparta, was "not at a loss" (*ouk apálamnos*)—that is, wise—when he used to say "Money makes the man." It is obvious that the pessimistic emphasis on human frailty found in the next to last verse

of the poem ("the race of fools [*alithíon*] has no end"; cf. v. 11, "all of us / whom the broad earth nourishes with its fruits") follows directly from the assertions that precede. It is as if the poet wanted to justify those assertions with the implied comment: numerous, too numerous are the incompetents I would have to deal with were I prone to faultfinding. *Alíthios* ("stupid, senseless") is an intensification of the preceding *apálamnos*.

22. Svenbro (1976, pp. 141ff.) understands *hygiés, apálamnos*, and *onasípolis díka* in an economic sense, and takes the whole poem as a tacit invitation to Simonides' new Thessalian patron to spend his money well by rewarding the poet who is praising him. The analysis, however, represents a type of reading that runs the risk of distorting the basic meaning of the text. Cf. Gentili 1981b, pp. 98–104.

23. Schaerer 1938, p. 128.

24. As Pietro Giannini points out to me, the subtle semantic discussion of *chalepón* = *kakón* launched by Socrates may not have been an entirely unmotivated one. According to a notice transmitted by the *Suda* (s.v. "Πιττακός"), Pittacus came out with the dictum *chalepòn esthlòn émmenai* when he was being forced, even though already old, to take up arms once more for a military campaign. In that case the sense of the phrase would not have been the generic one "it is difficult" but rather "it is *burdensome* to be a man of worth" (when necessity forces someone who is no longer young to show the virtues expected of a commander in confronting the dangers of war). It is only in isolation from its specific context and actual referent that the phrase takes on the absoluteness of a general maxim on the attainability of human excellence. Was Plato familiar with the anecdote? One would be tempted to reply in the affirmative. That way it would be possible to see an implicit motive for a seriocomic semantic debate that Socrates himself is shown at the end not to take seriously: his only purpose, he explains, was to test Protagoras's ability to defend his own thesis. It is obvious, of course, that Simonides himself interprets Pittacus's dictum without reference to the occasion that gave rise to it.

25. If the poet had wished to make a distinction between becoming and being he would have said γενέσθαι rather than ἔμμεναι in v. 5, and used γίνεται in v. 7 rather than requiring ἐστί to be understood (cf. also vv. 9–10 τὸ μὴ γενέσθαι δυνατόν); cf. Fränkel 1960, p. 72n.7. Further confirmation is provided by fr. 541 P. (cf. above), which restates the same formulation with slight variations (v. 7): οὐ γὰρ ἐλαφρὸν ἐσθλ[ὸν ἔμμεν (better metrically than ἔμμεναι), "it is not easy to be worthy."

26. *Biáomai* or *biázomai*, which refers to the overbearing power of falsehood, lies, and, in general, everything that causes damage or destruction; cf. *Il.* 23, 576; Simon. frr. 541, 8; 598 P.; Pind. *Nem.* 8, 34; Parmen. 28 B 7, 3 D.-K.; Emped. 31 B 3, 6 D.-K.

27. One need only think of Anacreon's poems addressed to Artemon, the parvenu from the lower classes (fr. 82 Gent.); to the girl as filly (fr. 78 Gent.); and to Erotima (fr. 60 Gent.), on which see Serrao 1968.

28. Cf. Gentili 1964, pp. 293ff. and n.42.

29. Fr. 581, 4 P.: ἀντιθέντα μένος στάλας (ἀντιθέντα codd., ἀντία θέντα Bergk); cf. chap. 8.

30. Von Fritz 1943.

31. Τὸ γὰρ αὐτὸ νοεῖν ἐστίν τε καὶ εἶναι (fr. 3). The Parmenidean formulation should be interpreted with due regard for context in fr. 2, which identifies two ways of investigation—that of being and that of seeming (v. 2)—both of which it is possible to *noeîn* (v. 2). The fragment goes on to say that it is impossible to know (*gignóskein*, v. 7) that which is not, because only being is knowable. It is thus evident that the *noeîn* identified with being in fr. 3 is not equivalent to the *noeîn* of fr. 2, where it has the archaic meaning of "perceive" or "intend": the ways of investigation of being and not being are both perceivable, but only being is knowable. If *noeîn* and *eînai* are the same thing, as they are in fr. 3, *noeîn* must mean "know" (*gignóskein*): the identity of being and knowing follows from the fact that only being is knowable. For other interpretations proposed for fr. 3, see Tarán 1965, pp. 41ff., and, most recently, Capizzi 1975, p. 77.

32. Fr. 542, 15 and 34 P. = vv. 8 and 15 in Gentili 1965a; cf. n.18.

33. It is in this restrictive sense that Svenbro (1976, p. 160) understands the Simonidean phrase.

34. Havelock 1978b, pp. 308ff.

35. Cf. Bowra 1961, p. 335.

36. Fr. 53 D. = p. 310 P.

37. See Christ 1941, pp. 76ff., and above all the observations of Detienne 1967, pp. 110ff.; 123.

38. Fränkel 1939.

39. Fr. 26, 11ff. V.:

>               ]. αν, ἔγω δ᾽ ἔμ᾽ [αὔτᾳ
> τοῦτο σύ]νοιδα.

The state of the text does not allow an exact determination of the reference of τοῦτο. It seems certain, however, that it was something that affected Sappho personally: cf. vv. 2–4:

>               ὄ]ττινα[ς γὰρ
> εὖ θέω, κῆνοί με μά]λιστα πά[ντων
>               σίνοντα]ι.

Here she refers to persons who mistreat her, who behave offensively toward her (contrary to the way she behaves toward them), and who thus cause her to suffer (cf. v. 10 τοῦ]το πάθη[v: Hunt's supplement may be regarded as certain; cf. Treu 1976, p. 44). The state described is one full of tension and recrimination between her and people very close to her of which she shows a full awareness—a *con-scientia* shared with herself (for τοῦτο in v. 12, cf. v. 10). See, further, the pertinent comments of Snell 1930, p. 24; Seel 1953; Cancrini 1970, pp. 41ff.

40. This schematic contrast, whose influence is apparent in a large number of the works devoted to the development of Greek culture from Homer to Plato, goes back, as is well known, to the hypothesis, advanced by Lévy-Bruhl 1910, of the presence in primitive societies of a "prelogical," "mythic" mentality that is unaware of the law of contradiction. Hence the distinction between mythical mentality and logical mentality as successive stages in the development of thought. The hypothesis is no longer acceptable, as has been shown, most recently, in Lévi-Strauss 1962; Lévi-Strauss 1966, pp. 407ff.; nor, for that matter, did it remain acceptable even to its original formulator. After a lapse of many years Lévy-Bruhl profoundly modified his views, considering his original hypothesis "without foundation" and unfortunate (1947, p. 258). It still provides, however, a theoretical ground for the recent study of Jarcho 1968.

The ideas of Lévy-Bruhl are discussed in M. Detienne, *L'invention de la mythologie* (Paris, 1981), pp. 200-209.

41. For the Homeric period, see the observations of Codino 1965, pp. 134ff.

## Six: The Ways of Love in the Poetry of *Thíasos* and Symposium

1. Merkelbach 1957.

2. Latte 1953, pp. 36ff.

3. See Peek 1960; Marzullo 1964; C. O. Pavese 1967b; and, above all, Calame 1977a, II, pp. 86ff.

4. See Page 1951; Garzya 1954; the review of Gerber 1968, pp. 325ff.; Gerber 1976, pp. 94ff.; and, most recently, the vast investigation of Calame 1977a.

5. For the interpretation of vv. 98ff., σιαὶ γάρ, ἀντ[ὶ δ' ἕνδεκα / παίδων δέ[κας ἄδ'ἀείδ]ει, see the analysis of G. Giangrande 1977, pp. 156ff.; what is involved is a kind of compliment in the superlative. The chorus praises Hagesichora for her qualities as a singer, which make her voice the equivalent of a choir of ten girls performing together. One may add that the papyrus commentary ad loc. seems to support this interpretation.

6. I cannot understand why some scholars continue to understand πεληάδες (v. 60) in the sense of "Pleiades" (so, most recently, Gianotti 1978) rather than "doves"; cf. the explanation of the *Schol. ad loc.*, where it is categorically stated that Agido and Hagesichora are compared to *peristeraí*, "doves." The ancient commentator's note may be supported by adducing a passage in Athenaeus (9, 394d), where it is said that the Dorians used the word *peleiádes* to refer to the sort of doves usually called *peristeraí*. Here the presence of doves—considered in antiquity the birds of Aphrodite *par excellence,* is fully justified by the erotic context of the poem. Those who, like A. Griffiths (1972), have sought to maintain at all costs the identification with the Pleiades (by common consent a fairly dim constellation) have had to go to enormous lengths—without reaching any plausible result—to show the validity of the comparison between them

and the gleaming star Sirius. But the comparison is perfectly appropriate for the beauty of the dove pair Agido-Hagesichora. Equally relevant in this context is the use of *aeíromai* to designate the flight of doves and winged creatures in general; cf. Theogn. 238: "I have given you wings that will lightly bear you aloft above all the earth to fly over the boundless sea."

7. In v. 7 I follow the papyrus in reading ορθριαι, which I prefer to take as the dative Ὀρθρίᾳ, "goddess of the morning" (cf. v. 87, Ἀῶτις), rather than as an adjective ὄρθριαι, modifying πελήαδες. For *pháros*, "plow," I follow the interpretation of Sosiphanes (*Schol.* A ad loc., p. 6 P. = p. 24 Calame) and Herodian (p. 5 P. = p. 15 Calame). At v. 77 I read with Lobel and Page τείρει rather than τήρει, even though the reading of the papyrus is not completely clear at this point. (Garzya 1954, p. 62, and A. Griffiths 1972, p. 22, are wrong in saying that τείρει does not yield satisfactory sense.) For the erotic connotations of *consume, afflict,* see Page 1951, p. 91, as well as Marzullo 1964, p. 205, C. O. Pavese 1967b, p. 130, and, most recently, Calame 1977a, II, p. 89n.82.

8. In this connection it is worth recalling the votive plows discovered in a temple of Hera in the course of the recent excavations at Gravisca; cf. Torelli 1971, pp. 52; 63.

9. The sense of v. 8, lacuna notwithstanding, is clear; the [δ' ἴκτ]αρ μένει proposed by the editors is a plausible reading.

10. Cf. Page 1951, pp. 76ff.

11. *Schol.* Arat. *Phaenom.* 451, p. 284 Martin.

12. Ibyc. fr. 331 P.

13. Vv. 34ff: "nocte latent fures, quos idem saepe revertens, / Hespere, mutato comprendis nomine Eous"; cf. Cic. *De nat. deor.,* 2, 20, 53: "stella Veneris, quae Φωσφόρος Graece, Lucifer Latine dicitur, cum antegreditur solem, cum subsequitur autem Ἕσπερος"; Plin. *Nat. hist.* 2, 36: "sidus appellatum Veneris . . . ante matutinum exoriens Luciferi nomen accepit . . . contra ab occasu refulgens nuncupatur Vesper." Further testimony in Pfeiffer 1949, to Callim. fr. 291.

14. *Schol.* Theocr. 18, p. 331 Wendel: τῶν δὲ ἐπιθαλαμίων τινὰ μὲν ᾄδεται ἑσπέρας ἃ λέγεται κατακοιμητικά, ἅτινα ἕως μέσης νυκτὸς ᾄδουσι·τινὰ δὲ ὄρθρια ἃ καὶ προαγορεύεται διεγερτικά.

15. A. Griffiths 1972.

16. Particularly worth noting is the term *cousin* (*anepsiá*), which recurs in v. 52 of the partheneion and is certainly an institutional designation for a girl who is a member of the community, just as in Sappho the word *hetaíra* refers to a companion in the *thíasos;* cf. Calame 1977a, II, pp. 84ff.

17. Himer. *Or.* 9, 4 Colonna = Sapph. Test. 194 V.

18. Aristaenet. *Ep.* 1, 10 = Sappho to fr. 71 V.; cf. *meilichóphonoi* in Aristaenetus's text and *mellichóphonos* in fr. 71, 6 V.

19. The only exception is a brief, passing reference in Snell 1965, p. 71n.22.

20. Cf. *sýzygos* in Aesch. *Choeph.* 599; Eur. *Alc.* 314.

21. Max. Tyr. 18, 9 = Sapph. Test. 219 V.: "just as Prodicus, Gorgias, Thra-

symachus, and Protagoras were rivals of Socrates, so were Gorgo and Andromeda rivals of Sappho."

22. The erotic connotation of "struggle" need hardly be insisted upon here.
The usage is common to all of archaic poetry, from Archilochus on (cf. Lanata
1966, pp. 68ff.; Lanata 1968).

23. For "peace" used in an erotic sense to designate the state of psycho-physi-
cal satisfaction that brings an end to the unrest of love, see Calame 1977a, II,
pp. 118ff., and n.141. Several recent studies of this partheneion (Puelma 1977;
Dunkel 1979; Hooker 1979) fail to contribute anything that has a bearing on
improved understanding of the general meaning and function of the poem.
The only merit of the first is to have formulated for v. 40 a conjecture
(ὁρῶσα) that is syntactically unexceptionable but does not affect the overall
significance of the text. The most obvious limitation they exhibit is a stubborn
refusal to assume that the erotic language—which pervades not only the first
partheneion but fr. 3 P. (= 26 Calame) as well—is not something accessory but,
as Calame 1977a among others has shown, contextually essential if one wishes
to understand the meaning of this poetic genre and its function in rites of initiation. For a methodological analysis devoted to recent works, see Vetta 1982.

24. *La force des choses* (Paris, 1963), p. 472.

25. Rösler 1975, p. 275. One wonders, however, whether fr. 27 V.—in sapphic
stanzas and certainly part of a marriage song according to Page 1955, p. 125—
does not belong properly to initiatory rites within the *thíasos*. This is likely in
view of its intimate tone and the phrases στείχομεν γὰρ ἐς γάμον and
παρθένοις ἄππεμπε ("let us proceed to the marriage," "let the girls proceed").

26. Cf. fr. 58, 25ff. V.: "I love splendor (*habrosýnan*) . . . love for the sun has
given me splendor and beauty as my lot."

27. Cf. n.46.

28. See, for example, the introductory essay of Barnstone 1965. There
(p. xxvii) the "universal condition" described by Sappho in poem 31 V. is said
to be "a passion" and "an ecstasy" of the sort that reappears in *El cántico
espiritual* of Saint John of the Cross, in Marvell, and in Guillén. The most such
"parallels" can do is to cast light on certain psychological constants in the
passion of love; otherwise they are worthless. Some notion of the various ways
in which French readers have responded to this famous ode, from 1500 to the
present day—and of their tendencies to modernize and universalize Sappho's
experience of love—can be got from Mora 1966, especially the chapter "Quatre
siècles autour d'un poème," pp. 168ff. For analysis of the poem itself, see
Privitera 1969; Manieri 1972; Segal 1974, pp. 146ff.

29. Cf. Page 1955, pp. 41ff.

30. Dion. Hal. *Ant. Rom.* 2, 68.

31. Dodds 1951, p. 116.

32. See the interesting documentation in Dodds 1951, p. 130n.82, with the
references to the specialized literature of the subject given there.

33. Latte 1946, pp. 154ff.

34. Further instances in Dodds 1951, pp. 117ff.

35. Cf. Xenophan. 21 A 52 D.-K.

36. Eliot 1950, p. 204.

37. Pound 1952, p. 126.

38. 1 V.; frr. 65; 159 V.

39. Page 1955, p. 42.

40. Snell 1931, p. 83n.2; Page 1955, pp. 12; 85ff.

41. The textual problem here is still unsolved: see Nicosia 1976, pp. 210ff.; the ε]ἰσάγην (with intransitive meaning) proposed by Heitsch 1967 would be plausible if attestations of intransitive εἰσάγω were not confined to the Homeric *Scholia*. I read, very doubtfully, Gallavotti's ἁ]ψ F'ἄγην. The much-discussed crux in v. 19 may now have a solution in V. Di Benedetto's suggestion ("Saffo fr. 1, 18–20," *Riv. filol. class.* III [1983]: 30–43) that we read τίνα δηῦτε πείθωμ᾽ / ἁψ ἄγην ἐς σὰν φιλότατα; "Whom am I now again to be persuaded to lead back to your love?"

42. Fr. 71, 3 V.: a girl, Mica, has opted for the love of one of the Pentilidai— Andromeda (Schadewaldt 1936, p. 365n.1) or Gorgo (Treu 1976, p. 146n.32).

43. Fr. 155 V.: an ironic greeting to the daughter of Polyanactes, Gorgo or Andromeda. There is no evidence that would make the identification with Andromeda (Treu 1976, loc. cit.) the more likely one.

44. We learn from Maximus of Tyre 18, 9 (= Sapph. Test. 219 V.) that there were times when Sappho honored Andromeda and Gorgo, and times when she censured them or treated them with irony and sarcasm.

45. Diog. Laert. 1, 81 = Alc. Test. 429 V.; cf. Alc. frr. 70, 6; 75, 10 V.

46. Fr. 98b, 1–3 V. In spite of the extreme skepticism of Page (1955, p. 102), the interpretation of these verses offered by Vogliano 1939, pp. 277ff., is still valid; cf. Vogliano 1941. See also Gallavotti–Pugliese Carratelli 1942, p. 168; Mazzarino 1943, p. 44; Treu 1976, p. 216.

47. *Marmor Parium*, *FGrHist* 239 A 36 = Sapph. Test. 251 V. For Sappho's exile, cf. Bauer 1963.

*For an up-to-date discussion of the notion of ἁβροσύνη and its social implications in the Lesbian and Ionian world of the archaic period, see M. Lombardo, "Habrosyne e habra nel mondo greco arcaico," in *Forme di contatto e processi di trasformazione nelle società antiche: Atti del Convegno di Cortona* (24–30 May 1981) (Pisa and Rome, 1983), especially pp. 1079ff.

48. Plutarch (*Sept. sap. conv.* 153e) records a symptomatic exchange of discourtesies between him and the Lydian king Alyattes.

49. Diod. 9, 12, 2; Plut. *De frat. am.* 484c; Diog. Laert. 1, 75 and 81. The contacts with Croesus—if they did in fact occur (cf. also Herodt. 1, 27)—must be placed for chronological reasons in the period beginning in 575, when Croesus was still very young and governing the city of Adramytteum in the Troad for his father, Alyattes; cf. Nicol. Damasc. *FGrHist* 90 F 65.

For ancient testimony on the life and activity of Pittacus, see B. Gentili-C.

Prato, *Poetarum elegiacorum testimonia et fragmenta* II (Leipzig, 1985), pp. 31–41.

50. We know of the third exile of Alcaeus from *P. Oxy.* 2506, fr. 98 = Alc. fr. 306Ae V. It coincided with the war between Alyattes and Astyages the Mede, which is to be dated, apparently, between 583/582 and 573/572; see Kaletsch 1958; Treu 1966, pp. 30ff.; Barner 1967b, p. 21. On the relations of Alcaeus and his brother Antimenides with the Lydians and Asia Minor in general, see *P. Oxy.* 2506, frr. 77; 102 = Alc. frr. 306Ab; 306Af V. (cf. also fr. 350 V.); Treu 1966, pp. 20ff.; Barner 1967b, pp. 3ff.; 25ff.

51. Vetta 1980, pp. xli ff.; Vetta 1982.

52. Cf. n.42.

53. Rivier 1967; Vetta 1980, p. xlii.

54. Cf. chap. 3. In the light of the parallel with Theognis and the very meaning of the words *díke, adikía, adikéo,* it is obviously unnecessary to consider the conjectures for v. 24 offered by Blomfield (κωὖκ ἐθέλοισαν) and A. D. Knox (κωῦ σε θέλοισαν), concerning which too much, if anything, has already been written—and continues to be written. See, for example, Saake (1971), who devotes fully seven pages (68–74) to a tedious—and, for all that, incomplete—listing of various views on the question, without the slightest attempt at a new approach to the text. As for the parallel with *Il.* 6, 165 ὅς (Bellerophon) μ' ἔθελεν φιλότητι μιγήμεναι οὐκ ἐθελούσῃ (Antea), a reference to the fine observations in Dawson 1966, p. 49 (not cited by Saake), should be sufficient. The omissions of the direct object in the peremptory formulations of the goddess ("if she flees [you], she will soon pursue [you]" etc.: cf. p. 112) take on, structurally and syntactically, the elliptical, formulaic character of judicio-sacral language; for several obvious parallels, see the Laws of Gortyn, in Guarducci 1978, no. 72. Cf. also Sokolowski 1969.

55. A. Capellano, *Trattato d'amore,* twelfth-century Latin text with two fourteenth-century Tuscan translations, ed. S. Battaglia (Rome, 1947), rule 9: "Amare nemo potest nisi qui amoris suasione compellitur"; rule 26: "Amor nil posset amori denegare"; cf. Contini 1976, p. 46, and especially Avalle 1977, pp. 39ff.

56. Fra Giordano da Pisa, 45: "There is no one but that, on perceiving that he be loved by someone, is not drawn incontinent to love that person in return"; Saint Catherine of Siena: "the soul is naturally drawn to love that by which it sees that it is itself beloved," cf. Avalle 1977, p. 41.

57. Page (1955, pp. 94ff.) deserves the credit for having definitively eliminated from the interpretation of these verses all the superstructures that modern idealism had built upon them. Already in 1935, however, Perrotta (pp. 66ff.) had correctly noted that the landscape described here is real, not imaginary, and that the flowers, so far from being "decorative details, are the landscape itself."

58. I read σὲ θέα«ι»σ' ἰκέλαν Ἀριγνώτα in vv. 4–5. Cf., for the use of the proper name, Gentili 1965a, pp. 157ff., and Snell 1965, p. 97n.69.

59. Note the resumption, in vv. 21-23, of the initial theme of vv. 3-5, a not infrequent stylistic and structural feature in Sappho's odes. Cf., in poem 16 V., the way the fifth strophe concludes with the initial theme of the first: v. 1, "an army of horsemen and infantry," and v. 19ff., "the chariots of the Lydians and infantry fighting under arms."

60. Cf. below.

61. Exhaustively documented in Turyn 1929, p. 65.

62. On the value attached to remembrance in archaic societies, see, among most recent studies, Vernant 1966, pp. 51ff. (Eng. trans., pp. 75ff.), and Eliade 1963, pp. 119ff.

63. That is, once your *psyché* is flown away from here (*ekpepotaména*); cf. *Il.* 16, 856, with Snell 1965, p. 99n.71.

64. Vv. 3 and 4 show that Sappho hoped for a continuation of life after death for herself and her companions, and that she would not have an obscure life, but the same privileged one she had lived on earth: celebrated among men after death and celebrated in the world of the "souls" in Hades. While not wishing to endorse completely Usener's view (1948, p. 329n.13) that Sappho actually expected to live after death like a heroine among the gods, I cannot see what vv. 3-4 can mean if we exclude the idea of a *life* beyond the grave—if, for example, we think that Sappho simply wished to express an idea more or less like that of Horace (3, 30, 6ff.): "non omnis moriar, multaque pars mei / vitabit Libitinam" (W. S. Barrett, *ap.* Page 1955, p. 137n.3). Snell (1965, p. 100n.72) is quite right in not accepting this interpretation, noting that the idea of one's own literary work as a *monumentum* is a Roman one, not typical of the Greeks in general, much less Sappho. He goes on, however, to show an extreme caution in crediting Sappho with belief in the afterlife—a cautiousness that is excessive and makes his own meaning unclear when he speaks of "definite hopes for the afterlife" and "eschatological expectations" in Sappho's circle. These expectations cannot possibly refer solely to earthly fame after one's death but—as v. 3 makes clear—to renown in the world beyond the grave.

65. Fr. 147 V.: "I say that even in the future someone will remember us."

66. Fr. 150 V; cf. Lanata 1966, p. 67.

67. Fr. 94, 1 V: "I wish with all my heart to die."

68. Arist. *Rhet.* 2, 1398b = Sapph. Test. 207 V.: "Sappho says that death is an evil: the gods decided that this was so, otherwise they would have died themselves."

69. The impatience is underlined by repeated instances of "once again" that appear in quick succession beginning with v. 15.

70. Maximus of Tyre's citation of the fragment (18, 9) makes it clear that the *persona loquens* is Aphrodite.

71. Fr. 22, 11ff. V. In v. 15 I read καὶ γὰρ αὖτα δή πο[τ']ἐμεμφ[ετ' ἄμμι Κ]υπρογέν[ηα, accepting Milne's supplement ἄμμι, which seems to fit the sense: Sappho is happy over the splendid dress her friend now wears because *at one time* (ποτά) Aphrodite had evidently complained of the girl's lack of

elegance, something for which Sappho herself shared the responsibility. I find impossible both Wilamowitz's interpretation (1935, p. 387: "since Aphrodite herself would be annoyed at this") and that of Treu (1976, p. 191), which would require the addition of a negative particle for which there is no room in the text. Schadewaldt (1950, p. 65) interprets correctly: "and so Kyprogenea herself at first found fault"; cf. also Pontani 1969, p. 189: "She herself, at one time, was the one who found fault with us, / the goddess of Cyprus. . . ."

72. *Od.* 8, 364ff. (cf. 18, 193ff.); *Hymn. Ven.* 61ff.

73. *Od.* 18, 193ff.; *Cypr.* fr. 4 Kinkel.

74. Himer. *Or.* 46, 6 Colonna = Sapph. Test. 208 V.

75. 1 V.; frr. 127; 128 V.

76. Fr. 32 V.: "[The Muses] who have bestowed all honors upon me through the gift of their works (i.e., of their art)."

77. We know from Aelius Aristides (*Or.* 28, 51 = Sapph. Test. to fr. 55 V.) that in reply to some women who considered themselves rich and fortunate Sappho boasted that the Muses had granted it to her to be "rich and an object of envy." This testimony seems to confirm the hypothesis of Treu (1966, pp. 12ff.), based on the newly discovered commentary published in *P. Oxy.* 2506, fr. 48 = Sapph. fr. 213Ag V., that Sappho received material remuneration from her companions. Particularly significant is the parallel with lines 12ff. of the papyrus, where the presence of the words *téchne* and *ólbos* suggests that the anonymous commentator touched on an argument linking wealth to the cultivation of the arts which went on within the *thíasos;* cf. also the fragment cited in the preceding note. It is very probable that it was the daughters of the Ionian aristocracy in particular (cf. *SLG* fr. 261a P.) who were most lavish when they came to Mytilene to join Sappho's community, paying her with luxury products from the trade with Lydia.

78. Cf. chap. 9.

79. Fr. 58 V., with the supplements of Stiebitz 1926, col. 1259.

On Sappho fr. 58, see V. Di Benedetto, "Il tema della vecchiaia e il fr. 58 di Saffo," *Quad. Urb.*, n.s. 19 [48] (1985): 145–63, who proposes for v. 25 the supplement [ἴστε δὲ] τοῦτο (pp. 153ff.).

80. V. 25ff., the final lines in the poem. I do not share the extreme skepticism of Page (1955, p. 130n.1), who firmly maintains his inability to see the sense connection between these verses and what precedes; cf. Perrotta 1935, p. 36, and Snell 1975, p. 74.

81. Fr. 16 V. On the structure of the poem (general maxim in customary *Priamel* form in the incipit, mythic *exemplum,* application to present situation), see the excellent analysis of Fränkel 1960, pp. 91ff., and 1969, p. 212.

82. The name of the goddess does not appear in the text of v. 11 (ἀλλὰ παράγαγ᾽ αὔταν), but Cypris is clearly the subject, and she must have been named in vv. 12 or 13, now mostly illegible. Sappho is here following the epic tradition preserved in the *Cypria* (p. 17 Kinkel), according to which it was Aphrodite who made Helen fall in love with Paris.

83. Cf. Snell 1965, p. 102, where the essential bibliography is given.

84. Mimnermus, fr. 2 Gent.-Pr.; Theognis 255; cf. Gentili 1965b, p. 381.

85. So Snell 1975, p. 60: "Sappho prefers inner feeling to external splendor," though on p. 65 he says: "For her [Sappho] love is not a feeling which wells up from within but the intervention of a god from without." I am equally reluctant to see Sappho as a precursor in this poem of Protagoras's view of man as the measure of all things (Fränkel 1969, p. 212 [Eng. trans., p. 187]). Free moral choice and man as an autonomous moral agent are notions of which there is no clear trace in the archaic Greek consciousness before Simonides. The rare references to the voluntary quality of an action are confined either to the juridical sphere (false oath taken voluntarily and so prosecutable as a crime against *díke:* Hesiod, *Theog.* 232; *Op.* 282) or to mentions of action that leads to disaster (Sol. fr. 15 Gent.-Pr.; cf. *Od.* 1, 29ff.).

86. Helen is for Sappho the measure of superlative beauty, equal in this respect to a goddess, these being the two terms of comparison she uses. See, for example, fr. 23, 3ff. V.: "when I look [face to face] at you [I think] that Hermione was not beautiful like you, but that you are a worthy likeness of the fair Helen"; cf., for the text, Page 1955, pp. 138ff.

87. Frr. 283; 42 V.; in the second poem the adulterous love of Helen, cause of Troy's final misfortune, is contrasted with the lawful marriage rites of Peleus and Thetis, honored by the presence of the gods and blessed by the birth of Achilles, greatest of heroes.

88. See the analysis in chap. 12.

89. Cf. *kallipáreoi* and *melíphonoi,* which Philostratus, *Im.* 2, 1, 3 (= Sapph. Test. 217 V.), quotes from Sappho's poems, and *mellichóphonos* in fr. 71, 6 V.

*On the symposium in archaic Greek culture, see the volume *Poesia e simposio nella Grecia antica: Guida storica e critica a cura di M. Vetta* (Rome and Bari, 1983), and the articles of O. Murray, "The Greek Symposium in History," in *Tria corda: Scritti in onore di A. Momigliano,* ed. E. Gabba (Como, 1983), pp. 257–72; and E. L. Bowie, "Early Greek Elegy, Symposium and Public Festival," *Journ. Hell. Stud.* 106 (1986): 13–35.

90. Fr. 33, 7–11 Gent.; on the interpretation of the fragment as a whole, see Pretagostini 1982a.

91. Fr. 148 Gent.

92. Fr. 15 Gent.

93. Frr. 26; 71 Gent.

94. Fr. 7 Gent.

95. *Schol.* Pind. *Isthm.* 2, 1b (III p. 213 Drachm.).

96. Such as, for example, "the most beautiful thing is the most just," in the epigram inscribed on the temple of Leto at Delos, cf. Theogn. 255; Aristot. *Eth. Nicom.* 1, 1099a; *Eth. Eud.* 1, 1214a.

97. Cf. Privitera 1972b, pp. 133ff.

98. This interpretation, proposed in 1895 by Giovanni Pascoli (*Prose* I [Milan, 1956]³, p. 666), passed unnoticed until Schwyzer's article (1930), and even today

is only being accepted with difficulty. Bowra's view (1961, p. 290) is implausible. The *pélekys* of v. 2 is, as Schwyzer demonstrated (1930), the hammer, not the axe.

99. Fr. 38 Gent. In v. 3 I now read (with Athen. 11, 782a, where the fragment is cited) ὡς μή ... πυκταλίζω, which is better suited to the context; cf. G. Giangrande 1967, pp. 113ff.

100. Fr. 65 Gent. For problems of text and interpretation, see Gentili 1958a, pp. 202ff.; Privitera 1970, p. 116.

101. In v. 1 the epithet *damáles,* "colt," refers not only to the violence, but to the playful fancifulness, of the god.

102. This erotic symbolism, which is not strictly literary at all but, rather, a product of the everyday experience of the symposium, reappears in poetry only at Apollonius Rhodius 3, 117ff., and in the epigrammatists (cf. Lasserre 1946, p. 48). It is extensively developed, however, in Attic painting from the end of the fifth century on. Among the boy god's preferred games (ball, chess, *morra*), that of dice stands out—as, for example, in the handsome London crater illustrated in Hampe 1951, plate 13. See, for an exhaustive documentation, Greifenhagen 1957.

103. See the documentation in Papaspyridi-Karouzou 1942-43 and, most recently, the red-figured crater in the National Museum of Copenhagen attributed to the Kleophrades painter: *Corpus Vasorum Antiquorum* Denmark, 8 (1963), p. 259, plates 331-33; Immerwahr 1965.

104. Fr. 132 Gent.

105. Fr. 8 Gent.

106. Fr. 48 Gent.

107. Fr. 6 Gent.

108. See Gentili 1973, 1976a; G. Giangrande 1973, 1976, 1981; Komornicka 1976.

109. The use of *lesbía,* in the sense of *tribás,* "female homosexual," goes back to the Byzantine scholar Areta (ninth to tenth centuries); cf. Cassio 1983. It did not become current in modern Europe until the first part of the nineteenth century: Battisti-Alessio 1952, s.v. "lesbico"; Bloch-Wartburg 1950, s.v. "lesbien"; *A Supplement to the Oxford English Dictionary* (Oxford, 1976), s.vv. "Lesbian" and "Lesbianism"; "tribadismo" in Italian belongs to the technical vocabulary of medicine (see *Lessico Universale Italiano,* XXIII, s.v.), though it was part of ordinary usage in English literature of the Victorian period.

110. Page 1955, pp. 142ff.

111. Theopomp. com. fr. 35 Kock; cf. Aristoph. *Eccl.* 920; Pherecrat. fr. 149 Kock.

112. On the meaning of *lesbiázein,* it should be sufficient to cite the energetic but too often forgotten observation of Wilamowitz (1913, p. 72): "Anyone who confuses λεσβιάζειν with female homosexuality should consult a dictionary: it has nothing to do with Sappho"; cf. his further remark (1913, p. 73n.1): "But the confusion of τριβάδες and λεσβίδες is a common one, even among scholars."

113. See *Eros in Grecia,* text by J. Boardman and E. La Rocca, photographs by A. Mulas (Milan, 1975).

114. Cf. Wigodsky 1962.

115. Cf. *Il.* 9, 129; 271.

116. Fr. 89 Gent.

117. Fr. 113 Gent.

118. Fr. 119 Gent.

119. Fr. 86 Gent.

120. Fr. 72 Gent.

121. Cf. Gentili 1958a, pp. 215ff.

122. Cf. Anacr. fr. 179 Gent. and Gentili 1958a, loc. cit.

123. Slater has made the interesting suggestion (1978) that the poem be seen as a good-natured exercise in formal *psógos* to accompany a transvestite ritual inside a fraternity of "friends"; see, to the contrary, Davies 1981.

More solid objections to Slater's proposal (1978) are raised by C. Brown, "From Rags to Riches: Anacreon's Artemon," *Phoenix* 37 (1983): 1–15. While I also am against interpreting fr. 82 along the lines suggested by Slater, a transvestite ritual as part of a *kômos* scene does seem to be the subject of fr. 138 Gent. (= 458 Page): cf. the words *saûla baínein,* with my commentary ad loc. Ancient sources interpret the phrase as referring to a "mincing, coquettish gait"—compare the scene represented on a Louvre amphora (G. 220) by the Flying Angel Painter (c. 480: *ARV²,* p. 220, 11; *Corpus Vasorum Antiquorum* Louvre, plate 42, 3–4 and, in this volume, figures 5–6). On one side a bearded young man in female dress (chiton with long sleeves and *himation*) and a turban on his head minces along with an umbrella in his hand. The other side shows a bald man with beard and a *mitre* (diadem) about his head and a *skýphos* for wine in his right hand, singing and accompanying himself on the lyre (Anacreon? cf. Papaspyridi-Karouzou 1942–43). Equally indicative are the well-known representation of Anacreon on a crater by the Kleophrades painter (*ARV²,* p. 285, 32), and Aristophanes' allusions (placed in the mouth of Agathon at *Thesm.* 161ff.) to the Tean poet's effeminate dress and way of life.

124. Fr. 82 Gent. In v. 1 βερβέριον καλύμματ᾽ ἐσφηκωμένα, the meaning of βερβέριον is uncertain. It is usually taken in the generic sense of "garment," "cloak" (cf., most recently, Chantraine 1968, s.v. "βερβέριον"). The appositional phrase that follows suggests rather a "wasp's-tail" piece of headgear, "a beret made from a handkerchief tied in a point"; cf. Lavagnini 1932, p. 22; Gerber 1970, p. 233.

125. Cf. Andrewes 1956, p. 113.

126. On the implications of Anacreontic poetry for our understanding of the cult of Dionysus, see especially, besides Gentili 1958a, pp. xxi ff., 202ff., Privitera 1970.

127. Fränkel 1969, p. 325 (Eng. trans., pp. 285–86).

128. Of the two fragments the first belonged certainly to a group of poems called *paídeia* or *paidiká,* a poetic genre (cf. chap. 7) also cultivated, according

to Chamaeleon (fr. 25 Wehrli), by Stesichorus. Chamaeleon cites, among other passages, fr. 286 P. of Ibycus and Pindar's encomium to Theoxenos (fr. 123 Sn.-Maehl.).

The new Oxyrhynchus fragments (*P. Oxy.* 3538 in *The Oxyrhynchus Papyri*, L, ed. E. Lobel [London, 1983], pp. 67–78) seem to come from the same type of song–plausibly attributed, on the basis of style and meter, to Ibycus (cf. M. L. West, "New Fragments of Ibycus' Love Songs," *Zeitschr. f. Pap. u. Epigr.* 57 [1984]: 23–32).

129. *Suda,* s.v. "Ἴβυκος"; cf. Cic. *Tusc.* 4, 33, 71.

130. In vv. 3–4 one must follow Schneidewin in reading *apeírona* for the transmitted *ápeira,* which makes no sense metrically in view of the anapestic structure of the first four verses. *Apeíron* traditionally means nothing more than "without end," "boundless," "innumerable" in a purely spatial or temporal sense. By a semantic extension not actually attested earlier, though in some sense implied, it seems in the present context to acquire the added meaning of inextricability–most appropriately applied to a net and, in particular, the net of Aphrodite within which Eros by the power of his glance ensnares his prey; cf. Gentili 1966. See, besides Lasserre 1946, p. 57 and n.2, the observations of Detienne in Detienne-Vernant 1974, p. 278 and n.70, who reads *apeírona* and locates Ibycus's image within the semantic system of the net and *dólos.* On the net of Aphrodite, see Privitera 1967, pp. 15ff. Davies 1980 adds nothing new–only a few lexical parallels with poets in the *Palatine Anthology.*

131. *Kyáneai* is the adjective applied to the brows of Zeus (*Il.* 1, 528) and the beard of Odysseus (*Od.* 16, 176).

132. This is the meaning of the verb *dérkomai:* "strike or fix with one's gaze"; cf. Snell 1975, pp. 13ff.

133. Fr. 3, 61 P. (= 26, 61 Calame) τακερώτερα δ' ὕπνω καὶ σανάτω ποτιδέρκεται: "fixes me with a gaze more devastating than sleep and death."

134. For the text of v. 12 ἐγκρατέως πεδόθεν φυλάσσει / ἡμετέρας φρένας, see Gentili 1967b (cf. G. Giangrande 1971, pp. 106ff.), where I defend the reading *phylássei* against the emendation *laphýssei* proposed in West 1975b, p. 307, and taken up by Borthwick 1979. The *loci similes* adduced by the latter in support of *laphýssei* (consume, tear) do not seem relevant. A different parallel is relevant, however–that with Meleager, *Anth. Pal.* 12, 157 (not yet examined in this context), where the theme of Eros as guard reappears: Ἔρως δ' οἴακα φυλάσσει / ἄκρον ἔχων ψυχῆς ἐν χερὶ πηδάλιον. Cypris is the captain of the ship and Eros is her pilot, "keeping watch at the helm"; that is, guiding the ship across the stormy sea with his hand gripped tight around the handle of the tiller of the (poet's) heart. Beckby's translation (1958, p. 95) shows a correct understanding of the sense of the image: "Eros [is] my helmsman; he governs my soul and holds its handle tight within his hand." For the meaning *pedóthen,* see Fränkel's thorough note (1960, p. 47n.2).

On the text of v. 12 of Ibycus 286 P. see B. Gentili, "Eros custode: Ibico, fr. 286 P. e Meleagro Anth. P. 12, 157," in *Aphoreta philologica E. Fernández*

*Galiano a sodalibus oblata,* I (Mantuae Carpetanorum, 1984), pp. 191-97.
135. On the Pindaric passage, see C. O. Pavese 1972, pp. 240ff.
136. Cf. chap. 5.


SEVEN: PRAISE AND BLAME


1. I find incredible the notion that *amachanía* in v. 54 is a reference to Archilochus's ineptness in composing poems of praise, as Wilamowitz (1922, p. 289), Schroeder (1922, p. 19), and, most recently, Miller (1981, p. 140) maintain, following one of the interpretations offered by the ancient commentators (*Schol. ad loc.* II p. 48 Drachm.). For this to be so one would have to join σοφία with πλουτεῖν in v. 56 (τὸ πλουτεῖν δὲ σὺν τύχᾳ πότμου σοφίας ἄριστον) and translate "to be wealthy in *sophía*"–an implausible interpretation, given the word order and also the context created by the verses that follow (57ff.), in honor of the generosity of Hieron. The interpretation that joins *sophía* and *áriston* ("To grow rich in accordance with divine will is the height of wisdom") is also unlikely to be correct; see the analysis of Burton 1962, p. 120. Péron's interpretation (1974a, pp. 13ff.) ignores the fact that the blame/poverty link recurs elsewhere in (anecdotal) Greek literature; see, for Xenophanes, chap. 9. Archilochus's poverty is, moreover, a subject on which the whole ancient biographical tradition is unanimous; see chap. 10.

2. Cf. *Ol.* 9, 38.

3. Fr. 181 Sn.-Maehl. ὁ γὰρ ἐξ οἴκου ποτὶ μῶμον ἔπαινος κίρναται, cf. *Schol. Nem.* 7, 89b (III p. 128 Drachm.).

4. Cf. *Schol. cit.*

5. *Nem.* 7, 61ff.

6. *Poet.* 1448b 25.

7. For a history of the use of these terms in ancient criticism, see Koster 1980, pp. 7-21.

8. Cf. Detienne 1967, pp. 18-27; Ward 1973; Nagy 1976; Nagy 1979, pp. 222-64. On the theme of praise and blame in Homeric epic, see the discussion in Vernant 1979, especially pp. 1367, 1370. It is important to note how praise and blame continue to constitute an indivisible pair through the centuries: they are still to be found in the poetry of Byzantine Egypt; cf. Cameron 1965, pp. 478ff.

9. Plut. *Lyc.* 8, 3; 25, 3; cf. 14, 5; 26, 6. The praise-blame opposition also pervaded other aspects of the ritual life of the Spartan community: see Alcman, 1 P. (= 3 Calame), vv. 43ff. ἐμὲ δ' οὔτ' ἐπαινῆν οὔτε μωμήσθαι νιν ἁ κλεννὰ χοραγὸς οὐδ' ἁμῶς ἐῇ.

10. Seriocomic (*spoudaiogéloion*) is defined by Bakhtin (1976, pp. 200ff.; 1984, pp. 106ff.) in relation to the genesis of the novel, the basic presuppositions for which he finds in the Socratic dialogue and other Greek literary genres such as mime, bucolic poetry, biographical memoir (Ion of Chios), and so

forth. The implications of the genre postulated by Bakhtin can, I believe, be studied at a deeper level and traced back, as has been shown here, to a remoter period in the history of Greek culture. For a summary discussion of the serio-comic in archaic poetry, see L. Giangrande 1972, pp. 72ff. Koster's investigation (1980, pp. 55–62) of the role of *psógos* in the archaic period is inadequate. For a more incisive presentation, see the morphological analysis of iambic poetry in Pellizer 1981b.

11. Cf. Archil. fr. 207 T.; Pind. *Ol.* 9, 1.

12. In the sense of *enybrízo*; cf. *Nem.* 7, 103, and *Schol. ad loc.* III p. 137 Drachm.

13. Procl. *Chrest.* 29 Severyns.

14. *Hymn. Dem.* 195.

15. Cf. n.22.

16. Democritus of Chios made fun of (*éskope*) the poet Melanippides for having composed long dithyrambic preludes, which, in his opinion, did others no good, and their author even less (Aristot. *Rhet.* 3, 1409b 26ff. = Melanipp. Test. 3 Del Grande).

17. Not exclusively: cf. the two verses (iambic trimeter and hexameter) of fr. 17 Gent.-Pr.

18. On the character of Hipponactean poetry, see Degani 1977a, pp. 122ff. Demetrius, in an important passage (*De eloc.* 301 Rhy Roberts), mentions Hipponax as an example of the broken style, the one most suited for *psógos*.

19. Cf. chap. 6.

20. Frr. 20; 44; 86; 98 Gent.; cf. Gentili 1958a, pp. 215ff.

21. *Rhet.* 3, 1418b 23.

22. So Hermias (fifth century A.D.), correctly commenting (*in* Plat. *Phaedr.* 267a, p. 238, 1 Couvreur) on the meaning of the passage: παρεπαίνους δὲ λέγει (*scil.* Evenus) ἵνα ἄντκρυς μὴ ἐπαινῇ, δοκῇ δὲ ἐπαινεῖν· ὁμοίως δὲ καὶ ψέγειν. The word *ántikrys* leaves no doubt that *parépainos* and *parápsogos* mean *indirect* praise and blame. Ast (*Lex. Plat.* s.vv. "parépainos," "parápsogos") and L. S. J. s.vv. "parep." "paraps.," are incorrect in taking the two terms to mean "occasional" or "incidental" praise and blame.

23. On the use of the term *íambos* to refer to content and function rather than meter, see chap. 3.

24. Plat. *Phaedr. loc. cit.* οἱ δ' αὐτὸν καὶ παραψόγους φασὶν ἐν μέτροις λέγειν, μνήμης χάριν. Hermias *in* Plat. *Phaedr. loc. cit.*: τὸ δὲ μνήμης χάριν ἐπειδὴ τὰ ἔπη τῶν καταλογάδην εὐμνημονευτότερά ἐστιν.

25. For Simonides, see below.

26. In pre-Alexandrian authors the most general category was that of banquet songs or *skólia*, a term that referred specifically to the symposiastic occasion for the poem, not to its content; cf. Harvey 1955, pp. 161–74.

27. Thuc. 2, 34, 4; Plat. *Menex.* 234c; 235a. On encomiastic motifs in funeral orations see Loraux 1981, pp. 42–54 (Eng. trans., pp. 44–56).

28. On these mixed forms see Wilamowitz 1921, pp. 299–322; Gentili 1979a, pp. 15–29; Pretagostini 1980, p. 127–33.

29. Fränkel (1969, p. 352n.12 [Eng. trans., p. 308n.12]) is offering a mere hypothesis (and one already advanced—without conviction—by Wilamowitz [1913, p. 169]) when he suggests that the thematic orientation of the poem presupposes some failure or unfortunate undertaking on the part of Scopas.

30. Cf. Cic. *De nat. deor.* 1, 60.

31. Cf. Dickie 1978, p. 31.

32. For an extended interpretation of the whole poem, see Giannini 1979. The concluding portion of *Pythian* 4 is analyzed in C. Carey, "The Epilogue of Pindar's Fourth Pythian," *Maia* 32 (1980): 143–52. On the relationship between praise, envy, and blame see G. Kirkwood, "Blame and Envy in the Pindaric Epinician," in *Greek Poetry and Philosophy: Studies in Honour of Leonard Woodbury,* ed. D. E. Gerber (Chico, Calif., 1984), pp. 169–83.

33. Cf. chap. 8.

34. Cf. fr. 1 P. (= 3 Calame) and Nannini 1982, pp. 74ff.

35. Cf. Gentili 1977b, pp. 14ff.

36. For a more detailed presentation of Polybius's view of the relation between biography and history, see Gentili-Cerri 1983, pp. 69ff.

37. See, further, Gentili-Cerri 1983, pp. 88ff.

### EIGHT: POET-PATRON-PUBLIC: THE NORM OF THE POLYP

1. Aristot. *Rhet.* 3, 1405b 24.

2. Cf. chap. 9.

3. On the role and function of myth in the Pindaric epinician, see Köhnken 1979 and Lehnus 1981, pp. xiv–xliv.

4. See Defradas's review (1963) of Bundy 1962, and the methodological objections to this critical approach raised by Rose 1974; Bernardini 1979; Cingano 1979a; Cingano 1979b.

5. For a thorough analysis of the Bacchylidean account and the role of Heracles in *Epin.* 5 and *Dith.* 16 Sn.-Maehl., see Gentili 1958b, pp. 13–78. I am in full agreement with the pages of A. Pippin Burnett's *The Art of Bacchylides* (Cambridge, Mass., 1985) devoted to an interpretation of *Dithyramb* 16 (pp. 123–28, in the chapter "The Tragic Muse"). Burnett does not take any stand on the question of whether Bacchylides is here dependent, as some have claimed, on the *Trachiniae* of Sophocles. For the opposite view, already maintained by M. Pohlenz, that the dithyramb antedates the play, see the analysis in Gentili 1958b, pp. 51–57.

6. Cf. Robert 1898, p. 152; Jebb 1905, p. 472.

7. A comparison of the Croesus story in Bacchylides (*Epin.* 3) and Herodotus (1, 86ff.) provides an illuminating example of diversity in treatment of the

same theme determined by function within a larger work and the character of the work itself (poetry or history). Cf. Gentili 1958b, pp. 9off.; Segal 1971.

8. For a survey of trends in Pindaric criticism over the course of the last two centuries, see Young 1964.

Young's discussion should now be supplemented by J. K. Newman–F. S. Newman, *Pindar's Art: Its Tradition and Aims* (Hildesheim, Munich, and Zürich, 1984), pp. 1–38, and M. Heath, "The Origins of Modern Pindaric Criticism," *Journ. Hell. Stud.* 106 (1986): 85–98.

9. Fränkel 1969, pp. 557ff.

For an intelligent discussion of the subtle connections and correspondences by which mythological narrative becomes a function of the character of different celebratory occasions in Pindar, see C. Segal, "Naming, Truth, and Creation in the Poetics of Pindar," *Diacritics* (Summer 1986): 65ff., and *Pindar's Mythmaking: The Fourth Pythian Ode* (Princeton, 1986), pp. 3–14.

10. Without going into the problem of the birthplace (Matauros or Himera) or chronology of Stesichorus (see Vürtheim 1919, pp. 99ff.; Lesky 1971, p. 181; and, most recently, West 1971), I wish to emphasize my disagreement with the late dating favored by those who reject *sic et simpliciter* the dates in the *Suda* s.v. "Στησίχορος": 632–556. As for the birthplace, it is plausible that he was born at Matauros, a colony first of Zancle and then of Locris, and moved later to Himera. What is incontestable is the close character of his connection with Italian Locris: cf. Aristot. *Rhet.* 2, 1395a, with 3, 1412a 22.

11. According to ancient tradition (*Suda*, s.v. "Στησίχορος"), Stesichorus was a citharoede—that is, a performer of solo songs accompanied by a chorus that danced but did not sing. This does not, of course, exclude his having composed choral songs as well. C. O. Pavese (1972, pp. 239ff.) has advanced sound arguments for believing that the *Geryoneis* is citharoedic rather than choral—a thesis perfectly compatible with the triadic structure of the poem.

12. Page 1973; Carmignani 1982, pp. 27ff.

13. For analysis see, most recently, the study of Haslam 1974.

14. The vase paintings are discussed in Robertson 1969; Tiberi 1977; Brize 1980. Pisander's inclusion of the Geryon story in his poem on the labors of Heracles follows from Athenaeus 11, 469c (= Pisandr. fr. 5 Kinkel). Athenaeus refers explicitly to Heracles' voyage in the cup of the Sun (cf. Huxley 1969, p. 101), an episode narrated in the *Geryoneis*. For Pisander's chronology, cf. *Suda*, s.v. "Πείσανδρος," which places his *floruit* around 648; for further, more detailed discussion, see Huxley 1969, pp. 100ff.

15. Cf. Burkert 1977.

16. An island of the Hesperides located by Stesichorus (*SLG* fr. 7 P.) opposite the mouth of the Tartessus (now the Guadalquivir; cf. Robertson 1969). Herodotus is in general agreement (4, 8), situating it just off Cadiz. Pherecydes' view is different (*FGrHist* 3 F 18b); for him Erytheia is the Spanish city itself, not an island.

17. Cf. Gentili 1976d, pp. 745ff.

A bronze pectoral from the last quarter of the seventh century discovered at Samos (figure 7) throws a new light on the relationship between Stesichorus and the figurative arts (cf. P. Brize, "Samos und Stesichoros: Zu einem frü-harchaischen Bronzeblech," *Mitteil. deutsch. archäol. Inst.*, Athen. Abt. 100, 1985, pp. 53-90 and plates 15-21). It represents the same episode of the encounter between Heracles and Geryon narrated by Stesichorus and agrees with Ste-sichorus at several points—for example, the arrow shot, which pierces the fore-head of one of Geryon's three heads and makes it droop to the side. It is clear that both artist and poet go back to an early tradition for their version of the exploits of Heracles. These had been treated, even before Stesichorus, in Kre-ophylos of Samos's narrative (eighth to seventh centuries?) of the capture of Hecalia and in the *Heracleia* of Pisander of Rhodes (cf. n.14). The material was thus well known in the Ionian cultural area, whence it was transmitted to the west by Chalcidean colonists.

18. Cf. *SLG* fr. 15 col. I, 3 P.: δόλῳ leg. Musso 1969, p. 73; 8: λάθρᾳ πολεμε[ῖν; col. II, 6ff.: σιγᾷ δ᾽ ὅ γ᾽ ἐπικλοπάδαν.

19. Particularly in the Meleager section of poem 5. There, too, the narrative proceeds in a temporal line in the direction of a pathetic and dramatic point of culmination; cf. above.

20. Fr. 11 contains a long speech that should be assigned to Geryon (Page, Barrett). The sense emerges, notwithstanding lacunae, with the aid of several plausible supplements by Barrett: "If I must come to grim old age and live a mortal's life far from the gods, it is much nobler for me to face a heroic death now, and not consign to ignominy my own name and that of my children" (vv. 16-24; Diggle 1970, p. 5). But to whom is Geryon talking (cf. v. 16 αἰ δ᾽, ὦ φί[λε)? Not to Heracles, who shoots him from a distance with his arrow, but, as Bar-rett believes, to Menoites, the herdsman for the cows of Hades (cf. Apollod. *Bibl.* 2, 5, 9-10). In *Schol. ad Il.* 21 = Stesich. fr. 273 P., the commentator ob-serves, apropos of the Lycaon episode, that Priam's son drags out his prayer to Achilles in order to get him to spare his life; and that, like Lycaon, all those who are on the point of death are given to long speeches (*makrológoi*), thereby stealing time away from death; and that it is no different with the heroes of Stesichorus. As Page's apparatus to the scholiast's commentary observes, "apud Stesichorum nescio quis moriturus *makrologeî*," and we can now say with some certainty that the long-winded hero is Geryon.

21. For editions of the papyrus and commentaries, see, in addition to the *editio princeps* of Ancher-Boyaval-Meillier 1976, Bollack–Judet de la Combe-Wismann 1977; Gallavotti 1977a; Gentili 1977b; Comotti 1977; Pretagostini 1977; Parsons 1977; Meillier 1977a; Meillier 1977b; Meillier 1978a; Haslam 1978; West 1978b; Ancher 1978; Gentili 1979b; Carmignani 1982, pp. 44ff. On the version of Theban saga retold in the poem and its relation to the mythographic tradition as attested elsewhere, in particular in the *Phoenissae* of Euripides, see also Gostoli 1978; Meillier 1978b.

22. Heraclid. Pont. fr. 157 Wehrli in Ps.-Plut. *De mus.* 3, 1132b.

23. Gentili 1977b.

24. C. Pavese 1962, p. 195.

25. Fr. 193 P. (*P. Oxy.* 2506, *comm. in melicos*).

26. Fr. 192 P. (*ap.* Plat. *Phaedr.* 243a).

27. The Peripatetic Chamaeleon (cf. Stesich. fr. 193 P.) states that Stesichorus composed two palinodes on the Helen myth and cites the opening line of each. He goes on to say that in the first Stesichorus took issue with Homer for representing Helen as having gone to Troy, and in the second with Hesiod, adding that Stesichorus's own version was that "the 'image' (*eídolon*) went to Troy while the real Helen remained with Proteus" in Egypt. The report has caused surprise – though without good reason – because of its supposed incompatibility with several pieces of testimony which mention a single palinode; cf. the analysis of Sisti 1965. I refer in particular to Plat. *Phaedr.* 243a (= fr. 192 P.): "(Stesichorus), having composed in its entirety the so-called palinode, immediately recovered his sight." It is clear, however, from the Platonic context that the term *palinode* must refer to the second revised version, the palinode *par excellence* in which Helen was *totally* rehabilitated, thereby allowing the poet to recover his sight. Here the relevant evidence is supplied by a historian of the Augustan period, Conon (*FGrHist* 26 F 1, 18), who in specific reference to the "palinode" of Stesichorus speaks of "songs" (*hýmnoi*); that is, at least two poems of recantation. The passage has been totally ignored hitherto, except by Davison (1968, p. 223) and West (1971, p. 303n.9), though West only uses it to document the connection between Stesichorus and Locris. Stesichorus must therefore have rejected Homer's account in favor of the Egypt version in the first palinode, and in the second maintained, as against Hesiod, that Helen never even left Sparta (this is clear from the lines Plato cites), hence never arrived in Egypt. This hypothesis on the nature of the polemic with Hesiod is based on the precise testimony of fr. 358 Merk.-West, according to which Hesiod was the first to introduce the *eídolon* story. We are not told, it is true, from where Hesiod had the *eídolon* depart on its voyage to Troy, Sparta, or Egypt, but Chamaeleon's report of a divergence between Hesiod and Stesichorus is only explicable if one accepts the second alternative – an alternative that is also supported by Tzetzes' commentary to v. 13 of the *Alexandra* of Lycophron (II p. 59 Scheer): "they say that Proteus stole Helena away from Alexander (Paris) as he was passing through Egypt, giving him in exchange an image, with which he subsequently went to Troy, as Stesichorus says"; cf. also *Schol.* Aristid. *Or.* 131, 1 (III p. 150 Dindorf). I am in total disagreement with Woodbury's rejection of the authoritative testimony of Chamaeleon (1967, pp. 160ff.), followed by Gerber 1970, p. 150, and Arrighetti 1982, p. 108n.26. The notice is precise, and its author obviously knew the text of Stesichorus, given the fact that he cites the incipit of both palinodes verbatim. It is *certain*, moreover, that the citations are verbatim. V. 1 of the first palinode (fr. 193, 9–10 P.) Δεῦρ' αὖτε θεὰ φιλόμολπε (enoplion), has a close parallel in fr. 240 P. of Stesichorus Δεῦρ' ἄγε Καλλιόπεια λίγεια, which Eustathius expressly cites as

the initial verse of another poem (Eust. to *Il.* 9, 43). V. 1 (metrically identical) of the second palinode (fr. 193, 11 P.) Χρυσόπτερε παρθένε [Μοῖσα?]—the poem to which Plato refers—is an invocation to the same deity, a fact that is sufficient to guarantee its initial position. On both verses see, further, Alcman, *SLG* 1 P. (= 1 Calame) Χρυσοκόμα φιλόμολπε. It is difficult to imagine—for reasons having to do with reception by an audience if for no other—a single poem in which different versions of the same event directly followed each other. Further proof of the existence of two palinodes is provided by Cingano's analysis (1982) of other testimony (not yet taken into consideration in the scholarly literature); see also Rossi 1983, p. 25.

An additional verse, preserved in the commentary to Tzetzes' *Antehomerica* 149, may now be assigned to one of the two palinodes of Stesichorus: see E. Cingano-B. Gentili, "Sul 'nuovo' verso della prima palinodia di Stesicoro," *Zeitschr. f. Pap. u. Epigr.* 57 (1984): 37-40.

28. Cf. Sisti 1965.

29. Bowra 1934, p. 118; 1961, p. 111; he bases his hypothesis on the prestige that the cult of the goddess Helen enjoyed at Sparta.

30. Most recent datings of the battle vary between 580 and 565. On older, unacceptable, hypotheses favoring a date considerably earlier or later (beginning of the sixth century or c. 530), see Bicknell 1966 and Van Compernolle 1969.

For a review of ancient tradition on the battle of the river Sagra, see M. Giangiulio, "Locri, Sparta, Crotone e le tradizioni leggendarie intorno alla battaglia della Sagra," *Mél. école franç. Rome* (Antiquité) 95 (1983): 473-521. Giangiulio's dating agrees with the conclusions of Van Compernolle.

31. For a hypothesis as to the connection of the two versions, see the further discussion in Van Compernolle 1969.

32. Cf. the testimonies in the apparatus to fr. 192 P. On the presence of the cult of the Discouroi at Locri, a significant common element in the culture of Locri and Sparta, see the observations of Musti 1977, pp. 48ff., and Torelli 1977, p. 174.

33. *SLG* fr. 151 = fr. 282 P.; cf. Barron 1969, pp. 119ff.; Simonini 1979. For the chronology of Ibycus, I follow the notice in the *Suda*, s.v. "Ἴβυκος," according to which the poet went to Samos during the fifty-fourth Olympiad (564-560), during the reign of the tyrant Polycrates' father. On the acceptability of this dating in comparison with that offered by Eusebius, who places the *floruit* of the poet between 536 and 532, see the analyses of Sisti 1966 and Barron 1969, pp. 136ff.

To the bibliography on the encomium to Polycrates should be added J. Péron, "Le poème de Polycrate: Une 'palinodie' d'Ibycus?" *Rev. de philol.* 56 (1982): 33-56; and L. Woodbury, "Ibycus and Polycrates," *Phoenix* 39 (1985): 193-220, whose arguments, however, have not persuaded me to modify the view summarized on p. 129: that Ibycus's refusal to tell of episodes from the Trojan War has to do with the nature of the occasion, one which excludes any somber theme not suited to the joyous ceremonial of the symposium.

34. At v. 46 (τοῖς μὲν πέδα κάλλεος αἰέν) I reject the punctuation of the papyrus in favor of that of the editors who join the line to what follows. On the other hand, Barron (1969, p. 135) follows the scribe in placing a stop after αἰέν and interpreting: these men (the heroes famous for their beauty) will remain ever beautiful (in song)–that is, their beauty is eternal. In vv. 47ff. (καὶ σύ, Πολύκρατες, κλέος ἄφθιτον ἑξεῖς / ὡς κατ᾽ ἀοιδὰν καὶ ἐμὸν κλέος) I prefer to follow the majority of interpreters (cf., most recently, Gerber 1970, p. 213) in translating "you too, Polycrates, shall have undying fame, just as, through song, my fame also shall be undying," rather than "you too, Polycrates, shall have undying fame to the extent that my song and my fame can confer it" (Snell 1965, p. 121; Gianotti 1973, p. 408). The former interpretation produces a clear parallelism between "by virtue of song" and "by virtue of beauty" in reference to the *kléos* of Polycrates and that of the poet.

35. *Carm.* 1, 6; cf. Sisti 1967, pp. 67ff.

36. Cf. the programmatic formulations in Xenophan. fr. 1, 21ff. Gent.-Pr.; Anacr. fr. 56 Gent.

37. Schneidewin 1833, pp. 38ff.; Bowra 1961, pp. 252ff.; Sisti 1967, p. 76.

38. On the classification of *paidiká* as encomia, see chap. 7.

39. Snell 1965, p. 120.

40. Barron (1969, pp. 113ff.) gives a detailed analysis of the relationship between the Homeric passage and vv. 23–26 of the encomium.

41. On vv. 23–26 see Gentili 1967b and Gostoli 1979; and, for the *thnatós / dierós* combination, the observations of Williams 1975 and Bonanno 1978–79.

42. For an exhaustive analysis of the proem, see Verdenius 1972, pp. 93–125; Verdenius 1976; Braswell 1976.

43. On the Delphic elements in Pindar's thought, see Duchemin 1955.

44. On the meanings that the polyp image had for the Greeks, see the discussion in Detienne-Vernant 1974, pp. 45ff.

45. Of the two datings, 475 and 470, proposed by scholars for *Pythian* 2, the first is certainly the more plausible, as Musti (1977, pp. 65ff.) and Torelli (1977, pp. 151ff.) have shown, in view of the Locrian events of 477–476 alluded to in vv. 15–20 of the poem. The Locrian maidens' praise of Hieron refers to the intervention that had saved them both from the danger of war with the tyrant of Rhegium and from fulfillment of their fellow citizens' vow (made when the danger was at its height) to dedicate them as prostitutes on the holy day of Aphrodite. Woodbury's detailed analysis (1978, pp. 285–99) comes to the same conclusions; cf. also the arguments of Puech 1961a, p. 40.

46. The possibility that vv. 72–96 contain no politico-personal allusions and implications is rightly rejected by Fogelmark 1976, pp. 122ff. See also Cingano 1979a, pp. 174–77.

47. *Pyth.* 11, 53: "I condemn the condition of tyrant." Of the two possible dates for *Pythian* 11, 474 and 454, the earlier has the support of valid arguments

drawn both from the text and the scholia; cf. von der Mühll 1958; Burton 1962, p. 61; cf. below.

48. I do not think that ψυχράν (v. 9 ψυχρὰν φορεῖται πᾶσαν ὁδὸν θεραπεύων) should be considered corrupt (Sn.-Maehl.). See the convincing argument of Van Groningen 1960a, pp. 65ff.

49. Cf. Bowra 1964, pp. 69ff.

50. Fr. 169a Sn.-Maehl. My analysis shows a type of approach to the problems of the ode which is fundamentally different from that usually encountered in the extensive earlier literature, on which see Castagna 1971; Lloyd-Jones 1972. I have noted the germ of my interpretation in interesting portions of the essays of Ostwald 1965 and 1969, pp. 37ff.

51. Wilamowitz 1895, p. 97n.179.

52. For Heracles as son of Zeus, see *Pyth.* 9, 84, and *Nem.* 1; and cf., in addition, fr. 29, 4 Sn.-Maehl.: τὸ πάντολμον σθένος Ἡρακλέος.

53. On the meaning of *kairós* and its semantic value in Pindar, see Untersteiner 1951, pp. 35ff.; Thummer 1957, pp. 104ff.; Fränkel 1969, pp. 509ff.; Wilson 1980.

Cf. n.81.

54. Cf., for example, Ehrenberg 1921, pp. 119ff.

55. *Isthm.* 3/4, 73ff., cf. *Nem.* 3, 23ff. Heracles' gluttony (fr. 168 Sn.-Maehl.) is sometimes taken as a comico-burlesque aspect of his portrayal, but extraordinary appetite is not an exclusive prerogative of Heracles. It is part of the superhuman nature that all heroes share; cf. the note of Bernardini 1976.

56. Excellently analyzed by Kirk 1977; see also Lacroix 1974.

57. On the concept, see Dupront 1965, p. 8: "Acculturation is defined as the movement of an individual, a group, a society or even a culture toward another culture; it is thus a process of dialogue, instruction, confrontation, mingling, and—in the majority of cases—*trial of strength* [italics mine]. Two cultures or two civilizations are present. Their interaction—everything that is suggested by the prefix *ad*—is acculturation."

58. One need only think of the way the primitive is represented as a monstrous being in the figurative art of the early nineteenth century: cf., for example, J. Webber's *The Offering of a Human Sacrifice in Tahiti* (British Museum, Print Room). Wittkower's study (1942) of the history of the monster is equally interesting, both for its iconographic documentation and its frequent citation of ancient parallels.

59. Fr. 10 Kinkel; cf. n.14.

60. I think that one may accept the dates 490 and 487-485 proposed for *Paean 6* and *Nemean 7* by Wilamowitz (1908, p. 345), in spite of the many objections to them which have been raised (cf., most recently, Radt 1958, p. 90; Bowra 1964, pp. 410ff.; Fogelmark 1972, pp. 41-48, 83-86, 89ff.). The paean cannot possibly be later than 480 for a very fundamental reason: at vv. 124ff. it celebrates the maritime hegemony of Aegina, "glorious island that holds dominion over the Aegean." But, as is well known, Aegina was the leading mari-

time power only to the time of Themistocles, not thereafter (cf. Welter 1938, pp. 38ff.; De Sanctis 1975, p. 386). The praise would have made no sense if the poem had been performed in the third or fourth decade of the century, as proponents of a late dating would have it. Once this is granted, 490 is shown to be the most probable date by another argument of Wilamowitz—not at all, as has been claimed, an "illusory" one—based on the allusion to *Paean* 6 in the incipit of *Pythian* 6 (490) ἢ γὰρ ἑλικώπιδος Ἀφροδίτας ἄρουραν ἢ Χαρίτων ἀναπολίζομεν; cf. *Pae.* 6, 3–4, Χαρίτεσσίν τε καὶ σὺν Ἀφροδίτᾳ. Granted that ἀνά in ἀναπολίζω need not contain the idea of repetition, the burden of proof is with those who claim that it does not have this idea in the present instance. The parallel with τρὶς τετράκι τ᾽ ἀμπολεῖν at *Nem.* 7, 104 seems to support rather than impugn the suggestion that the idea of repetition is present; see Soph. *Phil.* 1238 δὶς ταὐτὰ βούλει καὶ τρὶς ἀναπολεῖν μ᾽ ἔπη, with the note of Jebb 1905, ad loc. and L. S. J. s.v. "ἀναπ-." If, then, *Paean* 6 dates to 490, the only possible date for *Nemean* 7 is 487–485, which Wilamowitz obtains by correcting the impossible ιδ᾽ (Nemead 14 = 547) given in *Schol. Nem.* 7 inscr., III p. 116, 6 Drachm. to μδ᾽ (Nemead 44); Hermann's νδ᾽ (467) is unacceptable because it requires a lapse of many years between the composition of the two poems.

61. The passage supports the biographical tradition concerning Pindar, according to which the priests at Delphi accorded special privileges to the poet (cf. *Vita Ambros.* p. 2, 14; *Vita Thom.* p. 5, 6; *Vita metr.* 16, p. 9 Drachm.). These passed to his descendants, who are said to have exercised them in connection with the same festival of the theoxeny for which the paean was composed (Plut. *De sera num. vind.* 13, 557f).

62. Vv. 62–65 with the scholiast ad loc. In spite of the lacunae in the first strophe of the second triad (vv. 62–82), we can get an idea of what appeared in the narrative: the origin of the theoxeny and its connection with the famine (cf. *Scholl.* Pind. *Nem.* 5, 17b, III p. 91 Drachm.; *Nem.* 8, 19a, III p. 142 Drachm.; Paus. 2, 29, 7), an episode of the Trojan War and the legends of the sons of Aeacus. For the skolion to vv. 62ff., see the editions of Turyn 1952, p. 257, and Radt 1958, p. 35*.

63. V. 74 Πάνθοο[ν (Grenfell-Hunt, Schroeder, Puech, Turyn); but παν θοὸ[ν (*scil.* Achilles: Sn.-Maehl.), πανθοο[ (Radt).

64. Cf. *Schol.* T *Il.* 12, 211ff. (III p. 344 Erbse); *Schol.* T *Il.* 15, 521ff. (IV p. 116 Erbse).

65. Vv. 125–40; 176ff. The only legible parts of the final triad are the first ten verses of the strophe and the last nine of the epode.

66. Thus Wilamowitz 1922, pp. 134ff.; cf. the contrary argument of Hoekstra 1962. Puech (1961b, p. 113) plausibly suggests that the poet brought the chorus with him from Thebes.

67. Cf. Paus. 2, 29, 7.

68. Cf. Sitzler 1911; Tosi 1929; Radt 1958, p. 132; Puech 1961b, pp. 115ff.; Hoekstra 1962.

69. The correct reading in v. 118 .]υρ [...] περὶ τιμᾶν is a much-discussed

textual problem that has troubled both ancient and modern critics. The solution cannot be considered independently of the link between this poem and *Nemean* 7. We learn from the ancient commentary to the later poem (*Schol. Pind. Nem.* 7, 94a, III pp. 129, 7ff. Drachm.) that the Aeginetans had accused Pindar of insulting the memory of Neoptolemus by the allusion made in precisely this verse of the poem to the hero's pillaging of the Delphic temple (*Schol. Nem.* 7, 150a, III p. 137, 5 Drachm.). The Aeginetans had thus interpreted the poet's words in the light of what was certainly a well-known fifth-century version of the myth (it appears in Eur. *Andr.* 51ff.; 1095; 1107ff.; *Or.* 1657), according to which Neoptolemus went to the sanctuary at Delphi after the Trojan War to demand from Apollo just compensation for the death of his father, Achilles, whom the god, disguised as Paris, had slain. In *Nemean* 7 Pindar replied to the Aeginetans, saying that their resentment was based on a mistake: he had not meant to suggest in the *Paean* that the object of the struggle with the priest of the god was the riches of the temple (*perì chremáton*). It was merely the question of the honors due to the priests. Basically, then, there had not been the slightest reference in his words to a request for compensation made by the hero. Excluding, therefore, the impossible *moiriân* (cf. the cogent discussion in Radt 1958, p. 164), and the banal *Pythiân* of the Alexandrian grammarian Zenodotos, two of the various supplements to v. 118 proposed by scholars are worth considering: *kyriân* (owed; cf. Housman 1908) and *myriân* (innumerable). Both are based on the passage just examined from the ancient commentary to *Nemean* 7 (III p. 129 Drachm.). The first is paralleled in the paraphrase περὶ τῶν νομιζομένων τιμῶν τοῖς Δελφοῖς, the second in the almost verbatim citation of the verse in the *Paean*. Both adjectives are ambiguous in combination with the word *honors*, which, as the papyrus commentary to *Paean* verse points out (cf. Radt 1958, p. 36*, *schol.* v. 118), could designate either the flesh of the victims distributed after the sacrifice (referred to explicitly in *Nem.* 7, 42) or the possessions of the temple. The adjectives do not eliminate the ambiguity, because "innumerable" could be said equally of the portions of meat and the treasures requested by the hero, and either could have been "owed" equally well to Neoptolemus or to the priests of Delphi. *Kyriân*, however, seems more subtle and more in keeping with Pindar's intention—to please his Delphic patrons without displeasing the Aeginetans. "Concerning honors owed" could be taken equally well by the Delphians as honors requested from Apollo by the impious and arrogant Neoptolemus (a direction in which the reference at vv. 79ff. to the murder of Achilles by the god was already pointing), or by the Aeginetans as honors owed to the Delphians: thus Neoptolemus's action would have been partially justified as directed toward an equitable distribution of the sacrificial meats. It is possible, of course, that the ambiguity was unintentional, in which case the second interpretation is simply the one that happened to provide the poet with greater leeway for his defense when in *Nemean* 7 he made explicit the reason for the quarrel over dividing the meat. Even this defense, however, retains a certain degree of ambiguity: the brevity of the reference to the priests' arrogant claim to all the sacrificial victims points to a desire not to cause offense in Delphian circles; and the desire comes out openly in the emphasis on the grief of the Delphians for the accidental death of the hero (*Nem.* 7, 43). On the importance of appropriate ritual formalities in Greek sacrificial practice, see Detienne 1979.

70. *Schol.* Pind. *Nem.* 7, 70, III p. 126 Drachm.; 150a, III p. 137 Drachm. For an analysis of the myth of Neoptolemus at Delphi as it relates to *Nemean* 7, see the discussion of Woodbury 1979; and, for a commentary on the *Scholl. ad locc.,* Tugendhat 1960; Fränkel 1961; Fogelmark 1972.

71. Cf. *Nem.* 8, 24, also composed for an Aeginetan athlete.

72. For the interpretation of vv. 31-34, see the long note in Farnell 1932, pp. 291ff.

73. Cf. *Schol.* Pind. *Nem.* 7, 47, III p. 123 Drachm.: ὅτι ἀδοκήτως αὐτῷ συνέβη (viz. death), and Gerber 1963, p. 187.

74. See once again Farnell 1932, pp. 294ff.

75. Des Places 1949, p. 25; Köhnken 1971, p. 39.

76. Cf. Defradas 1954, pp. 146ff.; Sordi 1958, pp. 69ff.; Woodbury 1979, pp. 98ff.

77. Bundy 1962, I pp. 4, 29n.70; Thummer 1968, pp. 95ff., 98; Slater 1969a, pp. 91-94; Slater 1977, pp. 203-8; Köhnken 1971, pp. 38ff.; Lee 1978; Lefkowitz 1980, pp. 38-48. For a criticism of such interpretations, see Cingano 1979a, pp. 169-71; 177-82.

78. Slater (1969a, pp. 91-94) is inclined to deny the presence of an implicit reference to *Paean* 6 at this point, appealing to the usual *locus communis* argument. But the analogous formulations in other Pindaric odes which he adduces in support of his thesis are not examined in relation to their individual contexts; cf. Cerri 1976. See also Fogelmark 1972, pp. 104-16, and Lasso de la Vega 1977, especially pp. 76-135. The line of interpretation in C. O. Pavese 1978 is different, but equally unpersuasive. On the basis of the explanation offered by a scholion (to v. 56a), he believes that the person mentioned at the end of the poem (v. 103) is a different Neoptolemus, not the hero but the trainer responsible for Sogenes' victory, thus eliminating any possible connection between *Paean* 6 and *Nemean* 7. Further proof of the link between the two odes is provided by a comparative analysis of their metrico-rhythmical structure: cf. Gentili 1979a, pp. 15ff.

79. On Pindar's allusion here to the idea of *atropía,* see Tugendhat 1960, p. 405.

80. Fr. 43 Sn.-Maehl.; cf. above.

81. Brelich 1969, pp. 231ff.; 255; Lloyd-Jones 1973, pp. 136ff.

The reference to *kairós* in the much-discussed lines (78ff.) of *Pythian* 9 deserves further consideration in the light of the recent essay of D. C. Young ("Pindar, Aristotle, and Homer: A Study in Ancient Criticism," *Class. Ant.* 2 [1983]: 156ff.). Young's examination of vv. 76-79 leads him to reaffirm the—to my mind—highly implausible interpretation of E. L. Bundy. The words ἀρεταὶ δ' αἰεὶ μεγάλαι πολύμυθοι· / βαιὰ δ'ἐν μακροῖσι ποικίλλειν / ἀκοὰ σοφοῖς· ὁ δὲ καιρὸς ὁμοίως παντὸς ἔχει κορυφάν are taken (*art. cit.* p. 161) as equivalent to the poet's assertion that "by judicious selection and treatment (καιρός) I can convey the spirit (κορυφάν) of the whole *just as well.*"

These verses function as a demarcation between the first part of the ode (vv. 1–75), dedicated to the Pythian victory of Telesicrates and the myth of Cyrene, and the second (vv. 79–124), which records the athlete's preceding victories, associating them with the culminating episode in the Iolaus myth and the tale of the marriage of the daughter of Antaeus with Alexidamos, one of the victor's ancestors. They make the point that, though great exploits always provide rich material for song, persons of discernment–those who are poets or, at any rate, cultivated judges of poetry (cf. Burton 1962, p. 45)–pay attention to the singer who selects a few points in a long narrative for artistic treatment and embellishment. "Long" is here used, in the Pindaric sense (cf. *Ol.* 13, 41ff.), to refer to the extent and duration of a song (cf. L. L. Nash, *Quad. Urb*, n.s. II {40} [1982]: 80). What follows in vv. 78ff. ("The opportune moment embodies in equal degree the highest point of everything") is equivalent to saying that opportuneness and suitability–in the context of a given occasion–provides the best norm for human conduct in every type of situation (cf. *kairòs d'epì pâsin áristos* in Hes. *Op.* 694 and *kairòs áristos* in Pind. *Ol.* 13, 48). It is this norm that must govern the poet's selection–with due regard for the occasion– of the particular episodes in the subsequent myths of Iolaus and Antaeus which highlight more than any others the boldness and prowess of the hero. For Iolaus this is the beheading of Eurystheus, and for Antaeus the devising of the sort of contest which would insure that the best of the suitors won his daughter's hand in marriage. It is also the norm that governs the hero's own selection of the right moment–the exact point at which divine aid was available for the completion of his exploit and which Iolaus did not scorn or neglect when he came back to life and punished Eurystheus, the persecutor of the sons of Heracles, by killing him. Obviously, I do not share the opinion of those scholars–and they are fairly numerous–who refer νιν in v. 80 to Telesicrates (ἔγνον ποτὲ καὶ Ἰόλαον οὐκ ἀτιμάσαντά νιν ἑπταπύλοι Θῆβαι: vv. 79–80). I am firmly convinced–along with the ancient commentators on Pindar (*Schol.* v. 138, III p. 234 Drachm.); cf., among the moderns, Heyne, Boeckh, Dissen, and, most recently, G. Kirkwood, *Selections from Pindar* (Chico, Calif., 1982), pp. 228ff.–that the reference is to the nearer word *kairós.*

Bundy's identification (1962, p. 17n.42) of νιν with Telesicrates is based on the parallel with an analogous syntactical combination in *Ol.* 7, 83–where, however, the structure involved is a rather different, more linear one. In *Pythian* 9, by contrast, the beginning of the fourth triad marks a break with what has gone before, serving to introduce a new subject for the poet's song. (The presence of an additional νιν at the close of the triad immediately preceding [line 78] creates further difficulties for Bundy's interpretation.) The use of the abstract *kairós* as the direct object of *atimázo* is sufficiently paralleled by the passages cited in L. S. J. s.v. "atimázo," I, 1; but here one cannot exclude the possibility that the reference is to the personified divinity *kairós*—already coupled with Athena in a Pythagorean context (= Nr. 7 in Stob. *Ecl.* I, 10, pp. 21ff. Wachsmuth; cf. W. Burkert, *Weisheit und Wissenschaft* [Nürnberg, 1962], p. 443, and L. Leurini, *Parola d. passato* 150 [1973]: 208) and then, as the youngest of the sons of Zeus, in a hymn by Ion of Chios (fr. 38 Blumenthal).

In the context of the particular occasion, then, opportuneness means that the poet will limit his discussion to the few points that highlight the excellence of an enterprise, whether heroic (Iolaus) or human (Telesicrates), elaborating them (*poikíllein, Pyth.* 9, 77) with the embellishments of his art—that is, with all the resources of poetic language. Cf. the important discussion in *Evagoras* 9, where Isocrates, with the Pindaric encomium obviously in mind (cf. *Antidosis* 166), spells out the role of *poikíllein* in poetry: *toîs mèn poietaîs . . . pâsin toîs eídesin diapoikîlai tèn poíesin.*

My interpretation of *kairós* in *Pythian* 9 diverges from H. Fränkel's view (1969, p. 509n.14 [Eng. trans., p. 447n.14]) that the word never has a temporal significance in Pindar. Although there is a basic tendency, even in contemporary discussions of the term, to deny that this meaning is detectable before the fifth century, and though the spatial sense certainly predominates in Homeric epic, one cannot exclude the possibility of some original, implicit temporal connotation. The word is a highly ambiguous one, which has no exact equivalent in any other language. Diogenes Laertius (1, 78) records Pittacus's saying that it is for intelligent men (*synetoí*) to foresee (*pronoêsai*) difficult situations before they arise, so as to avoid them, and for courageous men to deal with them once they do arise—a shrewd norm for politicians, well encapsulated in the dictum traditionally ascribed to him: "Know the proper moment (*kairòn gnôthi*) for action" (B. Snell, *Leben und Meinungen der Sieben Weisen* (Munich, 1952)², p. 102 = Pittacus, Test. 19a Gent.-Pr. in *Poetae Elegiaci* II p. 39). The notions of space and time are indissolubly linked in the Pindaric notion of *kairós*. As was noted earlier, a brief discourse is certainly brief in a spatial sense, but the reference is also temporal, to the duration of the performance. Analogous formulations are, moreover, fairly frequent in Pindar's work (cf. C. G. Heyne, *Pindari carmina*, I [London, 1824], p. 160, *ad Pyth.* 1, 157ff. [81ff.]), and are explicable in terms of the archaic poet's oral mode of communication. Unlike written discourse intended for reading, oral discourse shows a structure arising out of the occasion or performance situation, and in direct response to the expectations of the audience. This is precisely the point of the net metaphor at *Pythian* 1, 81ff. (*peírata syntanýsais:* cf. *Schol. ad loc.*): if one speaks opportunely (*kairòn ei phthénxaio*—here kairón = katà kairón: cf. *Schol. ad loc.*), combining the threads of many arguments into a brief discourse, then the listener will be less inclined to criticize and the audience less likely to grow tired. Pindar thus develops the same idea of *kairós* which will become, a few years later, the guiding principle of the rhetorical theory of Gorgias (cf., for example, *Palamedes* 22). It is an idea that has to do equally with time, with space, and with occasion (cf. G. Kennedy, *The Art of Persuasion in Greece* [Princeton, 1963], pp. 66ff.). For this and related problems as they appear in the study of Greek rhetoric, see M. Vallozza, "La retorica e il tempo: Le valenze di καιρός tra oratoria orale e scritta," in *Atti del Convegno su Studi di retorica oggi in Italia* (18-19 April 1985), Bologna, 1987, pp. 87ff., and T. Cole, "Le origini della retorica," *Quad. Urb*., n.s. 23 [52] (1986): 7ff.

82. The political significance of Eunomia in this "Corinthian" ode is indicated by a comparison with Herodotus 5, 92, which refers to the *isokratía* of the Corinthian oligarchy. The regime was founded on an equality of rights among the members of the ruling class which prevented the aggrandizement of any one individual at the expense of another.

83. Cf., in v. 1 of fr. 205 Sn.-Maehl.: Ἀρχὰ μεγάλας ἀρετᾶς (cf. chap. 9), and in Bacchyl. fr. 14, 2 Sn.-Maehl.: ἀνδρῶν δ᾽ ἀρετὰν σοφία τε / παγκρατής τ᾽ ἐλέγχει / ἀλάθεια.

84. Snell 1978, pp. 91ff.; Cole 1983.

85. Cf. vv. 81ff., and the comment of Burton 1962, pp. 87ff.

86. Cf. Fränkel 1969, p. 539 (Eng. trans., p. 472).

I reject, of course, the disjunctive interpretation of the opening ἓν ἀνδρῶν . . . ἓν θεῶν γένος of *Nemean* 6 offered by some scholars. The race of men and the race of gods is one, just as their mother is one. There can be no doubt that the common mother is Earth, as pointed out in the ancient commentary (*Schol. ad* Pind. *Nem.* 6, 1, III pp. 101ff. Drachm.), which compares Hesiod, *Theog.* 126ff.; cf., most recently, J. Pépin, *Idées grecques sur l'homme et sur Dieu* (Paris, 1971), pp. 36-38. Solon seems to be referring to the same genealogical tradition when (fr. 30, 4 Gent.-Pr.) he calls upon Earth as great mother of the Olympian gods to witness the extent of his commitment to reconciling the opposed interests of the people and the land-owning aristocracy. But even if man and gods belong to a single universe, they still constitute distinct races: body and mind are common to both (cf. *phýsin* and *nóon* in *Nemean* 6, v. 5), but one race is immortal, the other mortal; one is pure, the other impure, for the human body is intimately bound up with sleep, weariness, hunger, old age—the grim companions of death (cf. J.-P. Vernant, "Corps des Dieux," *Le temps de la réflexion* 7 [1986]: 19ff.).

87. F. Hölderlin, "Der Menschen Worte verstand ich nie . . . / Im Arm der Götter wuchs ich gross," *Sämtl. Werke* (Ausg. Fr. Beisner Gross. Stuttgart), I/1, 1946, p. 267.

88. Cf. *Ol.* 3, 4; *Nem.* 8, 19; *Pyth.* 10, 67.

89. In v. 95 ἐπάμεροι (creatures of the day) contains, as Fränkel has shown (1960, pp. 23-39; 1969, pp. 149, 570ff.), the archaic idea of "beings who change every day," or even "beings subject to the mutability of time," not "beings whose life is short." In the phrase τί δέ τις; τί δ᾽ οὔ τις, the words τις and οὔ τις mean "someone" and "no one" (so the ancient commentary [135ab, II p. 218 Drachm.] followed by some modern scholars [cf. Dissen 1830 ad loc. and most recently Giannini 1982b]), and define the opposite outcomes of the life of man.

He may be "no one"—that is, because of the precariousness and changeability of his situation, "dream" (or "shadow") "of a shadow" and so nothing at all; but he also may be "someone"—when light from the gods shines on the accomplishing of his deeds and allows him to achieve success and fame. For a correct interpretation of the combination σκιᾶς ὄναρ ἄνθρωπος (vv. 95ff.), cf. Bieler 1933 and especially Jüthner 1936.

My discussion of the crisis of aristocratic values—values whose decline Pindar recognizes even while making himself their spokesman—should be compared with the analysis of W. Donlan, *The Aristocratic Ideal in Ancient Greece* (Lawrence, Kans., 1980), pp. 95ff.

90. On the Pindaric studies of Wilamowitz, see Rossi 1973.

91. The most important representatives of this approach continue to be the works of Bundy 1962 and C. O. Pavese 1968.

92. Young 1968, pp. 1-26.

93. Wilamowitz 1922, p. 293. Péron (1976-77, pp. 78ff.) follows Young's interpretation.

Péron returns to its defense in "Pindare et la tyrannie d'après la XIe Pythique," *Rev. ét. grec.* (1986): 1ff.

94. Aristotle (*Pol.* 5, 1302b 29) refers to the fall of the democratic government at Thebes after the battle of Oenophyta (457). Before then, during the years 479-457, it would seem that Thebes was governed by a democracy—though the regime may have been, as a number of modern authors assume, a moderate oligarchy rather than a true democracy; cf. Schober 1934.

95. It is thus evident that the Bacchylidean epinician has a character of its own, both as regards the poet-patron relationship and extratextual referentiality; and that Bacchylidean poetry requires a different type of examination and different tools of analysis. The difference is one with which scholarship in recent years has been more concerned and readier to deal (see the studies of Lefkowitz 1969; Lefkowitz 1976, pp. 42-76, 125-42; Arrighetti 1976, pp. 305ff.; Segal 1976b; Bernardini 1979; Segal 1979), though earlier writers—Wilamowitz, Romagnoli, Perrotta—were not unaware of its existence. Stern 1970 gives a survey of Bacchylidean criticism.

See, among more recent studies, A. Pippin Burnett, *The Art of Bacchylides* (Cambridge, Mass., 1985).

96. Cf. Gentili 1958b, pp. 113ff.

97. Cf. the encomium for Alexander, son of Amyntas (fr. 121 Sn.-Maehl.): "It is the portion of noble men to be praised . . . in songs of surpassing beauty. This is the only way to immortal honors; in silence noble achievement dies."

98. Cf. Fränkel 1969, pp. 495ff. (Eng. trans., pp. 435ff.); Arrighetti 1976, p. 280.

99. Cf., once again, Fränkel 1969, p. 495n.20 (Eng. trans., p. 435n.20).

100. Cf. Pind. *Ol.* 9, 100ff.: "everything that is inborn is better; among men there are many who through excellence acquired by learning burn to gain glory"; *Nem.* 1, 25: "varied are the arts of men, but he who proceeds along right

paths should contend by means of the arts that he has by nature."

101. Cf. *Od.* 1,1 *polýtropos,* and the note in Janni 1976.

102. *Nem.* 7, 21; 8, 25ff.

103. Fränkel 1969, pp. 358ff. (Eng. trans., pp. 314ff.).

104. Gentili 1958b, pp. 24ff., and Gzella 1969–70.

105. Fr. 615 P. Cf. chap. 5.


## NINE: INTELLECTUAL ACTIVITY AND SOCIOECONOMIC SITUATION

1. Cf. chap. 1.

2. The only itinerant poet mentioned in Homer is the Thracian Thamyris (*Il.* 2. 594–600)–see Svenbro 1976, p. 34 and n.97.

3. Roehl 1882, nr. 502; Lazzarini 1976, p. 198 nr. 142.

4. *I.G.* IV 914; Plat. *Ion* 530a–b.

5. Cf. chap. 1. For rhapsodic contests, see Càssola 1975, pp. xiv–xvi; Humphreys 1978, p. 215.

6. Havelock 1963, pp. 45ff.

7. Cf. chap. 1, n.12.

8. Fr. 27 Gent.-Pr.; cf. also Test. 77.

9. Giannini 1982a, p. 62n.24.

10. One should note in this connection Humphreys's observations (1978, p. 228) on the poet's role as mediator and spokesman in communications between *dêmos* and governing aristocracy.

11. Plut. *Lyc.* 4. Cf. Diog. Babyl. in Philodem. *De mus.* p. 85, 36ff. Kemke = *S.V.F.* 232, 10 Arnim.

12. Aristot. fr. 545 Rose.

13. Philodem. *De mus.* p. 18, 35ff. Kemke with Wilamowitz's persuasive supplement τῶν [Λοκρῶ]ν; cf. Vallet 1958, p. 312, and Gigante 1977, p. 40.

14. Cf. Svenbro 1976, pp. 93ff.; 101.

15. *Gnomol. Par.* p. 18n.160 Sternbach; Plut. *Reg. apophth.* 175c = Xenophan. Test. 23 Gent.-Pr.

16. It is difficult, in the light of Diogenes Laertius 9, 18 (ἀλλὰ καὶ αὐτὸς ἐρραψῴδει τὰ ἑαυτοῦ), to deny that Xenophanes was an itinerant rhapsode (Xenophan. fr. 7 Gent.-Pr.) who combined recitation of epic poems with renderings of his own works in which there were polemical attacks on Homer (cf. Xenophan. Σίλλοι frr. 9–22 Gent.-Pr.): see Pfeiffer 1968, pp. 8ff. The contrary hypothesis of Svenbro (1976, p. 78) is not convincing.

17. Antip. Sid. *Anth. Pal.* 7, 745.

18. On the significance of these episodes, see the observations of Svenbro (1976, pp. 169ff.).

19. On the meaning of *ólbos* cf. De Heer 1969, with the more precise formulations in Lévêque 1982.

20. Fränkel 1969, p. 270n.35 (Eng. trans., p. 234n.35) has well understood the link between the invocation of the Muses and the request for prosperity, specifically identifying it with the practice of a poetry that was "the medium for both his [Solon's] political activity and his rise to power."

21. On the aristocratic distinction between gain (*kérdos*) that is "just" by virtue of deriving from a type of commerce that complements the activity of the farmer, and that which is the "unjust" result of the autonomous commercial ventures of the entrepreneur and the speculator, see, most recently, Mele 1979.

22. For a full analysis of the *Elegy to the Muses*, see Masaracchia 1958, pp. 201–43; cf. also p. 277.

A detailed analysis of the various interpretations of the *Elegy to the Muses* and the ideological presuppositions that govern it may now be found in A. Spira, "Solons Musenelegie," in *Gnomosyne: Festschrift für Walter Marg zum 70. Geburtstag* (Munich, 1981), pp. 177–96. One senses in his own investigation the call for an interpretative approach that is both more concrete and more suited to the pragmatic tasks of Solon's poem—far removed from the abstract and idealizing superstructures erected by other critics. He is right in emphasizing the anthropological aspects of the *Elegy to the Muses*, a poem that supplements the political orientation of the *Eunomia* by a detailed and effective analysis of human custom and characteristic modes of human behavior—but one closely linked, it should be emphasized, to the specific context of socioeconomic reality in the Athenian community of the late seventh and early sixth centuries.

23. Descat 1982, pp. 392ff.

24. Plut. *Sol.* 23, 15ff. = Martina 1968, pp. 362ff.; cf. also the comment of Piccirilli 1977, p. 246; Diog. Laert. 1, 55.

25. The role of guide for the community thereby assumed is well documented in Detienne 1967.

26. Ael. Aristid. *Or.* 28, 51 = Sapph. Test. ad fr. 55 V.; cf. *P. Oxy.* 2506, fr. 48 = Sapph. fr. 213Ag V., on which see Treu 1966, p. 13.

27. Cf. *P. Col.* 5860ab, fr. 1, 8ff., ed. Gronewald 1974 = *SLG* fr. 261a P, and the discussion in chap. 6, n.77.

28. Stob. 4, 31, 91, V p. 767 Hense.

29. Anacr. fr. 177 Gent.

30. Cf. chap. 8.

31. The relationship posited here was first suggested by me in an article published in 1965 (Gentili 1965d) and further explored in the later studies of Gzella 1971 (within the limits imposed by an excessively mechanical, biographically oriented mode of reading) and Svenbro 1976, pp. 175; 179–86; 192ff.

32. There is ample justification for using the word *intellectual* in such a context as this. It can refer to anyone who performs an intellectual activity with a sociopolitical function, whether he is a completely autonomous economic agent or works on commission from a patron. See the study of Longo 1980.

33. See the anecdote reported in chap. 8 (fr. 515 P.).

34. Moretti 1957, p. 75 no. 134.

35. *Gnomol. Par.* p. 16 no. 142 Sternbach.

36. *Gnomol. Par. App. Vat.* p. 79 no. 102 Sternbach.

37. Xenophan. fr. 21 Gent.-Pr.; Athen. 14, 656d = Chamael. fr. 33 Wehrli.

38. *Schol.* Pind. *Isthm.* 2, 9b (III p. 214 Drachm.). For collections and discussions of the testimony pertaining to the avarice of Simonides, see Christ 1941, pp. 61ff.; Bell 1978; cf. also Pellizer 1981a.

39. Cf. Gentili 1964, p. 283; Detienne 1967.

40. Plat. *Hipparch.* 228c.

41. *Schol. ad loc.* (III pp. 88ff. Drachm.).

42. Isocr. *Antid.* 166.

43. Donnay 1967; Lauter 1974.

44. Diyll. *FGrHist* 73 F 3 in Plut. *De Herodt. malign.* 26, 862b.

45. Euseb. *Chron.* p. 113, 15c Helm, who dates the event in 445/444.

46. Jeffery–Morpurgo Davies 1970; Van Effenterre 1973; Pugliese Carratelli 1976.

47. Cf. also *Nem.* 4, 13ff., where the poet, directing himself to the victor (Timasarchos of Aegina), says that the victor's father would, if still alive, repeat the present song to the accompaniment of the lyre in celebration of his son's triumph. *Ol.* 9, 1 contains an interesting reference to the reutilization of ancient encomiastic songs such as Archilochus's hymn for Heracles (fr. 207 T.) in the celebration of new occasions.

48. See Benjamin 1974, pp. 474ff.

49. Cf. also *Schol. ad Nem.* 5, 1 (III p. 89 Drachm.).

50. Aelian, *Var. hist.* 14, 17.

51. Istros in Athen. 8, 345d = *Epic. Gr. Fr.* p. 266 Kinkel = *FGrHist* 334 F 61.

52. Hor. *Epist.* 2, 1, 232ff.; Porphyr. ad loc.; *Suda*, s.v. "Χοιρίλος."

53. The state of the investigation and the diverse orientations of critical methodology which it reveals are now surveyed by Coarelli 1980.

54. Cf. Burckhardt 1919; Schweitzer 1963; Bianchi Bandinelli 1979.

55. Cf. Guarducci 1958; Guarducci 1962; Philipp 1968; Lauter 1974; Corchia 1981, pp. 541ff.

56. Cf. Himmelmann 1979. See, further, Bilinski 1979, p. 65, and Paribeni 1979.

57. See, for example, the use of the verb *ergázesthai,* which belongs properly to the vocabulary of the crafts, in reference both to the production of statues (*Nem.* 5, 1) and the composition of epinicians (*Isthm.* 2, 45ff.). On poetry seen as one of the crafts, cf. chap. 4.

58. Cf. chap. 4.

59. Philipp 1968, p. 58.

60. Cf., for example, *Nem.* 7, 11.

61. Diehl, *Anth. lyr. gr.*³ 1, pp. 110ff.

62. Isocrates, *Evag.* 73ff.; cf. Plut. *Cim.* 2.

63. Cf. chap. 2.

64. Fr. 205 Sn.-Maehl.:

Ἀρχὰ μεγάλας ἀρετᾶς,
ὤνασσ᾽ Ἀλάθεια, μὴ πταίσῃς ἐμὰν
σύνθεσιν τραχεῖ ποτὶ ψεύδει.

The poet—if, as is likely, he is the narrating "I" of the passage—is uncertain of his ability to speak truly, and so invokes Truth, personified as a goddess, so that he can avoid being tripped by falsehood. It is hard to see why Boeckh (1821, p. 66) and later commentators have taken the term *sýnthesis* to mean "faith, loyalty" (cf., most recently, Slater 1969b, s.v. "σύνθ."). More understandable, given the context, are renderings such as "speech" (Komornicka 1972, p. 236), "testimony" (Ortega 1970, p. 357n.10), or, better, "composition" (cf. *Ol.* 3, 8 *thésis epéon*, song). The last would be possible if a different sense were not documented in Pindar himself, that of "accord," "pact"—as in *Pyth.* 4, 168, where the subject is the pact that Pelias and Jason concluded over the expedition to seek the Golden Fleece. In fifth-century prose this meaning is often expressed by words derived from *títhemi: sýnthetos, synthéke, sýnthema*, and so forth. In *Pyth.* 11, 41 and *Nem.* 4, 75, *syntíthemi* is used in connection with the agreement between patron and poet for the composition of a victory poem. The agreement provided for a fee settled in advance between poet and patron, as in the case of the victory of Pytheas of Aegina celebrated in *Nemean* 5; cf. p. 162 and Gentili 1981a.

65. On these two passages, see C. O. Pavese 1966, p. 108, and Gzella 1971, pp. 120ff.

66. Diog. Laert. 9, 52. For a picture of Athenian culture in the time of the Sophists, see Capizzi 1982, pp. 451-85.

67. Plat. *Prot.* 328b.

68. *Suda*, s.v. "Γοργίας."

69. Plin. *Nat. hist.* 33, 83. See Bernardini-Veneri 1981.

70. Isocr. *Antid.* 155.

71. Plat. *Apol.* 20b.

72. Plat. *Hipp. mai.* 282c.

73. Plat. *Cratyl.* 384b; Aristot. *Rhet.* 3, 1415b.

74. Plat. *Hipp. mai.* 282d-e.

75. Cf. *Hypoth.* Isocr. *Evag.* and *Hypoth.* Isocr. *Ad Nicocl.* Pliny the Elder (*Nat. hist.* 7, 110) is probably referring to this work when he says that Isocrates sold one of his speeches for twenty talents.

76. Cf., especially, v. 331, with the commentary in Dover 1968, ad loc.; cf. also Ehrenberg 1951, p. 234.

77. Busolt-Swoboda 1926, pp. 1204ff.

78. Mossé 1962, p. 155.

79. Cf. Hemelrijk 1925. This is the only investigation dealing specifically with the subject, limited to a semantic study of terminology in isolation from the evolving social reality to which it corresponds. But the principle enun-

ciated by Euripides and now rediscovered by semioticians is as valid as it ever was: words remain the same, it is the reality behind them which changes (*Phoen.* 502).

80. Diog. Laert. 4, 8; *Gnomol. Par.* p. 15 no. 117; p. 32 no. 313 Sternbach.

81. Aristot. *Rhet.* 3, 1413b ff.; Gentili-Cerri 1983, p. 14.

82. Serrao 1977, p. 172.

83. Cf. G. Giangrande 1968, p. 497.

84. *Epigr.* 26, 32, 46 Pfeiffer.

85. Cf. Wilamowitz 1924, p. 11, and the commentary of McLennan 1977, pp. 133ff.

86. Callim. fr. 222 Pfeiffer. It is highly probable that the fragment comes from an epinician for Polycles of Aegina (*Iamb.* 8 Pfeiffer); cf. Lavagnini 1950, p. 108.

87. *Schol. Isthm.* 2, 9a (III p. 214 Drachm.).

88. Cf., most recently, Woodbury 1968, p. 529; Gianotti 1975, pp. 12ff.

89. The word *ergátis*, meaning "one who performs a service for pay," carries negative connotations here, just as it does in Callimachus (cf. Archil. fr. 244 T.). The phrase that immediately follows οὐδ' ἐπέρναντο γλυκεῖαι . . . ἀργυρωθεῖσαι . . . ἀοιδαί contemptuously underlines the venal way in which poetry is treated as if it were a piece of ordinary merchandise. Wilamowitz (1922, p. 311n.1) observes correctly that *epérnanto* here suggests *pórne;* cf. also Thummer 1969, p. 40.

90. *Schol. Isthm.* 2 inscr. a (III p. 212 Drachm.) = Simon. fr. 513 P.

91. On the various interpretations of the ode see Nisetich 1977 and, most recently, Privitera 1982, pp. 156ff.

92. Cf. Vetta 1979.

93. *Iamb.* 1; 3; 12 Pfeiffer; cf. the analysis of Tarditi 1978, pp. 1015ff., and Meillier 1979, pp. 155ff.

94. Cf. Tarditi 1978, p. 1013.

95. Cf. F. T. Griffiths 1979.

96. Stob. 3, 10, 38, III pp. 417ff. Hense; *Gnomol. Vat.* p. 189 no. 513 Sternbach; *Schol. hypoth.* Theocr. 16 p. 325 Wendel; cf. Christ 1941, pp. 63ff., and Bell 1978, pp. 68ff.

97. Cf. n.35.

98. These are dramatic professionals in the true sense of the word—the normal meaning for *tragoidós* from the fourth century on; cf. Pickard-Cambridge 1968, pp. 127ff.

99. An incomplete catalogue from the first half of the fourth century (*I. G.* II/III² no. 2311 = Dittenberger 1920, no. 1055) registers the prizes fixed for individual victories in the musical contests of the Great Panathenaia as follows: "For citharoedes: first prize a golden olive crown (of) 1,000 drachmas, 500 drachmas in coin; second prize 1,200 drachmas; third 600 drachmas; fourth 400 drachmas; fifth 300 drachmas." An inscription from Tanagra (90–80; cf. Guarducci 1969, p. 377) contains the prizes for the winners in a poetico-musical

contest in honor of Serapis: first prizes (awarded to those whose names appear on the list) consisted of gold crowns worth various amounts (between 168 ¾ drachmas and 101 ¼ drachmas), whereas second prizes were sums of money (50 or 40 drachmas). For further documentation of honors and fees, see Guarducci 1927–29, pp. 629–65, and Sifakis 1967, pp. 21ff., 103ff.

100. Guarducci 1927–29.

101. Sifakis 1967.

102. Gentili 1977a, pp. 5–22 (Eng. trans., pp. 17–31).

103. Cf. Sifakis 1967, pp. 71ff.; Gentili 1977a, pp. 13ff. (Eng. trans., pp. 22ff.).

104. For revivals using lyric texts of the archaic period, cf. also Athenaeus 14, 620c.

105. Cf. Gentili 1977a, pp. 7ff.; 13 (Eng. trans., pp. 18; 22ff.) and, most recently, *P. Oxy.* XLV, 3214 (cf. Luppe 1980, p. 245), which contains a Euripidean anthology on the theme of *gámos*.

106. Dittenberger 1920, no. 648B; cf. Gentili 1977a, pp. 17ff. (Eng. trans., pp. 127ff.).

107. Cf. Guarducci 1927–29, p. 662 no. XXXI.

108. Cf. n.103.

109. Cf. Gentili 1980.

110. Cf. Guarducci 1927–29, p. 655 no. XVII.

111. Cf. Guarducci 1927–29, p. 652 no. XII.

112. J. U. Powell, *Collectanea Alexandrina* (Oxford, 1925), pp. 132–73; Diehl, *Anth. Lyr. Gr.*² II, 6 pp. 108–39.

113. Cf. Pöhlmann 1970, pp. 58–76.

*It has only recently come to my attention that E. Rohde, in the discussion of various aspects of Greek civilization in the fourth and later centuries which he included in his famous work *Der griechische Roman und seine Vorläufer* ([Leipzig, 1914]³, pp. 326ff.), had already, more than a century ago, used the word *popular* to refer to the form of itinerant oral culture which flourished in various cities of the Hellenistic world contemporaneously with the literate culture of courts and poetic circles and coteries. It is indeed remarkable that these pages have not received the scholarly attention they deserve.

TEN: ARCHILOCHUS AND THE LEVELS OF REALITY

1. For a panorama of the earliest history of Thasos as it emerges from the excavations carried out by the French Archaeological School, see Pouilloux 1954; 1963; and, for recent controversy, Graham 1978, with Pouilloux's own reply (1982).

2. Fr. 88 T. Πανελλήνων ὀϊζὺς ἐς Θάσον συνέδραμεν.

3. Ghali-Kahil 1960.

4. A full account of the exploitation of the mines at Thasos, from the time of the Phoenician settlement, is provided by Herodotus 6, 46ff. (confirmed by

the most recent investigations conducted on the island by members of the Max Planck Institut of Heidelberg; cf. "Nachweis antiken Goldbergbaus auf Thasos: Bestätigung Herodots," *Naturwissenschaften* 66 [1979]: 613; cf. des Courtils–Koželj–Muller 1982, and Canfora 1983, p. 257. One should reject, therefore, the interpretation, in itself fairly implausible, that Holtzmann 1979 proposes for the passage).

*On the role of Archilochus in the colonization of Thasos and the character of Parian cults in the archaic period, see L. A. Stella, "Note archilochee," *Boll. dei classici dell'Accad. Naz. dei Lincei,* s. III [7] (1986): 81ff. Stella gives ample attention to the historical and archaeological framework within which the life and activity of the poet should be viewed. Archilochus as the poet of slander and the relations between his work and that of Hipponax are discussed in A. Pippin Burnett, *Three Archaic Poets: Archilochus, Alcaeus, Sappho* (London, 1983), pp. 55ff., 98ff.

5. Kontoleon 1965.

6. Kontoleon 1965, and Gasparri 1982.

7. Mendel 1912–14, pp. 304ff.; Fuchs 1969, p. 49. On the close iconographical connection between the two pieces, see the acute observations of Gasparri 1982.

8. 10, 28, 3 = Archil. Test. 121 T.

9. The sanctuary was discovered in the excavation campaigns of the years 1962–64. The identity of the gods to whom the altars were dedicated is clear from inscriptions containing their names (Zeus, Athena, Artemis, the Nymphs). The entire complex must have referred symbolically to the introduction of Greek gods into an island that had been hitherto non-Greek: cf. Rolley 1965.

10. Archil. fr. 246 T.; Oenom. in Euseb. *Praep. Ev.* 6, 7, 8 (I p. 314 Mras = Test. 116 T.).

11. I do not intend to reexamine in detail here the problem of the chronology of Archilochus. I cannot accept either the early dating proposed in Blakeway 1936, or the tendentiously late one (680–640) of Jacoby and, more recently, Graham (1978, pp. 73ff.), who places the activity of the poet around 650. The disagreement of modern scholars reflects discrepancies in our ancient sources. Eusebius (*Praep. Ev.* 10, 11, 4, I p. 596 Mras = Test. 63 T.) gives the twenty-third Olympiad (688) as Archilochus's *floruit,* whereas Xanthos of Lydia (Dion. Hal. fr. 3 in Clem. Alex. *Strom.* 1, 21, 131, II p. 81 Stählin = Test. 59 T.) gives the eighteenth (708) as the date of the foundation of Thasos, placing the γνωρίζεσθαι of the poet himself in the twentieth (700). However, Glaucos of Rhegium (in Ps.-Plut. *De mus.* 5, 1133a = Test. 145 T.) considers Archilochus more recent than Terpander, who is dated by his victory in the Carneia of 676, whereas Phainias (*ap.* Clem. Alex. *Strom.* 1, 21, 131, II p. 81 Stählin = Test. 123 T.) and possibly the author of the *Marmor Parium* as well (*FGrHist* 239 A 33, if one accepts Baumgarten's supplement Ἀρχίλοχ]ο[ς) disagree and make Terpander the more recent. My own view is that the *floruit* cannot be placed any later

than 660; see, most recently, Rankin 1977a, pp. 20ff.; Rankin 1977b; and Aloni 1981, pp. 145ff. I take this opportunity to note an inaccuracy—found also in several more recent works—in W. Schmid, *Geschichte der griechischen Literatur* (I/1, p. 390n.11), where the twenty-third Olympiad (Eusebius's date for the *floruit* of Archilochus) is identified as 665 rather than 688.

12. Crit. 88 B 44 D.-K. = Archil. Test. 46 T.

13. Oenom. *ap.* Euseb. *Praep. Ev.* 5, 31, 1 (I p. 279 Mras) = Archil. Test. 114 T.

14. Cf. chap. 7.

15. *I. G.* XII 5, 1 no. 445 = Archil. Test. 4 T. Miralles-Pòrtulas 1983 give a precise and detailed analysis of the inscriptional account insofar as it has a bearing on the poetic personality of Archilochus.

The latest addition to the Mnesiepes inscription—a highly fragmentary one that contains no new material of significance—was published by W. Peek, "Ein neues Bruchstück vom Archilochos—Monument des Sosthenes," *Zeitschr. f. Pap. u. Epigr.* 59 (1985): 13–17; see also M. L. West, "Archilochus: New Fragments and Readings," *Zeitschr. f. Pap. u. Epigr.* 61 (1985): 8ff.

16. Cf. the analysis of Pucci 1977, pp. 8ff.

17. On the recurrence of the same motif in the Homeric hymn to Hermes, see Kontoleon 1963; Breitenstein 1971, pp. 15ff.

18. Cf. Marius Victorinus (Aphthonius VI p. 143 Keil = Archil. Test. 105 T.), with the additional material printed in Test. 314–19 West = pp. 212–16 T.

19. Ps.-Plut. *De mus.* 10, 1134de = Archil. Test. 71 T.

20. Cf. Kontoleon 1963, p. 50.

21. The word *épea* in v. 6 of this epigram has been mistakenly used to support the contention that Archilochus wrote hexameters (Notopoulos 1966). In fact, as was correctly seen by Gow (1952, pp. 545ff.), *épea* is here Theocritus's general word for all the lyric compositions of Archilochus, as is shown by *emmelés* in v. 5. On the use of the term *épea*, cf. Gentili 1977b, pp. 35ff.

22. Cf. C. O. Pavese 1972, pp. 230ff.

23. Cf. chap. 8.

24. *Or.* 55, 6 = Archil. Test. 53 T.

25. Cf. the correct observations of Gerevini 1954.

26. Fr. 42 T.: ἀμισθὶ γάρ σε πάμπαν οὐ διάξομεν.

27. Cf. F. W. Schneidewin, in fr. 41 adn. Bergk⁴.

28. Cf. especially Test. 60; 66; 158 T. and pp. 188ff.

Fr. 23 W. (54 T.) may also be relevant to the discussion of the paradigmatic role played by Archilochus's poetry by mythological characters and real characters drawn from history. J. Strauss Clay takes the fragment, very plausibly, as part of a dialogue in iambic trimeters between Gyges and the wife of Candaules ("Archilochus and Gyges: An Interpretation of Fr. 23 West," *Quad. Urb.*, n.s. 24 [53] (1986): 7ff.). She rightly points out that its dialogue structure links it to the Cologne papyrus poem and, probably, to the episode of Heracles, Nessus, and Deianira crossing the river Evenos, where the single surviving trimeter (fr. 42. T.: "We shall not carry you across without reward") also implies a dialogue. Cf. also below.

29. 1448b 24.

30. Cf. chap. 7.

For a fuller discussion of the narrative "I" in the poems of Archilochus, see W. Rösler, "Persona reale o persona poetica? L'interpretazione dell'io' nella lirica greca arcaica," *Quad. Urb*, n.s. 19 [48] (1985): 131ff.

31. *P. Col.* 7511, ed. Merkelbach-West 1974 = *SLG* fr. 478 P.; cf. Kramer-Hagedorn 1978; Gentili 1976d. The present analysis follows the verse numeration in the edition of Page. Suggested interpretations and relevant textual supplements are surveyed in Degani 1977a, pp. 15ff., and Degani 1977b, pp. 3–22. See, most recently, Rankin 1977a, pp. 68ff.; Slings 1980; Aloni 1981, pp. 18ff.; Jarcho 1982; Miralles-Pòrtulas 1983.

32. I accept in my translation the supplements that seem to me certain: v. 5 γάμου (Merkelbach-West); v. 8 φίλην (Ebert-Luppe); v. 11 σαόφρονος (Bossi); v. 30 ἥβης (Lebek, Perusino); v. 35 γαμεῖν (Ebert-Luppe); v. 38 δόλους (Bonanno); for v. 44ff. δ[έ μιν / χλαί]νῃ (Merk.-West) cf. Gentili 1976b; v. 52 λευκ]όν (Degani, Merkelbach, Page); v. 53 τριχός (Merkelbach-West). For a correct interpretation of the next to last line in the fragment (52), see Van Sickle 1980.

The expression μαλθακῇ δ[έ μιν / χλαί]νῃ καλύψας of vv. 44ff. refers concretely to wrapping the girl in one's own cloak at the moment of erotic contact—evidently both a customary gesture and, at least from the fifth century on, a metaphorical way of referring to intercourse. See the model study, with full documentation, by G. Arrigoni, "Amore sotto il manto e iniziazione nuziale," *Quad. Urb*, n.s. 15 [44] (1983): 7–56.

33. Cf. the architrave and doors mentioned in v. 21.

34. The expression παρὲξ τὸ θεῖον χρῆμα has been taken in various ways, but its exact value is caught in the rendering suggested by Snell (in Merkelbach-West 1974, p. 105): "without the bond of marriage." Snell's intuition is confirmed by precise parallels with other passages. Degani deserves the credit for having pointed out a gloss in Hesychius, certainly going back to a commentary on this very poem, in which the expression is paraphrased by ἔξω τῆς μίξεως, "without sexual consummation." That *chrêma* ("matter, affair"; cf. the sexual meaning of Italian *affare* in the expression *aver affare con qualcuno*) may refer to intercourse is clear from the use of similar words in the same sense—for example, *prâxis* and *prâgma* (cf. Eur. *Hipp.* 1004; Plat. *Symp.* 206c). But this leaves imprecise the exact sense of *theîon*, which does not involve, as has been thought, the general meaning of "marvelous (ecstatic)"— that is, containing the maximum of sexual pleasure. Rather, it means "divine"— that is, linked to the religious ceremony of marriage. This is precisely the meaning of the expression *theîon prâgma* in the passage from Plato's *Symposium* already cited, where the reference is to sexual union in connection with the begetting of offspring. This connotation of *theîon* recurs in what can be

considered the antithesis to *theîon chrêma*—in the phrase *hágneuma theîon,* which in Eur. *El.* 256 designates the "ritual abstinence" that Orestes imagines as having prevented the farmer from consummating his marriage with Electra.

35. Koenen 1974, p. 506.

For temple sanctuaries as a preferred place for assignations, see Plutarch (*De mul. virt.* 249b)—on the girls of Ceos, who were in the habit of going to the temple and passing the entire day in each other's company, dancing and playing before the admiring gaze of their young suitors.

36. *Anth. Pal.* 7, 351 = Archil. Test. 60 T.

37. See the commentary of Degani 1977b, pp. 3ff.

38. It is precisely this poem which Athenaeus seems to refer to at 10, 415d when he says *en tetramétrois,* a phrase that could easily have been used to describe its asynartete metrical structure. The inclusion of the Athenaeus passage among the testimonia cited in Tarditi's apparatus at this point is thus perfectly appropriate.

39. Cf. Nagy 1979, p. 247.

40. Rubensohn 1949.

41. There is no altar of Hera among those dedicated to the ancestral (*patrôiai*) divinities in the sanctuary that was discovered on Thasos and may be identified with the Thesmophorion; cf. n.9.

42. Segal 1976b, p. 123.

43. Test. 4, $E_1$ col. II, 44ff. T.

44. Dion. Chrys. *Or.* 74, 16.

*J. Strauss Clay's interpretation (see n.28) indicates that the "I" who speaks in vv. 14ff. is Gyges. This does not, however, affect the paradigmatic value of the lines, either for the addressee or within the general context of Archilochean ethics.

45. Athen. 11, 505de; cf. Bernardini-Veneri 1981.

46. *Ap.* Athen. loc. cit. = Hermipp. fr. 63 Wehrli = Archil. Test. 76 T.

47. Bakhtin 1984, p. 140; Bakhtin 1976.

48. Crat. fr. 6 K.-A. = 6 Kock. On the significance of Cratinus's judgment, cf. Pretagostini 1982b.

49. Cf. n.13.

50. One should mention at this point the hypothesis, first put forward by West (1974, p. 27), according to which the proper names found in Archilochus—Lycambes and all the rest—are *redende Namen* and the persons to whom they refer fictitious creations. The hypothesis is methodologically ingenious, and in harmony with the linguistic and onomastic inventiveness that is a constant in the seriocomic mode. If Greek examples are desired, one need only think of Attic comedy and the epithets that it constantly attaches to real persons. But even granted that Lycambes and Neoboule are artificially invented names, it does not follow that they do not designate real persons: cf. Bonanno 1980a; Bossi 1981; and, for other objections to West, Rösler 1976, pp. 300–308. Anyone familiar with the village life of central and southern Italy knows how difficult

it is to identify a person by his name but how easy it is to locate him through the nickname known to the people of the area in which he lives. The progressive industrialization and urbanization of society is, inevitably, putting an end to this situation; but in the *psógos* culture of the past verbal abuse and *redende Namen* were complementary aspects of a single phenomenon.

My own argument is in accord with C. Carey's view ("Archilochus and Lycambes," *Class. Quart.* 36 [1986]: 60–67) of the pragmatic character of Archilochean invective. He is perfectly correct in maintaining (p. 67n.31) that "it is to be stressed that there is nothing Romantic about the tradition of Archilochus as the rejected and embittered suitor. A marital link with Lycambes no doubt offered political and social advantages.... The rejection may have damaged Archilochus' interest materially. Certainly it constituted a public affront; archaic Greek society regarded revenge for wrongs suffered as an important aspect of manhood . . . and Archilochus repaid a public affront with public humiliation."

51. Λυκαμβὶς ἀρχή, fr. 138 K.-A. = 130 Kock.

52. Cf. n.13.

53. Cf. Miralles 1981, pp. 37ff.

54. Cf. chap. 3. For Terpander, cf. Aristot. fr. 545 Rose; for Thaletas, cf. Plut. *Lyc.* 4; Diog. Babyl. in Philodem. *De mus.* p. 85, 36 Kemke = *S.V.F.* 23, 10 Arnim.

55. See, for example, frr. 8; 91; °92; 99; 120; 122; 124 T.

56. Cf. Tarditi 1958.

57. Fr. 2 T.; cf. Gentili 1965c; Gentili 1970; Gentili 1976b; Lasserre 1979; Bossi 1980; Gerber 1981.

58. Frr. 21; 22 Gent.-Pr.

59. Frr. 29; 29a; 29b Gent.-Pr.

60. So, for example, Breitenstein 1971, p. 59. But see, most recently, the observations of J. Russo, 1974.

61. Kontoleon 1963.

62. Pasquali 1935, pp. 102ff. = 1968, p. 311.

63. Cf. chap. 3.

64. Adrados 1979, p. 388.

65. Rostagni 1927, p. 14.

ELEVEN: THE SHIP OF STATE:
ALLEGORY AND ITS WORKINGS

1. We read in Strabo (13, 2, 3) that Alcaeus insulted Melanchros, Myrsilos, Pittacus, and others as well—although he suffered as a result of revolutionary violence himself.

2. Fr. 333 V.

3. *De imit.* 421, p. 205, 16 Us.-Raderm. = Test. 173 Gall.

4. Quintilian, *Inst. or.* 8, 6, 44: "Allegoria, quam inversionem interpretantur, aut aliud verbis, aliud sensu ostendit, aut etiam interim contrarium. Prius fit genus plerumque continuatis translationibus"; there follows the citation of the famous allegory of Horace, *Carm.* 1, 14.

5. For theoretical discussions of metaphor see, in addition to the investigation of Richards 1936, Groupe μ 1970; Henry 1971; Silk 1974; Weinrich 1976; Eco 1980.

6. Fr. 208a V.

7. For an objective survey of the critical literature on the subject, see Nicosia 1976, pp. 145ff.

8. *All. Hom.* 5, 9.

9. *P. Oxy.* 2306 col. II = fr. 305b V.: a commentary on fr. 208a V.

10. *P. Oxy.* 2306 col. I, 15ff. = fr. 305a, 15ff. V. The fragment begins with the citation of several words from a poem of Alcaeus (probably the opening ones, "Nor could there be war between you and me"), after which the commentator writes, "these words are directed to a person named Mnamon who supplied a boat for the return (*káthodos*) of Myrsilos. He (Alcaeus) says that he is not accusing him or quarreling with him over this matter." There follows another citation from Alcaeus's text ("he who wishes to set us at odds") and then a mention of Pittacus, perhaps the one responsible for the falling out between the two men (cf. the analysis of Barner 1967a, pp. 162ff.). The reference to the return of Myrsilos in col. II, 8 (fr. 305b, 8 V.) leaves no doubt about the connection between the boat episode and the conspiracy mentioned by Heraclitus. The poem cited in col. I must antedate, perhaps by a short period, the one (208a V.) commented upon in col. II. The news of the aid given by Mnamon had to come first, and then Myrsilos's attack on Alcaeus and his faction. The phrase "he who wishes to set us at odds" is certainly an unfriendly one. It may have been on precisely this occasion, therefore, that Pittacus broke the old alliance that a number of years earlier (612–609) had permitted him, acting in conjunction with the brothers of Alcaeus, to eliminate the tyrant Melanchros; cf. Diog. Laert. 1, 74; *Suda*, s.v. "Πιττακός."

11. Fr. 208a V. I read ἄγκυλαι (Unger) in v. 9, cf. Burzacchini 1977, p. 227; μένο[ιεν (Page, Snell) in v. 12, although Barner's μένω[σι(ν) cannot be excluded; and in v. 14 the supplement ἐκπεπ[ατ]άχμενα (Kamerbeek 1953, pp. 89ff.)–cf. Hesych. s.v. "ἐξεπατάχθη· ἐξεπλάγη."

12. V. 64; cf. 114; 1077 and Van Nes 1963, pp. 31ff.

13. See, most recently, Rösler 1980, p. 144.

14. *Comic. Gr. Fragm. in pap. rep.* 255 col. I, 14 and 16 Austin.

15. Cf. Hom. *Od.* 5, 260.

16. Cerri 1972.

17. Tyrt. 7, 31; 8, 21 Gent.-Pr.

18. For *sóizein* in a political sense, cf. Janni 1965, pp. 104ff.; Cerri 1969a, p. 98 and n.4.

*Cf. Solon fr. 3, 7–10 Gent.-Pr., a parallel acutely adduced by G. Nagy, "On

the Symbolism of Apportioning Meat in Archaic Greek Elegiac Poetry,"
*L'uomo* 9 (1985): 45ff.

19. V. 68ıff.: ταῦτά μοι ἠνίχθω κεκρυμμένα τοῖς ἀγαθοῖσιν / γινώσκοι
δ᾽ ἄν τις καὶ κακόν, ἄν σόφος ᾖ. As Nagy has shown (1982, p. 112), the
*kakón* of the manuscripts should not be corrected to *kakós* (Brunck).

20. See the Comparative Table.

21. V. 673ff.: ὑπερβάλλει δὲ θάλασσα / ἀμφοτέρων τοίχων.

22. V. 673: ἀντλεῖν δ᾽ οὐκ ἐθέλουσιν.

23. V. 675ff.: κυβερνήτην μὲν ἔπαυσαν / ἐσθλόν, ὅτις φυλακὴν εἶχεν
ἐπισταμένως. The *kybernétes* is either the pilot of the ship or the one who
guides the city, as in Eur. *Suppl.* 880; similarly *phylaké*, which may mean
"guarding a ship" or "guarding a city"; cf. Silk 1974, p. 125n.10.

24. V. 677: χρήματα δ᾽ ἁρπάζουσι βίη.

25. V. 677ff.: κόσμος δ᾽ ἀπόλωλεν, / δασμὸς δ᾽ οὐκέτ᾽ ἴσος γίνεται ἐς
τὸ μέσον. The word *kósmos* designates in general a condition of order and
equilibrium, or, in a more narrowly political sense, constitution. Here the
"vehicle" is order on board ship, a meaning already attested in epic (*Od.* 13,
76ff.), the "tenor" or underlying idea is order in a sociopolitical sense, oligarchic stability and equality (Herodt. 1, 65; Thuc. 8, 72, 2 ἐν τῷ ὀλιγαρχικῷ
κόσμῳ), which involved an "equitable division" (δασμὸς . . . ἴσος) of
power; cf. Cerri 1969a, pp. 97ff.

26. For *chrémata* (coin), cf. Alc. frr. 360, 3; 63, 7 (χε]λίοις στάτ[ηρας); 69,
2 (δισχελίοις στά[τηρας) V., Musti 1980–81 and Musti 1981, pp. 70ff.

27. Hom. *Od.* 13, 283; other examples in Silk 1974, loc. cit.

28. Alc. fr. 73, 1 V., see below.

29. Cf. Hes. *Op.* 643, 693; Herodt. 1, 1; 2, 179.

30. V. 679: φορτηγοὶ δ᾽ ἄρχουσι. For the nautical sense of *árchein*, cf.
Hom. *Od.* 14, 230; other examples in Silk 1974, loc. cit. I do not agree with Van
Groningen 1966, p. 266, who takes *phortegoí* as a synonym of *émporoi* (merchants) and regards *chrémata, phylaké,* and *kósmos* as terms that "lie outside the
metaphorical framework"; that is, that have only literal meanings.

31. V. 1: ἀσυννέτημμι τῶν ἀνέμων στάσιν, cf. above. For the meaning of
*stásis,* see Kassel 1973, pp. 102ff., and the note in Burzacchini 1977, p. 219.

32. This is the meaning of the phrase ὂν τὸ μέσσον (νᾶϊ φορήμεθα σὺν
μελαίνᾳ) in the context of the strophe; cf. Page 1955, p. 186; Gallavotti 1957a,
p. 146; Treu 1963a, p. 41: Alcaeus and his men are not borne along "on the high
sea" (Marzullo 1975, p. 32; Bonanno 1980b, pp. 181n.12, 187) but between two
waves that batter against the hull from both sides: a vivid and precise image of
enemy attack on two flanks.

33. Probably the confraternity of the Cleanactidai, if we are to believe the
skolion to fr. 112, 23 V. rather than Strabo's testimony (13, 2, 3), which seems to
draw a distinction between them and the party of Myrsilos.

34. Cf. n.10. References to Pittacus's betrayal and to his sharing of power
with Myrsilos appear in frr. 129, 13ff.; 70, 7 V.

35. V. 7: λαῖφος δὲ πᾶν ζάδηλον. I translate, "The sail is nothing but a transparent rag," because *laîphos* means "rag," not "sail"; cf. *Od.* 13, 399; 20, 206. The word was taken over by Alcaeus to suggest the dilapidated condition of the sail, furrowed with great rips (cf. v. 8). For *zádelon* (= *diádelon*) in the otherwise unattested sense of "transparent," cf. *diaeidés*, used of water at Theocritus 16, 62.

36. Fr. 305a, 10 V.

37. Cf. Gallavotti 1948, p. 112; Trumpf 1958, p. 48; Barner 1967a, p. 137n.1.

38. Fr. 6, 1–14 V.:

> Τόδ᾽ αὖτε κῦμα τῷ προτέρῳ ᾽νέμω
> στείχει, παρέξει δ᾽ ἄμμι πόνον πόλυν
> ἄντλην, ἐπεί κε νᾶος ἔμβᾳ
>     ] .όμεθ᾽ ε [            4
>     ].. [.. ]. [
> [                            ]
> φαρξώμεθ᾽ ὡς ὤκιστα[
>   ἐς δ᾽ἔχυρον λιμένα δρό[μωμεν        8

> ----
> καὶ μή τιν᾽ ὄκνος μόλθ[ακος ὑμμέων (Hunt)
> λάβῃ: πρόδηλον γὰρ μέγ᾽ [ἀέθλιον (Wil.)
> μνάσθητε τῶν πάροιθε μ[όχθων, (Hunt)
>   νῦν τις ἄνηρ δόκιμος γε[νέσθω        12

> ----
> καὶ μὴ καταισχύνωμεν[ ἀνανδρίᾳ (Hunt)
> ἔσλοις τόκηας γᾶς ὔπα κε[ιμένοις.

39. V. 17: ἄπ πατέρω[ν μάθος: Herodian. περὶ μονηρ. λέξ. II. p. 941, 28 Lentz; Gallavotti 1957a, p. 54; Treu 1963a, p. 42.

40. *All. Hom.* 5, 7.

41. For the phrase προτέρῳ ᾽νέμω in v. 1, cf. Horace, *Carm.* 1, 14, 1ff.: "novi fluctus"; Barner 1967a, p. 136, and Rösler 1980, p. 130.

42. Silk 1974, p. 144.

43. *Steíchein* in connection with inanimate things only begins to be attested in the fifth century: Pind. *Nem.* 5, 3; Aesch. *Sept.* 534; *Prom.* 1090; Soph. *Ant.* 10.

44. Cf. also Aesch. *Sept.* 297; other examples in Silk 1974, loc. cit.

45. Aristot. *Rhet.* 3, 1411b.

46. *Il.* 15, 566; *Od.* 5, 256 (ships); *Il.* 12, 263 (walls).

47. *Il.* 14, 413.

48. *Od.* 9, 386.

49. For *limén* in the sense of "place of refuge," cf. Theogn. 114; Aesch. *Suppl.* 471; Eur. *Andr.* 891; it reappears with specific reference to a faction or *hetairía* at Soph. *Aj.* 683.

50. Eco 1980, p. 195.

51. Ὥσπερ κεκλιμένη ναῦς παρὰ γῆν ἔδραμεν; cf. Van Groningen 1966, p. 325.

52. Cf. v. 27ff. μοναρχίαν δ.[ / μ]η̣δὲ δεκώμ[εθ᾽ (Hunt).

53. *All. Hom.* 5, 5–7.

54. Fr. 6 V. must, therefore, have been composed after rather than before fr. 208a V.; cf. Theander 1943, pp. 159ff.; and Martin 1972, p. 28.

55. Frr. 73; 306i col. II V.

56. *P. Oxy.* 2307 fr. 14, col. II = fr. 306i col. II V.

57. Fr. 306i col. I.

58. Fr. 73, 1–10 V.:

πᾶν φόρτι[ο]ν δ . .[
  δ᾽ ὄττι μάλιστα σάλ[

καὶ κύματι πλάγεισ[α
ὄμβρῳ μάχεσθαι . . [                          4
φαῖσ᾽ οὐδὲν ἰμέρρη[ν, ἀσάμῳ
  δ᾽ ἔρματι τυπτομ[ένα

κήνα μὲν ἐν τούτ[οισιν ἔοισ᾽ ἴτω (Page)
νόστω λελάθων, ὦ φ[ίλ᾽, ἔγω θέλω (Page)       8
σύν τ᾽ ὔμμι τέρπ[εσθ]α[ι συν]άβαις (L.-P.)
καὶ πεδὰ Βύκχιδος αὖ . . [

The fragmentary vv. 1–2 alluded to the loss of the cargo, as in the earlier allegory (208a, 14 V.; cf. pp. 199ff.); Diehl's δ[ὲ βάλλε πόντον is a possible supplement; cf. Treu 1963a, pp. 41 and 162. Possible supplements in v. 6 are ῥάγημεν (Diehl, Treu) or κατάχθην (Gallavotti), but not ὄλεσθαι (Page), because the commentary (306i col. I, 2–3 V.: ὑπὸ [ἔρμα]τος διερρηγυῖαν) absolutely excludes the idea of destruction: the ship does not say that she longs for death, but that she has been wrecked against a rock. The papyrus reads τούτων λελάθων in v. 8, but the correct reading is νόστω λελ. (Lobel, Page), as can be deduced from the commentary (306i, fr. 16: νό]στου λελ.); the substitution of τούτων for νόστω was evidently caused by the presence of ἐν τούτ[οισιν in the verse immediately preceding.

59. Cf. *Schol.* Pind. *Pyth.* 5, 12a (II p. 173 Drachm.).

60. Cf. *Schol.* Pind. *Isthm.* 5, 63a (III p. 247 Drachm.); Privitera 1982, ad loc.

61. Cf. Péron 1974b, p. 301.

62. Cf. Aristoph. fr. 235 K.-A. (223 Kock = 30 Cassio).

63. In v. 5 I take φαῖσ(ι) as third-person singular; if it is taken as a plural, there is an immediate parallel with Theogn. 673; cf. above. If it is a singular there is an equally obvious parallel (suggested to me by Gregorio Serrao) with Catullus 4, 1ff.: "Phaselus ille quem videtis, hospites, / ait fuisse navium celerrimus." It is very probable that Catullus was familiar with the Alcaean allegories under examination here, an assumption supported by the precise reference to the wind falling on the lower corners of the sail (v. 20ff. *utrumque in pedem*) and to the dignified old age (cf. below) that the boat, after many adventurous voyages, enjoys in the quiet of its retirement (v. 25ff. *nunc recondita senet quiete*).

64. Cf. the commentary in 306i col. I, 3 V.: ἀσήμου ἔρμα]τος and Hesych.

s.v. "ἕρμα . . . ἢ τὸν πετρώδη καὶ ἐπικυματιζόμενον, ὥστε μὴ βλέπειν," a notice explaining Alcaeus's use of the word.

65. Anacr. fr. 114 Gent. ἀσήμων ὑπὲρ ἑρμάτων φορεῦμαι.

66. Ἄφαντον ἕρμα, cf. Ed. Fraenkel 1950, p. 453.

67. *Il.* 1, 486; 2, 154.

68. *Il.* 16, 549; *Od.* 23, 121.

69. Herodt. 7, 183; Thuc. 7, 25, 7; Eur. *Hel.* 854.

70. Cf. Alcaeus's own usage as documented in fr. 359 V.

71. Cf. Greimas-Courtés 1979, p. 227.

72. Fr. 332 V.

73. *Schol.* fr. 114 V.

74. Fr. 70, 7 V., cf. Mazzarino 1943, p. 64; Page 1955, p. 237.

75. Fr. 141 V.

76. *Schol.* fr. 74 V.

77. *Pol.* 3, 1285a 30.

78. Diog. Laert. 1, 75.

79. Fr. 70 V.

80. Test. 429 V.

81. Fr. 348 V.

82. Similar datings in Gallavotti 1953, p. 169; Merkelbach 1956, p. 96; Trumpf 1958, pp. 69ff.; and Rösler 1980, pp. 123ff. There are unsurmountable objections to the hypothesis of Koniaris 1966, pp. 395ff.; Barner 1967a, pp. 143ff.; and Kirkwood 1974, p. 78, which places the poem in the period of the tyranny of Myrsilos.

83. Fr. 69, 6–7 V.

84. Fr. 70, 6 V.: κῆνος δὲ παώθεις Ἀτρεΐδα[ν.

85. Cf. fr. 335 V.

86. Lines 8–13: θλιβομένης αὐτῆς καὶ περαινομένης πολλὴ ἀκαθαρσία ἀναπορεύεται καὶ λευκή· εἴρηται δὲ τὸ λευκός διὰ τὸ ἔπαρμα. Λευκη and λευκος in lines 11 and 12 can be taken as: (*a*) the substantives λεύκη, λεῦκος, "white sickness" (Page 1955, p. 193), though λεῦκος is not otherwise attested; and (*b*) the adjectives λευκή and λευκός: in this case the former agrees with ἀκαθαρσία (for the position of the adjective, cf. in lines 19ff. διὰ τοὺς πολλοὺς πλοῦς καὶ πυκνούς), and the latter (λεῦκος with aeolic accentuation) can be understood as a citation from Alcaeus's text, introduced by the article τό, as is regular in the language of exegesis; cf., for example, Sapph. fr. 213, 3ff. V.: ἀντὶ τοῦ σ[ύν]ζυξ. See the discussion in Barner 1967a, pp. 151ff.

87. Lines 13–21: οἷα δὲ σκέλ⟨εα⟩ (σκέλη pap.) ἤδη κεχώρηκε αὖτα· καὶ τὰ σκέλη αὐτῆς πεπαλαίωται[· πόλλ]α τε καὶ θάμε[α] δρομ[οίσα· ὡς ἐ]πὶ τῆς ἀλληγορία[ς. . .]. πεπλευκυία αὐτῇ διὰ τοὺς πολλοὺς πλοῦς καὶ πυκνοὺς ἤδη π[α]λαιὰ γέγονε[ν. In line 13 it is uncertain whether the citation from the text begins with οἷα or σκέλη (transcribed by error for the correct dialectical form σκέλεα or σκέλε'): cf. the discussion in Barner 1967a, pp.

152ff. In lines 16 and 17 I accept the supplements of Gallavotti 1957a: θάμε[α], and ὡς ἐ]πί.

88. Lines 23–28: οὐ διὰ τὸ [πεπα]λαιῶσθ[αι αὐτή φησι κα]θορμισθῆναι ἤ[τοι τῆς] συνουσί[ας] (or τῶν συνουσιῶν?) πεπα[ῦσθαι]· ἡ ναῦς π[α]λαιὰ τοῦ [πάλιν]· πλεῖν κ[α]τίσχει. I have supplied αὐτή (i.e., the ship) φησι in line 24 in place of ἐθέλει (Gallavotti) or βούλεται (Merkelbach): it fits the gap left in the line (which should contain from seventeen to twenty letters), and ἐθέλει must be rejected if one accepts Hamm's πεπαῦσθαι, which fits the sense of the context (cf. below); for φησί, cf. the preceding allegory fr. 73, 5 V. In line 25 ἤτοι (Hamm) is explicative, according to normal grammatical usage: "viz.," "that is to say"; cf. Kühner-Gerth 1955, II, p. 163d.

89. Page 1955, pp. 193ff., and Merkelbach 1956, pp. 92ff., are incorrect in assigning frr. 73 V. and 306i col. II V. to the same poem. The objections of Koniaris 1966, pp. 385ff. are quite valid here; cf. Rösler 1980, p. 121. For col. I 8–14 and 24–26 (fr. 16 = 73, 8–10 V.) in 306i, which do not seem to come originally from the same column, see the hypothesis of Barner 1967a, pp. 138ff.

90. In σκέλη . . . κεχώρηκε the verb choréo is appropriate for the slackening and loosening of legs/ship sides in their old age; as the commentary explains in what immediately follows, "its sides have grown old." For the meaning of choréo cf. Herodt. 1, 120; 122 adopted by Barner 1967a, p. 157. He translates the entire phrase as follows: "Wie(?) die Seiten schon auseinandergegangen sind"; cf. Treu 1963a, p. 15: "Wie ihm die Spanten schon dahin sind."

91. Cf. Aristoph. Lys. 1170, with the comment in Wilamowitz 1927a, p. 290. See, further, in Horace's allegory (Carm. 1, 14, 4): nudum remigio latus.

92. Cf. above.

93. Merkelbach 1956, p. 94.

94. Followed by Stark 1959, p. 48n.12, and Barner 1967a, 152.

95. This is the Alcaean passage referred to in Hesychius s.v. "ψόμμος· ἀκαθαρσία. {καπνός}." E. Degani informs me (letter of 22 May 1978) that the gloss καπνός is not in its proper position here but refers to the lemma ψόλος (Hesych. ψ 243 Schm.).

96. Cf. lines 10–13. It is worth noting in this connection that the author of Schol. Hom. Od. 5, 403 (p. 205 Dind.) glosses the lemma ἁλὸς ἄχνη (the "sea foam" poured on the beach by the waves) with "impurity" (ἀκαθαρσία).

97. For akatharsía cf. Hippocr. Aff. 22; Epid. 5, 31; 1 Fract. 31. For éparma cf. Hippocr. Epid. 1, 2; 7, 4; Soran. 1, 48.

98. Cf. line 3 ὀστείχει in Alcaeus's text, glossed (line 10) by the author of the commentary as ἀναπορεύεται.

99. So Steffen 1959, p. 43, and especially Treu 1963a, p. 15, who translates, "das eingedrungene unsaubere Wasser"; by "dirty water" he understands water mixed with sand (= impurity; cf. n.96) that has penetrated into the ship.

100. Lines 11–13: the word "white" refers to the swelling.

101. Of the three meanings of the verb peraíno—(a) bring to conclusion or completion, (b) penetrate, and (c) perforate (cf. L. S. J. s.v.)—the second may

well be the only one that can fit the present context, and its connotations are erotic: cf. *Com. ad* fr. 14 Kock; *Anth. Pal.* 11, 339, 2; Diog. Laert. 2, 127. But the first cannot be excluded: "arriving at the end (of her voyages)." This possibility is suggested to me by Agostino Masaracchia, citing the parallel of Pind. *Pyth.* 10, 28.

102. Given the briefest of mentions by Lobel 1951, p. 120, the hypothesis was subsequently developed by Page 1955, p. 195, and Merkelbach 1956, p. 93; cf. also Barner 1967a, pp. 151, 153, 158ff., and Rösler 1980, pp. 121 and 236.

103. Merkelbach 1956, p. 95n.4; but as Barner observes (1967a, p. 160n.1): "Zur ausgeführten Allegorie gehört mehr als die Andeutung zweier möglicherweise verschiedener Bildbereiche."

104. *Anth. Pal.* 5, 204 (Meleager); 9, 416 (Philip).

105. Barner 1967a, p. 157.

106. E. M. Voigt (*ad* 306i col. II) adduces an interesting parallel with Plautus, *Men.* 403: "saepe tritam (θλιβομένης), saepe fixam (περαινομένης)." But this fails to take into account that the Greek text lacks the very word that is most crucial: some equivalent, *pollákis,* for example, to *saepe.* Without the idea of repetition the text remains unintelligible.

107. So Lobel 1951, p. 120; Page 1955, pp. 192ff.

108. Cels. *De med.* 5, 28, 19; cf. the analysis in Ebbell 1967, pp. 103ff.

109. Cf. L. S. J. s.v. "λεύκη."

110. Already in Herodotus 1, 138 there is a clear distinction between the diseases *leúke* and *lépre* (leprosy), just as there is in Hippocr. *Prorrh.* 2, 43. From the time of Plato (*Tim.* 85a 1) and Aristotle (*Hist. an.* 518a 12; *Gen. an.* 784a 26; *Probl.* 10, 4–5) the symptoms of *leúke* are the same as those described several centuries later by Paul of Aegina (a physician of the seventh century A.D.): ἡ λεύκη μεταβολή τίς ἐστι τοῦ χρωτὸς ἐπὶ τὸ λευκότερον, ὑπὸ γλίσχρου τε καὶ κολλώδους γινομένη φλέγματος. Cf. Poll. *Onom.* 4, 193.

My discussion of *leúke* and *lépre* should be supplemented by the analysis of M. D. Grmek, *Les maladies à l'aube de la civilisation occidentale* (Paris, 1983) (translated into English by Mireille Muellner–Leonard Muellner [Baltimore, 1988]).

111. Correcting οἷα δέ to διὰ δέ, Page (1955, p. 193) offers the following conjectural text for the poem: καὶ λεῦκος ὀστείχει, διὰ δὲ σκέλεα / ἤδη κεχώρηκ' [- -] αὖτα, but cf. Barner 1967a, p. 152.

112. Line 16ff.: on the use of τρέχειν in connection with the ship, see above.

113. Cf. above.

114. Diog. Laert. 1, 81 = Alc. Test. 429 V.

115. Zonar. 13 ἀγάσυρτος· ὁ ἀκάθαρτος.

116. Cf. Demosth. 21, 119.

117. Sotad. 9, 4 Pow.; cf. Hesych. s.v. "ἔπαρσις· ὑπερηφανία."

118. Line 8: θλιβομένης. The commentator's use of this verb is not accidental, for it may apply equally well to the ship actually pressed in by the sand and to the city figuratively pressed or cast down by the corruption of Pittacus

(cf. L. S. J. s.v. "θλίβω"). Like *akatharsía* and *éparma*, the word has been consciously chosen for the way it expresses the concrete, visual, and, at the same time, moral aspect of the allegorical action that is being explained.

119. Fr. 306g V., which is a peremptory call to seize the opportunity for delivering a stab in the back to Pittacus and putting an end to his regime of violence and outrage (κακῆς ὕβρεως). In point of fact, Pittacus held his position of head of state with extraordinary powers (*aisymnétes*) as a result of free election by his fellow citizens (pp. 208ff.); but this did not make him any less a tyrant in Alcaeus's eyes.

120. *Pol.* 5, 1313a 34ff.

121. Line 25ff.: τῆς συνουσίας πεπαῦσθαι. On the convivial, symposiastic character of the *synousía* see Herodt. 2, 78; Plat. *Symp.* 173a; *Leg.* 2, 652a; 672a.

122. Cf. above.

123. Fr. 130b, 3–6 V., where the institutions of assembly and council are recalled as tangible symbols of the oligarchical regime in which the poet's father and grandfather had had the privilege of living even during their old age.

124. See Finley 1977b.

125. *Ann.* 492 Vahl.² = 512 Skutsch.

126. Cf. the analysis of Bettini 1979, pp. 35ff.

127. This is certainly not the place to deal with the old and ongoing debate on the Alcaean motifs in 1, 14; see, most recently, Bonanno 1980b, with bibliography. I will only note that Horace has, *more suo,* kept the political situation of his own time in mind and linked it to a reelaboration of elements drawn not only from the first two allegories (cf. *novi fluctus,* with v. 1 of the second allegory and Barner 1967a, p. 136n.3), but also from the fourth. The peremptory injunction *fortiter occupa portum* (vv. 2–3) contaminates, in typical Horatian fashion, v. 8 of the second allegory ("let us run to a safe harbor") with the definitive "mooring place" of the fourth allegory (cf. Alfonsi 1954, p. 218)—the mooring place, that is, of peace. Horace's expression is, to be sure, at least a formal calque (cf. Bonanno 1980b, p. 187) of Alcaeus's phraseology in the second allegory, but its message is that of the fourth: a definitive renunciation on the part of the ship, now wearied and old, of any intention to take to the sea again or, figuratively, to face once more the grave risks of civil war. The port to which the ship in Horace's poem must resolutely hold is, as Quintilian saw, the port that will assure a sure and lasting peace to the Roman state.

128. Fr. 91 T., cited by Heraclitus (*All. Hom.* 5, 3) as an example of allegory. Archilochus, he explains, is involved in the dangerous enterprises connected with the war against the Thracians, and "compares the war to the waves of a stormy sea."

129. The Gyrai are the highest mountain chain on Tenos, one of the Cyclades; cf. Cic. *Ad Att.* 5, 12, 1, and Sandbach 1942, pp. 63ff.

130. Hom. *Il.* 4, 274; 23, 133 "cloud of foot-soldiers"; 17, 243 "cloud of war."

131. Fr. 302c, 5 V.; cf. the Comparative Table.

132. Fr. °92 T. I see no reason for doubting that these verses are by Archilo-

chus and come from the same poem as fr. 91 T.; this has been shown by Adrados 1955, p. 206, on the basis of both meter and context; cf. West 1974, p. 128. H. Wood 1966 denies Archilochean authorship on the basis of the nonarchaic use of *promethéomai* in v. 7, and Boserup 1966 argues that the poem, unlike 91 T., was in trimeters rather than tetrameters; but neither author's view is persuasive.

133. Cf. the Comparative Table.

134. The maritime metaphor ψυχὰς ἔχοντες κυμάτων ἐν ἀγκάλαις, "with one's life held in the arms of the sea" (Archil. fr. 21 T.), seems to belong to a similar allegorical context; see Pòrtulas 1982.

135. Fr. 249 V. In v. 9 *tòi paréonti tréchen anánka*, the verb *tréchen* is usually corrected for metrical reasons (the scansion *paréontĭ tr.*, with *correptio attica*, rather than the expected *paréontī tr.*). But Attic corruption appears in Sappho as well (fr. 16, 19 V.) and elsewhere in Alcaeus (fr. 332, 1 V.: *tínā pròs bían*). The decisive argument for retaining the text is that the verb *tréchein* in connection with ships is in the style of Alcaean allegory (cf. above). *Anémoi* must be understood with the instrumental dative *tòi paréonti;* cf. v. 5 *aném]o* (Page) *katéchen aétais.*

136. Cf. above.

137. Sol. fr. 1, 65–70 Gent.-Pr.

138. Cf. frr. 8; 120 T.

139. See Gerlach 1937; Kohlmeyer 1934.

## TWELVE: HOLY SAPPHO

1. Fr. 384 V. The attribution to Alcaeus may be considered certain. Hephaestion (p. 45, 12 Consbr.) cites it without indication of author; but it is his example of an alcaic dodecasyllable, hence, presumably from Alcaeus himself and, more particularly, given the way it functions as a model, from the beginning of a poem—Hephaestion's normal procedure in such situations.

2. On the ancient tradition, see Della Corte 1950 and, more recently, Treu 1966.

3. Ferrari 1940, pp. 38ff.

4. Ferrari 1940, p. 40. I see no reason to devote any further time to refuting the erroneous interpretation of ἄγνα presented in the study of Williger 1922, p. 47. Although he rightly acknowledges that ἁγνός in its secondary sense of "ritually pure," and thus "chaste, virginal" (= keusch, jungfräulich), appears clearly for the first time in the tragedians (pp. 44 and 47), he is nevertheless inclined to find this very meaning already present in Alcaeus. But Sappho could not be chaste and virginal and still have, as she did, a husband and a daughter (Cleis).

5. Cf. Moulinier 1952, p. 40n.6; Bowra 1961, p. 239; Treu 1963a, p. 180.

6. Ferrari 1940, p. 50.

7. Ed. Fraenkel 1950, p. 128.

8. Williger 1922.

9. Rudhardt 1958, pp. 39ff.

10. For *hierós*, see, in addition to the excellent observations of Wilamowitz 1931, pp. 21ff., and Pagliaro 1953, pp. 89–122, Wülfing–von Martitz 1959 and 1960–61, which is a welcome reaction against the old theory of a double etymology of the word ("sacred" or "pertaining to the god" on the one hand and, on the other, "large, strong") and rationalistic explanations that would make one of the two meanings the earlier one. The study of Chantraine-Masson 1954, pp. 103ff. is fundamental for ἁγνός, ἅγιος, and ἄγος. The same cannot be said for the article ἁγνός in Chantraine 1968, s.v. "ἅζομαι," which does not even mention in its incomplete bibliographical section the author's earlier study done in collaboration with Masson. Moulinier 1952 is useful for the fullness of its bibliography. Roloff 1952–53, p. 115, adds nothing new to the analysis in Williger 1922.

11. Cf. Chantraine-Masson 1954, p. 103.

12. For the meaning of the formula ἁγνῶς καὶ καθαρῶς (Hes. *Op.* 337; *Hom. hymn. Apoll.* 121), see the excellent observations of Williger 1922, p. 47. It should also be observed that v. 377 of the *Works* of Hesiod (cf. Stengel 1892, p. 447n.4) is—pace West (1978a, p. 241)—almost certainly interpolated.

13. Cf. Chantraine-Masson 1954, loc. cit.

14. Gerber 1965.

15. Fr. 577a P.:

ἔνθα χερνίβεσσιν ἀρύεται τὸ Μοισᾶν
καλλικόμων ὑπένερθεν ἁγνὸν ὕδωρ.

where holy water is drawn for lustral rites
from beneath the place of the fair-tressed Muses.

16. For a more detailed discussion see Flacelière's commentary (1962, p. 56) ad loc.

17. This is Edmonds's translation (1924, p. 315).

18. In fr. 577b P., from the same poem as 577a P., one should perhaps read ἁγνὰ ἐπίσκοπε (Κλειοῖ) χερνίβων rather than, with Diehl and Page, ἁγνὰν ἐ. χ. (αὖθις ὁ Σιμωνίδης τὴν Κλειὼ προσείπων 'ἁγνὰν ἐπίσκοπον χερνίβων κτλ.' Plut. *Mor.* 402d). For ἁγνός as an epithet of the Muses, see n.41.

19. Cf. Gentili 1964, p. 292.

20. Williger 1922, p. 47, and most commentators on Pindar, with the exception of Farnell.

21. Cf. Roloff 1952–53, p. 115.

22. Frr. 53; 103, 8 V.

23. See Lanata 1966, p. 68.

24. Cf. above.

25. Kazik-Zawadzka (1958, pp. 94ff.) notes that "mighty sound" echoes the

Homeric ἠχὴ θεσπεσίη and that *hagnós* applied to a religious song would represent an extension of the Homeric use attested in ἑορτὴ τοῖο θεοῖο ἀγνή (*Od.* 21, 258ff.). Just as a religious rite is "sacred," so is the ritual song that accompanies such a rite or ceremony.

26. The explanation is implicit, if not actually spelled out, by the analysis of Kazik-Zawadzka (1958, p. 95) when it cites Alcaeus's *íros* as a parallel to Sappho's *ágnon.*

27. Cf. Chantraine-Masson 1954, p. 103.

28. It is now generally agreed that the ceremony described in the song is modeled on those that actually took place (see, most recently, Page 1955, p. 71, with n.30 below). It is also probable that the poem was composed for the marriage of some companion in the Sapphic community (see, especially, Rösler 1975, p. 275).

29. Μέλος ἄγνον, ἄχω θεσπεσία, ἐλέλυσδον (= ὀλόλυζον); cf. ἄγνον in v. 22 (where a gap in the text makes it impossible to know whether the adjective is linked to a noun). On *ololygmós, ololygé, ololýzo* as words belonging to religious ritual, see Deubner 1941 and Ed. Fraenkel 1950, p. 296 (see *ad* v. 594ff.).

30. The structure is articulated according to the form of an actual religious ceremony: initial song (that of the maidens), cry of the women (*elélysdon*), song of the men in honor of Apollo and then of the bride and groom. The cry of the women marked the beginning of the sacrifice as the culminating moment of the entire ceremony (cf. *Od.* 3, 450, Alcaeus fr. 130b, 20 V., and Ed. Fraenkel 1950, loc. cit., who, however, cites the Alcaeus passage without mentioning Sappho). The presence of sacrifice as part of the ceremony described by Sappho is implicit in the brief reference to smoke and the scent of myrrh, cassia, and incense. For an instructive parallel to the ritual cry coming simultaneously with the beginning of a paean see Xenophon, *Anab.* 4, 3, 19.

31. Page 1955, p. 71.

32. As in the expressions θεσπεσίη φύζα and ἠχὴ θεσπεσίη (*Il.* 9, 2; 8, 159); cf. L. S. J. s.v. "θεσπ.2."

33. Fr. 130b, 20V. Here the reference to beauty contests as an annual rite is merely one episode among many. It touches the theme of the poem, the miseries of exile, only to the extent that it represents a happy interruption of the exile's grief. Emphasis is not on the sacral solemnity of the event but on the presence of its protagonists, the lovely women of Lesbos, who parade past in their long *péploi.* There is nothing except the culminating ritual cry to indicate that the ceremony is religious at all (cf. above).

34. The translations "sacred," "marvelous," and "ceremonial" are all very approximate and generic. Even "solemn" fails to catch the precise meaning of the epithet; "inspiring of reverence" is the closest rendering, but not sufficiently expressive—better "arcane," originally associated with the ideas of holiness and religious awe: cf. Battaglia 1961.

35. Simon. fr. 577b P. (cf. n.18); Aristoph. *Ran.* 875ff.; Crat. Theb. fr. 1, 10 D.³; *Orph. Hymn.* 76, 10 and 11 (ed. Quandt²).

36. Fr. 298, 17 V. ἄγνας Πάλλαδος.

37. The metaplastic form μελλιχόμειδε instead of μελλιχόμειδες and Σάπφοι in place of the original Ψάπφοι (without dissimilation of consonants). See, in addition to Treu 1963a, pp. 150ff., the note in Gentili 1965b, pp. 224ff.

38. *Il.* 3, 424; *Od.* 8, 362.

39. *Méllichos* appears as an attribute of the eyes of the bride (fr. 112, 4 V.), of the voice (frr. 71, 6; 185 V.), and of the wind (fr. 2, 11 V.) that blows in a spot sacred to Aphrodite: cf. Lanata 1966, pp. 68ff.

40. Gentili 1958a, pp. 184ff., gives full documentation; cf. Lanata 1966, p. 69. One should also note the equivalent *iostéphanos* used as an epithet of Aphrodite in *Hom. Hymn. Ven.* 18 and Solon, fr. 11, 4 Gent.-Pr.

41. Frr. 21, 13 V.; 103, 3 V.: Hebe (Lobel, Gallavotti) or Aphrodite (Treu 1976, p. 169).


APPENDIX: THE ART OF PHILOLOGY

1. Battaglia 1968, s.v. Cf. Pfeiffer 1968, p. 3: "Philology is the art of understanding, explaining and reconstructing literary tradition."

2. Battaglia 1968, s.v.

3. Fowler-Fowler 1964, s.v.

4. Wilamowitz 1927b, p. 1 (Eng. trans., p. 1 [altered to replace the word "scholarship" on its two occurrences with "philology" {translator's note}]).

5. Pasquali 1964, p. 50.

6. Usener 1907, pp. 1–35. These pages, which contain an enlarged and modified version of a lecture delivered by Usener at Bonn in October 1882, were republished on the occasion of the Fifth International Congress of the FIEC (Bonn, 1–6 September 1969) by Wolfgang Schmid 1969, pp. 13–36.

7. *Ars gramm.* 1 p. 5 Uhlig; cf. *Schol.* Dionys. Thr. p. 114, 28 Hilg.

8. Sext. Emp. *Adv. math.* 1, 252–53.

9. Quentin 1926.

10. Cf. Römer 1924, pp. 16, 179–81; Pfeiffer 1968, pp. 225ff. The tendency to view Aristarchus's methodological range as narrower than that of his master Aristophanes seems finally to have given way to a more just evaluation of the validity of his method: cf. Grube 1965, pp. 129ff.

11. On Lachmann's method, see Timpanaro 1981.

12. This is the orientation of Froger's attempt (1968) to translate textual criticism into the language of the theory of sets and mappings, and of Avalle's proposal (1978) that current terminology be transliterated "into more formalized notational systems" (p. viii), a proposal whose adoption would, he claims, have the advantage of eliminating "the obstacles which an essentially anthropomorphic terminology like the traditional one poses for the solution of certain problems that have been hitherto insoluble (or almost so), such as that of con-

tamination" (p. viii). For an evaluation of such research tools borrowed from the theory of functions I refer the reader to Segre 1979, p. 56: "One has the impression that the theory of functions does not contribute in any appreciable way to the understanding of the mechanisms of a textual tradition, but only to their representation and schematization." On the problems of contamination, selection, and the utilization of variant readings, see, most recently, Froger 1979 and Irigoin 1979; cf. Irigoin 1978.

13. See, for example, Segre 1979; and, on the applicability of such critical tools to the study of antiquity in general and archaic Greece in particular, Gentili 1969a and Calame 1971.

14. Cf. Bense 1960 and Bense 1971.

15. Fränkel 1964, p. 141n.1.

16. Waszink 1975, p. 23n.29.

17. Cf. Egenolff 1900, p. 618.

18. Ὁρικήν cod.: corr. Egenolff. As to whether σίοντα is the present participle σίοντα-σείοντα as attested in the two citations of the verse or the aorist *siónta* assumed by Ahrens and later interpreters, cf. Gentili 1958c, p. 157.

19. Frr. 60 str. 1; III Gent.

20. Egenolff 1900.

21. 18, 9 p. 233 Hob. = fr. 148 adn. Gent.: Anacreon's poetry is "full of the youthful bloom of Bathyllos" (Βαθύλλου ὥρας). The Anacreontic provenance of ὥρα is very likely in view of Maximus of Tyre's habit of sprinkling his paraphrases of lines or passages from early poets with words taken directly from the original texts. See, further, Gentili 1958c, p. 159.

22. II. παθῶν fr. 103 (II p. 205 Lentz) = fr. 148 adn. Gent.

23. Cf. Egenolff 1888, pp. 4ff.

24. Fr. 245 K.-A. = 235 Kock: ὡρικὸν δὲ μειράκιον; cf. *Ach.* 272.

25. Waszink 1975, p. 23.

26. Fr. 71 Gent.

27. Cf. Athen. 6, 250b; Luc. *Ver. hist.* 2, 15.

28. See, especially, Chamael. fr. 28 Wehrli *ap.* Athen. 14, 620b–d; cf. chap. 9.

29. Fr. 235 K.-A. (223 Kock = 30 Cassio); cf. Anacr. fr. 182 Gent.

30. *Contra Apionem* I, 12.

31. This is exactly the procedure adopted by Càssola 1975, p. 118.

32. 315–21 Allen.

33. *Schol.* Pind. *Nem.* 2, 1c (III p. 29, 13 Drachm.); cf. Càssola 1975, p. 101. I do not share the view of West (1975a, p. 165), who is inclined to regard the Delian portion of the hymn as more recent and modeled on the Delphic one. The phrase ἀνατέθεικεν αὐτῷ (or αὐτῷ) in the scholion relating to Cynaethos may also mean that, having written down the Hymn to Apollo, the rhapsode attributed it to Homer (αὐτῷ rather than αὐτῷ). That he attributed it to himself is the view of Wade-Gery 1952, pp. 21ff. and De Martino 1983.

34. For fuller discussion, cf. chap. 3.

35. Segre 1979, pp. 58ff.

36. Weinreich 1963.

37. Cf. Giannini 1977, p. 45.

38. Dawe 1964, especially chap. 6 (on the notion of an archetype) and Dawe 1973, especially chap. 1 (on the *stemma codicum*). For a critical evaluation of Dawe's thesis, cf. Irigoin 1966; Irigoin 1977; Irigoin 1980. Whatever view one takes of the principles on which it is based, the new Sophocles text is distinguished for correct lyric colometry and intelligent analysis of Sophoclean meters.

39. Cf. chap. 1.

40. Lord 1960.

41. Cianfogni 1748, pp. 84ff.

42. Cf. Gentili 1980, p. 37n.42.

43. Cf. Eco 1979, p. 178.

44. F. Nietzsche, "Morgenröthe," Vorrede V, in *Nietzsche Werke: Kritische Gesamtausgabe*, v/1, ed. G. Colli and M. Montinari (Berlin and New York, 1971), p. 9 (R. J. Hollingdale, trans., *Daybreak: Thoughts on the Prejudices of Morality* [Cambridge, 1982], p. 5).

# Bibliography of Works Cited

Adkins 1960 — A. W. H. Adkins. *Merit and Responsibility: A Study in Greek Values.* Oxford, 1960.

Adrados 1955 — F. R. Adrados. "Origen del tema de la nave del estado en un papiro de Arquíloco." *Aegyptus* 35 (1955): 206–10.

Adrados 1976 — F. R. Adrados. *Orígenes de la lírica griega.* Madrid, 1976.

Adrados 1979 — F. R. Adrados. *Historia de la fabula greco-latina,* I–II. Madrid, 1979.

Alfonsi 1954 — L. Alfonsi. "Il nuovo Alceo e Orazio." *Aegyptus* 34 (1954): 215–19.

Aloni 1981 — A. Aloni. *Le Muse di Archiloco.* Copenhagen, 1981.

Ancher 1978 — G. Ancher. "P. Lille III c et P. Lille 76 abc (+73)." *Zeitschr. f. Pap. u. Epigr.* 30 (1978): 27–35.

Ancher–Boyaval–Meillier 1976 — G. Ancher–B. Boyaval–C. Meillier. "Stésichore (?) (P.L. 76 abc)." *Cahier de Recherches de l'Institut de Papyrol. et d'Egypt. de Lille* 4 (1976): 287–351.

Andrewes 1956 — A. Andrewes. *The Greek Tyrants.* London, 1956.

Angeli Bernardini — See Bernardini.

Ardizzoni 1953 — A. Ardizzoni. Ποίημα: *Ricerche sulla teoria del linguaggio poetico nell'antichità.* Rome, 1953.

Arena 1967 — R. Arena. "La terminazione 'eolica' -οισα (-αισα)." *Acme* 20 (1967): 215–27.

Arrighetti 1976 — G. Arrighetti. "In tema di poetica arcaica e tardo-arcaica (Esiodo, Pindaro, Bacchilide)." *Studi class. or.* 25 (1976): 255–314.

311

Arrighetti 1982    G. Arrighetti. "Stesicoro, l'ispirazione divina e la
                   poetica della verità." In ΑΠΑΡΧΑΙ: *Nuove ricerche
                   e studi sulla Magna Grecia e la Sicilia antica in onore
                   di P. E. Arias*, I. Pisa, 1982, pp. 105–11.

Avalle 1977        D. S. Avalle. *Ai luoghi di delizia pieni.* Milan and
                   Naples, 1977.

Avalle 1978        D. S. Avalle. *Principi di critica testuale.* Padua, 1978².

Bakhtin 1976       M. Bakhtin. "Epos e romanzo: Sulla metodologia
                   dello studio del romanzo." In *Problemi di teoria del
                   romanzo.* Turin, 1976, pp. 179–221.

Bakhtin 1984       M. Bakhtin. *Problemy tvorchestva Dostoevskogo.*
                   Leningrad, 1929. Translated by C. Emerson, under
                   the title *Problems of Dostoevsky's Poetics.* Minne-
                   apolis, 1984.

Barner 1967a       W. Barner. *Neuere Alkaios-Papyri aus Oxyrhynchos.*
                   Hildesheim, 1967.

Barner 1967b       W. Barner. "Zu den Alkaios-Fragmenten von P. Oxy.
                   2506." *Hermes* 95 (1967): 1–28.

Barnstone 1965     W. Barnstone. *Sappho: Lyrics in the Original Greek.*
                   New York, 1965.

Barron 1969        J. P. Barron. "Ibycus: To Polycrates." *Bull. Inst.
                   Class. Stud. London* 16 (1969): 119–49.

Barthélemy 1788    J. J. Barthélemy. *Voyage du jeune Anacharsis en
                   Grèce vers le milieu du quatrième siècle avant Jésus
                   Christ,* 1788.

Bataille 1961      A. Bataille. "Remarques sur les deux notations
                   mélodiques de l'ancienne musique grecque." *Re-
                   cherches de papyrol.* 1 (1961): 5–20.

Battaglia 1961     S. Battaglia. *Grande dizionario della lingua italiana,*
                   I. Turin, 1961 (1980), pp. 617–18.

Battaglia 1968     S. Battaglia. *Grande dizionario della lingua italiana,*
                   V. Turin, 1968 (1972), pp. 1003–4.

Battisti-Alessio 1952  C. Battisti–G. Alessio. *Dizionario etim. it.,* III.
                   Florence, 1952, p. 2208.

Bauer 1963         O. Bauer. "Sapphos Verbannung." *Gymnasium* 70
                   (1963): 1–10.

Beazley 1963       J. D. Beazley. *Attic Red-figure Vase-Painters,* I². Ox-
                   ford, 1963.

Beckby 1958        H. Beckby. *Anthologia Graeca,* XII–XVI. Munich,
                   1958.

Becker 1937        O. Becker. *Das Bild des Weges und verwandte Vor-
                   stellungen in frühgriechischen Denken.* Berlin, 1937.

Bell 1978          J. M. Bell. "Κίμβιξ καὶ σοφός: Simonides in the
                   Anecdotal Tradition." *Quad. Urb.* 28 (1978): 29–86.

Benjamin 1974 W. Benjamin. "Das Kunstwerk in Zeitalter seiner technischen Reproduzierbarkeit." *Gesammelte Schriften*, I/2 (1936). Frankfurt am Main, 1974.

Bense 1960 M. Bense. *Programmierung der Schönen: Allgemeine Texttheorie und Textästhetik.* Baden-Baden and Krefeld, 1960.

Bense 1971 M. Bense. *Artistik und Engagement.* Cologne, 1971.

Bernardini 1967 P. Angeli Bernardini. "Linguaggio e programma poetico in Pindaro." *Quad. Urb.* 4 (1967): 80–97.

Bernardini 1976 P. Angeli Bernardini. "Eracle mangione: Pindaro, fr. 168 Sn.-Maehler." *Quad. Urb.* 21 (1976): 49–52.

Bernardini 1977 P. Angeli Bernardini. "Ancora sull'iscrizione agonistica di Kleomrotos." *Quad. Urb.* 26 (1977): 149–54.

Bernardini 1979 P. Angeli Bernardini. "Interpretazioni recenti delle odi di Pindaro e Bacchilide per Ierone di Siracusa con particolare riferimento al libro di M. R. Lefkowitz." *Quad. Urb.*, n.s. 2 [31] (1979): 193–200.

Bernardini-Veneri 1981 P. Angeli Bernardini–A. Veneri. "Il 'Gorgia' di Platone nel giudizio di Gorgia e l''aureo' Gorgia nel giudizio di Platone." *Quad. Urb.*, n.s. 7 [36] (1981): 149–60.

Bettinelli 1799 S. Bettinelli. *Opere edite e inedite in prosa e in versi,* III. Venice, 1799².

Bettini 1979 M. Bettini. *Studi e note su Ennio.* Pisa, 1979.

Bianchi Bandinelli 1979 R. Bianchi Bandinelli. "L'artista nell'antichità classica." In *Archeologia e cultura.* Rome, 1979², pp. 45–62 = *Artisti e artigiani in Grecia.* Historical and critical survey, ed. F. Coarelli. Rome and Bari, 1980, pp. 49–73.

Bicknell 1966 P. J. Bicknell. "The Date of the Battle of the Sagra River." *Phoenix* 20 (1966): 294–301.

Bieler 1933 L. Bieler. "Σκιᾶς ὄναρ ἄνθρωπος." *Wien. Stud.* 51 (1933): 143–45 = *Pindaros und Bakchylides,* ed. W. M. Calder III-J. Stern. Darmstadt, 1970, pp. 191–193.

Bilinski 1979 B. Bilinski. *Agoni ginnici, componenti artistiche e intellettuali nell'antica agonistica greca.* Accad. Polacca delle Scienze, Biblioteca e Centro di Studi di Roma, Conferenza 75, 1979.

Blackwell 1735 T. Blackwell. *An Inquiry into the Life and Writings of Homer.* London, 1735.

Blakeway 1936 A. Blakeway. "The Date of Archilochus." In *Greek Poetry and Life: Essays Presented to G. Murray.* Oxford, 1936, pp. 34–55.

Bloch-Wartburg 1950     O. Bloch-W. von Wartburg. *Dictionnaire étymol. de la langue franç.*, I². Paris, 1950, p. 348.

Blum 1969     H. Blum. *Die antike Mnemotechnik.* Hildesheim, 1969.

Boeckh 1821     A. Boeckh. *Pindari opera*, II/2. Leipzig, 1821.

Bollack–Judet de la     J. Bollack–P. Judet de la Combe–H. Wismann. "La
Combe–Wismann 1977     réplique de Jocaste: Papyrus Lille 73 et 76 abc." *Suppl. au Cahier de Philol.* 2 (1977): 1–17.

Bonanno 1973     M. G. Bonanno. "Osservazioni sul tema della 'giusta' reciprocità amorosa da Saffo ai comici." *Quad. Urb.* 16 (1973): 110–20.

Bonanno 1976     M. G. Bonanno. "Alcaeus fr. 140 V." *Philologus* 120 (1976): 1–11.

Bonanno 1978–79     M. G. Bonanno. "Ibyc. S. 151, 23 ss. P." *Mus. Crit.* 13–14 (1978–79): 143–46.

Bonanno 1980a     M. G. Bonanno. "Nomi e soprannomi archilochei." *Mus. Helv.* 37, no. 2 (1980): 65–88.

Bonanno 1980b     M. G. Bonanno. "Sull'allegoria della nave (Alcae. 208 V.; Hor. Carm. I 14)." *Riv. Class. medioev. (Miscellanea di studi in memoria di M. Barchiesi)* 1976 (1980): 179–92.

Borthwick 1979     E. K. Borthwick. "Φυλάσσω or λαφύσσω? A Note on Two Emendations." *Eranos* 77 (1979): 79–83.

Boserup 1966     J. Boserup. "Archiloque ou un Epigone Alexandrin? Sur l'authenticité du fr. 56 A (Diehl)." *Class. et Medioev.* 27 (1966): 28–38.

Bossi 1980     F. Bossi. "Archil. fr. 2 (e 4) W." *Quad. Urb.*, n.s. 5 [34] (1980): 23–27.

Bossi 1981     F. Bossi. "Appunti per un profilo di Archiloco." *Quad. di storia* 13 (1981): 117–42.

Bowra 1934     C. M. Bowra. "Stesichorus in the Peloponnese." *Class. Quart.* 28 (1934): 115–19.

Bowra 1960     C. M. Bowra. *Early Greek Elegists* (1935). Cambridge, Mass., 1960.

Bowra 1961     C. M. Bowra. *Greek Lyric Poetry.* Oxford, 1961².

Bowra 1964     C. M. Bowra. *Pindar.* Oxford, 1964.

Braswell 1976     B. K. Braswell. "Notes on the Prooemium to Pindar's Seventh Olympian Ode." *Mnemosyne* 29 (1976): 233–42.

Breitenstein 1971     T. Breitenstein. *Hésiode et Archiloque.* Odense, 1971.

Brelich 1969     A. Brelich. *Gli eroi greci.* Rome, 1969².

Brillante 1981     C. Brillante. *La leggenda eroica e la civiltà micenea.* Rome, 1981.

Brize 1980     P. Brize. *Die Geryoneis des Stesichoros und die frühe griechische Kunst.* Würzburg, 1980.

Broccia 1979     G. Broccia. *La questione omerica.* Florence, 1979.

Bundy 1962     E. L. Bundy. *Studia Pindarica*, I: *The Eleventh Olympian Ode;* II: *The First Isthmian Ode.* Berkeley and Los Angeles, 1962.

Burckhardt 1900     J. Burckhardt. *Griechische Kulturgeschichte*, ed. J. Oeri. Berlin and Stuttgart, 1900².

Burckhardt 1919     J. Burckhardt. "Die Griechen und ihre Künstler." In *Vorträge 1844–1887.* Basel, 1919, pp. 202–14.

Burkert 1977     W. Burkert. "Le mythe de Géryon: Perspectives préhistoriques et tradition rituelle." In *Il mito greco.* Atti del Convegno Internazionale (Urbino, 7–12 May 1973), ed. B. Gentili–G. Paioni. Rome, 1977, pp. 273–84.

Burkert 1979     W. Burkert. *Structure and History in Greek Mythology and Ritual.* Berkeley and Los Angeles, 1979.

Burr 1944     V. Burr, Νεῶν κατάλογος: *Untersuchungen zum homerischen Schiffskatalog.* Leipzig, 1944.

Burton 1962     R. W. B. Burton. *Pindar's Pythian Odes: Essays in Interpretation.* Oxford, 1962.

Burzacchini 1977     *Lirici greci.* Anthology edited by E. Degani–G. Burzacchini. Florence, 1977.

Busolt-Swoboda 1926     G. Busolt–H. Swoboda. *Griechische Staatskunde,* II. Munich, 1926.

Calame 1971     C. Calame. "Philologie et anthropologie structurale: A propos d'un livre récent d'Angelo Brelich." *Quad. Urb.* 11 (1971): 7–47.

Calame 1974     C. Calame. "Réflexions sur les genres littéraires en Grèce archaïque." *Quad. Urb.* 17 (1974): 113–28.

Calame 1977a     C. Calame. *Les choeurs des jeunes filles en Grèce archaïque*, I–II. Rome, 1977.

Calame 1977b     C. Calame. "Die Komposita mit ἀρτι- im frühgriechischen Epos." *Mus. Helv.* 34 (1977): 209–20.

Cameron 1965     A. D. E. Cameron. "Wandering Poets: A Literary Movement in Byzantine Egypt." *Historia* 14 (1965): 470–509.

Campbell 1964     D. A. Campbell. "Flutes and Elegiac Couplets." *Journ. Hell. Stud.* 84 (1964): 63–68.

Cancrini 1970     A. Cancrini. *Syneidesis: Il tema semantico della "conscientia" nella Grecia antica.* Rome, 1970.

Canfora 1983     Tucidide. *La guerra del Peloponneso,* I, ed. L. Canfora. Milan, 1983.

Cantilena 1981    M. Cantilena. *Ricerche sulla dizione epica,* I. Rome, 1981.

Cantilena 1983    M. Cantilena. "Oralisti di ieri e di oggi." *Quad. Urb,* n.s. 13 [42] (1983): 165–86.

Capizzi 1975    A. Capizzi. *La porta di Parmenide.* Rome, 1975.

Capizzi 1982    A. Capizzi. *La repubblica cosmica.* Rome, 1982.

Carandini 1979    A. Carandini. *Anatomia della scimmia.* Turin, 1979.

Carmignani 1982    L. Carmignani. "Stile e tecnica narrativa di Stesicoro." *Richerche di filologia classica* 1 (1982): 25–60.

Cassio 1983    A. C. Cassio. "Post-classical Λέσβιαι." *Class. Quart.* 33 (1983): 296–97.

Càssola 1975    *Inni omerici,* ed. F. Càssola. Milan, 1975.

Castagna 1971    L. Castagna. "Pindaro, fr. 169a Sn.³: interpretazione e proposta di datazione." *Studi it. filol. class.* 43 (1971): 173–98.

Cerri 1968    G. Cerri. "Metodologie strutturalistiche nello studio della grecità arcaica: Due indagini di Marcel Detienne." *Quad. Urb.* 6 (1968): 131–35.

Cerri 1969a    G. Cerri. "Ἴσος δασμός come equivalente di ἰσονομία nella silloge teognidea." *Quad. Urb.* 8 (1969): 97–104.

Cerri 1969b    G. Cerri. "Il passaggio dalla cultura orale alla cultura di comunicazione scritta nell'età di Platone." *Quad. Urb.* 8 (1969): 119–33.

Cerri 1972    G. Cerri. "Un'espressione tirtaica in un contesto allegorico di Alceo: Un caso di ambivalenza espressiva." *Quad. Urb.* 14 (1972): 65–70.

Cerri 1976    G. Cerri. "A proposito del futuro e della litote in Pindaro: 'Nem.' 7, 102 sgg." *Quad. Urb.* 22 (1976): 83–90.

Cerri 1980    G. Cerri. Review of F. R. Adrados, *Orígenes de la lírica griega.* Madrid, 1976. In *Gnomon* 52 (1980): 605–9.

Cerri 1985    G. Cerri. "G. B. Vico e l'interpretazione oralistica di Omero." In *Oralità, cultura, letteratura, discorso.* Atti del Convegno Internazionale (Urbino, 21–25 July 1980), ed. B. Gentili–G. Paioni. Rome, 1985, pp. 233–52.

Chadwick-Baumbach 1963    J. Chadwick–L. Baumbach. "The Mycenaean Greek Vocabulary." *Glotta* 41 (1963): 157–271.

Chantraine 1968    P. Chantraine. *Dictionn. étym. de la langue grecque,* I. Paris, 1968.

Chantraine 1970    P. Chantraine. *Dictionn. étym. de la langue grecque,* II. Paris, 1970.

Chantraine-Masson 1954    P. Chantraine–O. Masson. "Sur quelques termes du vocabulaire religieux des Grecs: La valeur du mot ἄγος et de ses dérivés." In *Festschrift A. Debrunner.* Bern, 1954, pp. 85–107.

Christ 1941    G. Christ. *Simonidesstudien.* Freiburg, 1941.

Cianfogni 1748    D. Cianfogni. *Saggi di poesie dette all'improvviso e parte scritte dal Cavaliere Bernardino Perfetti,* I. Florence, 1748.

Cingano 1979a    E. Cingano. "Problemi di critica pindarica." *Quad. Urb.,* n.s. 2 [31] (1979): 169–82.

Cingano 1979b    E. Cingano. "L'analisi formale dell'epinicio nel volume di R. Hamilton." *Quad. Urb.,* n.s. 2 [31] (1979): 183–91.

Cingano 1982    E. Cingano. "Quante testimonianze sulle palinodie di Stesicoro?" *Quad. Urb.,* n.s. 12 [41] (1982): 21–33.

Coarelli 1980    F. Coarelli. Introduction to *Artisti e artigiani in Grecia.* Historical and critical survey, ed. F. Coarelli. Rome and Bari, 1980, pp. v–xxx.

Codino 1965    F. Codino. *Introduzione ad Omero.* Turin, 1965.

Cole 1983    T. Cole. "Archaic Truth." *Quad. Urb.,* n.s. 13 [42] (1983): 7–28.

Colletti 1974    L. Colletti. *Intervista politico-filosofica: Con un saggio su "marxismo e dialettica."* Rome and Bari, 1974.

Comotti 1977    G. Comotti. "'Muta cum liquida' nel nuovo Stesicoro (Pap. Lille 76 a, b, c)." *Quad. Urb.* 26 (1977): 59–61.

Comotti 1979    G. Comotti. *La musica nella cultura greca e romana.* Turin, 1979.

Contini 1976    G. Contini. *Un'idea di Dante.* Turin, 1976.

Corchia 1981    R. Corchia. "Genealogia dedalica e scultura arcaica: Un 'canone' in forma di mito?" *Mélanges école française Rome* 93 (1981): 533–45.

Cunningham 1954    M. P. Cunningham. "Medea ἀπὸ μηχανῆς." *Class. Philol.* 49 (1954): 151–60.

Davies 1980    M. Davies. "The Eyes of Love and the Hunting-Net in Ibycus 287 P." *Maia* 32 (1980): 255–57.

Davies 1981    M. Davies. "Artemon Transvestitus? A Query." *Mnemosyne* 34 (1981): 288–99.

Davison 1962    J. A. Davison. "The Transmission of the Text." In *A Companion to Homer,* ed. A. J. B. Wace–F. H. Stubbings. London, 1962, pp. 215–33.

Davison 1968    J. A. Davison. *From Archilochus to Pindar.* London, 1968.

Dawe 1964     R. D. Dawe. *The Collation and Investigation of Manuscripts of Aeschylus.* Cambridge, 1964.

Dawe 1973     R. D. Dawe. *Studies in the Text of Sophocles,* I. Leiden, 1973.

Dawson 1966     Ch. M. Dawson. "ΣΠΟΥΔΑΙΟΓΕΛΟΙΟΝ: Random Thoughts on Occasional Poems." *Yale Class. Stud.* 19 (1966): 39–76.

Defradas 1954     J. Defradas. *Les thèmes de la propagande delphique.* Paris, 1954.

Defradas 1963     J. Defradas. "Studia pindarica." *Rev. ét. gr.* 76 (1963): 193–202.

Degani 1975     E. Degani. "ΠΑΡΕΞ ΤΟ ΘΕΙΟΝ ΧΡΗΜΑ nel nuovo Archiloco di Colonia." *Quad. Urb.* 20 (1975): 229.

Degani 1977a     *Poeti greci giambici ed elegiaci.* Critical essays, ed. E. Degani. Milan, 1977.

Degani 1977b     *Lirici greci.* Anthology edited by E. Degani–G. Burzacchini. Florence, 1977.

De Heer 1969     C. De Heer. Μάκαρ, εὐδαίμων, ὄλβιος, εὐτυχές: *A Study of the Semantic Field Denoting Happiness in Ancient Greece to the End of the Fifth Century* B.C. Amsterdam, 1969.

Della Corte 1940     F. Della Corte. "Elegia e giambo in Archiloco." *Riv. filol. class.* 68 (1940): 90–98 = *Opuscula,* I. Genoa, 1971, pp. 4–9.

Della Corte 1950     F. Della Corte. *Saffo.* Turin, 1950.

De Martino 1983     F. De Martino. "Cineto, Testoride e l'eredità di Omero." *Quad. Urb,* n.s. 14 [43] (1983): 155–61.

De Sanctis 1975     G. De Sanctis. *Atthis: Storia della Repubblica ateniese dalle origini alla età di Pericle.* Florence, 1975³.

Descat 1982     R. Descat. "Les Grecs et le travail du VIIIᵉ au Vᵉ siècle av. J. C." Thesis, Univ. Besançon, 1982.

des Courtils–Koželj–     J. des Courtils–T. Koželj–A. Muller. "Des mines d'or
Muller 1982     à Thasos." *Bull. corresp. hell.* 106 (1982): 409–17.

Des Places 1949     E. Des Places. *Pindare et Platon.* Paris, 1949.

Detienne 1967     M. Detienne. *Les maîtres de verité dans la Grèce archaïque.* Paris, 1967.

Detienne 1977     M. Detienne. *Dionysos mis à mort.* Paris, 1977. Translated by M. Muellner–L. Muellner, under the title *Dionysos Slain.* Baltimore, 1979.

Detienne 1979     M. Detienne. "Il coltello da carne." *Dialoghi d'archeologia,* n.s. 1 (1979): 6–16.

Detienne 1980　　　　M. Detienne. "La territoire de la mythologie." *Class.*
　　　　　　　　　　　　*Philol.* 75 (1980): 107–11.

Detienne-Vernant 1974　M. Detienne–J. P. Vernant. *Les ruses de l'intelli-*
　　　　　　　　　　　　*gence–La métis des Grecs.* Paris, 1974. Translated by
　　　　　　　　　　　　J. Lloyd, under the title *Cunning Intelligence in*
　　　　　　　　　　　　*Greek Culture and Society.* Atlantic Highlands, N.J.,
　　　　　　　　　　　　1978.

Deubner 1941　　　　　L. Deubner. "Ololyge und Verwandtes." *Abhandl.*
　　　　　　　　　　　　*Preuss. Akad. Wissenschaft.* 1 (1941): 1–28.

Dickie 1978　　　　　　M. Dickie. "The Argument and Form of Simonides
　　　　　　　　　　　　542 PMG." *Harv. Stud. Class. Philol.* 82 (1978): 21–33.

Diggle 1970　　　　　　J. Diggle. "Notes on Greek Lyric Poets." *Class. Rev.*
　　　　　　　　　　　　20 (1970): 5–6.

Diller 1956　　　　　　H. Diller. "Der philosophische Gebrauch von
　　　　　　　　　　　　κόσμος und κοσμεῖν." In *Festschr. B. Snell.*
　　　　　　　　　　　　Munich, 1956, pp. 47–60.

Di Marco 1973–74　　　M. Di Marco. "Osservazioni sull'iporchema." *Heli-*
　　　　　　　　　　　　*kon* 13–14 (1973–74): 326–48.

Di Nola 1971　　　　　*Canti erotici dei primitivi,* ed. A. M. Di Nola.
　　　　　　　　　　　　Milan, 1971.

Dissen 1830　　　　　　L. Dissen. *Commentarius in Pindari Carmina.*
　　　　　　　　　　　　Gotha and Erfurt, 1830.

Di Tillio 1969　　　　　Z. Di Tillio. "Confronti formulari e lessicali tra le
　　　　　　　　　　　　iscrizioni esametriche ed elegiache dal VII al V sec.
　　　　　　　　　　　　a.C. e l'epos arcaico, I: Iscrizioni sepolcrali." *Quad.*
　　　　　　　　　　　　*Urb.* 7 (1969): 45–73.

Dittenberger 1920　　　W. Dittenberger. *Sylloge Inscriptionum Graecarum,*
　　　　　　　　　　　　III. Leipzig, 1920³ (Hildesheim, 1960).

Dodds 1951　　　　　　E. R. Dodds. *The Greeks and the Irrational.*
　　　　　　　　　　　　Berkeley and Los Angeles, 1951.

Donlan 1969　　　　　　W. Donlan. "Simonides, fr. 4 D. and P. Oxy. 2432."
　　　　　　　　　　　　*Trans. Am. Philol. Assoc.* 100 (1969): 71–95.

Donnay 1967　　　　　　G. Donnay. "Les comptes de l'Athéna chryséléphan-
　　　　　　　　　　　　tine du Parthénon." *Bull. corresp. héll.* 91 (1967): 50–
　　　　　　　　　　　　86.

Doria 1967　　　　　　　M. Doria. "Strumentali, ablativi e dativi plurali in
　　　　　　　　　　　　miceneo: Alcune precisazioni." In *Atti e mem. del I*
　　　　　　　　　　　　*Congr. Internaz. di Micenologia,* II. Rome, 1967, pp.
　　　　　　　　　　　　764–80.

Dorson 1964　　　　　　R. M. Dorson. "Oral Styles of American Folk Nar-
　　　　　　　　　　　　rators." In *Style in Language,* ed. T. A. Sebeok.
　　　　　　　　　　　　Cambridge, Mass., 1964², pp. 27–51.

Dover 1963　　　　　　K. J. Dover. "The Poetry of Archilochos." In

|  | *Archiloque, Entr. Hardt,* X. Vandoeuvres-Geneva, 1963, pp. 181–222. |
| Dover 1968 | K. J. Dover. *Aristophanes: "Clouds."* Oxford, 1968. |
| Drachmann 1903 | A. B. Drachmann. *Scholia vetera in Pindari carmina,* I. Leipzig, 1903; II, 1910; III, 1927. |
| Duchemin 1955 | J. Duchemin. *Pindare poète et prophète.* Paris, 1955. |
| Dunkel 1979 | G. Dunkel. "Fighting Words: Alcman, 'Partheneion' 63 μάχονται." *Journ. Indo-Europ. Stud.* 7, nos. 3–4 (1979): 249–72. |
| Dupront 1965 | A. Dupront. "De l'acculturation." In *Comité International des Sciences Historiques, XII<sup>e</sup> Congrès International des Sciences Historiques* (Vienna, 29 August–5 September 1965), *Rapports:* I, *Grands Thèmes.* Horn-Vienna, 1965, pp. 7–36. |
| Durante 1971 | M. Durante. *Sulla preistoria della tradizione poetica greca,* I: *Continuità della tradizione poetica dall'età micenea ai primi documenti.* Rome, 1971. |
| Durante 1976 | M. Durante. *Sulla preistoria della tradizione poetica greca,* II: *Risultanze della comparazione indoeuropea.* Rome, 1976. |
| Düring 1945 | I. Düring. "Studies in Musical Terminology in Fifth Century Literature." *Eranos* 43 (1945): 176–97. |
| Ebbell 1967 | B. Ebbell. *Beiträge zur ältesten Geschichte einiger Infektionskrankheiten.* Oslo, 1967. |
| Eco 1979 | U. Eco. *Lector in fabula: La cooperazione interpretativa nei testi narrativi.* Milan, 1979. |
| Eco 1980 | In U. Eco. *Enciclopedia Einaudi,* IX. Turin, 1980, pp. 191–236, s.v. "Metafora." |
| Edmonds 1924 | J. M. Edmonds. *Lyra Graeca,* II. London, 1924 (1964). |
| Egenolff 1888 | P. Egenolff. *Die orthogr. Stücke d. byzant. Literatur.* Progr., Heidelberg, 1888. |
| Egenolff 1900 | P. Egenolff. "Zu Anakreon." *Philologus* 59 (1900): 618–20. |
| Ehrenberg 1921 | V. Ehrenberg. *Die Rechtsidee im frühen Griechentum.* Leipzig, 1921. |
| Ehrenberg 1951 | V. Ehrenberg. *The People of Aristophanes.* Oxford, 1951². |
| Eliade 1963 | M. Eliade. *Myth and Reality.* New York, 1963. |
| Eliot 1950 | T. S. Eliot. *Selected Essays.* New York, 1950². |
| Else 1958 | G. F. Else. "Imitation in the Fifth Century." *Class. Philol.* 53 (1958): 73–90. |
| Fabi Montani 1843 | F. Fabi Montani. *Elogio storico di F. Gianni.* Rome, 1843. |

Fantuzzi 1980a     M. Fantuzzi. "Oralità, scrittura, auralità: Gli studi sulle tecniche della comunicazione nella Grecia antica." *Lingua e Stile* 15 (1980): 593–612.

Fantuzzi 1980b     M. Fantuzzi. "La contaminazione dei generi letterari nella letteratura greca ellenistica: Rifiuto del sistema o evoluzione di un sistema?" *Lingua e stile* 15 (1980): 433–50.

Färber 1936     H. Färber. *Die Lyrik in der Kunsttheorie der Antike.* Munich, 1936.

Farnell 1932     R. L. Farnell. *The Works of Pindar,* II. London, 1932.

Fernow 1806     K. L. Fernow. *Römische Studien,* II. Zürich, 1806.

Ferrari 1940     W. Ferrari. "Due note su ἁγνός." *Studi it. filol. class.* 17 (1940): 33–53.

Ferrin Sutton 1983     D. Ferrin Sutton. "Dithyramb as Δρᾶμα: Philoxenus of Cythera's 'Cyclops or Galatea.'" *Quad. Urb.,* n.s. 13 [42] (1983): 37–43.

Finley 1957     M. I. Finley. "Homer and Mycenae: Property and Tenure." *Historia* 6, no. 2 (1957): 133–59.

Finley 1965     M. I. Finley. "Myth, Memory and History." *History and Theory* 4 (1965): 281–305 = *The Use and Abuse of History.* London, 1975, pp. 11–33.

Finley 1977a     M. I. Finley. "The Ancient City: From Fustel de Coulanges to Max Weber and Beyond." *Comparative Studies in Society and History: An International Quarterly* 19, no. 3 (1977): 305–27 = *Mythe, mémoire, histoire.* Paris, 1981, pp. 89–120.

Finley 1977b     M. I. Finley. *The World of Odysseus.* New York, 1977².

Finnegan 1970     R. Finnegan. *Oral Literature in Africa.* Oxford, 1970.

Finnegan 1977     R. Finnegan. *Oral Poetry.* Cambridge, 1977.

Flacelière 1962     R. Flacelière. *Plutarque: Dialogue sur les oracles de la Pythie.* Paris, 1962.

Fogelmark 1972     S. Fogelmark. *Studies in Pindar with Particular Reference to Paean VI and Nemean VII.* Lund, 1972.

Fogelmark 1976     S. Fogelmark. "Pindar, Nemean 7, 50–52." *Antiquité class.* 45 (1976): 121–32.

Forssman 1966     B. Forssman. *Untersuchungen zur Sprache Pindars.* Wiesbaden, 1966.

Fowler-Fowler 1964     *The Concise Oxford Dictionary of Current English,* ed. H. W. Fowler-F. G. Fowler. Oxford, 1964⁵.

Ed. Fraenkel 1950     Ed. Fraenkel, *Aeschylus: Agamemnon,* II. Oxford, 1950.

Fränkel 1939     H. Fränkel. "W. Marg. Der Charakter in der

Sprache der frühgriechischen Dichtung (Homer, Semonides, Pindar)." *Am. Journ. Philol.* 60 (1939): 475–79.

Fränkel 1960    H. Fränkel. *Wege und Formen frühgriechischen Denkens.* Munich, 1960².

Fränkel 1961    H. Fränkel. "Schrullen in den Scholien zu Pindars Nemeen 7 und Olympien 3." *Hermes* 89 (1961): 385–97.

Fränkel 1964    H. Fränkel. *Einleitung zur kritischen Ausgabe der Argonautika des Apollonios.* Göttingen, 1964.

Fränkel 1969    H. Fränkel. *Dichtung und Philosophie des frühen Griechentums.* Munich, 1969³. Translated by M. Hadas–J. Willis, under the title *Early Greek Poetry and Philosophy.* New York, 1975.

Franchi 1984    S. Franchi. "Prassi esecutiva musicale e poesia estemporanea italiana: Aspetti storici e tecnici." In *Oralità: Cultura, letteratura, discorso.* Atti del Convegno Internazionale (Urbino, 21–25 July 1980), ed. B. Gentili–G. Paioni. Rome, 1985, pp. 409–24.

Friedländer 1948    P. Friedländer. *Epigrammata: Greek Inscriptions in Verse from the Beginnings to the Persian Wars.* Berkeley and Los Angeles, 1948.

Frisk 1960    H. Frisk. *Griechisches Etymologisches Wörterbuch,* I. Heidelberg, 1960.

Frisk 1972    H. Frisk. *Griechisches Etymologisches Wörterbuch,* II. Heidelberg, 1972.

Froger 1968    J. Froger. *La critique des textes et son automatisation.* Paris, 1968.

Froger 1979    J. Froger. "La méthode de dom Quentin, la méthode des distances et le problème de la contamination." In *La pratique des ordinateurs dans la critique des textes* (Colloque Intern. du Centre Nat. de la Recherche Scient. n. 579, Paris, 29–31 March 1978). Paris, 1979, pp. 13–22.

Frontisi-Ducroux 1975    F. Frontisi-Ducroux. *Dédale: Mythologie de l'artisan en Grèce ancienne.* Paris, 1975.

Frye 1969    N. Frye. "Mythos and Logos." *Yearbook of Comparative and General Literature* 18 (1969): 5–18.

Fuchs 1969    W. Fuchs. *Die Skulptur der Griechen.* Munich, 1969.

Führer 1967    R. Führer. *Formproblem: Urtersuchungen zu den Reden in der frühgriechischen Lyrik.* Munich, 1967.

Pseudo-Gadda 1969    Pseudo-Gadda. "Inderogabili norme e cautele." *Il Caffè* 16, no. 1 (1969): 3–19.

Gallavotti 1948     C. Gallavotti. *Storia e poesia di Lesbo nel VII-VI sec. a. C.*, I: *Alceo di Mitilene*. Bari, 1948.

Gallavotti 1953     C. Gallavotti. "Auctarium Oxyrhynchium." *Aegyptus* 33 (1953): 159–71.

Gallavotti 1957a    C. Gallavotti. *Saffo e Alceo: Testimonianze e frammenti*, II. Naples, 1957².

Gallavotti 1957b    C. Gallavotti. "Ares e Areios prima di Omero." *Riv. filol. class.* 35 (1957): 225–33.

Gallavotti 1967     C. Gallavotti. "Tradizione micenea e poesia greca arcaica." In *Atti e mem. del I Congr. Internaz. di Micenologia*, II. Rome, 1967, pp. 831–61.

Gallavotti 1972     C. Gallavotti. "Le pernici di Alcmane." *Quad. Urb.* 14 (1972): 31–36.

Gallavotti 1977a    C. Gallavotti. "Un poemetto citarodico di Stesicoro nel quadro della cultura siceliota." *Boll. Class. Lincei*, n.s. 25 (1977): 1–30.

Gallavotti 1977b    C. Gallavotti. "L'iscrizione arcaica di Sicino e la metrica stesicorea." *Quad. Urb.* 25 (1977): 75–86.

Gallavotti 1979     C. Gallavotti. *Metri e ritmi nelle iscrizioni greche* (Suppl. Boll. Accad. Naz. Lincei). Rome, 1979.

Gallavotti–Pugliese    C. Gallavotti–G. Pugliese Carratelli. "Rilievi storici
Carratelli 1942     sulla nuova ode di Saffo." *Studi it. filol. class.* 18 (1942): 161–74.

Gallo 1974         I. Gallo. "L'epigramma biografico sui nove lirici greci e il 'canone' alessandrino." *Quad. Urb.* 17 (1974): 91–112.

Gangutia Elícegui 1972    E. Gangutia Elícegui. "Poesía griega 'de amigo' y poesia arábigo-española." *Emerita* 40 (1972): 329–96.

Garzya 1954        A. Garzya. *Alcmane: I frammenti*. Naples, 1954.

Gasparov 1978      B. M. Gasparov. "Ustnaja reč kak semiotičeskij ob'ekt [Oral Discourse as Semiotic Object]." In *Semantika nominacii i semiotika ustnoj reči* [The Semiotics of "Nominatio" and the Semiology of Oral Discourse]. *Učěnye zapiski Tartuskogo gosudarstvennogo universiteta*. Tartu, 1978, pp. 63–113.

Gasparri 1982      C. Gasparri. "Archiloco a Taso." *Quad. Urb.*, n.s. 11 [40] (1982): 33–41.

Gebhard 1926       W. Gebhard. *Die Pharmakoi in Ionien und die Sybakchoi in Athen*. Diss., Munich, 1926.

Gentili 1950       B. Gentili. *Metrica greca arcaica*. Messina and Florence, 1950.

Gentili 1958a      *Anacreonte*. Critical edition with introduction, translation, and a study of the papyrus fragments, by B. Gentili. Rome, 1958.

Gentili 1958b          B. Gentili. *Bacchilide: Studi.* Urbino, 1958.

Gentili 1958c          B. Gentili. "Anacreonte, fr. 47 D.²." *Maia* 10 (1958): 157–60.

Gentili 1961           B. Gentili. Review of *The Oxyrhynchus Papyri,* XXV, edited with translation and note by E. Lobel–E. G. Turner, with a contribution by R. P. Winnington-Ingram. London, 1959. *Gnomon* 33 (1961): 331–43.

Gentili 1964           B. Gentili. "Studi su Simonide, II: Simonide e Platone." *Maia* 16 (1964): 278–306.

Gentili 1965a          G. Perrotta–B. Gentili. *Polinnia: Poesia greca arcaica.* Messina and Florence, 1965².

Gentili 1965b          B. Gentili. "Mimnermo. Interventi di: F. Della Corte, V. De Marco, A. Garzya, A. Colonna, L. Alfonsi, B. Gentili." *Maia* 17 (1965): 366–87.

Gentili 1965c          B. Gentili. "Interpretazione di Archiloco fr. 2 D = 7 L.-B." *Riv. filol. class.* 93 (1965): 129–34.

Gentili 1965d          B. Gentili. "Aspetti del rapporto poeta, committente, uditorio nella lirica corale greca." *Studi Urb.* 39 [n.s. B1] (1965): 70–88.

Gentili 1966           B. Gentili. "Sul testo del fr. 287 P. di Ibico." *Quad. Urb.* 2 (1966): 124–27.

Gentili 1967a          B. Gentili. "Epigramma ed elegia." In *L'Épigramme grecque, Entr. Hardt,* XIV. Vandoeuvres-Geneva, 1967, pp. 37–90.

Gentili 1967b          B. Gentili. "Metodi di lettura (su alcune congetture ai poeti lirici)." *Quad. Urb.* 4 (1967): 177–81.

Gentili 1969a          B. Gentili, "L'interpretazione dei lirici greci arcaici nella dimensione del nostro tempo: Sincronia e diacronia nello studio di una cultura orale." *Quad. Urb.* 8 (1969): 7–21. Translated under the title "The Interpretation of Greek Lyric Poets in Our Time." In *Contemporary Literary Hermeneutics and Interpretation of Classical Texts,* ed. S. Kresic. Ottowa, 1981, pp. 109–20.

Gentili 1969b          B. Gentili. Review of V. Pisani, *Storia della lingua greca;* C. Del Grande, *La metrica greca, Enciclopedia classica,* II/5, Turin, 1960. *Gnomon* 41 (1969): 533–44.

Gentili 1970           B. Gentili. "La lancia di Archiloco e le figurazioni vascolari." In *Studia Florentina A. Ronconi sexagenario oblata.* Rome, 1970, pp. 115–20, plates 1 and 2.

Gentili 1971           B. Gentili. "I frr. 39 e 40 P. di Alcmane e la poetica delle mimesi nella cultura greca arcaica." In *Studi in onore di V. De Falco.* Naples, 1971, pp. 57–67.

Gentili 1972a      B. Gentili. "Il 'letto insaziato' di Medea e il tema dell''adikia' a livello amoroso nei lirici (Saffo, Teognide) e nella 'Medea' di Euripide." *Studi class. or.* 21 (1972): 60–72.

Gentili 1972b      B. Gentili. "Lirica greca arcaica e tardo arcaica." *Introduzione allo studio della cultura classica*, I. Milan, 1972, pp. 57–105.

Gentili 1973       B. Gentili. "La ragazza di Lesbo." *Quad. Urb.* 16 (1973): 124–28.

Gentili 1976a      B. Gentili. "Addendum (a G. Giangrande, 'On Anacreon's Poetry')." *Quad. Urb.* 21 (1976): 47.

Gentili 1976b      B. Gentili. "Nota ad Archiloco, P. Col. 7511; fr. 2 Tard., 2 West." *Quad. Urb.* 21 (1976): 17–21.

Gentili 1976c      B. Gentili. "Il 'Partenio' di Alcmane e l'amore omoerotico femminile nei tiasi spartani." *Quad. Urb.* 22 (1976): 59–67.

Gentili 1976d      B. Gentili. Review of *Poetae Melici Graeci*, ed. D. L. Page. Oxford, 1962; *Lyrica Graeca Selecta*, ed. D. L. Page. Oxford, 1968; *Supplementum Lyricis Graecis*, ed. D. L. Page. Oxford, 1974. *Gnomon* 48 (1976): 740–51.

Gentili 1977a      B. Gentili. *Lo spettacolo nel mondo antico.* Rome and Bari, 1977. Translated by the author as *Theatrical Performances in the Ancient World: Hellenistic and Early Roman Theatre.* Amsterdam, 1979.

Gentili 1977b      B. Gentili. "Preistoria e formazione dell'esametro." *Quad. Urb.* 26 (1977): 7–37.

Gentili 1979a      B. Gentili. "Trittico pindarico." *Quad. Urb.*, n.s. 2 [31] (1979): 7–33.

Gentili 1979b      B. Gentili. "Molossus + Bacchius in the New Stesichorus Fragment (P. Lille 76 abc)." *Gr. Rom. Byz. Stud.* 20 (1979): 127–31.

Gentili 1980       B. Gentili. "Cultura dell'improvviso: Poesia orale colta nel Settecento italiano e poesia greca dell'età arcaica e classica." *Quad. Urb.*, n.s. 6 [35] (1980): 17–59.

Gentili 1981a      B. Gentili. "Verità e accordo contrattuale (σύνθεσις) in Pindaro, fr. 205 Sn." *Ill. Class. Stud.* 6 (1981): 215–20.

Gentili 1981b      B. Gentili. "*La parola e il marmo:* Una discussione." *Dialoghi d'archeologia*, n.s. 2 (1981): 32–38; 94–108.

Gentili 1983       B. Gentili. "L'asinarteto nella teoria metrico ritmica degli antichi." In *Festschrift für R. Muth.* Innsbruck, 1983, pp. 135–43.

Gentili-Cerri 1983    B. Gentili–C. Cerri. *Storia e biografia nel pensiero antico.* Revised and enlarged version of 1975 edition. Rome and Bari, 1983.

Georgiev 1966    V. I. Georgiev. *Introduzione allo studio delle lingue indo-europee.* Rome, 1966.

Gerber 1963    D. E. Gerber. "Pindar, Nemean VII, 31." *Am. Journ. Philol.* 84 (1963): 182–88.

Gerber 1965    D. E. Gerber. "The Gifts of Aphrodite (Bacchylides 17, 10)." *Phoenix* 19 (1965): 212–13.

Gerber 1968    D. E. Gerber. " A Survey of Publications on Greek Lyric Poetry since 1952." *Class. World* 61 (1968): 265–79; 317–30; 373–85.

Gerber 1970    D. E. Gerber. *Euterpe: An Anthology of Early Greek Lyric Poetry.* Amsterdam, 1970.

Gerber 1976    D. E. Gerber. "Studies in Greek Lyric Poetry, 1967–1975." *Class. World* 70 (1976): 65–157.

Gerber 1981    D. E. Gerber. "Archilochus, fr. 4 West: A Commentary." *Ill. Class. Stud.* 6 (1981): 1–11.

Gerevini 1954    S. Gerevini. "L'Archiloco perduto e la tradizione critico-letteraria." *Parola d. passato* 9 (1954): 256–64.

Gerlach 1937    W. Gerlach. "Staat und Staatschiff." *Gymnasium* 2 (1937): 127–39.

Ghali-Kahil 1960    L. Ghali-Kahil. *La céramique grecque (Fouilles 1911–1956, Etudes Thasiennes, VII).* Paris, 1960.

G. Giangrande 1967    G. Giangrande. "Sympotic Literature and Epigram." In *L'Épigramme grecque. Entr. Hardt,* XIV. Vandoeuvres-Geneva, 1967, pp. 91–174.

G. Giangrande 1968    G. Giangrande. "Théocrite, Simichidas et les Thalysies." *Antiquité class.* 37 (1968): 491–533.

G. Giangrande 1971    G. Giangrande. "Interpretationen griechischer Meliker." *Rh. Mus.* 114 (1971): 97–131.

G. Giangrande 1973    G. Giangrande. "Anacreon and the Lesbian Girl." *Quad. Urb.* 16 (1973): 129–33.

G. Giangrande 1976    G. Giangrande. "On Anacreon's Poetry." *Quad. Urb.* 21 (1976): 43–46.

G. Giangrande 1977    G. Giangrande. "On Alcman's Partheneion." *Mus. Philol. Lond.* 2 (1977): 151–64.

G. Giangrande 1981    G. Giangrande. "Anacreon and the 'Fellatrix' from Lesbos." *Mus. Philol. Lond.* 4 (1981): 15–18.

L. Giangrande 1972    L. Giangrande. *The Use of Spoudaiogeloion in Greek and Roman Literature.* The Hague and Paris, 1972.

Gianni 1807-8    F. Gianni. *Raccolta delle poesie di F. Gianni.* Milan, 1807-8 (vol. V of Silvestri ed.).

| | |
|---|---|
| Giannini 1973 | P. Giannini. "Espressioni formulari nell'elegia greca arcaica." *Quad. Urb.* 16 (1973): 7–78. |
| Giannini 1977 | P. Giannini. "Preistoria e formazione dell'esametro." *Quad. Urb.* 26 (1977): 38–51. |
| Giannini 1979 | P. Giannini. "Interpretazione della 'Pitica' 4 di Pindaro." *Quad. Urb.*, n.s. 2 [31] (1979): 35–63. |
| Giannini 1982a | P. Giannini. "Senofane fr. 2 Gentili-Prato e la funzione dell'intellettuale nella Grecia arcaica." *Quad. Urb.*, n.s. 10 [39] (1982): 57–69. |
| Giannini 1982b | P. Giannini. "'Qualcuno' e 'nessuno' in Pind. 'Pyth.' 8, 95." *Quad. Urb.*, n.s. 11 [40] (1982): 69–76. |
| Gianotti 1973 | G. F. Gianotti. "Mito ed encomio: Il carme di Ibico in onore di Policrate." *Riv. filol. class.* 101 (1973): 401–10. |
| Gianotti 1975 | G. F. Gianotti. *Per una poetica pindarica.* Turin, 1975. |
| Gianotti 1978 | G. F. Gianotti. "Le Pleiadi di Alcmane (Alcm. fr. 1, 60–63 P.)." *Riv. filol. class.* 106 (1978): 257–71. |
| Gigante 1977 | M. Gigante. "Atakta II." *Cron. Ercol.* 7 (1977): 40–42. |
| Goody 1977 | J. Goody. "Mémoire et apprentissage dans les sociétés avec et sans écriture: La transmission du Bagre." *L'Homme* 17 (1977): 29–52. |
| Goody 1980 | J. Goody. "Les chemins du savoir oral." *Critique* 34 (1980): 189–96. |
| Gostoli 1978 | A. Gostoli. "Some Aspects of the Theban Myth in the Lille Stesichorus." *Gr. Rom. Byz. Stud.* 19 (1978): 23–27. |
| Gostoli 1979 | A. Gostoli. "Osservazioni metriche sull'encomio a Policrate di Ibico." *Quad. Urb.*, n.s. 2 [31] (1979): 93–99. |
| Gow 1952 | A. S. F. Gow. *Theocritus,* II. Cambridge, 1952². |
| Graham 1978 | A. J. Graham. "The Foundation of Thasos." *Ann. Brit. School at Athens* 73 (1978): 61–98. |
| Greifenhagen 1957 | A. Greifenhagen. *Griechische Eroten.* Berlin, 1957. |
| Greimas-Courtés 1979 | A. J. Greimas-J. Courtés. *Sémiotique: Dictionnaire raisonné de la théorie du language.* Paris, 1979. |
| A. Griffiths 1972 | A. Griffiths. "Alcman's 'Partheneion': The Morning after the Night Before." *Quad. Urb.* 14 (1972): 7–30. |
| F. T. Griffiths 1979 | F. T. Griffiths. *Theocritus at Court.* Lugduni Batavorum, 1979. |
| Grinbaum 1968 | W. S. Grinbaum. "Mikenskaja kojne i problema obrazovanija jazyka drevne-grečeskoi chorovoj liriki [The Mycenaean *Koine* and the Problem of |

the Formation of the Language of Early Greek Choral Lyric]." In *Atti e mem. del I Congr. Internaz. di Micenologia*, II. Rome, 1968, pp. 875–79.

Gronewald 1974     M. Gronewald. "Fragmente aus einem Sappho-kommentar: Pap. Colon. inv. 5860." *Zeitschr. f. Pap. u. Epigr.* 14 (1974): 114–18.

Groupe μ 1970     Groupe μ. *Rhétorique générale*. Paris, 1970. Translated by P. B. Burrell–E. M. Slotkin, under the title *A General Rhetoric*. Baltimore, 1981.

Grube 1965     G. M. A. Grube. *The Greek and Roman Critics*. London, 1965.

Guarducci 1927–29     M. Guarducci, "Poeti vaganti dell'età ellenistica." *Atti R. Accad. Lincei*. Cl. Sc. mor., s. 6, vol. 2, 1927–29, pp. 629–65.

Guarducci 1958     M. Guarducci. "Ancora sull'artista nell'antichità classica." *Archeol. class.* 10 (1958): 138–50.

Guarducci 1962     M. Guarducci. "Nuove osservazioni sull'artista nell'antichità classica." *Archeol. class.* 14 (1962): 237–39 = *Artisti e artigiani in Grecia*. Historical and critical survey, ed. F. Coarelli. Rome and Bari, 1980, pp. 75–101.

Guarducci 1967     M. Guarducci. *Epigrafia greca*, I. Rome, 1967.

Guarducci 1969     M. Guarducci. *Epigrafia greca*, II. Rome, 1969.

Guarducci 1978     M. Guarducci. *Epigrafia greca*, IV: *Epigrafi sacre, pagane e cristiane*. Rome, 1978.

Gzella 1969–70     S. Gzella. "The Competition among the Greek Choral Poets." *Eos* 58 (1969–70): 19–32.

Gzella 1971     S. Gzella. "Problem of the Fee in Greek Choral Lyric." *Eos* 59 (1971): 189–202.

Hamm 1958     E. M. Hamm. *Grammatik zu Sappho und Alkaios*. Berlin, 1958².

Hampe 1951     R. Hampe. "Die Stele aus Pharsalos im Louvre." *Berl. Winkelmannsprogr.* 107 (1951): plate 13.

Harrison 1912     J. E. Harrison. *Themis: A Study of the Social Origins of Greek Religion*. Cambridge, 1912.

Harvey 1955     A. E. Harvey. "The Classification of Greek Lyric Poetry." *Class. Quart.*, n.s. 5 [29] (1955): 157–75.

Haslam 1974     M. W. Haslam. "Stesichorean Metre." *Quad. Urb.* 17 (1974): 7–57.

Haslam 1978     M. W. Haslam. "The Versification of the New Stesi-chorus (P. Lille 76 abc)." *Gr. Rom. Byz. Stud.* 19 (1978): 29–57.

Hausrath 1890     A. Hausrath. "Philodemi περὶ ποιημάτων libri secundi quae videntur fragmenta." *Jahrb. f. klass. Philol.* Suppl. 17 (1890): 213–76.

Havelock 1963    E. A. Havelock. *Preface to Plato.* Oxford, 1963.

Havelock 1978a    *Communication Arts in the Ancient World,* ed. E. A. Havelock–J. P. Hershbell. New York, 1978, pp. 3–21.

Havelock 1978b    E. A. Havelock. *The Greek Concept of Justice.* Cambridge, Mass., 1978.

Havelock 1980    E. A. Havelock. "The Oral Composition of Greek Drama." *Quad. Urb.,* n.s. 6 [35] (1980): 61–113 = *The Literate Revolution in Greece and Its Cultural Consequences.* Princeton, 1982, pp. 261–313.

Havelock 1982    E. A. Havelock. *The Literate Revolution in Greece and Its Cultural Consequences.* Princeton, 1982.

Heitsch 1967    E. Heitsch. "Zum Sappho-Text." *Hermes* 95 (1967): 385–92.

Hemelrijk 1925    J. Hemelrijk. Πενία en πλοῦτος. Diss., Utrecht, 1925.

Hemmerdinger 1982    D. Hemmerdinger. "A propos d'un livre récent sur la musique grecque." *Quad. Urb.,* n.s. 12 [41] (1982): 145–63.

Henry 1971    A. Henry. *Métonymie et métaphore.* Paris, 1971.

Himmelmann 1979    N. Himmelmann. "Zur Entlohnung künstlerischer Tätigkeit in klassischen Bauinschriften." *Jahrb. Deutsch. archäol. Inst.* 94 (1979): 127–42 = *Artisti e artigiani in Grecia.* Historical and critical survey, ed. F. Coarelli. Rome and Bari, 1980, pp. 131–52.

Hoekstra 1957    A. Hoekstra. "Hésiode et la tradition orale: Contribution à l'étude du style formulaire." *Mnemosyne,* s. IV [10] (1957): 193–225.

Hoekstra 1962    A. Hoekstra. "The Absence of the Aeginetans: On the Interpretation of Pindar's Sixth Paean." *Mnemosyne,* s. IV [15] (1962): 1–14.

Holtzmann 1979    B. Holtzmann. "Des mines d'or à Thasos." *Bull. corresp. hell.* Suppl. V, *Thasiaca* (1979): 345–49.

Hooker 1979    J. T. Hooker. "The Unity of Alcman's Partheneion." *Rh. Mus.* 122, nos. 3–4 (1979): 211–21.

Housman 1908    A. E. Housman. "On the Paeans of Pindar (Grenfell and Hunt, 'Oxyrhynchus Papyri,' Part V, pp. 24–81)." *Class. Rev.* 22 (1908): 8–12.

How-Wells 1928    W. W. How–J. Wells. *A Commentary on Herodotus,* II. Oxford 1928².

Huchzermeyer 1931    H. Huchzermeyer. *Aulos und Kithara in der grie-*

*chischen Musik bis zum Ausgang der klassischen Zeit.*
Emsdetten, 1931.

Humphreys 1978     S. C. Humphreys. *Anthropology and the Greeks.*
London, 1978.

Huxley 1969     G. L. Huxley. *Greek Epic Poetry.* London, 1969.

Immerwahr 1964     H. R. Immerwahr. "Book Rolls on Attic Vases." In
*Class. Mediaev. Renaiss. Stud. in Honour of B. Ull-
man,* I. Rome, 1964, pp. 17–48.

Immerwahr 1965     H. R. Immerwahr. "Inscriptions on the Anakreon
Krater in Copenhagen." *Am. Journ. Archaeol.* 69
(1965): 152–54.

Innis 1950     H. Innis. *Empire and Communications.* Oxford,
1950, pp. 53–83.

Irigoin 1952     J. Irigoin. *Historie du texte de Pindare.* Paris, 1952.

Irigoin 1966     J. Irigoin. Review of R. D. Dawe, *The Collation and
Investigation of Manuscripts of Aeschylus. Rev. ét. anc.*
68 (1966): 135–38.

Irigoin 1977     J. Irigoin. "Quelques réflexions sur le concept
d'archétype." *Rev. hist. text.* 7 (1977): 235–45.

Irigoin 1978     J. Irigoin. "La pratique des ordinateurs dans la critique des textes." *Rev. hist. text.* 8 (1978): 337–40.

Irigoin 1979     J. Irigoin. "Table ronde sur les problèmes de sélec-
tion et d'utilisation des variantes. 1. Rapport de J.
Irigoin." In *La pratique des ordinateurs dans la critique des textes* (Colloque Intern. du Centre Nat. de
la Recherche Scient. n. 579, Paris, 29-31 March 1978).
Paris, 1979, pp. 265–71.

Irigoin 1980     J. Irigoin. Review of R. D. Dawe, *Studies on the Text
of Sophocles,* III: *Women of Trachis—Antigone—Phi-
loctetes—Oedipus at Colonus.* Leiden, 1978. *Gnomon*
52 (1980): 51–53.

Jacoby 1941     F. Jacoby. "The Date of Archilochos." *Class. Quart.*
35 (1941): 97–109 = *Kleine Philologische Schriften,* I.
Berlin, 1961, pp. 249–67.

Janni 1965     P. Janni. "ΣΩΤΕΙΡΑ e ΣΩΤΗΡ in Pindaro." *Studi
Urb.,* n.s. 39 [B 1] (1965): 104–9.

Janni 1976     P. Janni. "Euripide, 'Troiane' 281 sgg." *Quad. Urb.* 21
(1976): 97–102.

Jarcho 1968     V. N. Jarcho. "Zum Menschenbild der nachhome-
rischen Dichtung." *Philologus* 112 (1968): 147–72.

Jarcho 1982     V. N. Jarcho. "Novyi epod Archiloca [A New
Epode of Archilochus]." *Vestnik drevnej istorii* 153,
no. 1 (1982): 64–80.

Jauss 1967        H. R. Jauss. *Literaturgeschichte als Provokation der
                  Literaturwissenschaft.* Konstanz, 1967.
Jebb 1905         R. C. Jebb. *Bacchylides.* Cambridge, 1905 (1967).
Jeffery 1961      L. A. Jeffery. *The Local Scripts of Archaic Greece.*
                  Oxford, 1961.
Jeffery-Morpurgo  L. H. Jeffery-A. Morpurgo Davies. "Ποινικαστάς
Davies 1970       and ποινικάζειν: 'BM' 1969 4-2, 1, A New Archaic
                  Inscription from Crete." *Kadmos* 9 (1970): 118-54.
Jüthner 1936      J. Jüthner. "Zu Pyth. VIII, 96." *Wien. Stud.* 53 (1936):
                  142-43.
Kaibel 1898       G. Kaibel. *Die Prolegomena* περὶ κωμῳδίας. Ber-
                  lin, 1898 (*Abhandl. Gött. Gesellsch. Wiss.* Phil. hist.
                  Kl., N.F., II/4).
Kaletsch 1958     H. Kaletsch. "Zur lydischen Chronologie." *Historia*
                  7 (1958): 1-47.
Kamerbeek 1953    J. C. Kamerbeek. "Alcaica quaedam." *Mnemosyne,* s.
                  IV [6] (1953): 89-92.
Kassel 1973       R. Kassel. "Kritische und exegetische Kleinigkeit-
                  en," IV. *Rh. Mus.* 116 (1973): 97-112.
Kazik-Zawadzka 1958  I. Kazik-Zawadzka. *De Sapphicae Alcaicaeque elocu-
                  tionis colore epico.* Wroclaw, 1958.
Kirk 1962         G. S. Kirk. *The Songs of Homer.* Cambridge, 1962.
Kirk 1977         G. S. Kirk. "Methodological Reflexions on the
                  Myths of Heracles." In *Il mito greco.* Atti del Con-
                  vegno Internazionale (Urbino, 7-12 May 1973), ed.
                  B. Gentili-G. Paioni. Rome, 1977, pp. 285-97.
Kirkwood 1974     G. M. Kirkwood. *Early Greek Monody.* Ithaca, 1974.
Koenen 1974       L. Koenen. In "Ein wiedergefundenes Archilochos-
                  Gedicht?" *Poetica* 6 (1974): 468-512.
Kohlmeyer 1934    J. Kohlmeyer. *Seesturm und Schiffbruch als Bild im
                  antiken Schrifttum.* Diss., Greisswald, 1934.
Köhnken 1971      A. Köhnken. *Die Funktion des Mythos bei Pindar.*
                  Berlin and New York, 1971.
Koller 1954       H. Koller. *Die Mimesis in der Antike.* Bern, 1954.
Koller 1963       H. Koller. *Musik und Dichtung im alten Griechen-
                  land.* Bern and Munich, 1963.
Komornicka 1972   A. M. Komornicka. "Ἀλήθεια et ψεῦδος chez Pin-
                  dare." *Eos* 60 (1972): 235-53.
Komornicka 1976   A. M. Komornicka. "A la suite de la lecture 'La ra-
                  gazza di Lesbo.'" *Quad. Urb.* 21 (1976): 37-41.
Koniaris 1966     G. L. Koniaris. "Some Thoughts on Alcaeus Fr. D
                  15, X 14, X 16." *Hermes* 94 (1966): 385-97.
Kontoleon. 1963   N. M. Kontoleon, "Archilochos und Paros." In

| | *Archiloque, Entr. Hardt,* X. Vandoeuvres-Geneva, 1963, pp. 37–73. |
|---|---|
| Kontoleon 1965 | N. M. Kontoleon. "Ἀρχαικὴ ζῳφόρος ἐκ Πάρου." In *Charisterion Orlandos,* I. Athens, 1965, pp. 348–418. |
| Koster 1980 | S. Koster. *Die Invektive in der griechischen und römischen Literatur.* Meisenheim am Glan, 1980. |
| Kramer-Hagedorn 1978 | *Kölner Papyri,* VII, 2, ed. B. Kramer–D. Hagedorn. Opladen, 1978. |
| K. Kraus 1955 | K. Kraus. *Beim Wort genommen,* ed. H. Fischer. Munich, 1955. |
| W. Kraus 1955 | W. Kraus. "Die Auffassung des Dichterberufs im frühen Griechentum." *Wien. Stud.* 68 (1955): 65–87. |
| Kristeva 1969 | J. Kristeva. Σημειωτική: *Recherches pour une semanalyse.* Paris, 1969. |
| Kühner-Gerth 1904 | R. Kühner–B. Gerth. *Ausführliche Grammatik der griechischen Sprache.* Syntax II. Hanover, 1904³ (1966). |
| Kühner-Gerth 1955 | R. Kühner–B. Gerth. *Ausführliche Grammatik der griechischen Sprache.* Syntax I. Hanover, 1955⁴. |
| Labarbe 1968 | J. Labarbe. "Une épigramme sur les neuf lyriques grecs." *Antiquité class.* 37 (1968): 449–66. |
| Lacroix 1974 | L. Lacroix. "Héraclès héros voyageur et civilisateur." *Bull. Acad. Roy. Belgique,* s. V [60] (1974): 34–59. |
| Lanata 1963 | G. Lanata. *Poetica preplatonica: Testimonianze e frammenti.* Florence, 1963. |
| Lanata 1966 | G. Lanata. "Sul linguaggio amoroso di Saffo." *Quad. Urb.* 2 (1966): 63–79. |
| Lanata 1968 | G. Lanata. "Archiloco 69 D." *Quad. Urb.* 6 (1968): 33–35. |
| Lanza 1981 | D. Lanza. "Una scimmia piuttosto complicata." *Quad. d. storia* 13 (1981): 55–77. |
| Lanza 1983 | D. Lanza. "Aristotele e la poesia: Un problema di classificazione." *Quad. Urb.,* n.s. 13 [42] (1983): 51–66. |
| Lasserre 1946 | F. Lasserre. *La figure d'Eros dans la poésie grecque.* Lausanne, 1946. |
| Lasserre 1954 | F. Lasserre. *Plutarque: De la musique.* Olten-Lausanne, 1954. |
| Lasserre 1967 | F. Lasserre. "Mimésis et mimique." In *Atti del II Congresso di Studi sul dramma antico.* Rome and Syracuse, 1967, pp. 245–63. |
| Lasserre 1979 | F. Lasserre. "Archiloque frg. 2 West." *Graz. Beitr.* 8 (1979): 49–56. |

Lasso de la Vega 1977    J. S. Lasso de la Vega. "La séptima Nemea y la uni-
dad de la oda pindarica." *Estud. clas.* 21 (1977): 59–
139.

Latacz 1966    J. Latacz. *Zum Wortfeld "Freude" in der Sprache
Homers.* Heidelberg, 1966.

Latacz 1979    J. Latacz. "Tradition und Neuerung in der Homer-
forschung: Zur Geschichte der Oral poetry-Theor-
ie." In *Homer: Tradition und Neuerung,* ed. J.
Latacz. Darmstadt, 1979, pp. 25–44.

Latte 1946    K. Latte. "Hesiods Dichterweihe." *Antike u. Abend-
land* 2 (1946): 152–63.

Latte 1953    K. Latte. Review of H. Fränkel, *Dichtung und Phi-
losophie des frühen Griechentums.* New York, 1951.
*Gött. gel. Anz.* 207 (1953): 30–42 = *Kleine Schriften,*
Munich, 1968, pp. 713–26.

Lauter 1974    H. Lauter, "Zur gesellschaftliche Stellung des bil-
denden Künstlers in der griechischen Klassik."
*Erlang. Forsch., F. A.* 23 (1974): 5–25.

Lavagnini 1932    B. Lavagnini. *Nuova antologia dei frammenti della
lirica greca.* Turin, 1932.

Lavagnini 1950    B. Lavagnini. *Da Mimnermo a Callimaco.* Turin,
1950.

Lazzarini 1976    M. L. Lazzarini. *Le formule delle dediche votive
nella Grecia arcaica.* Rome, 1976.

Lee 1978    H. M. Lee. "The 'Historical' Bundy and Encomiastic Relevance in Pindar." *Class. World* 72 (1978):
65–70.

Lefkowitz 1969    M. R. Lefkowitz. "Bacchylides' Ode 5: Imitation
and Originality." *Harv. Stud. Class. Philol.* 73 (1969):
45–96.

Lefkowitz 1976    M. R. Lefkowitz. *The Victory Ode: An Introduction.*
Park Ridge, N.J., 1976.

Lefkowitz 1980    M. R. Lefkowitz. "Autobiographical Fiction in
Pindar." *Harv. Stud. Class. Philol.* 84 (1980): 29–49.

Le Goff 1979    J. Le Goff. In *Enciclopedia Einaudi,* VIII. Turin,
1979, pp. 1068–1109.

Lehnus 1981    *Pindaro: Olimpiche.* Translated, with notes, commentary, and critical essay, by L. Lehnus. Milan,
1981.

Lesky 1971    A. Lesky. *Geschichte der griechischen Literatur.* Bern,
1971³.

Lévêque 1982    P. Lévêque. "Ὄλβιος et la félicité des initiés."
*Rayonnement grec (Hommage à C. Delvoye)* 83 (1982):
113–26.

Lévi-Strauss 1962     C. Lévi-Strauss. *La pensée sauvage.* Paris, 1962. Translated under the title *The Savage Mind.* Chicago, 1966.

Lévi-Strauss 1966     C. Lévi-Strauss. *Du miel aux cendres.* Paris, 1966. Translated by John Weightman–Doreen Weightman, under the title *From Honey to Ashes.* New York, 1974.

Lévy-Bruhl 1910     L. Lévy-Bruhl. *Les fonctions mentales dans les sociétés inférieures.* Paris, 1910.

Lévy-Bruhl 1947     L. Lévy-Bruhl. "Les 'Carnets' de Lucien Lévy-Bruhl." *Rev. philos.* 137 (1947): 257–81.

Lloyd 1966     G. E. R. Lloyd. *Polarity and Analogy.* Cambridge, 1966.

Lloyd-Jones 1968     H. Lloyd-Jones. "The Cologne Fragment of Alcaeus." *Gr. Rom. Byz. Stud.* (1968): 125–39.

Lloyd-Jones 1972     H. Lloyd-Jones. "Pindar fr. 169." *Harv. Stud. Class. Philol.* 76 (1972): 45–56.

Lloyd-Jones 1973     H. Lloyd-Jones. "Modern Interpretation of Pindar: The Second Pythian and Seventh Nemean Odes." *Journ. Hell. Stud.* 93 (1973): 109–37.

Lobel 1951     E. Lobel. *The Oxyrhynchus Papyri,* XXI. London, 1951.

Longo 1978     O. Longo. "Scrivere in Tucidide: Comunicazione e ideologia." In *Studi in onore di A. Ardizzoni,* I, ed. E. Livrea–G. A. Privitera. Rome, 1978, pp. 519–54.

Longo 1980     O. Longo. "Per la definizione di una figura d'intellettuale nell'antica Atene." In *Il comportamento dell'intellettuale nella società antica.* Genoa, 1980, pp. 9–32.

Loraux 1981     N. Loraux. *L'invention d'Athènes.* Paris, 1981. Translated by A. Sheridan, under the title *The Invention of Athens.* Cambridge, Mass., 1986.

Lord 1960     A. B. Lord. *The Singer of Tales.* Cambridge, Mass., 1960.

Lord 1985     A. B. Lord. "Memory, Meaning and Myth in Homer and Oral Epic Tradition." In *Oralità: Cultura, Letteratura, discorso.* Atti del Convegno Internazionale (Urbino, 21–25 July 1980), ed. B. Gentili–G. Paioni. Rome, 1985, pp. 37–63.

Lotman 1978     J. M. Lotman. "Ustnaja reč v istoriko-kul'turnoj perspektive." In *Semantika nominacii i semiotika ustnoj reči [The Semantics of "Nominatio" and the Semantics of Oral Discourse], Učënye zapiski Tartuskogo gosudarstvennogo universiteta.* Tartu, 1978, pp.

113–21 [Ital. trans., "La lingua orale nella prospettiva storico-culturale." *Quad. Urb.*, n.s. 6 {35} (1980): 7–16].

Luck 1961  G. Luck. *Die römische Liebeselegie.* Heidelberg, 1961.

Luppe 1980  W. Luppe. "Literarische Texte unter Ausschluss der christlichen Drama." *Archiv. f. Papyrusforsch.* 27 (1980): 233–50.

McLennan 1977  *Callimachus: Hymn to Zeus.* Introduction and commentary by G. R. McLennan. Rome, 1977.

McLuhan 1962  M. McLuhan. *The Gutenberg Galaxy: The Making of Typographic Man.* Toronto, 1962.

Maddoli 1977  G. Maddoli. Introduction to *La civiltà micenea.* Historical and critical survey, ed. G. Maddoli. Rome and Bari, 1977, pp. v–xxxv.

Maehler 1963  H. Maehler. *Die Auffassung des Dichterberufs im frühen Griechentum bis zum Zeit Pindars.* Göttingen, 1963.

Manieri 1972  F. Manieri. "Saffo: Appunti di metodologia generale per un approccio psichiatrico." *Quad. Urb.* 14 (1972): 46–64.

Marazzi-Tusa 1976  M. Marazzi–S. Tusa. "Nuove testimonianze micenee nell'isola di Vivara." *Parola d. passato* 31 (1976): 472–85.

Martin 1972  H. Martin. *Alcaeus.* New York, 1972.

Martina 1968  *Solone.* Literary and biographical testimonia, ed. A. Martina. Rome, 1968.

Marzullo 1958  B. Marzullo. *Studi di poesia eolica.* Florence, 1958.

Marzullo 1964  B. Marzullo. "Il primo Partenio di Alcmane." *Philologus* 108 (1964): 174–210.

Marzullo 1975  B. Marzullo. "Lo smarrimento di Alceo (fr. 208 V.)." *Philologus* 191 (1975): 27–38.

Masaracchia 1958  A. Masaracchia. *Solone.* Florence, 1958.

Massenzio 1985  M. Massenzio. "Il poeta che vola: Conoscenza estatica, comunicazione orale e linguaggio dei sentimenti nello 'Ione' di Platone." In *Oralità: Cultura, letteratura, discorso.* Atti del Convegno Internazionale (Urbino, 21–25 July 1980), ed. B. Gentili–G. Paioni. Rome, 1985, pp. 161–74.

Mattioli 1965  E. Mattioli. "Introduzione al problema del tradurre." *Il Verri* 19 (1965): 107–28 = *Studi di poetica e di retorica.* Modena, 1983, pp. 135–63.

Mazzarino 1943  S. Mazzarino. "Per la storia di Lesbo nel VI secolo a. C. (A proposito dei nuovi frammenti di Saffo e Alceo)." *Athenaeum* 21 (1943): 38–78.

Mazzarino 1966 — S. Mazzarino. *Il pensiero storico classico,* I. Bari, 1966.

Meillier 1977a — C. Meillier. "P. Lille 73 (et P. Lille 76a et c)." *Zeitschr. f. Pap. u. Epigr.* 26 (1977): 1–5.

Meillier 1977b — C. Meillier. "Quelques conjectures à Stésichore." *Zeitschr. f. Pap. u. Epigr.* 27 (1977): 65–67.

Meillier 1978a — C. Meillier. "Stésichore, P. L. 76a (+ 'P. L.' 73): Quelques conjectures possibles." *Studi class. or.* 28 (1978): 35–47.

Meillier 1978b — C. Meillier. "La succession d'Oedipe d'après le P. Lill. 76a + 73, poème lyrique probablement de Stésichore." *Rev. ét. gr.* 91 (1978): 12–43.

Meillier 1979 — C. Meillier. *Callimaque et son temps.* Lille, 1979.

Mele 1979 — A. Mele. *Il commercio greco arcaico: Prexis ed emporie (Cahiers du Centre Jean Bérard, IV).* Naples, 1979.

Mendel 1912–14 — G. Mendel. *Catalogue des sculptures grecques, romaines et byzantines,* II. Constantinople, 1912–14 (Rome, 1966).

Merkelbach 1956 — R. Merkelbach. "Griechische literarischen Papyri." *Archiv. f. Papyrusforsch.* 16 (1956): 82–129.

Merkelbach 1957 — R. Merkelbach. "Sappho und ihr Kreis." *Philologus* 101 (1957): 1–29.

Merkelbach-West 1974 — R. Merkelbach–M. L. West. "Ein Archilochos-Papyrus." *Zeitschr. f. Pap. u. Epigr.* 14 (1974): 97–112.

Mette 1963 — H. J. Mette. *Der verlorene Aischylos.* Berlin, 1963.

Miller 1981 — M. M. Miller. "Pindar, Archilochus and Hieron in P. 2. 52–56." *Trans. Am. Philol. Assoc.* 111 (1981): 135–43.

Miralles 1981 — C. Miralles. "L'iscrizione di Mnesiepes (Arch. Test. 4 Tarditi)." *Quad. Urb,* n.s. 9 [38] (1981): 29–46.

Miralles-Pòrtulas 1983 — C. Miralles–J. Pòrtulas. *Archilochus and the Iambic Poetry.* Rome, 1983.

Monteverdi 1954 — A. Monteverdi. *Studi e saggi sulla letteratura italiana dei primi secoli.* Milan and Naples, 1954.

Mora 1966 — E. Mora. *Sappho.* Paris, 1966.

Moretti 1957 — L. Moretti. *Olympionikai, i vincitori negli antichi agoni olimpici.* Rome, 1957.

Morpurgo-Tagliabue 1967 — G. Morpugo-Tagliabue. *Linguistica e stilistica di Aristotele.* Rome, 1967.

Mossé 1962 — C. Mossé. *La fin de la démocratie athénienne.* Paris, 1962.

Moulinier 1952 — L. Moulinier. *Le pur et l'impur dans la pensée des Grecs d'Homère à Aristote.* Paris, 1952.

Müller 1908

G. Müller. *De Aeschyli Supplicum tempore atque indole*. Diss., Halle, 1908.

Mureddu 1983

P. Mureddu. *Formule e tradizione nella poesia di Esiodo.* Rome, 1983.

Musso 1969

O. Musso. "Due note papirologiche." *Aegyptus* 49 (1969): 72–74.

Musti 1977

D. Musti. "Problemi della storia di Locri Epizefirii." In *Atti del XVI Convegno di Studi sulla Magna Grecia* (Taranto, 3–8 October 1976). Naples, 1977, pp. 23–146.

Musti 1980–81

D. Musti. "Χρήματα nel fr. 90 D.-K. di Eraclito: Merci o monete?" *Annali Ist. It. Numismatica (*1980–81): 9–22.

Musti 1981

D. Musti. *L'economia in Grecia*. Rome and Bari, 1981.

Muth 1966

R. Muth. "Randbemerkungen zur griechischen Literaturgeschichte. Zur Bedeutung von Mündlichkeit und Schriftlichkeit der Wortkunst." *Wien. Stud.* 79 (1966): 246–60.

Nagler 1974

M. N. Nagler. *Spontaneity and Tradition: A Study in the Oral Art of Homer.* Berkeley and Los Angeles, 1974.

Nagy 1976

G. Nagy. "'Iambos': Typologies of Invective and Praise." *Arethusa* 9 (1976): 191–205.

Nagy 1979

G. Nagy. *The Best of the Achaeans: Concepts of the Hero in Archaic Greek Poetry.* Baltimore, 1979.

Nagy 1982

G. Nagy. "Theognis of Megara: The Poet as Seer, Pilot, and Revenant." *Arethusa (American Classical Studies in Honour of J.-P. Vernant)* 15 (1982): 109–28.

Nannini 1982

S. Nannini. "Lirica greca arcaica e 'recusatio' augustea." *Quad. Urb.,* n.s. 10 [39] (1982): 71–78.

Nicosia 1976

S. Nicosia. *Tradizione testuale diretta e indiretta dei poeti di Lesbo.* Rome, 1976.

Nida 1964

E. Nida. "Linguistics and Ethnology in Translation-Problems." In *Languages in Culture and Society: A Reader in Linguistics and Anthropology,* ed. D. Hymes. New York, 1964, pp. 90–100.

Nisetich 1977

F. J. Nisetich. "Convention and Occasion in 'Isthmian' 2." *Calif. Stud. Class. Ant.* 10 (1977): 133–56.

Notopoulos 1949

J. A. Notopoulos. "Parataxis in Homer: A New Approach to Homeric Literary Criticism." *Trans. Am. Philol. Assoc.* 80 (1949): 1–23.

Notopoulos 1966

J. A. Notopoulos. "Archilochus, the Aoidos." *Trans. Am. Philol. Assoc.* 97 (1966): 311–15.

| | |
|---|---|
| Ong 1967 | W. J. Ong. *The Presence of the Word.* New Haven, 1967. |
| Ortega 1970 | A. Ortega. "Poesía y verdad en Píndaro." *Helmantica* 21 (1970): 353-72. |
| Ostwald 1965 | M. Ostwald. "Pindar: Nomos and Heracles (Pindar, frg. 169 [Snell²] + P. Oxy. No. 2450, frg. 1)." *Harv. Stud. Class. Philol.* 69 (1965): 109-38. |
| Ostwald 1969 | M. Ostwald. *Nomos and the Beginnings of the Athenian Democracy.* Oxford, 1969. |
| Paduano 1968 | G. Paduano. *La formazione del mondo ideologico e poetico di Euripide.* Pisa, 1968. |
| Page 1936 | D. L. Page. "The Elegiacs in Euripides' Andromache." In *Greek Poetry and Life: Essays Presented to G. Murray.* Oxford, 1936, pp. 393-421. |
| Page 1951 | D. L. Page. *Alcman: The Partheneion.* Oxford, 1951. |
| Page 1952 | D. L. Page. *Euripides: Medea.* Oxford, 1952. |
| Page 1955 | D. L. Page. *Sappho and Alcaeus: An Introduction to the Study of Ancient Lesbian Poetry.* Oxford, 1955. |
| Page 1963 | D. L. Page. "Archilochus and the Oral Tradition." In *Archiloque, Entr. Hardt,* X. Vandoeuvres-Geneva, 1963, pp. 117-64. |
| Page 1973 | D. L. Page. "Stesichorus: The Geryoneïs." *Journ. Hell. Stud.* 93 (1973): 138-54. |
| Pagliaro 1953 | A. Pagliaro. *Saggi di critica semantica.* Messina and Florence, 1953. |
| Papaspyridi-Karouzou 1942-43 | S. Papaspyridi-Karouzou. "Anacréon à Athènes." *Bull. corresp. hell.* 66-67 (1942-43): 248-54. |
| Paribeni 1979 | E. Paribeni. "Artisti e artigiani nella Pentecontaetia." In *Storia e civiltà dei Greci,* II/4. Milan, 1979, pp. 501-15. |
| Parry 1965 | H. Parry. "An Interpretation of Simonides 4 (Diehl)." *Trans. Am. Philol. Assoc.* 96 (1965): 297-320. |
| Parsons 1977 | P. J. Parsons. "The Lille 'Stesichorus.'" *Zeitschr. f. Pap. u. Epigr.* 26 (1977): 7-37. |
| Pasquali 1935 | G. Pasquali. *Pagine meno stravaganti.* Florence, 1935 = *Pagine stravaganti,* I. Florence, 1968. |
| Pasquali 1964 | G. Pasquali. *Filologia e storia.* Florence, 1964² (with preface by A. Ronconi). |
| C. Pavese 1962 | C. Pavese. "Il mestiere di poeta." In *Poesie edite e inedite,* ed. I. Calvino. Turin, 1962. |
| C. O. Pavese 1966 | C. O. Pavese. "Χρήματα, χρήματ' ἀνήρ ed il motivo della liberalità nella seconda 'Istmica' di Pindaro." *Quad. Urb.* 2 (1966): 103-12. |

C. O. Pavese 1967a  C. O. Pavese. "La lingua della poesia corale come lingua d'una tradizione poetica settentrionale." *Glotta* 45 (1967): 164–85.

C. O. Pavese 1967b  C. O. Pavese. "Alcmane, il 'Partenio' del Louvre." *Quad. Urb.* 4 (1967): 113–33.

C. O. Pavese 1968  C. O. Pavese. "Semantematica dell poesia corale greca." *Belfagor* 23 (1968): 389–430.

C. O. Pavese 1972  C. O. Pavese. *Tradizione e generi poetici della Grecia arcaica.* Rome, 1972.

C. O. Pavese 1974  C. O. Pavese. *Studi sulla tradizione epica rapsodica.* Rome, 1974.

C. O. Pavese 1978  C. O. Pavese. "La settima 'Nemea' di Pindaro: A Sogenes di Aigina, nel pentathlon dei ragazzi." In *Studi in onore di A. Ardizzoni,* II, ed. E. Livrea– G. A. Privitera. Rome, 1978, pp. 661–88.

Peek 1955  W. Peek. *Griechische Vers-Inschriften,* I. Berlin, 1955.

Peek 1960  W. Peek. "Das neue Alkman Parthenion." *Philologus* 104 (1960): 163–80.

Pellizer 1978  E. Pellizer. "'...E il bello e il turpe distingue': Simonide, fr. 36 P. M. G. 541." *Quad. Urb.* 28 (1978): 87–91.

Pellizer 1981a  E. Pellizer. "Simonide κίμβιξ e un nuovo trimetro di Semonide Amorgino." *Quad. Urb.,* n.s. 9 [38] (1981): 47–51.

Pellizer 1981b  E. Pellizer. "Per una morfologia della poesia giambica arcaica." In *I canoni letterari: Storia e dinamica.* Trieste, 1981, pp. 35–48.

Péron 1974a  J. Péron. "Pindare et Hiéron dans la II^e Pythique (vv. 56 et 72)." *Rev. ét. gr.* 87 (1974): 1–32.

Péron 1974b  J. Péron. *Les images maritimes de Pindare.* Paris, 1974.

Péron 1976–77  J. Péron. "Le thème du φθόνος dans la XI^e Pythique de Pindare (v. 29–30, v. 55–56)." *Rev. ét. anc.* 78–79 (1976–77): 65–83.

Perrotta 1935  G. Perrotta. *Saffo e Pindaro.* Bari, 1935.

Pfeiffer 1949  R. Pfeiffer. *Callimachus,* I. Oxford, 1949 (1965).

Pfeiffer 1968  R. Pfeiffer. *History of Classical Scholarship from the Beginnings to the End of the Hellenistic Age.* Oxford, 1968.

Pfohl 1967  G. Pfohl. *Greek Poems on Stones,* I: *Epitaphs from the Seventh to the Fifth Centuries B.C.* Leiden, 1967.

Philipp 1968  H. Philipp. *Tektonon Daidala.* Berlin, 1968.

Piccirilli 1977  *Plutarco: La vita di Solone,* ed. M. Manfredini–L. Piccirilli. Milan, 1977.

Pickard-Cambridge 1962    A. Pickard-Cambridge. *Dithyramb, Tragedy and Comedy.* Oxford, 1962².

Pickard-Cambridge 1968    A. Pickard-Cambridge. *The Dramatic Festivals of Athens.* Oxford, 1968².

Pöhlmann 1960    E. Pöhlmann. *Griechischen Musikfragmente.* Nuremberg, 1960.

Pöhlmann 1970    E. Pöhlmann. *Denkmäler altgriechischer Musik.* Nuremberg, 1970.

Pöhlmann 1976    E. Pöhlmann. "Die Notenschriften in der Uberlieferung der griechischen Bühnenmusik." *Würzb. Jahrbb. f. d. Altertumswiss.,* N. F. 2 (1976): 53–73.

Pontani 1969    F. M. Pontani. *I lirici greci.* Turin, 1969.

Pòrtulas 1982    J. Pòrtulas. "Archilochus fr. 213 West = 21 Tarditi." *Quad. Urb.,* n.s. 11 [40] (1982): 29–32.

Pouilloux 1954    J. Pouilloux. *Recherches sur l'histoire et les cultes de Thasos,* I: *De la fondation de la cité a 196 avant J. C.* (*Etudes Thasiennes* III). Paris, 1954.

Pouilloux 1963    J. Pouilloux. "Archiloque et Thasos: Histoire et poésie." In *Archiloque, Entr. Hardt,* X. Vandoeuvres-Geneva, 1963, pp. 3–27.

Pouilloux 1982    J. Pouilloux. "La fondation de Thasos: Archéologie, littérature et critique littéraire." *Rayonnement grec* (Hommage à C. Delvoye) 83 (1982): 91–101.

Pound 1952    E. Pound. *The Spirit of Romance.* London, 1952.

Prato 1968    *Tirteo.* Critical edition with introduction, testimonia, and commentary, by C. Prato. Rome, 1968.

Prato 1978    C. Prato, "L'oralità della versificazione euripidea." In *Problemi di metrica classica.* Genoa, 1978, pp. 77–99.

Pretagostini 1977    R. Pretagostini. "Sticometria del 'Pap. Lille' 76a, b, c (Il nuovo Stesicoro)." *Quad. Urb.* 26 (1977): 53–58.

Pretagostini 1980    R. Pretagostini. "Considerazioni sui cosiddetti 'metra ex iambis orta' in Simonide, Pindaro e Bacchilide." *Quad. Urb.,* n.s. 6 [35] (1980): 127–36.

Pretagostini 1982a    R. Pretagostini. "Anacr. 33 Gent. = 356 P.: Due modalità simposiali a confronto." *Quad. Urb.,* n.s. 10 [39] (1982): 47–55.

Pretagostini 1982b    R. Pretagostini. "Archiloco 'salsa di Taso' negli 'Archilochi' di Cratino (fr. 6 K.)." *Quad. Urb.,* n.s. 11 [40] (1982): 43–52.

Prier 1976    R. A. Prier. *Archaic Logic: Symbol and Structure in Heraclitus, Parmenides and Empedocles.* The Hague and Paris, 1976.

Privitera 1965    G. A. Privitera. *Laso di Ermione.* Rome, 1965.

| | |
|---|---|
| Privitera 1967 | G. A. Privitera. "La rete di Afrodite: Ricerche sulla prima ode di Saffo." *Quad. Urb.* 4 (1967): 7-58. |
| Privitera 1969 | G. A. Privitera. "Il commento del περὶ ὕψους al fr. 31 L. P. di Saffo." *Quad. Urb.* 7 (1969): 26-35. |
| Privitera 1970 | G. A. Privitera. *Dioniso in Omero.* Rome, 1970. |
| Privitera 1972a | G. A. Privitera. "Il ditirambo da canto cultuale a spettacolo musicale." *Cultura e scuola* 43 (1972): 55-56. Reprinted, in abridged form, in *Rito e poesia corale in Grecia.* Historical and critical survey, ed. C. Calame. Rome and Bari, 1977, pp. 27-37. |
| Privitera 1972b | G. A. Privitera. "Saffo, Anacreonte, Pindaro." *Quad. Urb.* 13 (1972): 131-40. |
| Privitera 1982 | *Pindaro: Le Istmiche,* ed. G. A. Privitera. Milan, 1982. |
| Pucci 1977 | P. Pucci. *Hesiod and the Language of Poetry.* Baltimore, 1977. |
| Pucci 1980 | P. Pucci. *The Violence of Pity in Euripides' Medea.* Ithaca, 1980. |
| Puech 1961a | *Pindare,* II: *Pythiques,* ed. and trans. A. Puech. Paris, 1961[4]. |
| Puech 1961b | *Pindare,* IV: *Isthmiques et Fragments,* ed. and trans. A. Puech. Paris, 1961[3]. |
| Puelma 1977 | M. Puelma. "Die Selbstbeschreibung des Chores in Alkmans grossen Partheneion-Fragment." *Mus. Helv.* 34 (1977): 1-55. |
| Pugliese Carratelli 1976 | G. Pugliese Carratelli. "Cadmo: Prima e dopo." *Parola d. passato* 31 (1976): 5-16. |
| Quaglio 1970 | A. E. Quaglio. *La letteratura italiana: Storia e testi,* I/1 (*Il Duecento*). Bari, 1970. |
| Quasha 1977 | G. Quasha. "Dialogos: Between the Written and Oral in Contemporary Poetry." *New Literary History* 8 (1977): 485-506. |
| Quentin 1926 | H. Quentin. *Essais de critique textuelle (Ecdotique).* Paris, 1926. |
| Radt 1958 | S. L. Radt. *Pindars Zweiter und Sechter Paian.* Amsterdam, 1958. |
| Rankin 1977a | H. D. Rankin. *Archilochus of Paros.* Park Ridge, N. J., 1977. |
| Rankin 1977b | H. D. Rankin. "Archilochus' Chronology and Some Possible Events of His Life." *Eos* 65 (1977): 5-15. |
| Reitzenstein 1893 | R. Reitzenstein. *Epigramm und Skolion.* Giessen, 1893. |

Reitzenstein 1907    R. Reitzenstein. *R. E.*, VI/1 (1907), cols. 75ff., s.v. "Epigramma."

Richards 1936    I. A. Richards. *The Philosophy of Rhetoric.* Oxford, 1936.

Risch 1946    E. Risch. "Sprachliche Bemerkungen zu Alkaios." *Mus. Helv.* 3 (1946): 253–56.

Ritoók 1962    Zs. Ritoók, "Rhapsodos." *Act. Ant. Acad. Scient. Hung.* 10, nos. 1–3 (1962): 225–31.

Rivier 1967    A. Rivier. "Observations sur Sappho 1, 19 sq." *Rev. ét. gr.* 80 (1967): 84–92 = *Etudes de littérature grecque.* Geneva, 1975, pp. 235–42.

Robert 1898    C. Robert. "Theseus und Meleagros bei Bakchylides." *Hermes* 33 (1898): 130–59.

Robertson 1969    M. Robertson. "'Geryoneis': Stesichorus and the Vase-Painters." *Class. Quart.* 19 (1969): 207–21.

Rochette 1817    R. Rochette. "De l'improvisation poétique chez les Anciens et particulièrement chez les Grecs et les Romains." *Class. Journ.* 15 (1817): 249–57.

Rochette 1818    R. Rochette. "De l'improvisation poétique chez les Anciens et particulièrement chez les Grecs et les Romains." *Class. Journ.* 16 (1818): 96–109; 357–71.

Roehl 1882    H. Roehl. *Inscriptiones Graecae antiquissimae praeter Atticas in Attica repertae.* Berlin, 1882 (Chicago, 1978).

Rolley 1965    C. Rolley. "Le sanctuaire des dieux patrôoi et le Thesmophorion de Thasos." *Bull. corresp. hell.* 89 (1965): 441–83.

Roloff 1952–53    K.-H. Roloff. "Caerimonia." *Glotta* 32 (1952–53): 101–38.

Römer 1924    R. Römer. *Die Homerexegese Aristarchs in ihren Grundzügen.* Paderborn, 1924.

Rose 1974    P. W. Rose. "The Myth of Pindar's First Nemean: Sportsmen, Poetry and Paideia." *Harv. Stud. Class. Philol.* 78 (1974): 145–75.

Rosenmeyer 1968    T. G. Rosenmeyer. "Elegiac and Elegos." *Calif. Stud. Class. Ant.* 1 (1968): 217–31.

Rösler 1975    W. Rösler. "Ein Gedicht und sein Publikum: Uberlegungen zu Sappho Fr. 44 Lobel-Page." *Hermes* 103 (1975): 275–85.

Rösler 1976    W. Rösler. "Die Dichtung des Archilochos und die neue Kölner Epode." *Rh. Mus.* 119 (1976): 289–310.

Rösler 1980    W. Rösler. *Dichter und Gruppe.* Munich, 1980.

Rossi 1971    L. E. Rossi. "I generi letterari e le loro leggi scritte e non scritte nelle letterature classiche." *Bull. Inst. Class. Stud.* 18 (1971): 69–94.

Rossi 1973 · · · L. E. Rossi. "Rileggendo due opere di Wilamowitz, 'Pindaros' e 'Griechische Verskunst.'" *Ann. Scuola Norm. Pisa* 3 (1973): 119–45.

Rossi 1981 · · · L. E. Rossi. "La parola e il marmo: Una discussione." *Dialoghi d'archeologia*, n.s. 2 (1981): 39–42.

Rossi 1983 · · · L. E. Rossi. "Feste religiose e letteratura: Stesicoro o dell'epica alternativa." *Orpheus* 1 (1983): 5–31.

Rostagni 1927 · · · A. Rostagni. "Poesia ed estetica classica." *Riv. filol. class.* 55 (1927): 1–23.

Rubensohn 1949 · · · P. Rubensohn. *R. E.*, XVIII/4 (1949), cols. 1781–1872, s.v. "Paros."

Rudhardt 1958 · · · J. Rudhardt. *Notions fondamentales de la pensée religieuse et actes constitutifs du culte dans la Grèce classique*. Geneva, 1958.

Ruijgh 1967 · · · C. J. Ruijgh, *Etudes sur la grammaire et le vocabulaire du grec mycénien*. Amsterdam, 1967.

J. Russo 1971 · · · J. Russo. "The Meaning of Oral Poetry. The Collected Papers of Milman Parry: A Critical Reassessment." *Quad. Urb.* 12 (1971): 27–39.

J. Russo 1974 · · · J. Russo. "The Inner Man in Archilochus and the Odyssey." *Gr. Rom. Byz. Stud.* 15 (1974): 139–52.

J. Russo-Simon 1968 · · · J. Russo–B. Simon. "Homeric Psychology and the Oral Epic Tradition." *Journ. Hist. Ideas* 29 (1968): 483–98; rev. and enl. in B. Simon, *Mind and Madness in Ancient Greece*. Ithaca, 1978, pp. 53–88.

Saake 1971 · · · H. Saake. *Zur Kunst Sapphos*. Munich, Paderborn, and Vienna, 1971.

Sambursky 1956 · · · S. Sambursky. *The Physical World of the Greeks*. London, 1956.

Sandbach 1942 · · · F. H. Sandbach. "Άκρα Γυρέων Once More." *Class. Rev.* 36 (1942): 63–65.

Schadewaldt 1936 · · · W. Schadewaldt. "Zu Sappho." *Hermes* 71 (1936): 363–73.

Schadewaldt 1950 · · · W. Schadewaldt. *Sappho*, I. Darmstadt, 1950.

Schaerer 1938 · · · R. Schaerer. *La question platonicienne*. Neuchâtel, 1938.

Schlegel 1798 · · · F. Schlegel. *Geschichte der Poesie der Griechen und Römer*. Berlin, 1798.

Wilhelm Schmid 1929 · · · W. Schmid. *Geschichte der griechischen Literatur*, I/1. Munich, 1929.

Wolfgang Schmid 1969 · · · W. Schmid. *Wesen und Rang der Philologie, Zum*

*Gedenken an H. Usener und F. Bücheler.* Stuttgart, 1969.

Schmidt 1854 — M. Schmidt. *Didymi fragmenta.* Leipzig, 1854.

Schneidewin 1833 — F. G. Schneidewin. *Ibyci Rhegini Carminum Reliquiae.* Göttingen, 1833.

Schober 1934 — F. Schober. *R. E.,* V A 2 (1934), cols. 1423–1553, s.v. "Thebai-Boiotien."

Schroeder 1922 — O. Schroeder. *Pindars Pythien.* Leipzig and Berlin, 1922.

Schweitzer 1963 — B. Schweitzer. "Der bildende Künstler und der Begriff des Künstlerischen in der Antike." In *Ausgewählte Schriften,* I. Tübingen, 1963, pp. 18–40.

Schwyzer 1930 — E. Schwyzer. "Axt und Hammer: Zu Anakreon fr. 47 Bergk (45 Diehl)." *Rh. Mus.* 79 (1930): 314–18.

Sebeok 1964 — T. A. Sebeok. "Decoding a Text: Levels and Aspects in a Cheremis Sonnet." In *Style in Language,* ed. T. A. Sebeok. Cambridge, Mass., 1964², pp. 221–35.

Seel 1953 — O. Seel. "Zur Vorgeschichte des Gewissensbegriffes im altgriechischen Denken." In *Festschr. Dornseiff.* Leipzig, 1953, pp. 312ff.

Segal 1971 — C. Segal. "Croesus on the Pyre: Herodotus and Bacchylides." *Wien. Stud.* 84 (1971): 39–51.

Segal 1974 — C. Segal. "Eros and Incantation: Sappho and Oral Poetry." *Arethusa* 7 (1974): 139–60.

Segal 1976a — C. Segal. "Pindar, Mimnermus and the 'Zeus-given Gleam': The End of 'Pythian' 8." *Quad. Urb.* 22 (1976): 71–76.

Segal 1976b — C. Segal. "Bacchylides Reconsidered: Epithets and the Dynamics of Lyric Narrative." *Quad. Urb.* 22 (1976): 99–130.

Segal 1979 — C. Segal. "The Myth of Bacchylides 17: Heroic Quest and Heroic Identity." *Eranos* 77 (1979): 23–37.

Segal 1982 — C. Segal, "Tragédie, oralité, écriture." *Poétique* 50 (1982): 131–54 = *Oralità: cultura, letteratura, discorso.* Atti del Convegno Internazionale (Urbino, 20–25 July 1980), ed. B. Gentili-G. Paioni. Rome, 1985, pp. 199–226.

Segre 1979 — C. Segre. *Semiotica filologica: Testi e modelli culturali.* Turin, 1979.

Serrao 1968 — G. Serrao. "L'ode di Erotima: Da timida fanciulla a donna pubblica (Anacr. fr. 346, 1 P. = 60 Gent.)." *Quad. Urb.* 6 (1968): 36–51.

Serrao 1977 — G. Serrao. "Antimaco di Kolophòn primo 'poèta

doctus.'" In *Storia e civiltà dei Greci*, III/5. Milan, 1977, pp. 299–310.

Sifakis 1967  G. M. Sifakis. *Studies in the History of Hellenistic Drama.* London, 1967.

Silk 1974  M. S. Silk. *Interaction in Poetic Imagery, with Special Reference to Early Greek Poetry.* Cambridge, 1974.

Simon 1978  B. Simon. *Mind and Madness in Ancient Greece.* Ithaca, 1978.

Simonini 1979  L. Simonini. "Il fr. 282 P. di Ibico." *Acme* 32 (1979): 285–98.

Sisti 1965  F. Sisti. "Le due Palinodie di Stesicoro." *Studi Urb.*, n.s. 39 [B 1] (1965): 301–13.

Sisti 1966  F. Sisti. "Ibico e Policrate." *Quad. Urb.* 2 (1966): 91–102.

Sisti 1967  F. Sisti. "L'ode a Policrate: Un caso di 'recusatio' in Ibico." *Quad. Urb.* 4 (1967): 59–80.

Sitzler 1911  J. Sitzler. "Zum sechsten Päan Pindars." *Wochenschr. klass. Philol.* 28 (1911): 1015–18.

Skafte Jensen 1980  M. Skafte Jensen. *The Homeric Question and the Oral-formulaic Theory.* Copenhagen, 1980.

Slater 1969a  W. J. Slater. "Futures in Pindar." *Class. Quart.* 19 (1969): 86–94.

Slater 1969b  W. J. Slater. *Lexicon to Pindar.* Berlin, 1969.

Slater 1977  W. J. Slater. "Doubts about Pindaric Interpretation." *Class. Journ.* 72 (1977): 193–208.

Slater 1978  W. J. Slater. "Artemon and Anacreon: No Text without Context." *Phoenix* 32 (1978): 185–194.

Slings 1980  R. S. Slings. "Archilochus, eerste Keulse epode." *Lampas* 5 (1980): 315–35.

Snell 1930  B. Snell. Review of F. Zucker, *Syneidesis-Coscientia: Ein Versuch zur Geschichte des sittlichen Bewusstseins im griechischen und griechisch-römischen Altertum.* Jena, 1928. *Gnomon* 6 (1930): 21–30 = *Gesammelte Schriften.* Göttingen, 1966, pp. 9–17.

Snell 1931  B. Snell. "Sapphos Gedicht Φαίνεταί μοι κῆνος." *Hermes* 66 (1931): 71–90 = *Gesammelte Schriften.* Göttingen, 1966, pp. 82–97.

Snell 1952  B. Snell. "Bakchylides' Marpessa-Gedicht (Fr. 20 A)." *Hermes* 80 (1952): 156–63 = *Gesammelte Schriften.* Göttingen, 1966, pp. 105–11.

Snell 1963  B. Snell. In *Archiloque, Entr. Hardt*, X. Vandoeuvres-Geneva, 1963, passim.

Snell 1965  B. Snell. *Dichtung und Gesellschaft.* Hamburg, 1965.

|  | = *Poetry and Society: The Role of Poetry in Ancient Greece.* Bloomington, Ind., 1961. |
| Snell 1969 | B. Snell. *Tyrtaios und die Sprache des Epos.* Göttingen, 1969. |
| Snell 1975 | B. Snell. *Die Entdeckung des Geistes.* Göttingen, 1975[4]. Translated by T. G. Rosenmeyer, under the title *The Discovery of the Mind in Early Greek Philosophy and Literature.* Cambridge, Mass., 1953. |
| Snell 1978 | B. Snell. *Der Weg zum Denken und zur Wahrheit.* Göttingen, 1978. |
| Sokolowski 1969 | F. Sokolowski. *Lois sacrées des cités grecques.* Paris, 1969. |
| Sordi 1958 | M. Sordi. *La lega tessala fino ad Alessandro Magno.* Rome, 1958. |
| Stanford 1967 | W. B. Stanford. *The Sound of Greek.* Berkeley and Los Angeles, 1967. |
| Stark 1959 | R. Stark. "Textgeschichtliche und literarkritische Folgerungen aus neueren Papyri." *Ann. Univ. Sarav.* 8 (1959): 31–49. |
| Steffen 1959 | W. Steffen. "Die neuen Papyruskommentare zu Alkaios." In *Philol. Vorträge,* ed. J. Irmscher–W. Steffen. Wroclaw, 1959, pp. 35–46. |
| Stengel 1892 | P. Stengel. "Zum Saecularorakel." *Hermes* 27 (1892): 447–51. |
| Stern 1970 | J. Stern. "An Essay on Bacchylidean Criticism." In *Pindaros und Bakchylides,* ed. W. M. Calder III–J. Stern. Darmstadt, 1970, pp. 290–307. |
| Stiebitz 1926 | F. Stiebitz. "Zu Sappho 65 Diehl." *Philol. Wochenschr.* (1926), cols. 1259–62. |
| Stoneman 1979 | R. Stoneman. "The Niceties of Praise: Notes on Pindar's 'Nemeans.'" *Quad. Urb.,* n.s. 2 [31] (1979): 65–77. |
| Svenbro 1976 | J. Svenbro. *La parole et le marbre.* Lund, 1976. |
| Taillardat 1965 | J. Taillardat. *Les images d'Aristophane: Etude de langue et de style.* Paris, 1965. |
| Taplin 1978 | O. Taplin. *Greek Tragedy in Action.* Berkeley and Los Angeles, 1978. |
| Tarán 1965 | L. Tarán. *Parmenides.* Princeton, 1965. |
| Tarditi 1958 | G. Tarditi. "Motivi epici nei tetrametri di Archiloco." *Parola d. passato* 13 (1958): 26–46. |
| Tarditi 1968 | *Archiloco.* Critical edition with biographical and literary testimonia, introduction, and translation, by G. Tarditi. Rome, 1968. |

| | |
|---|---|
| Tarditi 1969 | G. Tarditi. "Ľἀσέβεια di Aiace e quella di Pittaco." *Quad. Urb.* 8 (1969): 86–96. |
| Tarditi 1978 | G. Tarditi. "Le Muse povere (Call. 'Ia.' I, fr. 191, 92–93 Pf.)." In *Studi in onore di A. Ardizzoni*, II, ed. E. Livrea–G. A. Privitera. Rome, 1978, pp. 1013–21. |
| Taylour 1958 | W. C. Taylour. *Mycenaean Pottery in Italy and Adjacent Areas.* Cambridge, 1958. |
| Theander 1943 | C. Theander. "Lesbiaca." *Eranos* 41 (1943): 139–68. |
| Thummer 1957 | E. Thummer. *Die Religiosität Pindars.* Innsbruck, 1957. |
| Thummer 1968 | E. Thummer. *Pindar: Die Isthmischen Gedichte,* I. Heidelberg, 1968. |
| Thummer 1969 | E. Thummer. *Pindar: Die Isthmischen Gedichte,* II. Heidelberg, 1969. |
| Tiberi 1977 | L. Tiberi. "Stesicoro e le raffigurazioni vascolari." *Archeol. class.* 29 (1977): 175–79. |
| Timpanaro 1981 | S. Timpanaro. *La genesi del metodo del Lachmann.* Padua, 1981². |
| Torelli 1971 | M. Torelli. "Il santuario di Hera a Gravisca." *Parola d. passato* 136 (1971): 44–67. |
| Torelli 1977 | M. Torelli. "I culti di Locri." In *Atti del XVI Convegno di Studi sulla Magna Grecia* (Taranto, 3–8 October 1976). Naples, 1977, pp. 147–84. |
| Tosi 1929 | T. Tosi. "Ancora sul sesto peana di Pindaro." *Studi it. filol. class.* 7 (1929): 199–201. |
| Treu 1955 | M. Treu. *Von Homer zur Lirik.* Munich, 1955. |
| Treu 1963a | *Alkaios,* ed. M. Treu. Göttingen, 1963². |
| Treu 1963b | M. Treu. In *Archiloque, Entr. Hardt,* X. Vandoeuvres-Geneva, 1963, passim. |
| Treu 1966 | M. Treu. "Neues über Sappho und Alkaios (P. Oxy. 2506)." *Quad. Urb.* 2 (1966): 9–36. |
| Treu 1976 | *Sappho,* ed. M. Treu. Munich, 1976⁵. |
| Trumpf 1958 | J. Trumpf. *Studien zur griechischen Lyrik.* Diss., Köln, 1958. |
| Tsagarakis 1979 | O. Tsagarakis. "Oral Composition, Type-Scene and Narrative Inconsistencies in Homer." *Graz. Beitr.* 8 (1979): 23–48. |
| Tugendhat 1960 | E. Tugendhat. "Zum Rechtfertigungsproblem in Pindars 7. Nemeischen Gedicht." *Hermes* 88 (1960): 385–409. |
| Turner 1952 | E. G. Turner. *Athenian Books in the Fifth and Fourth Centuries B.C.* London, 1952. Italian translation, revised by the author, "I libri nell'Atene del V e IV secolo a. C." In *Libri, editori e pubblico nel mondo* |

*antico.* Historical and critical survey, ed. G. Cavallo. Rome and Bari, 1975, pp. 3–24.

Turyn 1929      A. Turyn. *Studia sapphica.* Leopoli, 1929.

Turyn 1952      A. Turyn. *Pindari carmina cum fragmentis.* Oxford, 1952.

Untersteiner 1951      M. Untersteiner. *La formazione poetica di Pindaro.* Messina and Florence, 1951.

Usener 1907      H. Usener. *Vorträge und Aufsätze.* Leipzig and Berlin, 1907.

Usener 1948      H. Usener. *Götternamen. Versuch einer Lehre von der religiösen Begriffsbildung.* Third edition (unaltered), with introductory remarks, by M. P. Nilsson–E. Norden. Frankfurt am Main, 1948³.

Vagnetti 1970      L. Vagnetti. "I Micenei in Italia: La documentazione archeologica." *Parola d. passato* 25 (1970): 359–80.

Vagnetti 1980      L. Vagnetti. "Mycenaean Imports in Central Italy." In E. Peruzzi, *Mycenaeans in Early Latium.* Rome, 1980.

Vallet 1958      G. Vallet. *Rhégion et Zancle.* Paris, 1958.

Van Compernolle 1969      R. Van Compernolle. "Ajax et les Dioscures au secours des Locriens sur les rives de la Sagra (ca. 575–565 av. notre ère)." In *Hommage à M. Renard,* II. Brussels, 1969, pp. 733–66.

Van Effenterre 1973      M. Van Effenterre. "Le contrat de travail du scribe Spensithios." *Bull. corresp. hell.* 97 (1973): 31–46.

Van Groningen 1953      B. A. Van Groningen. *In the Grip of the Past.* Leiden, 1953.

Van Groningen 1960a      B. A. Van Groningen. *Pindare au banquet.* Leiden, 1960.

Van Groningen 1960b      B. A. Van Groningen. *La composition littéraire archaïque grecque.* Amsterdam, 1960².

Van Groningen 1966      B. A. Van Groningen. *Théognis: Le premier livre.* Amsterdam, 1966.

Van Nes 1963      D. Van Nes. *Die Maritime Bildersprache des Aischylos.* Groningen, 1963.

Van Otterlo 1944      W. A. A. Van Otterlo. *Untersuchungen über Begriff, Anwendung und Entstehung der griechischen Ringkomposition.* Amsterdam, 1944.

Van Sickle 1980      J. Van Sickle. "On the Cologne Epode's End Again: An Antinote." *Class. Journ.* 75 (1980): 225–28.

Vansina 1961      J. Vansina. *De la tradition orale: Essai de méthode historique.* Tervuren, 1961.

Veneri 1977      A. Veneri. "'Unmetrical metres' nell'analisi di P. A. Hansen." *Quad. Urb.* 26 (1977): 157–64.

Verdenius 1972     W. J. Verdenius. *Pindar's Seventh Olympian Ode: A Commentary* (Med. Nederl. Akad., n.s. 35 [2]). Amsterdam, 1972.

Verdenius 1976     W. J. Verdenius. "Pindar's Seventh Olympian Ode: Supplementary Comments." *Mnemosyne* 29 (1976): 243–53.

Vernant 1966     J. P. Vernant. *Mythe et pensée chez les Grecs.* Paris, 1966. Translated under the title *Myth and Thought among the Greeks.* London, 1983.

Vernant 1968     J. P. Vernant. "Structure géométrique et notions politiques dans la cosmologie d'Anaximandre." *Eirene* 7 (1968): 5–23.

Vernant 1979     J. P. Vernant. "ΠΑΝΤΑ ΚΑΛΑ: D'Homère à Simonide." *Ann. Scuola Norm. Pisa* 9 (1979): 1365–74.

Vetta 1979     M. Vetta. "La 'giovinezza giusta' di Trasibulo: Pind. 'Pyth.' VI 48." *Quad. Urb.,* n.s. 2 [31] (1979): 87–90.

Vetta 1980     *Teognide.* Critical edition of book II of the elegies, with introduction, translation, and commentary, by M. Vetta. Rome, 1980.

Vetta 1982     M. Vetta. "Il P. Oxy. 2506 fr. 77 e la poesia pederotica di Alceo." *Quad. Urb,* n.s. 10 [39] (1982): 7–20.

Vitagliano 1905     A. Vitagliano. *Storia della poesia estemporanea nella letteratura italiana dalle origini ai nostri giorni.* Rome, 1905.

Vogliano 1939     A. Vogliano. "Nuove strofe di Saffo." *Philologus* 93 (1939): 277–86.

Vogliano 1941     A. Vogliano. *Saffo: Una nuova ode della poetessa.* Milan, 1941.

von Fritz 1943     K. von Fritz. "ΝΟΟΣ and ΝΟΕΙΝ in the Homeric Poems." *Class. Philol.* 38 (1943): 79–93.

von der Mühll 1958     P. von der Mühll. "Wurde die elfte Pythie Pindars 474 oder 454 gedichtet?" *Mus. Helv.* 15 (1958): 141–46.

Vürtheim 1919     J. Vürtheim. *Stesichoros' Fragmente und Biographie.* Leiden, 1919.

Wade-Gery 1952     H. T. Wade-Gery. *The Poet of the Iliad.* Cambridge, 1952.

Ward 1973     D. Ward. "On the Poets and Poetry of the Indo-Europeans." *Journ. Ind. Europ. Stud.* 1 (1973): 127–44.

Waszink 1975     J. H. Waszink. "Osservazioni sui fondamenti della critica testuale." *Quad. Urb.* 19 (1975): 7–24.

Webster 1939     T. B. L. Webster. "Greek Theories of Art and Literature down to 400 B.C." *Class. Quart.* 33 (1939): 166–79.

Wegner 1949            M. Wegner. *Das Musikleben der Griechen*. Berlin,
                       1949.
Weil-Reinach 1900      H. Weil–T. Reinach. *Plutarque: De la musique*. Paris,
                       1900.
Weinreich 1963         U. Weinreich. *Languages in Contact*. The Hague,
                       1963².
Weinrich 1976          H. Weinrich. *Metafora e menzogna: La serenità
                       dell'arte*. Bologna, 1976.
Welcker 1845           F. G. Welcker. "Aöden und Improvisatoren." In
                       *Kleine Schriften zur griechischen Literaturgeschichte*,
                       II. Bonn, 1845 (1820 or 1821).
Welter 1938            G. Welter. *Aigina*. Berlin, 1938.
West 1966a             M. L. West. *Hesiod: Theogony*. Oxford, 1966.
West 1966b             M. L. West. "Conjectures on Forty-six Greek
                       Poets." *Philologus* 110 (1966): 147–68.
West 1971              M. L. West. "Stesichorus." *Class. Quart.* 21 (1971):
                       302–14.
West 1974              M. L. West. *Studies in Greek Elegy and Iambus*. Ber-
                       lin and New York, 1974.
West 1975a             M. L. West. "Cynaethus' Hymn to Apollo." *Class.
                       Quart.* 25 (1975): 161–70.
West 1975b             M. L. West. "Shorter Notes: Some Lyric Fragments
                       Reconsidered." *Class. Quart.* 25 (1975): 307–9.
West 1978a             M. L. West. *Hesiod: Works and Days*. Oxford, 1978.
West 1978b             M. L. West. "Stesichorus at Lille." *Zeitschr. f. Pap. u.
                       Epigr.* 29 (1978): 1–4.
Wigodsky 1962          M. Wigodsky. "Anacreon and the Girl from Les-
                       bos." *Class. Philol.* 57 (1962): 109.
Wilamowitz 1895        U. von Wilamowitz. *Euripides Herakles*, II. Berlin,
                       1895².
Wilamowitz 1900        U. von Wilamowitz. *Die Textgeschichte der griechi-
                       schen Lyriker*. Berlin, 1900.
Wilamowitz 1908        U. von Wilamowitz. "Pindars siebentes nemeisches
                       Gedicht." *Sitzungsber. Berl. Akad.* (1908): 328–52.
Wilamowitz 1913        U. von Wilamowitz. *Sappho und Simonides*. Berlin,
                       1913.
Wilamowitz 1914        U. von Wilamowitz. "Neue lesbische Lyrik (Oxy-
                       rhynchos-Papyri X)." *Neue Jahrb.* 33 (1914): 225–47.
Wilamowitz 1921        U. von Wilamowitz. *Griechische Verskunst*. Berlin,
                       1921.
Wilamowitz 1922        U. von Wilamowitz. *Pindaros*. Berlin, 1922.
Wilamowitz 1924        U. von Wilamowitz. *Hellenistische Dichtung*, II.
                       Berlin, 1924.

Wilamowitz 1927a     U. von Wilamowitz. *Aristophanis Lysistrata.* Berlin, 1927 (1964).

Wilamowitz 1927b     U. von Wilamowitz. *Geschichte der Philologie.* Leipzig, 1927. Translated by Alan Harris, and edited with introduction and notes by Hugh Lloyd-Jones, under the title *History of Classical Scholarship.* Baltimore, 1982.

Wilamowitz 1931     U. von Wilamowitz. *Der Glaube der Hellenen,* I. Berlin, 1931 (Darmstadt, 1959).

Wilamowitz 1935     U. von Wilamowitz. *Kleine Schriften,* I. Berlin, 1935.

Williams 1975     F. Williams. "Five Problems in Callimachus' 'Hymn to Apollo.'" *Quad. Urb.* 19 (1975): 127–43.

Williger 1922     E. Williger. *Hagios: Untersuchungen zur Terminologie des Heiligen in den hellenisch-hellenistischen Religionen.* Giessen, 1922.

Wilson 1980     J. R. Wilson. "Kairos as Due Measure." *Glotta* 58 (1980): 177–204.

Winnington-Ingram 1936     R. P. Winnington-Ingram. *Mode in Ancient Greek Music.* Cambridge, 1936 (Amsterdam, 1968).

Wittkower 1942     R. Wittkower. "Marvels of the East: A Study in the History of the Monster." *Journ. Warburg and Courtauld Inst.* 5 (1942): 159–97.

Wolf 1795     F. A. Wolf. *Prolegomena ad Homerum.* Halle, 1795 (Hildesheim, 1963). Translated by Anthony Grafton–Glenn Most–James Zetzel, under the title *Prolegomena to Homer.* Princeton, 1985.

H. Wood 1966     H. Wood. "On a Fragment Falsely Ascribed to Archilochus." *Mus. Helv.* 23 (1966): 228–33.

R. Wood 1769     R. Wood. *Essay on the Original Genius of Homer.* London, 1769.

Woodbury 1967     L. Woodbury. "Helen and the Palinode." *Phoenix* 21 (1967): 157–76.

Woodbury 1968     L. Woodbury. "Pindar and the Mercenary Muse: Isthm. 2. 1–13." *Trans. Am. Philol. Assoc.* 99 (1968): 527–42.

Woodbury 1978     L. Woodbury. "The Gratitude of the Locrian Maidens: Pindar, 'Pyth.' 2. 18–20." *Trans. Am. Philol. Assoc.* 108 (1978): 285–99.

Woodbury 1979     L. Woodbury. "Neoptolemus at Delphi: Pindar, 'Nem.' 7.30ff." *Phoenix* 33 (1979): 95–133.

Wülfing-von Martitz 1959     P. Wülfing-von Martitz. "Ἱερός bei Homer und in der älteren griechischen Literatur." *Glotta* 38 (1959): 272–307.

| | |
|---|---|
| Wülfing-von Martitz 1960–61 | P. Wülfing-von Martitz. "Ἱερός bei Homer und in der älteren griechischen Literatur." *Glotta* 39 (1960–61): 24–43. |
| Yates 1966 | F. A. Yates. *The Art of Memory.* London, 1966. |
| Young 1964 | D. C. Young. "Pindaric Criticism." *Minnesota Rev.* 4 (1964): 584–641 = *Pindaros und Bakchylides,* ed. W. M. Calder III–J. Stern. Darmstadt, 1970, pp. 1–95. |
| Young 1968 | D. C. Young. *Three Odes of Pindar.* Leiden, 1968. |
| Zumthor 1972 | P. Zumthor. *Essai de poétique médiévale.* Paris, 1972. |
| Zumthor 1979 | P. Zumthor. "Pour une poétique de la voix." *Poétique* 40 (1979): 514–24. |

# Index of Words and Subjects

# Index of Passages Cited

FLAVIUS JOSEPHUS
*Contra Ap.* I, 12: 17, 308n.305

GLAUCOS OF RHEGIUM
*ap.* Ps.-Plut. *De mus.* 5, 1133a:
291n.11

GNOMOLOGIUM PARISINUM
p. 15 no. 117 Sternbach: 289n.80
16 no. 142: 161 and 287n.35
18 no. 160: 285n.15
32 no. 313: 289n.80
*App. Vat.* p. 79 no. 102: 161 and
287n.36

GNOMOLOGIUM VATICANUM
p. 189 no. 513 Sternbach: 289n.96

GORGIAS
*Palam.* 22: 282n.81
82 A 15a D.-K.: 108, 245n.33
B 11, 9ff. D.-K.: 54f. and 251n.35
B 23: 55 and 251n.36

HELIODORUS
*Ethiopica:* 187

HEPHAESTION
p. 45, 12 Consbr.: 304n.1
51, 21: 244n.4
*perì poiem.* p. 70, 11: 248n.83
71, 16ff.: 248n.84

HERACLIDES PONTICUS
fr. 157 Wehrli: 15 and 239n.51,
273n.22

HERACLITUS
*All. Hom.* 5, 3: 303n.128
5, 5: 198
5, 5–7: 206 and 299n.53
5, 7: 247n.62, 298n.40
5, 9: 198 and 296n.8
22 B 42 D.-K.: 238n.19, 240n.76
B 87: 252n.49

HERMESIANAX
fr. 7, 37ff. Pow.: 245n.31

HERMIAS
*in* Plat. *Phaedr.* 267a, p. 238, 1
Couvreur: 270nn. 22, 24

HERMIPPUS
fr. 63 Wehrli: 192 and 294n.46

HERODIANUS
περὶ μονηρ. λέζ. II, p. 941, 28
Lentz: 298n.39
942, 9: 259n.7
περὶ παθῶν fr. 103 (II p. 205
Lentz): 308n.22

HERODOTUS
1.1: 297n.29
1, 23–24: 159
1, 27: 261n.49
1, 65: 297n.25
1, 86ff.: 271n.7
1, 120: 301n.90
1, 122: 301n.90
1, 138: 302n.110
2, 78: 303n.121
2, 93: 255n.16
2, 179: 297n.29
3, 37, 2: 249n.9
3, 38, 20: 138
3, 121: 160
3, 131: 162
4, 8: 272n.16
4, 32: 237n.17
5, 58: 17
5, 67: 156, 237nn. 12, 17
5, 92: 283n.82
6, 46ff.: 290n.4
7, 183: 300n.69

HESIOD
*Op.* 282: 265n.85
286ff.: 219
337: 305n.12
643: 297n.29

Poetry and Its Public in Ancient Greece

Designed by Chris L. Smith.
Composed by A. W. Bennett, Inc., in Garamond Antiqua text and display.
Printed by the Maple Press Company, Inc., on S. D. Warren's 50-lb. Sebago
Eggshell Cream offset paper and bound in Holliston's Roxite A and Linden-
meyr's Elephant Hide.